The Asbury Theological Seminary Series in Christian Revitalization Studies

This volume appears within the publication project of the Christian Revitalization Studies Series at Asbury Theological Seminary. There are several sub-series within this publishing project, which together have produced more than 75 volumes devoted to research in revitalization movements within Christianity, since its inception in 1989. This significant study of Canadian Pentecostalism appears in the Pentecostal and Charismatic Studies sub-series of the project.

A key contribution of Butler's timely research is its longitudinal interpretation of the Pentecostal Assemblies of Canada in light of theological and cultural shifts which have occurred since its inception in the nineteenth century until the present day. The analysis of continuities and discontinuities with the Charismatic Renewal, from the 1960s forward, places the discussion in a larger ecclesial framework. Important issues are addressed regarding shifts from a concern for conversion to commitment, and from personal to social holiness, which is viewed as coming at the expense of the historic concern for Christology and atonement. At the same time, this study makes clear that the contributions of the Charismatic Renewal to Canadian Pentecostalism rise higher than a concern for enthusiasm to enabling it to recover its own early roots as a movement of renewal of persons and cultures that is not burdened by parochialism and protectionism.. This volume is presented as an important contribution to that ongoing conversation.

—J. Steven O'Malley
Series Editor

Sub-Series Foreword

Pentecostal and Charismatic Studies

Pentecostalism has, arguably, made the most significant impact on global Christianity of any movement to have emerged out of the renewal traditions. The beginning of the 20th century saw a theologically and spiritually distinctive tradition beginning to develop in numerous centers around the world (India, Chile, and Korea, for example) but this revival erupted into an explosive movement as a result of the catalytic Azusa Street Revival in Los Angeles, California, in 1906. The Pentecostal movement became a global one from that time onward and within one hundred years it was widely acknowledged that Pentecostalism, including the related Charismatic and neo-Pentecostal movements, had become the fastest-growing movement within Christendom. It is now believed that there are an estimated 600 million adherents worldwide, representing 25% of all Christians. In North America, Europe, and especially in the majority world, Pentecostals are noted for their vibrant worship services, marked by lively music and preaching, charismatic manifestations, such as speaking in tongues (glossolalia) and prophetic speech, and for their belief in miracles, including healing.

It is the intersection of these related but distinctive movements, the Pentecostal and Charismatic, that is the subject of this study, *Canadian Winds of the Spirit: Holiness, Pentecostal, and Charismatic Currents* by Ewen H. Butler. The intersection was inevitable, and in Canada was engaged and welcomed, but, sometimes met with resistance and struggle. One may argue, that tension is also an inevitability. As Avery Dulles warned in *Models of the Church,* "When paradigms shift, people suddenly find the ground cut out from under their feet. They cannot begin to speak the new language without already committing themselves to a whole new set of values that may not be to their taste."[1]

As a participant-observer of a similar, but somewhat less distinguishable, merger between the two movements in the churches of Canada's southern neighbor, I sensed a familiarity in the findings of this research; it sometimes felt as if I was sitting at a family reunion, hearing stories of my northern cousins. As a historian, I am intrigued by the interplay of ecclesiastical politics and the vitality of spiritual renewal, a recurring theme in the history of the Christian traditions. As a confessional Pentecostal, I am aware of both the warning and the promise revealed in these pages.

—Kimberly Ervin Alexander, Sub-Series Editor

---

[1] Avery Dulles, *Models of the Church* (New York: Doubleday Image Classics, 2000), 23.

Canadian Winds of the Spirit

Holiness, Pentecostal and Charismatic Currents

Ewen H. Butler

The Asbury Theological Seminary Series in
World Christian Revitalization Movements in Pentecostal/Charismatic Studies

EMETH PRESS
www.emethpress.com

Canadian Winds of the Spirit, Holiness, Pentecostal and Charismatic Currents

Copyright © 2018 Ewen H. Butler
Printed in the United States of America on acid-free paper

All rights reserved. No part of this book may be reproduced, or stored in a retrieval system or transmitted in any form or by any means, electronic, mechanical, photocopying, recording, scanning or otherwise, except as permitted by the 1976 United States Copyright Act, or with the prior written permission of Emeth Press. Requests for permission should be addressed to: Emeth Press, P. O. Box 23961, Lexington, KY 40523-3961.
http://www.emethpress.com.

Library of Congress Cataloging-in-Publication Data

Names: Butler, Ewen H., author.
Title: Canadian winds of the spirit : holiness, Pentecostal and Charismatic currents / Ewen H. Butler.
Description: Lexington : Emeth Press, 2018. | Series: The Asbury Theological Seminary series in world Christian revitalization movements in Pentecostal/Charismatic studies | Includes bibliographical references.
Identifiers: LCCN 2018021188 | ISBN 9781609471231 (alk. paper)
Subjects: LCSH: Pentecostalism--Canada. | Pentecostal Assemblies of Canada--History.
Classification: LCC BR1644.5.C2 B88 2018 | DDC 277.1/082--dc23
LC record available at https://lccn.loc.gov/2018021188

Contents

Acknowledgments	vii
Foreword	ix
Introduction	xi
1) Anchor Points	1
Deep Roots	2
Unintended Transformation	4
Early Writings	5
Denominational Response	6
PAOC and Global Renewal	8
2) Beginnings	13
Early Renewal Spreads North	13
Long Reach of the Holiness Movement	15
Phoebe Palmer	16
Two Canadian Holiness Leaders	19
The Holiness Legacy	22
Pentecostalism Spreads into Canada	27
The Hebden Mission	27
Azusa, Hebden and Canadian Holiness	29
A New Latter Rain	33
3) Neo-Pentecostalism Threatens a Near Monopoly	47
More Winds from the South	47
New Associations and Denominational Accommodation	50
Success of Canadian Renewal	57
Initial Intersection of Charismatic Movement and PAOC	61
4) Quebec Revisionism, Charismatic Renewal and the PAOC	71
Societal and Ecclesial Transformation	71
The Charismatic Renewal Reaches Quebec	74
PAOC Accelerated Evangelism	79
Assessing PAOC Involvement	83

Renewal Begins to Wane	87
5) David Mainse: The Bridge Between Two Movements	97
Catalyst for Greater Understanding	97
Community to National Television Pastor	100
The Pastor - Evangelist Embraces New Wave of Renewal	104
Ambivalence Towards *Crossroads*	110
Philosophy of Ministry as Bridge to Charismatic Movement	113
A Canadian Incarnation of Billy Graham and David du Plessis	117
Ecumenical and Charismatic Legacy	118
6) Youth of the PAOC—Another Bridge Between Two Movements	125
The Toronto Catacombs: A Jesus Movement—Charismatic Phenomenon	125
Artistic Worship Environment	128
Venue, Style and Substance	130
Impact on PAOC Worship Style	133
Charismatic Worship in the Spirit	136
Where Pentecostals and Jesus People—Charismatics Converged	138
Intersections with PAOC Leadership	140
Fracturing of the Catacombs	144
Enduring Implications	150
New Renewal and University Ministry	151
Long Term Consequences of Youth Involvement	157
7) Shift in Theological Loci	165
Disappearance of Doctrinal Emphasis	165
Five Classical Pentecostal Doctrines and the Charismatic Movement	166
Salvation Through Christ's Atonement	168
Sanctification	171
Baptism in the Spirit and Initial Evidence	174
Divine Healing	180
Expectation of Christ's Second Coming	182
8) Facing the Dilemma	191
Vacillating Perspectives	191
Official Responses	199
Impact of Changes	205
9) Reflections and Recommendations	211
Two Generations Encounter Renewal	213
Two Generations Changed by Renewal	215
The Road Ahead	217
Bibliography	221

Acknowledgements

My roots in Pentecostalism run deep. My paternal great-grandfather and great-grandmother came under the influence of the early Pentecostal revival during the difficult years of the 1930s. As life-long dedicated Pentecostal church members, my parents always encouraged excellence, truth, and experiencing the Spirit. The historical line of my Pentecostal heritage reaches to the work of Alice Bell Garrigus and her founding of Bethesda Mission in St. John's, Newfoundland in 1910 from which radiated evangelism efforts reaching to the remotest corners of the windswept, rugged island on the extreme east coast of Canada. Decades later, the intersection of the Pentecostal and Charismatic movements with the myriad of leaders, pastors, and other influences shaped my thinking and appreciation for the work of the Spirit.

The quality of theological scholarship under which I have been privileged to study has been well beyond my dreams. I am indebted to the late Robert E. Webber, my mentor at the Wheaton College Graduate School for helping me understand more clearly the relationship between the worship of the Pentecostal/Charismatic tradition, its orthopraxy and traditional church sacraments. Dr. Stanley M. Burgess and Dr. H. Vinson Synan have not only been inspiring Pentecostal scholars but models of spirituality, integrity, and humility. I am deeply grateful to Dr. Kimberly Ervin Alexander as my doctoral advisor for her energetic interest in my work and her patient, relentless support of this project. My appreciation goes to James Craig, archivist at the Pentecostal Assemblies of Canada Archives for his encyclopedic knowledge of Canadian Pentecostal history and tireless efforts in digging up and referring me to pertinent sources. Linda Wood provided some much appreciated transcription of oral resources all completed within an astonishingly rapid turnaround time. Over numerous country breakfasts, Dr. Ronald A. Kydd, a valued friend and former colleague offered helpful insights from his wealth of research and experience in both Pentecostal history and the broader Canadian ecclesiastical scene.

If it does not take a village to write a book, it must assuredly does take family and friends. Over the course of research and writing this project I have had occasion to interact with numerous acquaintances within church ministry and education circles—currently retired pastors, laypeople, denominational leaders and college professors. They have all had a part in helping to shape and reshape my perspective on the relationships among Canadian renewal movements. The greatest credit goes to my wife Donna for her unfailing encouragement, financial sacrifice, and time commitment. As a capable teacher, writer, and editor in her own right, she was instrumental in suggesting revisions and helping to edit the document. Along with our sons, André and Jonathan who both have been supportive in every way, my family has been my most valuable asset. Jonathan's smart technical skills were instrumental in formatting the final draft.

Finally the book is dedicated to students of Pentecostalism in the hope that those who have a special interest in renewal movements find it to be a platform from which numerous other trajectories might be launched. But more than anything, it is dedicated to the church with a prayer that while the past can never be recovered, lessons may be learned and new desires kindled for the fresh winds of the Spirit. "Veni Creator Spiritus!"

Foreword

When Monsignor Ronald Knox died in 1957 many in England took note. Famous in lecture halls, on radio, and in print, he was granted a 1500 word obituary. I wonder if people knew he thought himself haunted, haunted by what he called "enthusiam." He used the word to refer to the heart of spiritual movements that flared into existence, glowed white hot, then in time, for the most part, sputtered out. The prophets of Cévenne in southern France in the late seventeenth century would be one; the early New Apostolic Church in England another. But what would you call a movement that looked something like one of those, was well into its second century, and had become a bona fide global phenomenon? Maybe "Pentecostalism." And then what would you say when it and another movement of the Spirit were to be found in the same place at the same time? Then you should talk to Dr. Ewen Butler.

Butler's work is devoted to probe in depth "significant crossover points" between the Pentecostal Assemblies of Canada and the Charismatic Renewal. The former is a denomination with roots in various places globally, but particularly in the southern United States in the early twentieth century and the latter, a movement that burgeoned also in the United States in the 1960s, but rapidly spread far beyond. Both would qualify for Knox's label "enthusiam" in that they emphasized, and continue to emphasize in various ways, intimate encounters with God the Holy Spirit. Butler's study examines the convergence of these two movements in Canada from about 1960 on. It is based on the consultation of a wide range of sources one would expect, both literary and oral, and in both English and French.

The leitmotif running throughout is the interaction of two specific religious movements, but many other facets grip attention. Looking at formative influences, Butler discusses Methodism and the Holiness movements in Canada with reference to Ralph C. Horner and Phoebe Palmer among others. Focus is given to both movements in French-speaking Quebec. To help understand the interaction, the innovative ministry of David Mainse on national television is recounted and assessed thoroughly, and Merve and Merla Watson's "The Catacombs" is highlighted. This was a ministry in the 1970s primarily to young people, "hippies" as well as church kids, with up to 2500 attending Thursday night after Thursday night and meeting in the largest Anglican church in Toronto.

How did these Pentecostals and "Charismatics" get along? The relationship oscillated between encouragement and suspicion. As Butler proceeds it becomes obvious that influence flowed both ways, but the current seems to have been stronger from the charismatics to the PAOC than the other way around. How positive this has been is open to interpretation. Butler's treatment is engaging, accurate, and bold.

Toward the end of his book on enthusiasm, Monsignor Knox pondered, "Perhaps it a closed chapter, this chapter in the history of religion." Butler's navigation of the entanglements of Pentecostals and charismatics makes clear that it was not.

Ronald Kydd, Ph.D., Tyndale University College and Seminary, Toronto, ON.
January, 2018.

Introduction

"A historian has many duties. Allow me to remind you of two which are important. The first is not to slander; the second is not to bore," *Voltaire.*

The French philosopher might well have added several others, not the least of which is the duty to reconstruct pictures in an effort to provide as fair a representation as possible of the events and in the end certainly to avoid his two chief negatives. Even then, the representation of any piece of history is never perfect because there is so much that the interpreter does not know and can never know. Like the writing of all histories, portraying revival movements is a task riddled with potential pitfalls. The goal of objectivity, as worthy as it is, can never be fully realized. The inability of the historian, who while examining the wider picture of renewal in any context, to fully grasp, compile and present all the details makes that goal elusive. Not every detail of every context can be recovered, leaving some of the finer nuances and unrecorded conversation entombed in history.

Although the parameters of the current project are limited to approximately three decades of one denomination's history, The Pentecostal Assemblies of Canada (PAOC), to gain some understanding it is necessary to trace the roots. These were years of transformation and challenge as they were for other Pentecostal constituencies in the Western world. At least two major sociological factors working together changed the revival landscape. First, increasing individualization and desire for privacy appears to have run counter to the more corporate understanding of the early revivalist impulse. The youth and young adults of the 1960s, 1970s and 1980s signalled a trend whereby people were less inclined to become aligned for life with any particular religious organization than were their parents. Second, the postmodern culture has turned out to be a formidable force against any attempt to establish theological propositions as universal guidelines and compelling loyalty. The loss of a communal self-understanding and the relativistic conditioning of a subsequent generation placed the PAOC, in particular, in a veritable no man's land.

While both the Jesus Movement and the Charismatic Movement of those decades were renewal phenomena characterized by high degrees of corporate belonging and conservative biblical perspectives, neither of them morphed into formal structures with loyal followings. Yet, ironically both influences together resulted in numerous conversions, Spirit baptisms and commitments to ministry and many individuals out of both eventually landed in PAOC churches. The impact was both positive and at times questionable. The transformation though is indisputable but its extent is left to further research.

The Charismatic Movement arose at a time when the PAOC had already come of age. The denomination had come into existence during the modernist era and so carried with it not just a robust belief in the dynamic of the supernatural but combined it with fundamentalist elements including literalistic approaches to biblical interpretation. Charismatics brought a refreshing reminder of the blessing of experiencing the Spirit but for many classical Pentecostals also a bewildering lack of emphasis on the *ordo salutis* and denominational distinctives. It was the experience of the Spirit and the new music that attracted a new generation of Pentecostals for whom the initial revival impulse was perceived as having faded. The reticence of PAOC leadership in the new environment is abundantly clear as later chapters of this book will demonstrate. Classical Pentecostals may not have actually believed they had a monopoly on the baptism of the Spirit and glossolalia, but there seems at least to have been the underlying assumption that those who experience the Spirit and practice tongues would eventually leave their mainline Protestant and Catholic roots and join the ranks of the Pentecostals.

The reluctance to fully embrace a phenomenon that was both familiar and unfamiliar for Pentecostals from the older tradition reached to the individual level. My first encounter with the Charismatic Movement occurred in 1972 while an undergraduate student. A minister who spoke in tongues and smoked a pipe was an oxymoron for a young Pentecostal. Holiness influences, firm doctrinal guidelines regarding conversion and subsequent blessing, and the perplexing formulaic manner of praying to receive the Spirit was cause for consternation and caution, if not avoidance.

It was these concerns and others such as differing views over demonology that unsettled PAOC leadership as they sought to still affirm the global moving of the Spirit. Responses at the time must not be judged too severely from the present perspective of wider renewal. The ambivalence was justifiable in view of the times, the denomination's history, and the conscientiousness and integrity of many of its leaders, some of whom are still living.

The years 1960-1985 constitute roughly the span of time during which the Charismatic Movement was having its most potent impact. As non-classical Pentecostal renewal did not formalize, the Charismatic Movement slowly waned and many of its prayer groups retreated to their own denominational structures. It could be argued that the same eagerness for spiritual renewal though evolved into other forms such as in the so-called Toronto Blessing that began approximately a decade later in January 1994.

With or without official endorsement the Charismatic Movement permanently transformed the Pentecostal landscape both in Canada and beyond its borders. Attempts to return to primitive roots have had minimal success at best. It was at the grassroots where it became increasingly clear where the future of the PAOC lay. It was the local pastor and layperson who were listening to and embracing the emerging musical idioms, attending the conferences, and watching the television programs where popular preachers of the Movement were attracting their followers. No one could have imagined the far-reaching impact of dizzying communication advancement that would make established loyalties to denominational structures and theological stances difficult to maintain.

Observation of the current PAOC ambience reveals the profound influence of a Charismatic worship style with the rapid importation of new songs, many characterized by an individual focus and chord patterns foreign to an earlier generation accustomed to the traditional piano and organ. Revival-style preaching common to the early Pentecostal movement generally has evolved into teaching and preaching series along the lines of the Charismatic conference mode with extensive borrowing from popular psychology trends. The result is that a noticeable convergence in style, language, and substance has developed among both older Pentecostal and Charismatic-type churches and has even spilled over into some evangelical churches in Canada. There appears to be a more common and generic language of the Spirit as it relates to the individual and corporate life, more favorable perspectives on divine healing, and while the term 'sanctification' is rarely used, the need for Spirit-empowerment for a life of holiness as central to Christian life is not uncharacteristic in any of those contexts. Although denominational lines have traditionally been clearly defined in Canada, the historical line of demarcation between a PAOC and non-PAOC adherent does not appear to be as relevant as it once was as some groups within mainline denominations and even outside them have emerged with climates that are discernibly Pentecostal-Charismatic in tone.

Although the metamorphosis of the revival movement from its early beginnings into something that looks quite different can be painful for those who remember its inception, the cycle of revival, decline, and institutionalization must not be seen as necessarily altogether negative. This book attempts to lay out the context within which the PAOC underwent a significant modification—a process not without precedent. It highlights at times the long-term impact of successive Wesleyan, Holiness, Pentecostal, and Charismatic currents from the United States. The established Methodist Church in Canada in the mid-19th century was clearly seen as having become too urban and overly concerned with being relevant. The Holiness movement self identified as a return to true Methodist roots, so preparing the way for the era of Pentecostalism. As our own Holiness forebears discerned the need to return to what was seen as neglected, Pentecostals recognized the need for a third blessing in addition to conversion and sanctification. Finally, Charismatics discerned the need for a greater emphasis on experiencing the Spirit than either they were experiencing in their own churches or even as Pentecostals were supposedly experiencing.

I have attempted to develop a brief contextual history of each successive movement within the Canadian social and religious landscape leading up to the outbreak of the Charismatic Movement with specific reference to the province of Québec where its ripples were especially noticeable. Initial official responses from PAOC leadership were generally positive and even celebratory. Nobody seemed to know where it was headed although the new wave of renewal appeared to be validating what Pentecostals had always believed and practiced. The period can be described as a high water mark in Québec religious history as both the PAOC and the Catholic Charismatic Renewal were together responding to a climate of spiritual search and riding a wave of spiritual renewal.

Arguably, the pivotal crossover between these older and new movements in Canada is the ministry of David Mainse and Crossroads Christian Communications (CCC). Mainse was intentional and explicit about his mission to be wherever the Spirit was working regardless of denominational affiliation. His passion never waned and he was astonishingly able to maintain stellar relationships with his denominational leadership. Despite serious health challenges at the time of my research, Mainse graciously permitted access to his recollection of the events leading up to and surrounding the growth years of his television ministry at the height of the Charismatic Movement when he invited several non-PAOC Charismatic individuals to be part of his ministry. Mainse passed away September 25, 2017 after a lengthy battle with leukemia.

The impetus for renewal found its energy largely among PAOC youth. Some participation in The Catacombs community in Toronto and in other less prominent events and contexts points to an appetite among youth for spiritual experience as they faced an increasingly uncertain future. College and university campus ministry while as yet not widespread across the country served as a catalyst for interaction with the new renewal, in particular, through the life and ministry of Bernice Gerard in Vancouver BC.

There is ample evidence of interface between the two movements through events, television ministry, and youth interaction, the long-range impact of which is difficult to measure. Nevertheless, it is the evidence left from the time by leadership that points to nothing less than the beginnings of a significant alteration in PAOC substance and style. Historians are always left with only relics of a past time. In a case such as this, one assumes that its official monthly publication is a fair reflection of the thinking of a denomination. The disappearance of emphasis on historic PAOC doctrines over the period in question points to a shift in what theological points were considered essential to perpetuate. More than anything, it is in the boardroom and conference hall where direction is usually established by majority or consensus. The surviving relics—records of annual meetings and official publications of those gatherings during the 1960s through the 1980s proved to be invaluable sources of information while recognizing that these do not fully capture and reflect the context, tone, conversation, and atmosphere of any meeting. Definite reactions of the PAOC to the Charismatic Movement are preserved in those official publications and documents.

It was surprisingly difficult to find any serious research on perspectives from the Charismatic side or primary sources apart from an abundance of devotional materials by specific leaders and teachers. Few Charismatic leaders wrote about their experiences, thus leaving the historian to tease out the story from oral testimony, any relevant documentation and publications by mainstream clergy and laity who were present and/or actively involved in some way in the new renewal.

In the end, a look through the eyes of those who were part of the classical Pentecostal-Charismatic phenomenon of the 1960s to 1980s as evidenced in available individual recollection and written sources might provide an enhanced awareness of where Pentecostals are today, insight into analyzing the current situation, specifically within the PAOC environment, and more than anything, clarification of some implications for our response to ongoing global renewal. Debates over music with its cultural conditionings, differing uses of the *charismata* including tongues as 'prayer language', angels and demons, even to appearance and dress while not unimportant, are ever subordinate to the global issues of justice, poverty, and war. To these the Spirit is speaking as always, seeking human instruments of liberation while groaning for the restoration of all creation. (Rom. 8:19-21)

1

Anchor Points

The scarcity in volume and depth of research into the roots of Spirit renewal in Canada has been well known among Canadian church historians. For an emerging generation of renewal scholars, the situation is at the same time frustrating, challenging and yet engaging. While serious interpretive scholarship beyond the chronicling of events has been slow in coming, prospects for serious research are now quite promising. At least on the surface, the ground appears to be rich with potential for scholarly excavation. Renewal historians in this country have become increasingly awakened to the existence of valuable primary sources and been able to share materials and insights more rapidly through the use of the Internet and social media.

While vaguely attempting to anchor the Pentecostal movement in the nineteenth century holiness revivals and the 1904-1905 Welsh Revival in Great Britain, most Pentecostals have assumed connections to the Azusa Street revival that broke out in 1906 in the United States. However, Canadian Pentecostals have also inherited the assertion from their forebearers that the Pentecostal revival was of supernatural origin with minimal human causation. They have essentially been caught between what Augustus Cerillo Jr. and Grant Wacker call "the image of a revival focal point radiating outward around the earth" with that of "causally unconnected stirrings simultaneously springing up all around the world."[1] Cerillo and Wacker outline four interpretive approaches that historians have taken toward Pentecostal origins: the providential approach defined as God working with and through human agents and the structures of society; the genetic approach that sees Pentecostalism as the product of diverse religious and social strands within a process of historical continuity; the multi-cultural approach that explains the rise of Pentecostalism as the impulse for the creation of an egalitarian community with the elimination of race, gender, and class distinctions; and the functional approach that uses social analysis theories to account for Pentecostalism based on economic and social deprivation.[2] The current generation of Pentecostals within the Pentecostal Assemblies of Canada (PAOC) would likely place themselves somewhere between the first two approaches. They understand that what happened for the creation of their movement was providential but at the same time genetic in that it reaches well back into the nineteenth century.

Deep Roots

Few within classical Pentecostalism or within newer Charismatic-type groups in Canada seem to be aware of the actual intertwining roots of Canadian renewal movements, the reciprocal influence of their various theological ideas, and the general impact of renewal on the Canadian religious landscape. The popular perspective seems to be that the various renewal phenomena occurred independently while recognizing some individual interconnections: the Holiness movement in central Canada of the mid to late nineteenth century; the Hebden Mission in East Toronto and the overflow of the Azusa revival together resulting in the emergence of the PAOC in 1919; the Latter Rain revival in North Battleford, Saskatchewan in 1946-48; the Charismatic Renewal of the 1960s and 1970s; and the Toronto Blessing beginning in 1994.

Canadian Pentecostalism emerged out of a matrix of theological ideas imported from Britain and the United States. While the earlier movement is a child of the Azusa revival, some argue that the Toronto Hebden Mission that slightly preceded Azusa was an independent Pentecostal revival led by a British couple, James and Ellen Hebden. In any case, early twentieth century Canadian holiness leaders visited the Azusa Mission and W.H. Durham's work in Chicago and were impacted by the spread of the revival across the continent. Likewise, leaders associated with the revival visited Canada frequently. A similar pattern occurred during the Charismatic Renewal when Canadian Catholic leaders visited Charismatic hotspots in the US and Renewal leaders frequently were invited to Canada.

The PAOC generally recognizes its roots within Methodism and later Holiness revivals, but not so much any connection with subsequent movements such as the Charismatic Movement that arose from within mainline denominations [3] and the later Toronto Blessing. The Pentecostal Assemblies of Newfoundland and Labrador (PAONL), a sister organization to the PAOC, likewise has its origins in the Holiness tradition, American revivalism, and the Azusa event through the influence of its founder, Alice Belle Garrigus from New England. Evidence exists, however, pointing toward relationship and influence traceable from one movement to another, that though perhaps overlooked, or subtly denied, is nonetheless real. In subsequent chapters, these interconnections will be highlighted, specifically focusing on the Charismatic Movement from the mid-1960s to mid-1980s as it interfaced with the PAOC.

At least until recently, the common belief expressed among grassroots classical Pentecostals namely that the early twentieth century revival was a providential last-days outpouring of the Spirit, meant that no further waves of renewal were considered necessary. There developed, therefore, a culture of parochialism and protectionism. The hope, if not the assumption, seemed to be that any renewal that focused on experiencing the Spirit would automatically align itself with the PAOC. Yet, one might argue that ambivalence, suspicion, and even rejection of the Charismatic Movement was also due in part to the PAOC having become both weary and wary of the controversies involving the Latter Rain phenomenon[4] and some of the healing evangelists of the 1950s and 1960s. If that is so, it might also explain to some degree how the PAOC sought to retreat behind, and entrench itself within, the salvation-sanctification-Spirit baptism-divine healing-second coming theological form. Although within PAOC official documentation there is clear evidence of attempts to defend itself against perceived aberrations of doctrine, the new wave of renewal in the Charismatic Movement was generally ignored, as much as possible, out of fear and the conviction that no true Pentecostal could possibly grow in faith within the confines of mainline denominations that did not appear to recognize the moving of the Spirit or fully support fundamental evangelical doctrines. Moreover, there was a high level of discomfort over different musical styles and a non-traditional version of the *charismata*.

Although the outbreak of the second wave of renewal in the twentieth century can be argued as having its roots within classical Pentecostalism, it nonetheless spread and flourished in Canada for a time without the endorsement of the PAOC or any official connection with it. Meanwhile, many Pentecostals began to frequent places where the Charismatic Movement was happening. Whether they were becoming somewhat dissatisfied with the routinization of renewal[5] in their own churches, or perhaps out of sheer curiosity, regardless of denominational affiliation or the lack thereof, people were drawn to the unusual work of the Spirit. Renewal was occurring at such places as the Toronto Catacombs and in prayer groups across the country. Furthermore, some within the Renewal eventually ended up settling within PAOC circles, bringing their experiences and perspectives with them. The responses of the PAOC, some of the perspectives of key clergy leadership and also laity as they engaged with the Charismatic Movement provide a window on the interconnections and influences prevalent at the time.

While the story of the relationship between both movements needs to be examined, it is important to recognize the risk of painting too broadly the idea of the PAOC as being steeped in its own history, unable or unwilling to concede the reality of other genuine workings of the Spirit outside itself. Although the generation of leaders that found itself compelled to evaluate the Charismatic Movement has now retired, the research confirms that most are still very interested and concerned for the future of their denomination. Also, they have been followed by another generation of leaders who appear anxious to engage in serious self-evaluation and the examination of possibilities for constructive engagements outside their ranks. Assuming as far as possible the absence of bias and naiveté in trying to draw the distinction between what Michel-Rolph Trouillot calls the Geschichte and the Geschichtschreibung—what actually happened and what was said to have happened, (or more precisely what was ignored as having happened),[6] enough time has elapsed since that period to examine the evidence and reach some logical and judicious conclusions. In any case, it is clear that the PAOC has changed dramatically over the past few decades—a transformation that can be attributed largely, though not exclusively, to subsequent waves of renewal.

Unintended Transformation

In discerning and articulating areas of actual interface between the PAOC and the Charismatic Movement, the transformational influence of the latter upon the former and possible reasons for the evolution of the PAOC climate, it is essential to recognize, as well, influences that flowed northward from the United States, and how a common desire to recover the place of the Spirit within the broad Christian community resulted in the Charismatic Movement modifying the PAOC mainly through its youth. Other key factors in the matrix of events include especially the major contribution of David Mainse, founder and former president of Crossroads Christian Communications (CCC) as a key cross-denominational link.

The changes were manifested in the creation of an environment characterized by remarkable uniformity among the youth in musical tastes, perspectives on spirituality and lifestyle, and reaction against what Pentecostalism was perceived to be with its alleged legalism and restrictive doctrinal stand. This resulted in a need for response: in some cases, the PAOC determined to assert its distinctiveness, an effort that proved to be arduous and of questionable success. In other cases, leaders were ambivalent with a 'live and let live' approach, or they looked for acceptable elements and built on those.

The outcome of investigation of mainly primary material consisting of denominational archival sources such as records of official meetings of PAOC committees and conferences; publications, especially *The Pentecostal Testimony*;[7] and interviews with individuals actually involved or with verifiable knowledge from the years 1960 to 1985 demonstrate threads and influences linking both the classical Pentecostal and Charismatic renewal movements. As the spillover of the nineteenth century holiness revivals in the United States prepared soil north of the border for early Pentecostalism to flourish, so the classical Pentecostal movement in Canada became the backdrop for the Charismatic Movement. Yet, in this case, the new renewal was not an offshoot of the PAOC, but emerged from the outside, and was decidedly not affected by it. However, the older movement itself over time has been re-shaped by the broad conditions of the later renewal. The two movements interfaced by means of the involvement of key figures and ecumenical events resulting in significant modifications of PAOC culture. A different style and ambiance, new approaches to ministry, and different theological ideas and emphases have all contributed to a far less monolithic Pentecostal landscape at present than historic PAOC denominational lines would appear to convey.

Early Writings

In setting parameters, it is appropriate to note that the emergence and development of the earlier Pentecostal movement in Canada, manifested predominantly in the current PAOC, is generally well documented, though it could be argued that historical analysis is sparse. The events have been chronicled in two official histories: the first by Gloria G. Kulbeck, *What God Hath Wrought*, published by the PAOC in 1958 and the second by Thomas W. Miller, *Canadian Pentecostals: History of the Pentecostal Assemblies of Canada* released in 1994, to date the most popular and trusted resource for Pentecostalism in Canada. Miller makes frequent references to historical connections with the United States, particularly in relation to camp meetings, conventions, and conferences. His chapter, "'Classical Pentecostals' in Canada" points to abundant cross-border contact involving not only the impact of the Azusa Revival but also the Jesus Movement and the Charismatic Movement.

At least two unofficial works have appeared over the years. *The Third Force* by Gordon F. Atter, a mid-twentieth century leader in the PAOC and Bible college professor, was published in 1962. It gives a basic survey of the origin and development of the Pentecostal movement and includes helpful chapters on the arrival of Pentecostalism into Canada, organizational developments in North America, and the development of Pentecostal doctrine. A much later volume, *When the Spirit Came Upon Them: Highlights from the Early Years of the Pentecostal Movement in Canada* by Douglas Rudd appeared in 2002. Rudd, a retired pastor and archivist, presents a fairly extensive series of short biographical sketches of events associated with the pre-1925 days of Canadian Pentecostalism. He makes frequent references to personalities within American Pentecostalism and their impact upon the movement to the north. His documentation is helpful in pointing to numerous original journal articles, letters, and booklets written by early leaders.

Historiography on later twentieth century renewal is likewise far from voluminous. The Charismatic Movement in Canada was documented in 1979 by an Anglican priest, Al Reimers, in his work *God's Country*, and by Richard Dunstan in *Fire in the North: A History of the Catholic Charismatic Renewal in Canada* (n. d.). Reimers' book, now in its second edition, is an account of the early days of the Canadian Charismatic Movement, a collection of personal experiences surrounding the outbreak of a wave of spiritual renewal that, at least in part, had as its catalyst the visits of Charismatic personalities to Canada such as that of Dennis and Rita Bennett to Vancouver and Toronto in the early 1960s. The work by Dunstan, a journalist and religious studies professor, is specifically about renewal among Catholics.[8] Apart from those efforts, much of which contains vital first-hand information, attempts to establish substantial interrelationships among renewal movements in Canadian religious history have been scanty to this point. Whether ideas or practices that may possibly have trickled down from earlier Pentecostalism into subsequent movements, or renewal influences that have flowed back into PAOC churches, they have either been the by-product of other research agendas or cursorily overlooked.

Publications of the Canadian Conference of Catholic Bishops are available and provide helpful insight, in particular, a lengthy pastoral letter on the occasion of the 35th anniversary in 2003 of the Charismatic Renewal in Canada. The original official response of the bishops to the Renewal, along with those of mainstream Protestant church leaders contained in Killian McDonnell's *Presence, Power, Praise,* serves as a valuable source of primary material on responses to the Charismatic Movement from both Catholic and Protestant perspectives.[9] Secondary source material is likewise not at all extensive, thus making reliance vital on primary sources such as letters, journal entries, sermons, denominational publications, conference/council minutes and personal interviews with key leaders. The few available surveys and anecdotal-type histories of the Pentecostal movement and the Charismatic Movement in Canada are helpful in providing context and some clues to the roots of current pneumatological thought and practice.

Denominational Response

The notes, papers, and minutes left by a denomination's leadership in an official capacity are a clear indication of the path taken by that tradition. The PAOC archives are an excellent repository, containing a range of documents including minutes of the General Executive and its related committees.[10]

Reflection on doctrine of the Spirit and reaction to newer perspectives and practices brought by the Charismatic Movement are naturally evident in *The Pentecostal Testimony*.[11] Throughout the 1960s and 1970s, various contributors, especially PAOC leadership responded to what they perceived as pneumatological excesses. Although there had been initial delight that finally the experience of Spirit baptism with tongues had begun to be highlighted everywhere, it soon became apparent that the Charismatic view of tongues as a prayer language gift and, furthermore, not as the only sign of having received the Spirit were viewed as serious points of divergence.

The PAOC also saw the need to address what it considered to be confusion over demonology and exorcism. Emphasis on the basics of Pentecostal doctrine was in all likelihood an attempt to re-discover and articulate its raison d'être in the face of burgeoning Spirit renewal in other denominations. In retrospect, it seems that retreating behind established doctrinal positions in publications and at official consultations had little impact one way or other on either the existing Pentecostal movement, except perhaps to hasten its growing institutionalization, or on the new wave of renewal. A fresh rediscovery of spiritual gifts among older Protestant groups and the emergence of new styles of worship eventually altered the PAOC as both an older generation of Pentecostals to some degree, but especially a younger generation, crossed over into the realm of the Charismatic Movement.

David Mainse, a PAOC pastor, was able for more than four decades to establish a television ministry that clearly spanned both movements and flourished in spite of ambivalence, if not sometimes opposition, toward his venture outside the four walls of his traditional Pentecostalism. He strategically appointed a Charismatic minister from each of the major Canadian denominations to be involved with him on his daily national television program, *100 Huntley Street*. His unprecedented step outside his own denomination, while keeping himself grounded firmly within it, allowed Mainse to experience minimal negative reaction toward him personally. The nature of his approach to other denominational traditions, his relationship with PAOC leaders, his theology of the Spirit, the church and evangelism were strategic.

The PAOC was the parent body of Mainse's television ministry during its formative years and joint meetings were regularly held. Official minutes from those meetings are kept in the PAOC archives at the national headquarters in Toronto. These are vital in obtaining a clearer picture of the growing pains of Mainse's very successful ministry.[12] Three non-PAOC and Charismatic figures worked with Mainse during those early years: Gordon Williamson of the United Church of Canada, Al Reimers of the Anglican Church of Canada, and Father Bob MacDougall of the Roman Catholic Church.[13]

During the late1960s and early 1970s, at the height of the Charismatic Movement, a group emerged in Toronto known as The Catacombs at St. Paul's Anglican Church. For a time, this gathering drew between two and three thousand people per week, predominantly youth. Over two thousand were baptized in the makeshift basement tank; many of them eventually went into full-time Christian service in many parts of the world.[14] There was some influence at the leadership level that had deep roots in the earlier Pentecostal movement but more importantly, many participants who attended The Catacombs fellowship in some way had direct ties to PAOC churches. While national PAOC leadership did not tend to respond to specific local Charismatic expressions, there was widespread ambivalence regarding the Pentecostal legitimacy of the Catacombs.

A scholarly reflection on the interface between the PAOC and the later renewal is contained in a short journal article by Ronald Kydd, "The Impact of the Charismatic Movement upon Classical Pentecostalism in Canada."[15] Although, as Kydd observes, when Bennett and other mainline denominational leaders began to share their experiences quickly providing social validation among Pentecostals for what they had already been experiencing,[16] initial enthusiasm soon turned to caution and distance and it continued that way. Meanwhile, young PAOC churchgoers, in particular, appear to have interacted with the Charismatic Movement with relative ease.

Those in PAOC leadership and its constituency generally responded in writing that often was reactionary rather than proactive. The voices of former and current PAOC leaders, pastors and laypeople who had some involvement with the denomination during the peak years of the Charismatic Movement help in understanding the nature of the PAOC response at the time. Local newspaper coverage of the period also helps illuminate the message that was being conveyed to the public regarding events that were difficult to ignore.[17]

PAOC and Global Renewal

Social, religious, and cultural interaction on a global scale has long ago accelerated to the point where investigation of a particular brand of renewal does not seem to be of much benefit without reference to the wider scene. Discerning the relationship between one renewal group and another means moving beyond the confines of a specific pneumatological perspective to recognize the wider church. It seems clear that during the years from 1960 to 1985, the PAOC sought to reinforce the doctrinal parameters around itself and, it might be argued, largely succeeded in doing so on an official level. However, at the grassroots of its constituency, the story was quite different and the effects have continued to this day. While on the surface, it may appear that the earlier and later waves of renewal remained different and widely separate, such was not the case, at least not in as stark relief as is often conceived. Ripples from the second wave of Pentecostalism altered the first. The two renewals in Canada are connected as they frequently are elsewhere and the interface needs to be examined even if some leading figures in both movements might deny, ignore, or perhaps not even be fully aware of any influence. Since the study of Canadian renewal history is only now coming into its own, crucial points of departure need to be highlighted in order to facilitate the pursuit of other avenues.[18]

Modern Canadian renewal is one piece of a large picture where the Spirit continues to transcend race, gender, and church organizational boundaries. Whether those involved in the Charismatic Movement and the earlier Pentecostal churches over-managed renewal or over-reacted to it, not exercising due sensitivity to both the Spirit's work and to people of different persuasions, is a matter of speculation. Overall, the more foundational outcomes of Canadian renewal might better be seen as affective ones—a new appreciation for the work of the Spirit even in the recent past and anticipation for greater things in the future.

Going forward, determining what renewal looks like in a rapidly changing global culture is a formidable but exciting challenge. It is of particular interest how all of this relates, not just to those given to researching, reflecting, writing, and teaching, but also to the local and global church where people live. While recognizing that both a theoretical and practical pneumatology that stays true to biblical and historical faith is complex, the hard work must be done to facilitate the next generation to grasp the reality of God as Spirit as well as Son and Father for all aspects of human existence.

Therefore, the hope is that those in classical Pentecostal contexts will begin to appreciate more the wideness of God's Spirit and the unbounded nature of the triune God. Identifying Pentecostalism mainly in terms of dogmatics and one specific pneumatological hermeneutic seems to do injustice to that wideness as evidenced in the obvious diversity within contemporary global Pentecostalism. Humbly admitting that the edges are more obscure than previously thought will help classical Pentecostals to engage with the burgeoning global Pentecostal movement. It will not mean that a Pentecostal apologetic needs to be abandoned entirely as much as a willingness to admit that God still works in mysterious ways. Maintaining a rigid view of the Spirit no longer seems to be a productive option as the history of the Charismatic Movement in relation to the PAOC has demonstrated. Identifying Pentecostalism along the lines of a rationalistic approach to Scripture will continue to become more challenging.

While recognizing that most of global Pentecostalism is understood to focus on a transformational experience, it is critical to also affirm that it is a phenomenon with a multitude of different worship/music styles and local customs, not to mention the varying emphases on the use of the *charismata*. This will contribute to understanding renewal, not as any particular expression of the Spirit, but rather as a plethora of expressions within global Pentecostalism of the Spirit. In that regard, if the Spirit is seen as moving in distinct waves, each occurring in a different context, temporally and spatially, renewal embraces them all, of which the PAOC-Charismatic interface is but one small example.

Much work remains to be done in the history and theology of Canadian Pentecostalism, particularly in regard to the Toronto Blessing, as well as the influx of an increasing number of immigrant Pentecostals from Latin America and Asia. There presently appears to be somewhat less resistance to diverse Pentecostal groups than would have been the case during the days of the Charismatic Movement. At any rate, the arrival of the Charismatics proved to be the second major challenge to the PAOC, following the Latter Rain controversy, and began a transformation of the denomination that appears to be continuing under the influence of Third Wave phenomenon.

Notes

1. Augustus Cerillo, Jr. and Grant Wacker, "Bibliography and Historiography of Pentecostalism in the United States," in Stanley M. Burgess and Eduard M. Van Der Maas, eds. *New International Dictionary of Pentecostal and Charismatic Movements,* rev. ed. (Zondervan, 2004): 395.

2. Ibid, 397-405.

3. Traditional Canadian denominationalism still retains relatively distinct identities. "Mainline" here would refer primarily to the Roman Catholic, Anglican, United Church of Canada, and Presbyterian groups. The United Church of Canada was formed in 1925 out of the merger of the Methodist Church of Canada, the Congregational Union of Ontario and Quebec and two-thirds of the Presbyterian Church in Canada.

4. In connecting the Latter Rain Movement, works that provide background include Richard M. Riss's *The Latter Rain Movement* (Honeycomb Visual Productions, 1987) and *Winds From the North: Canadian Contributions to the Pentecostal Movement* (Brill, 2010) edited by Peter Althouse and Michael Wilkin-

son, particularly chapters by David W. Faupel, "The New Order of the Latter Rain" and Mark Hutchinson "The Latter Rain Movement and the Phenomenon of Global Return." Faupel's book, *The Everlasting Gospel: The Significance of Eschatology in the Development of Pentecostal Thought*, Journal of Pentecostal Theology, Supplement Series 10 ((Sheffield, England: Academic Press 1996) as well as his work, *The American Pentecostal Movement: A Bibliographical Essay, Vol. 2.*, Asbury Theological Seminary, May 2012 are leading sources. L. Thomas Holdcroft, a PAOC minister and Bible college teacher, wrote an unflattering portrayal of the Latter Rain Movement published in *PNEUMA* (Fall 1980). Holdcroft's perspective would presumably mirror the official PAOC stance.

5. Max Weber, *The Theory of Social and Economic Organization* (New York, NY: The Free Press, 1947): 363-381. Weber referred to it famously as the routinization of charisma.

6. Michel-Rolph Trouillot, *Silencing the Past: Power and the Production of History* (Boston, MA: Beacon Press, 1995): 5.

7. The perspectives and experiences of Pentecostals are best reflected in the official magazine of the PAOC, *The Pentecostal Testimony* (now *The Testimony*) that includes writings by both local pastors and lay people. Fortunately, all of the issues from that period are available and accessible electronically. *Good Tidings*, a publication of the PAONL also contains both pastoral and lay submissions and is readily available.

8. http://thebreadoflife.ca/Books.html Peter Couglin, an original Canadian Catholic Charismatic leader says of Dunstan's works, "Richard has captured the human response of individuals who experienced the first outpourings of the Holy Spirit infilling their hearts and lives. He followed the move and lead of the Holy Spirit across Canada. This book is a wonderful overview and glimpse into the Spirit's work, a work that continues to this day . . . ." Couglin is still actively involved in Catholic renewal and spiritual leader of the Bread of Life Renewal Centre founded in 1975. He has written several books on renewal including *Explosion of Fire: Holy Spirit Ministry*, a compendium of materials from various writers celebrating the outbreak of the Catholic Renewal in February 1967, (accessed September 24, 2104). In conversation with the author, Couglin verified that written records are sparse with no formal statistics and that each region of Canada was unique in how the Catholic Renewal unfolded.

9. Roman Catholic Church, Canada 1975, "Charismatic Renewal: Message of the Canadian Bishops Addressed to all Canadian Catholics." *Presence, Power, Praise. Vol.II.* Continental, National, Regional Documents. Edited by Kilian McDonnell. Collegeville, MN: The Liturgical Press, 1980: 84-98. The three-volume set remains a very useful collection of denominational documents reflecting early responses to the Charismatic Movement. The Catholic Charismatic Renewal Council still continues to serve the renewal segment of the Catholic Church in Canada with some of the original Renewal-centered worship and teaching still appearing to be ongoing. The archbishop of Toronto, Thomas

Cardinal Collins, for instance, is a well-known Charismatic who presided over Feast of Pentecost celebrations in May 2012 and "stressed to the community of believers to catch the fire of the Holy Spirit and be one of the instruments of the divine grace." http://www.ccrctor.com/ (accessed September 24, 2014). The Catholic Charismatic Renewal was particularly strong in Quebec where its publication *Selon Sa Parole* has continued since 1976.

10. The PAOC has also been a longtime member of broader Pentecostal organizations such as the Pentecostal Fellowship of North America (PFNA) and the Pentecostal World Fellowship (PWF). In spite of the denomination's historic uneasiness with the Charismatic Renewal, it continues to retain membership in the newly formed replacement organization, Pentecostal/Charismatic Churches of North America in 1994.

11. The Canadian Pentecostal environment in recent years has seen a reaction especially among a younger generation against open reference to the label "Pentecostal." The PAOC's current publication, *Testimony*, is one example of the tendency to distance ministry from usage of this identification.

12. One example of the challenges of those formative years comes from a meeting held September 16, 1979. Letters had been written to the PAOC expressing concern over the "Roman Catholic presence" on the program.

13. Father Bob MacDougal who was arguably the most popular personality passed away in 2004. It was highly unusual for Pentecostals to witness the presence of a Catholic priest on daily Christian television, or anywhere else for that matter, who had experienced the Spirit while remaining within his own tradition.

14. http://www.mervandmerla.com/home.cfm (accessed September 24, 2014).

15. Ronald Kydd, "The Impact of the Charismatic Movement upon Classical Pentecostalism in Canada," PNEUMA (18:1): 55-68.

16. Ronald A.N Kydd, "Canada," *International Dictionary of Pentecostal Charismatic Movements,* ed. Stanley M Burgess and Eduard M. Van Der Maas, (Grand Rapids, MI: Zondervan, 2003): 49.

17. *Maclean's* Canada's national newsmagazine wrote cynically in 1979 during the climate of the Charismatic Movement: These days...we are swamped in a wave of fundamentalist, Bible-thumping evangelism which has brought with it the highly seductive instant spirituality of born-again Christians, the toothy assurances of Praise-to-the-Lord television preachers who sell religion like soap suds and the group-grope of the charismatic prayer sessions. For proof that religion, like Elastoplast, sells, listen to the phone-in after a daily religious talk show like *100 Huntley Street*.... For further proof, follow the fans of the new entertainers—the faith healers who advertise their next engagement. Angela Ferrante, "The New Believers," *Maclean's* (January 1, 1979): 26.

18. Recently, the fine research of such scholars as Michael Wilkinson and Peter Althouse has been a welcomed contribution to a Canadian Pentecostal historiography that had been largely anecdotal and chronological rather than analytical.

2

Beginnings

Early Renewal Spreads North

The histories of revival and renewal in the United States and Canada have always been interwoven. As early as the years immediately following the First Great Awakening of the early to mid-eighteenth century, the revivalist impulse from the south soon began to make its way into Canada, taking firm root in the Canadian religious landscape. Perhaps the most notable and influential figure of the time was Henry Alline, born in Newport, Rhode Island, but who relocated with his parents to Nova Scotia in 1760. His conversion as a youth was more than an evangelical assent to doctrine, but rather a "traumatic 'New Birth'" experience that took place within the context of personal struggle over commitment to the American Revolutionary cause.[1]

The uneasiness and ambivalence toward independence being experienced by early settlers in Nova Scotia, the majority of whom in the 1760's were immigrants from New England, appears to have made a perfect audience for a preacher like Alline who was mystically oriented, pietistic, and apolitical. Although Alline was anti-Calvinistic and in retreat from the political arena, his revivalism with its emphasis on a transformational new birth experience earned him the title, "Whitefield of Nova Scotia."[2] George Whitefield and Jonathan Edwards's Great Awakening was essentially rekindled in the eastern provinces by Alline's New Light evangelism that emphasized the inner light of personal experience.[3] He was essentially viewed as a genuine renewalist: "His contemporaries regarded him… as a powerful instrument of the Almighty, charismatic and uniquely spiritual. Historians in the nineteenth and twentieth centuries have been, almost to a person, overwhelmed by Alline's mystical theology, his creative powers, and his unusual ability to communicate to others his profound sense of Christian ecstasy."[4] In his writings, Alline described himself as being "ravished" by the "Divine ecstasy" and having been "married" to his Saviour by the redeeming power of the Holy Spirit.[5] His focus on the "New Light" experience of a sudden transforming regeneration was one that left a long-term impact upon the evangelical tradition of the Canadian Maritimes.[6]

The Second Great Awakening of the late eighteenth and early nineteenth centuries was a much broader movement in the United States but it too resonated with the growing pains of the Canadian religious, political and social environment. As with the earlier awakening, concern for personal salvation and worldwide renewal continued as revivalists within the North Atlantic triangle communicated with each other. In both revivals, "a network of correspondents arose who learned from each other and rejoiced or sorrowed as revivals waxed or waned in the Atlantic community."[7] In Canada, this later renewal energy was particularly manifested in the rise and spread of Methodism.

While there is some evidence that the first Methodist preacher in Canada was a soldier in the British regiment in 1780, most subsequent Methodist influence came via the young American nation.[8] Wesley's emphasis on holiness especially in his later sermons compelled him in a sermon on "The Signs of the Times" to rejoice over the spread of the revival throughout "various parts of Europe, particularly England, Scotland, Ireland, in the Islands, in the North and South, from Georgia to New England and Newfoundland."[9] Laurence W. Wood sees Wesley as casting this in Pentecostal imagery when reference is made to the "extraordinary work of God" as signs "that the day of God's power is approaching" and that Christ is seeking to "set up his kingdom over the earth" as well as to people experiencing "inward and outward holiness" and "righteousness, peace, and joy in the Holy Ghost."[10] While it would be an over-simplification to conclude that such experiential and transformational language associated with both awakenings served to directly prepare the way for later renewal, as these movements spread into the Atlantic region and Upper Canada from both America and England, even with all of the twists and turns of denominational history, they left remnants of revival that provided the backdrop for the later Holiness, Pentecostal and Charismatic Movements.[11] They laid the groundwork for an ongoing mistrust of religious tradition especially among the poor and marginalized:

> To Methodists, only a deep and personal commitment to God through the redeeming power of Jesus Christ could truly renew the individual and advance society. At the same time, emotional fervor appeared to provide a legitimate catalyst for gaining access to God's re-creative force. In early-nineteenth-century North America, tradition and reason as sources of religious authority, were at least partially abandoned. Experience reigned instead.... These shifts in emphasis were especially understandable in light of pioneer conditions in British America. The early settlers, whether isolated in Atlantic fishing ports, in embryonic villages, or on primitive farms carved out of the threatening forests, were ever conscious of their own insignificance.[12]

Nevertheless, at the time of Wesley's death in 1791, Upper and Lower Canada (now Ontario and Quebec) could only boast of one organized circuit, one preacher and only about sixty members. Along with the Maritimes and Newfoundland, the total was unimpressive with just four circuits, four preachers, and a membership of about eight hundred.[13]

Just over half a century later, however, all of the branches of Canadian Methodism had a total membership exceeding that of all other Protestant denominations in the country. The difference was largely due to the growing influence of revivalism that "became instrumental in shaping Methodism's perception of both its tradition and religious identity."[14] That transformation came not from across the ocean but from the south and was to prove extremely effective particularly in rural communities for many decades to come. A conversion experience in response to revivalist preaching rather than assent to a set of cardinal doctrines or a religion of sacramentality became the core of Methodist piety. Methodist leaders proclaiming individual transformational experience eventually followed by their Holiness successors would travel and preach, increasingly in a south-north direction on the North American continent.

Francis Asbury made at least one trip into Canada, preaching in towns along the shores of the St. Lawrence River and into eastern Ontario in 1811.[15] His travelling companion, Henry Boehm recounts that he himself preached to two thousand people on one occasion while Asbury who by that time was not in good health preached six times and delivered numerous lectures to societies.[16] Boehm refers to the visit as a "time of power; many of God's people rejoiced, and some mourners found converting grace.... Everywhere the bishop was treated as the angel of the Churches."[17] For many years Asbury had had an ardent desire to visit Canada. Boehm was with the bishop in July 1809, near Lake Champlain, when he ordained "a native Canadian" named Joseph Sampson to be "a missionary to his countrymen."[18] Asbury said at the time of that ordination, "The day of small things will be great; but the day is not yet come, rather it is still afar off. Patience, my soul! Do I not feel for the lost sheep? Yea, verily."[19] He recorded in 1811 that there were three thousand Methodists in Upper and Lower Canada.[20] A century later, Clara McLeister recorded that "the name of Francis Asbury became revered, and his ministry fruitful from the Atlantic to the Mississippi, and from Canada to the Gulf."[21] In any case, Asbury's influence appears to have been deep and far-reaching upon early Canadian Methodism.

Out of rural Methodist piety expressed in the teaching and worship of small community gatherings but particularly manifested in the emerging camp-meeting movement grew the later holiness emphasis on the way to the development of early Canadian Pentecostalism. Mid-twentieth century Pentecostals would warm up to the Charismatic Movement, perceiving in it a return to a higher life focus and to more primitivistic teaching and practice of the Spirit life unencumbered by institutional formality.

Long Reach of the Holiness Movement

American Protestant culture during the mid-nineteenth century was obsessed with Christian perfectionism and the resulting holiness impulse emerging out of Methodism would soon make itself felt in Canada. Originating in the United States, the Holiness Movement took root along the north shore of the St. Lawrence River spreading into the Ottawa area and Quebec. There was theological tension within

Methodism over how Christian perfection or sanctification ought to be conceived, whether gradually or through a second 'crisis' experience following conversion, resulting in the widespread holiness awakening—a revival that soon spread into Canada as hundreds who had experienced conversion came to Methodist altars to seek a subsequent experience of sanctification. While Wesley's doctrine of "entire sanctification" was well known within Canadian Methodist circles, it did not really begin "to catch fire" until the 1850's.[22] Highly successful holiness camp and revival meetings were held in the Maritimes, Western Canada, and Quebec as holiness preachers such as James Caughey and Phoebe and Walter Palmer invited thousands to experience sanctification.[23]

Caughey, an Irish-American Methodist preacher, made numerous trips to Canada over two decades beginning in 1835 preaching not only justification but also sanctification that could be received in an instant. His ministry had an immediate impact, particularly upon Methodism in Ontario. In 1851, Caughey arrived in Toronto and stayed for eight months during which he preached seven sermons a week and around 2000 were converted. Membership in Wesleyan Methodist churches in the city grew from 714 to 1,537. Peter Bush concludes that Caughey left three marks on Canada and in particular on Canadian Methodism:

> As the first professional evangelist to visit the Canadas, he prepared the way for future evangelists, providing a model which people such as Dwight Lyman Moody could follow. Secondly, the combined ministry of Caughey and Walter and Phoebe Palmer, lay evangelists from New York who visited Canadian camp meetings between 1852 and 1858, increased the impact of the Holiness movement in Canada. This success opened the door to groups such as the Church of the Nazarene, the Keswick movement, and ultimately the Pentecostal movement. Thirdly, as a result of Caughey's ministry in Hamilton in 1853 a group of young men decided to become Wesleyan Methodist ministers. They went to Victoria College, Cobourg, and within a year a revival broke out among the students there.[24]

From mid-century on, the annual pastoral address of the Wesleyan Methodist Church in Canada was explicit in its intent that each member was to take responsibility for seeking the blessings of entire sanctification.[25] This emphasis would continue and eventually cause breakage from the mother church that for holiness advocates had become formalistic and lax in its standards. In the latter part of the century, numerous holiness groups would emerge.

Phoebe Palmer

The Canadian Holiness Movement especially came under the impact of the strong ongoing ministry of Walter and Phoebe Palmer. The Palmers became known among Canadian Wesleyans through columns in the Methodist official publication, *Christian Guardian*. One of Phoebe's letters was featured each week in it for more than a year.[26] The Palmers made several visits during the mid-nineteenth century, the first of which was to Napanee in eastern Ontario in 1853. Mrs. Palmer wrote, "The Mayor of Kingston was powerfully blest, over five hundred professed conversion, and nearly as many obtained the full assurance of faith.

That meeting gave new life, and a fresh impetus to camp-meetings in Canada."[27] For several years in succession, the Palmers conducted four camp meetings in Canada annually with hundreds of conversions. Her assessment was that "the whole history of revival efforts shows no more grateful record than that of those summer visits to the sister Canadian churches."[28] The Wesleyan Conference, according to Palmer, reported an increase of six thousand that year—a significant spiritual awakening by any account.

The most notorious of the Palmer visits included an extended period of revival meetings in Hamilton, Ontario in late 1857. From June through October, they had conducted camp meetings in Ontario, Quebec, and the Maritimes with crowds of 5,000 and more. While waiting for their train connection back to New York, a local Wesleyan minister convinced them to speak at a nearby Methodist church. They were invited back the following evening and ended up staying for a few weeks during which several hundred people experienced conversions.[29] Mrs. Palmer recorded in her journal that "the revival has been progressing ten days, and nearly four hundred souls have been gathered into the fold of Christ."[30] She added that while no attempt had been made to count the number of the "wholly sanctified," from observation, they were convinced that "many scores have received the baptism of the Holy Ghost."[31] A subsequent issue of her publication, *Beauty of Holiness* (1857), carried a hurried two-line insert: "Glorious News From Hamilton, C.W. too late for insertion: 700 converted and sanctified."[32]

Some have made the broad but usually unsubstantiated suggestion that the result of the events triggered the beginning of the Third Great Awakening south of the border.[33] It is difficult to see this as much more than conjecture, nevertheless J. Edwin Orr argues that the visit of the Palmers to Hamilton in the fall of 1857 while prayer meetings were already going on in three different locations, was instrumental in the outbreak of the 1858 revival.[34] *The Christian Advocate*, a New York newspaper, reporting a month later on the events in Hamilton noted: "The work is taking within its range persons of all classes...and even little children are seen humbly kneeling together pleading for grace. The mayor of the city, with other persons of like position, are not ashamed to be seen bowed at the altar there beside the humble servant."[35] Orr's view is that it sparked the beginning of the famous Fulton Street prayer meeting in New York, the effects of which spread across the United States: "Spiritual awakenings are exceedingly infectious, and proximity in time and place adds to the stimulation of desire for similar blessing."[36] The revival in New York was also reported in the New York Times, March 20, 1858.[37] D. William Faupel argues as well that the 1857-1858 Revival began with Palmer's meetings in Hamilton, characterized by holiness teaching and expectation of the immediate dawning of the millennial kingdom, and spread quickly throughout North America.[38] In the final analysis, it is more likely that factors such as the economic conditions of the time, specifically the October 1857 stock market crash and the ensuing financial panic resulted in an emphasis on prayer out of which revival occurred in several places at the same time.

Repentance of sin and entire holiness by means of the 'shorter way' impacted deeply ordinary folk who thrived on a religion of experience more than social engagement. The Palmers conducted this type of meetings in the Maritime Provinces of Nova Scotia, New Brunswick, and Prince Edward Island the following summer with many conversions. This was especially true at Saint John and Charlottetown where around 400 and 700 converts respectively were recorded under the Palmers' preaching.[39] Mrs. Palmer reported at the time,

> We are now at Charlottetown, Prince Edward's Island, and here we are witnessing one of the most glorious revivals we have ever seen. A flame burst forth which we trust will envelope the whole island. Nightly, when the invitation to seekers is given, from seventy to one hundred present themselves. The most of these are broken-hearted penitents, and then to witness the glorious triumphs of faith as these newly converted ones sing....[40]

Following meetings at Peel, Ontario in 1868, she wrote, "Not only were many of the disciples baptized with the Holy Ghost, but many unsaved pricked to the heart. It was only to give an invitation for seekers of pardon or purity to present themselves, and from one to two hundred would come flocking forward."[41] As late as 1871, she led revival services in the "largest Wesleyan church in Toronto" where meetings were held twice each day with increasing attendance and altars crowded at each meeting with "earnest seekers "[42] and then finally in London and back to Toronto in 1873.[43] Desire for the experience of present personal holiness continued to be clearly the driving force behind this revival and gave impetus to later holiness groups.

In 1836 in New York City, Phoebe Palmer and her sister, Sarah Worrall Lankford, had founded what became a regularly occurring Tuesday afternoon prayer group, known as the Tuesday Meeting for the Promotion of Holiness, lasting for many years and inspiring nationwide prayer meetings.[44] Melvin Easterday Dieter observes that the Palmers' special promotion of holiness had an essential dynamic best captured by the one word heard most at the Tuesday meetings—"definite."[45] The language perhaps best reflects the emerging modernism in renewal piety that would be in full bloom by the time of the Pentecostal revival a few decades later and would impact its doctrine of the Spirit by attempting to articulate it in an objective way. However, compulsion to develop clear definitions of the Spirit's work had begun to fade somewhat by the time of the outbreak of the Charismatic Movement. Similarly Palmer's 'shorter way' to sanctification had broken ranks with Wesley's subjective approach and, while paving the way for classical Pentecostalism's objective view of the reception of Spirit-Baptism, the trend had appeared to cycle back to a more subjective understanding in the Charismatic Movement with its widespread view of experiencing the Spirit apart from any reference to definite initial evidence.

While lacking precise parameters, Christian perfection, holiness, and entire sanctification as roughly synonymous concepts for an experience of post-conversion grace was an impulse that was all-pervasive in Methodist circles in Canada during the mid to late nineteenth century, as it was in the United States. It was more the positive side of holiness understood as love made perfect, as opposed to the more negative angle of cleansing the heart from evil, a notion that occupied the preaching and writings of Holiness leaders.[46] As Methodist camp meetings and the religious fervor associated with those ideas began to decline, the Holiness Movement signaled a return to a more personal and pietistic approach to religion and, in so doing, anticipated the embracing of a personal experience of the Spirit among hundreds within the institutional structure of Catholicism and mainstream Protestantism many decades later. Holiness groups became concentrated largely in southwestern and eastern Ontario as well as in the Prairie Provinces.

Two Canadian Holiness Leaders

Two Ontario Methodist ministers, Nelson Burns and Ralph Cecil Horner, actively promoted holiness within their denomination by organizing autonomous holiness associations, a practice which led to each being deposed from the Methodist ministry in 1894 and 1895 respectively.[47] The earliest of those groups is commonly known as the Canadian Holiness Association with Nelson Burns as its first president and was active mainly in southwestern Ontario from Toronto to London and the Niagara Peninsula.[48] As an organization within Canadian Methodism, it was launched in 1879 with the explicit purpose of "reviving the teaching of Wesley, John Fletcher and Adam Clarke on the subject of entire sanctification"[49] and, meanwhile to join with the same Holiness Movement already taking place in England and the United States, naming its official publication, *The Expositor of Holiness*.[50]

As a boy, Burns had read Phoebe Palmer's writings and had subsequently experienced the blessing of entire sanctification.

> When about the age of fourteen I came across "Faith and Its Effects," a book published by the late Mrs. Palmer of New York. Those familiar with that publication will remember that its chief burden was the "blessing of holiness," as it was called, in harmony with the teaching of John Wesley. I read it with great appreciation, and, according to my practical nature, at once essayed to seek and obtain the experience. I was successful, following closely the directions of the writer, and secured what I considered was that blessing.[51]

His later writings indicate that he was deeply impacted by her ministry.

Notwithstanding this direct influence of Palmer's ministry, Burns' thinking and that of his associates began to shift. In his landmark work on the Holy Spirit as the source of direct revelation, *Divine Guidance or the Holy Guest*, Burns included the testimony of another Holiness minister, Rev. B. Sherlock, in which a window is opened on the motivation and progress of his changing perspective:

> We honestly thought at that time, that the methods of work, and mode of presenting the subject which had been adopted and used by the late Mrs. Palmer, Dr. Foster, Bro. Inskip and others, were as nearly right as possible. But after a few years our President, Rev. N. Burns, began to see that the Holy Spirit of God was not receiving due honor and recognition, neither by us, nor by the Church generally.[52]

While the Canadian holiness revival claimed to revive and restore true Methodism, the version being preached was, in reality, one more derived from Phoebe Palmer. Burns was very much aware that the sanctification teaching brought by Palmer was a definite shift away from mainstream Methodism—a direction with which he did not entirely agree. In his view, she had "impressed her characteristics and experience upon the movement; so much so that the whole movement in the States and Canada might at this time been correctly named 'Palmerism.'"[53] The term was his cynical assessment of Palmer's mechanistic method of achieving holiness:

> Mrs. Palmer professed to represent the experience which John Wesley taught in his writings on the subject of holiness, but, in my estimation, she added considerably to his thoughts on the subject. Unlike John Wesley, she pointedly and continuously professed to practise what she taught on that subject. The improvements she made was to make the seeking and gaining of a definite experience easier of securement, that is, as the outcome of definite faith rather than as a chance outcome of vague teaching concerning ascetic practices. Hence it followed that she was able to lead a vast number into a definite experience on the subject, as she insisted on the acceptance of the blessing of holiness by cold, intellectual faith.[54]

Burns did not seem to be opposing Palmer's theology of holiness as much as her methodology of faith that for him was the vulnerable point in her ministry because "failure to retain the experience was inevitable."[55] For Burns, "the whole matter might be summed up as accepting an experience by faith, and striving to retain it by abounding labors."[56] Nevertheless, the 'shorter way' to holiness preached by Palmer became the common property of all three North Atlantic countries: the United States, Britain and Canada.[57] Her periodical, *Guide to Holiness*, had a deep impact generally upon the emerging Canadian Holiness Movement, receiving mention in the *Christian Guardian*.[58]

Burns seemed to gradually acquire the notion of a divinely given authority over his own organization and became preoccupied with the private guidance of the Holy Ghost.[59] He wrote in 1889 that "the Holy Spirit, as guide into all truth, would supersede all laws, whether human or Divine, and be to each and every one, so receiving him, the law of God, written on his heart...."[60] Furthermore, his holiness emphasis based on a second blessing experience of instantaneous sanctification quickly ran into trouble with the Methodist commitment to holiness as part of the everyday life of ordinary Christians. His eventual assertion that *divine guidance* would result in a Christian making no regrettable mistakes resulted in his deposition from the Methodist Church at its 1894 conference in Guelph, Ontario.[61]

Although the movement led by Burns was slightly earlier, the Holiness Movement Church in Eastern Ontario was perhaps the most prominent. David Bebbington observes, "These organisations were self-consciously part of an international impulse to rediscover the source of early Methodist power."[62] Caughey's evangelism endeavors from south of the border had already paved the way for the ministries of later Canadian Holiness leaders, especially that of Ralph Cecil Horner,[63] "an ambitious young Methodist clergyman whose mesmerizing and emotional services led to a break with that church in 1895."[64]

It became clear following Horner's conversion and experience of entire sanctification at a Methodist revival in 1872 that he was determined to lean on his own interpretation of the will of God and not on obedience to the religious hierarchy.[65] Following his ordination in 1887 with the Montreal conference of the Methodist Church, Horner soon ran into trouble for insubordination to the Conference that had assigned him a specific circuit, choosing instead to follow the "leadings of the Spirit" in his own evangelistic ministry.[66] He began to advocate a third blessing of empowerment for evangelism, believing he had received a "Tongue of Fire," in addition to conversion and entire sanctification, and was quite comfortable with wild physical manifestations much to the dismay of his Methodist superiors.[67] Donald Dayton argues that in addition to B. H. Irwin, Horner was a pivotal figure in addressing the tension between entirely sanctified and empowered by the Spirit by articulating his doctrine of "three blessings" or "works of grace." He proposes:

> R. C. Horner is particularly interesting because he reveals a more extensive and sophisticated knowledge of Wesley, having at one point written an extensive refutation of the emerging attacks on Christian Perfection in the Methodist Episcopal Church. In one sense it may be said that Horner understood Wesley better than the mainstream of the holiness movement. As Horner put it, "Wesley taught that holiness was salvation from inbred sin, and he knew that the disciples were not told to wait for cleansing. He collected and quoted prayers that had been offered up for the entire sanctification of God's people, but did not intimate that any of these prayers were answered on the day of Pentecost.[68]

Horner's reference to being "baptized with the Holy Ghost" anticipated the language of Pentecostalism that would become common in the following century among early Pentecostals and later to some degree with Charismatics. In fact, both Burns and Horner spoke respectively of a 'full-orbed Pentecostal experience' and 'a Pentecostal flame'.[69] Horner described his own experience of entire sanctification on a campground where "instantly the second work of grace was wrought and God seemed to let the whole heavens upon me, and the witness of the Spirit was received. A heaven of love was upon my head, and love went through me to the sole of my feet. It destroyed the body of sin and purged out all carnal affections."[70] He describes his third blessing as "Tongues of Fire": "The extra gift for soul winning has been the aggressive element in my experience…It's Fire brought all the dormant powers of my soul into activity, and energized all my faculties in the vineyard of the Lord."[71]

This experience propelled him into an aggressive evangelistic ministry that preached holiness principles while at the same time criticized institutional Methodism for its loss of Wesley's vision of complete holiness. In essence, the language of Horner's teachings and writings on the *ordo salutis* clearly set the stage for the soon emergence of Pentecostalism. His work, Pentecost, for instance, was an effort to convince followers of the need for seeking a 'baptism of fire'—as much their privilege as the early Christians.[72] Nevertheless, Horner's ouster from the Methodist Church followed his increasing unwillingness to submit to its discipline and hold to its doctrines, arguing instead that it had forsaken the genuine theology of holiness. As Brian Ross suggests, "The Methodist Church finally had no place for Ralph Horner only because he simply had no place for it."[73] Ross's no-holds barred assessment of Horner takes into account the latter's view of himself as a new John Wesley: "Horner viewed himself confronting the hostility of established Methodism, even as Methodism's founder had faced the hostility of the established Church of England. Eventually the fate which Wesley escaped overtook Horner - he was removed from the ministry to which the Church had ordained him."[74]

Horner had become a member of the Wesleyan Methodist Connection of America in 1894, tried unsuccessfully to have it incorporated in Canada and then in 1897, he finally founded the Holiness Movement Church (HMC) with himself as bishop. Thousands had already been converted under his ministry in the Ottawa Valley and surrounding area and now scores of disenchanted Methodists and other evangelical Christians became attracted to the holiness impulse under his leadership. A report on one of Horner's extended missions by the circuit minister to the Methodist paper noted: "A peculiar feature of our meetings was the number who were prostrated. Sometimes as many as twelve were unable to rise from the altar of prayer, being overcome by the power of God."[75] In his autobiography, Horner recalled that such phenomenon was common, with people falling over immediately upon being prayed for while others danced or shook with uncontrollable fits of laughter and one instance of a man roaring like a lion.[76] When criticism came against him at the Montreal Conference in 1893, his defense was that he was not deliberately encouraging such manifestations but that "under the mighty outpouring of the Holy Ghost such scenes would follow."[77]

The movement spread to western Canada as some of its members eventually migrated there.[78] Nevertheless, by the turn of the twentieth century, of the 2,772 people listed in the official Canadian census who declared themselves followers of the HMC, 2,139 of them lived in Ontario.[79] They were to constitute the small demographic out of which the early Pentecostal movement in eastern Ontario emerged.

The Holiness Legacy

In retrospect, Horner's church organization arose in the context of "the synergistic forces of urbanisation and industrialization"[80] occurring within Canadian life that went hand in hand with transition away from emphasis on personal crisis experiences of conversion and sanctification toward formality and respectability in religion. The Hornerite schism "...forced Horner and his followers to justify the separate existence of the Movement by developing a systematic critique of Methodism that caricatured the church as a spiritually bereft, worldly, elitist organization that had abandoned the values of both 'Old-time Methodism' and 'true believers.'"[81] The simplicity of the rural island of nineteenth century agrarian Canada caused Horner and his associates to advocate separation from worldly practices and resulted in widespread appeal to people from rural non-industrial society. The typical follower of Horner's movement would have been a common rural individual "unhappy with how the Methodist Church was meeting his spiritual and emotional needs"[82] and wanted to experience a "more emotional, old-fashioned salvation which was totally opposed to the social gospel, industrial capitalism, and modernism."[83]

Yet in his later years, Horner came to believe that even the church he founded had also slipped by not staying true to Wesleyan theology. As with many Pentecostals in the second half of the twentieth century when faced with growing institutionalization within their own ranks on the one hand, and what was perceived as strange manifestations of the Spirit within some circles on the other, there was a fervent desire to return to the past. Horner too believed firmly in Methodist theology as it was practiced in the earlier part of his own century. His "vision economically, socially, and culturally was firmly fixed on the past. He wished to hold tightly to those strands of Methodism, nurturing and protecting them and applying them to his generation so that change would be neither necessary nor possible."[84] That coupled with his style of episcopacy, his view that having been wholly sanctified, he was incapable of making wrong decisions, and his insistence on external dress as evidence of inner change led him and a small group of members of the church in 1916 to form the Standard Church of America. Eventually, Horner started a small Bible college in Brockville, Ontario that also served as a high school following his split from the HMC that he had founded. The 1947 edition of its yearbook lists Roy L. Mainse as Principal and David, his son as a student. The new organization's most stable mission work was in Egypt where, in the 1930s to 1940s, Roy Mainse was one of its main missionaries. David would become a PAOC minister and the preeminent classical Pentecostal leader in the interface of Canadian Pentecostalism and the emerging Charismatic Movement.[85]

Meanwhile, there continued to be widespread disagreement within Methodist circles, not so much over the validity of the doctrine of entire sanctification, but over how it is to be attained—suddenly or gradually, and its necessity for salvation. Many leaders and members were not prepared to relate its attainment to excessive displays of enthusiasm and emotion. As would be the tendency in the next century when classical Pentecostals would try to respond to the Charismatic Movement, there was suspicion over claims of direct communication with the Holy Spirit. Moreover, as early Pentecostals originally saw themselves as the vanguard of the full gospel with its fundamentalist values that had gotten lost in the formality and institutionalization characteristic of mainstream Protestantism, so Hornerite holiness envisioned itself as a counter-cultural movement against Methodism's compromise with modernity.[86] Methodism's lack of revivalist-type piety, its formalism, emphasis on higher education, and friendship with worldly practices[87] had created a perfect mix unpalatable to the Holiness taste.

As with the later Charismatic Movement that would spread trans-denominationally and so become a true ecumenical renewal, the Holiness Movement was not a phenomenon confined to the Methodist church only but drew in many from other denominational groups. *The Expositor of Holiness*, circulated mainly among Methodists when it was launched in 1882, described itself as 'Thoroughly Wesleyan in Doctrine, yet not Sectarian - hence suitable to the Lovers of Holiness in every Denomination.'[88] This was true for both Burns and Horner's holiness groups in that Presbyterians and Congregationalists participated and testimonies were heard from Lutherans, Anglicans, and ex-Catholics.[89] An ecumenical spirit seems to have been somewhat pervasive during this period while the Holiness Movement was still firmly attached to its Methodist roots.

American influence upon renewal in Canada, particularly evident in the Canadian Holiness Movement, continued throughout the remainder of the nineteenth century—an impact reinforced, it seems, by the lengthy tradition of camp meetings reaching back at least as far as 1810 with the spread of the Stone-Campbell Movement into the Maritime Provinces. Through the migration of Baptists from Scotland, a significant work had started in Halifax in the mid-1820s that became increasingly important as "a conduit for early influence from the United States."[90] Similarly in Ontario, Baptist immigrants also from Scotland had brought their traditions that interacted with the ideas of Barton W. Stone and Alexander Campbell and over time merged with the wider revival. While the Stone-Campbell Movement continued to have its own character, by the end of the nineteenth century, the shape of the tradition was being determined largely by events in the United States[91] and the Second Great Awakening would make effective use of the camp meeting approach.

Nevertheless, some Canadian scholars continue the claim to independent and indigenous renewal as echoed in this case by Leroy Garrett, a leading researcher in the American Restorationist Movement, who suggests:

> The Movement started in Canada as early, or almost as early, as it did the United States, and from independent sources.... The heirs of the Movement in the United States today are prone to overlook the history of their counterparts to the north as not all that significant. They are to be informed that the basic history of the Canadian movement, The Disciples of Christ in Canada Since 1930 (Toronto, 1949) by Reuben Butchart with its 700 pages is longer than most American histories and is filled with exciting stories of how the work began and grew, with the American movement.[92]

He observes that Canadians have their own heroes and pioneers and their own publications and institutions. Butchart emphasized this independence in his preface while admitting that the impact of the American movement was strong. Looking back on his life within the Movement, Butchart reminisced, "The Campbells and Barton W. Stone enlarged, qualified, and to a large extent developed, what had already begun. Especially did it add soul and depth to what was sometimes rigid, literalistic, and legalistic."[93]

The long history of rural Methodist camp meetings helped to sustain the vibrancy of the Wesleyan tradition of holiness for a longer period of time than in areas where increased urbanization was chipping away at the emphasis on entire sanctification and replacing it with the desire for respectability and a more formal, less emotional approach to piety. One such camp meeting took place just outside Toronto at which Methodists from the areas of Yonge Street and the Toronto Township gathered for several days where "a spirit of conviction rested on all the unconverted" and the preacher spoke with "the Holy Ghost sent down from heaven."[94] The language easily found its way into Canadian Pentecostalism particularly in places like the province of Newfoundland and Labrador where many Pentecostals had direct roots in the holiness traditions of the Salvation Army.

Except for the usual cultural moratorium brought about military upheaval, in this instance by the War of 1812-14, there was generally an uninterrupted circulation of literature and personnel within the circles of Methodism and subsequently in its offspring Holiness Movement. American Methodism was arguably more doctrinally conservative than its British counterpart and its influence in Canada during the mid to late nineteenth century tended to reinforce already received teaching on sanctification.[95]

In 1884, the Canadian Holiness Association launched its own series of camp meetings, inspired no doubt by the hugely successful camp meetings to the south initiated by the National Holiness Camp Meeting Association. Several of the leaders tried to keep the Canadian movement along American lines and although Burns tried to resist this, not so much it seems from an anti-American sentiment as from a desire to impose his own spiritual authority, the impetus came from the burgeoning holiness revival in the United States.[96] The 'United States Holiness Camp-Meeting Association' was invited to and did conduct at least one of its camp meetings in Canada in 1888 which Burns and his followers attended, albeit reluctantly.[97] Burns appears to have been in constant conflict with the "holiness creed movement" and referred openly to the "whole lengthened conflict between Palmerism and Burnsism."[98] His softer position on the issue of dress, seeing it as matter of each individual being led by the Holy Spirit, not only put him at odds with close followers of Palmer but also resulted in American holiness periodicals condemning The Expositor as a dangerous publication.[99] He soon became charged by the editor of the denominational paper, *Christian Guardian*, as 'an infallible oracle' and was even accused of heresy in reducing the force of Christ's divinity.[100]

As is frequently the case in times of renewal, frustration with denominational structures coupled with a self-understanding that the old is being divinely rejected in favor of the new prevailed in the disruption that was taking place in Canadian Methodist life. The followers of Burns and Horner came to be seen as supporting lone rangers leading organizations outside the control of denominational authorities and with attitudes of super-spirituality. John Carroll, the well-known Methodist preacher of perfect love, wrote to the *Christian Guardian*, warning about making a "specialty" of the Wesleyan doctrine of Scriptural holiness and against those who "talk by the hour to a very small coterie of illuminati who pique themselves on a terminology peculiar to themselves."[101]

Holiness leaders were appealing to a wide segment of Canadians that saw Canadian society moving away from a focus on personal piety as exemplified in old Methodist revivalism toward a social and community-oriented gospel, which for many was a shift from the sacred to the secular. After 1860 with the continuing economic and social changes associated with the pervading spirit of progress, in Methodism 'relevancy' became the buzzword as it attempted to make religion relevant to all aspects of society and so to join the sacred and the secular realms. Methodism was removing itself further from the ordinary citizen and gradually becoming more elitist and institutional.[102] By the end of the century, Methodist evangelist Hugh T. Crossley was preaching a hyper-positive post-millennialism: "Look on the bright side of the world. Some people think and teach that the world is getting worse and will continue to do so.... The world is getting better.... The Church and the world are coming together; but it is the world that is advancing nearer to the Church...."[103] It was this changing socio-religious environment that was perfect soil for the Holiness Movement to flourish.

For Horner, the connection between society and the sacred was not at the point of the institution but at the point of an experience of sanctification, resulting in true social responsibility. It appears that entire sanctification still did not entirely equip a person for living and engaging with Canadian society but life needed to progress within a legalistic ethos, governed by rules for living that resulted in a closed and super-spiritual society, doomed to survive on the fringes and eventually to devolve into almost total oblivion. Going forward, it was to be at least in part also the increasing institutionalization of Canadian Pentecostalism that resulted in many Pentecostals becoming attracted to the more open and spontaneous approach to the things of the Spirit manifested in the Charismatic Movement that they perceived as lying at the root of their own movement's origins.

Just as there was for some years no clear line of demarcation between the Canadian Holiness tradition and the Methodist tradition, so there would be significant overlapping of the Holiness and Pentecostal movements, and an eventual interfacing of the Pentecostal and Charismatic movements. Ironically, while the Holiness and Pentecostal movements built upon what remained of an already established renewal environment and conditioned it, the Charismatic Movement was a renewal from within the established liturgical and sacramental tradition. Nevertheless, it too was to be the agent for a widespread transformation of the former waves of renewal through individuals who emerged as leaders either from that tradition or frequently from previous revival traditions. Each movement had direct influence upon the next largely because the later wave of renewal was an attempt to recover what the previous one was seen to have lost. It is likely, therefore, that each movement is not as distinct as might be commonly perceived, or reported by its followers, but rather, part of an ongoing renewal impulse. In particular, the early Pentecostal revival in Canada by the 1960s was morphing into a very different brand of Pentecostalism. The Charismatic Movement, as well as the Jesus Movement, largely transformed the PAOC—a process that continued further with the Toronto Blessing.

By the end of the twentieth century, there had developed within the ranks of the PAOC at least three different 'Pentecostal' trajectories. Long-established congregations especially in rural areas continued to hold to the older doctrinal emphases, style, and ethos of the Holiness and Azusa Street revivals or wanted to return to a bygone revivalist era if possible. Other churches embraced a less traditional Pentecostal and more radical trans-denominational or non-denominational Charismatic approach, manifested especially in immigrant congregations though by no means confined to them. The third expression was an apparent rejection of both traditional Pentecostalism and contemporary Charismatic worship and practice in favor of a safer evangelical position that downplayed Pentecostal-Charismatic emphasis on glossolalia and the supernatural.

Pentecostalism Spreads into Canada

The Hebden Mission

For years, historians and students of Pentecostal history have searched for the origins of Canadian Pentecostalism. Perhaps in an effort to demonstrate its more indigenous origin, research has focused on the Hebden Mission in Toronto, a ministry founded by English immigrants James and Ellen Hebden in May 1906. Ellen had experienced conversion and sanctification at an early age in England and referred to it as "the baptism in the Holy Spirit." However, six months after the establishment of what also became known as the East End Mission, Ellen claimed she experienced a baptism in the Holy Spirit accompanied by speaking in tongues, an event totally unlike the experience of sanctification she remembered and one that was indeed common to others within the North Atlantic Holiness environment.[104] Her husband received the same experience shortly thereafter followed by between seventy and eighty individuals in the next five months. Students of Canadian Pentecostal history have been quick to point out that the importance of the events that transpired at the Hebden Mission is that no historical evidence exists to suggest that the Hebdens had any knowledge of the revival that had already started in April 1906 at Azusa Street. Adam Stewart argues, "In other words, both Ellen's Spirit baptism and the beginning of Pentecostalism in Canada appear to have originated independently from the influence of Pentecostalism in the United States."[105] As news of the East Toronto revival spread throughout the Holiness world of Canada and the United States, people from across the continent began to visit the mission to experience the Pentecostal baptism. Early Pentecostal leaders, including Frank Bartleman, William H. Durham, and Aimee Semple McPherson also made the journey to Toronto and spoke at the mission. From the revival, evangelists spread out across Ontario to establish new churches and missions.[106]

As was common among early Pentecostal groups, the mission very soon ran into organizational controversy, resisting attempts to consider affiliation with anything connected with denominationalism. As early PAOC historian Gloria Kulbeck observed, "They failed to distinguish between the ecclesiastical restrictions which they considered a form of bondage, and an organization such as was outlined in the New Testament."[107] The primitive independent nature of this early renewal movement in Canada is clear from the February 1909 edition of *The Promise*, the mission's publication:

> The work is undenominational but claims a place as the Church of God, at 651 Queen St. E., and being one in spirit with all the body of Christ all over the earth, with the Holy Ghost as leader and teacher, and the Word of God as the only creed, Jesus Christ being the savior, Sanctifier and baptizer, with the Holy Ghost and the Head over all things to the Church and the only foundation, or name, or gathering and the person to whom the gathering is made.[108]

The effect of anti-denominationalism was isolation and among other internal factors, including an increasing emphasis on a "prophetic ministry,"[109] resulted in the eventual demise of the Mission.

Meanwhile, the events surrounding the short life of the Hebden Mission constitute some firsts in Canadian Pentecostalism—Ellen as the first known individual to have received Pentecostal Spirit baptism; the first Canadian Pentecostal periodical, *The Promise*; the first camp meeting; and the first Pentecostal missionary from Canada.[110] But it is at this point that the roots of the current PAOC become less clear. Was the Hebden Mission a distinctive "Canadian Azusa" or was there an unknown connection with the Los Angeles phenomenon? And what part did the American Azusa really play in the emergence of Canadian Pentecostalism? The evidence appears scanty thus making any firm conclusion risky.

While some Canadian scholars, as noted previously, view the Hebden Mission as an independent Pentecostal phenomenon, it has been speculated that Ellen Hebden had first heard of the Spirit at Azusa Street through some tracts and correspondence. However, Miller reports that she gave no indication of it in her early writings and was initially opposed to tongues speaking. He notes that reports of the events in Toronto did reach as far as Los Angeles and received mention in Seymour's paper. It was widely believed at the time that spontaneous manifestations of Holy Spirit power were taking place all over the world.[111] Frank Bartleman visited the Hebden Mission in 1908 later recalling, "The Spirit wrought very deeply in the meetings at Toronto." Yet his expression of the revival was obviously at odds with what was happening in Toronto: "But the leader was very much tried with me because he did not understand the Spirit. He expected things done the old way, new wine in the old wineskins."[112]

One of Toronto's evangelical leaders, George Chambers, who initially was opposed to the events at the Hebden Mission eventually received Spirit baptism with tongues and later became a founding member of the PAOC in 1919 and was its first General Superintendent.[113] The report of Ellen having received Spirit baptism and speaking in tongues was sent to William J. Seymour, leader of the Azusa Street mission, and published in his paper, *The Apostolic Faith*. A longer account of Ellen's experience was also reprinted in the paper that she founded in early 1907, *The Promise*. Further reports of the events in Toronto spread throughout southern Ontario and even as far away as Los Angeles. Another report in Seymour's paper stated that a "Bro. O. Adams" of Los Angeles was in Toronto in 1906 to investigate the outbreak of glossolalia there.[114] In any case, Toronto and a short time later, Winnipeg, came under the influence of Azusa Street, both becoming the centers of early Canadian Pentecostal renewal.

Toronto, in particular, was a hub of activity with Pentecostal workers' conventions being held and foreign missions work initiated with the deployment among others of Charles and Emma Chawner to Africa, a couple whom the PAOC still claim as its first missionaries. Miller claims that before 1919, the Hebden Mission was clearly the leading Pentecostal work in eastern Canada. Yet in that year when Pentecostal leaders gathered in Ottawa to seek incorporation of the PAOC, the Hebdens were not present.[115] Among them were two individuals, Robert Edward McAlister, and Andrew Harvey Argue, both who were to become significant figures in the early history of the PAOC. Kulbeck reports that Ward recounted the first actual attempt of Canadian Pentecostals to become a denomination had taken place in 1909 when the Pentecostal Missionary Union was formed: "We chose this name to conform with the similar organization of the Americans at Alliance, Ohio, and also with the British organization of the same name."[116] McAlister became the leading spokesman in Ontario and Argue in Winnipeg, Manitoba. Both figures were strongly impacted by the Azuza Revival.

Azusa, Hebden and Canadian Holiness

It is necessary to turn briefly to the contribution of the Azusa revival upon early Canadian Pentecostalism, which appears to have blended and overlapped with the influence of the Hebden mission in an environment where Holiness and Pentecostal experiences of the Spirit were tending to merge. The leading edge of the Azusa influence in Canada seems to have been the ministry of W. H. Durham from Chicago who along with Robert Semple and his future renowned evangelist wife, Aimee Semple held Pentecostal meetings in London, ON in 1907 and 1909-1910. Durham's mission in Chicago would continue to have a far-reaching influence upon Canadian Pentecostalism through Argue's work in Winnipeg who himself was involved in the Holiness Movement. Argue visited Durham's mission in 1907 and received the Pentecostal baptism with tongues. He recalls, "At the end of 21 days,... I was filled with the Holy Ghost, speaking with other tongues as the Spirit gave utterance."[117] In time, it was Durham's Finished Work theology that would become the official doctrinal position of the PAOC. Argue maintained a close relationship with the Azusa Street Mission, sending at least one report of his meetings to Seymour in 1908 and in 1912 moved his family to Los Angeles to become better acquainted with the work there.[118]

The Los Angeles revival found its most direct vehicle in Canada in the Holiness Movement of eastern Ontario. McAlister's Scottish Presbyterian roots ran deep in the movement with its strict governance of behavior and dress. While living in Winnipeg, he had heard of the events at Azusa Street and was determined to travel there to see if the revival was genuine as reported. It was on the journey back home in December 1906 that he received his experience of Spirit baptism with tongues. By late 1908, he had started a small congregation in Ottawa and from there for several years itinerated through Ontario and Western Canada. The work in Ottawa was referred to as the "Apostolic Faith", a title most likely borrowed from Seymour's mission in Los Angeles. Always with a compulsion for publishing as a means of spreading news of the progress of the Pentecostal Movement, McAlister eventually was instrumental in launching *The Good Report*, shortly thereafter becoming *The Pentecostal Testimony*.[119] It became the official publication of the PAOC and its chief means of reinforcing its core doctrinal positions, unifying the fledging movement, as well as disseminating news of camp meetings, missionary reports and testimonies of miracles. The early fluidity of Pentecostal thought found McAllister associated with the Oneness wing of Pentecostalism and not until the formal organization of the PAOC in 1919 did he formally renounce Oneness doctrine. He and his colleagues were reluctant to be seen as starting another denomination but were nonetheless determined through the acquisition of a federal charter to "protect doctrine" and in some way to preserve the fruits of the great apostolic revival.[120]

In the same year, a convention was held in Moose Jaw, Saskatchewan at which J.W. Welch, General Superintendent of the Assemblies of God was invited to speak and to organize the Pentecostal churches of the four western provinces. As a result, the Western Canada District Council of the Assemblies of God, USA was formed. Two years later (1921), a conference of the fledging movement was held in Montreal and again Welch was invited to be present representing the American AG. Emerging from this meeting the Eastern Canadian group known as the Pentecostal Assemblies of Canada became the Eastern Canadian District of the Assemblies of God, USA. Before long, however, it became clear that it was not practical for Canadian Pentecostal churches to continue to be part of the American AG and the arrangement was dissolved by mutual agreement.[121]

While large segments of the Holiness Movement rejected Pentecostalism and shunned those who would not renounce their experience of tongues, it was a ready-made foundation for much of early Pentecostalism and the context in which a fresh, new experience of the Spirit took place. Direct connection between McAlister and Horner's Holiness group in the Ottawa area is not easy to establish with certainty. However McAlister had been converted in one of Horner's meetings around 1900 in a former Methodist church that became part of HMC after Horner was expelled from the Methodist denomination in 1895.[122] Given the short span of time between McAlister's personal spiritual encounter and news of the events in Los Angeles, it is difficult to imagine that his theology and practice had not been shaped significantly by the Holiness environment. Yet, in spite of the attempts by some PAOC historians to establish a direct link between Horner and PAOC founders, there are those who are not so convinced. Earl Conley of the Standard Church, a small splinter group from the HMC formed in 1916, insists that the connection does not exist and that Horner had absolutely no influence on Pentecostals.[123] The distancing that frequently occurs, especially on the part of the majority group when a renewal segment establishes itself separately is arguably at play here. The PAOC would later find itself compelled to follow a similar pattern in its response to the Charismatic Movement as it faced what it deemed to be aberrations of Pentecostal orthodoxy.

Nevertheless, maintaining distance and isolation as a natural reaction to threatened position and authority can frequently be at odds with reality. As late as 1958 when Kulbeck published her history of the PAOC, no mention is made of either Horner or the HMC as factors in the formative years of the denomination. Yet, Horner's renewal position was practically identical to that of the early Pentecostals in Toronto, Winnipeg, and the Ottawa area. His third work of grace, a 'baptism of fire' seen as "the extra gift for soul winning" that "brought all the dormant powers of [his] soul into activity, and energized all [his] faculties for efficiency in the vineyard of the Lord"[124] parallels the long accepted view in PAOC circles of Spirit baptism primarily as empowerment rather than as a sanctifying experience. Fortune observes that prostration and intense feelings of ecstasy associated with Holiness piety were exactly what early Pentecostals experienced except that they were delighted to express those same emotions through speaking in tongues.[125] The widened gap between the majority of Holiness churches and Pentecostals was largely the effect of the former's rejection of the doctrine of glossolalia, not its doctrine of Spirit baptism as an 'anointing' for service following sanctification.[126] Dieter argues:

> Horner observed that had Wesley not been convinced that the apostles had already been sanctified and that the Acts passages referred to a "baptism for service," he would most certainly have used those passages, for they would have been his strongest texts. Horner concluded that the experience of the holiness movement to his time was the practical proof that sanctification did not bring spiritual power.[127]

While historical lines of actual contact with the Canadian Holiness Movement, specifically the HMC denomination are difficult to document, the similarity in pneumatological thought is striking.

Both Argue and McAlister had become part of the new wave of renewal emerging out of the Holiness Movement; McAlister out of a Hornerite revival and Argue through a more loose connection with Holiness groups, the latter stating in 1932 that previous to his Pentecostal experience he "had been much interested in the various Holiness Movements and enjoyed the experience of holiness."[128] Further, early interfacing of the Holiness and Pentecostal movements is no better illustrated than in the case of Herbert E. Randall, the first missionary of Horner's HMC, deployed to Egypt in 1899. He visited the Hebden Mission in March 1907 and while he held that he had been wholly sanctified, there he experienced the baptism of the Spirit with tongues: "And right there, I let go my profession, which I had held until then of having the baptism of the Holy Ghost. When I let it go, I was conscious of no loss, and I saw that hitherto I had been cleansed from all sin, and had received many outpourings, or anointings of the Spirit, but had not received the real baptism with the Holy Ghost.[129]

McAlister reprinted the story in his own early paper, *The Good Report* [130] which preceded his founding of *The Pentecostal Testimony*. While there was in no way any merging of the HMC and the early beginnings of the PAOC, some of Horner's people had definite connections with the emerging Pentecostal movement. In fact, of the early leaders surveyed in Gordon A. Atter's *The Third Force*, whom he believes "deserve mention," he observes that at least half have direct roots in the Holiness Movement.[131]

Why there still seems to be little knowledge within the PAOC about its Holiness origins is a matter of speculation but few know little, if anything, about Phoebe Palmer's ministry or even of the subsequent Hornerite holiness revival. The distance that grew over the decades may be due to several factors, not the least of which may have been the general rejection of tongues by the Holiness Movement and the associated rift that appears to have occurred between some new "come-outers" such as McAlister and their theological parent. McAlister's report of his baptism in the Spirit in *The Good Report* suggests that indeed such a divorce was underway. His rhetoric is strong and incisive: "Well, I see I have all you Holiness people shouting when I talk about the wind and fire. But now I read the fourth verse which says, 'And they were ALL filled with the Holy Ghost and began to speak with other tongues as the Spirit gave them utterance.' What's the matter now? You have all dropped your heads, and not an amen in the crowd."[132] McAlister then satirically refers to an unnamed Holiness leader as "Brother Loyalty" (presumably Horner) who keeps resisting when one of McAlister's own group "...would break through the restraint and receive the fullness, speaking in other tongues....But as soon as it was known the ecclesiastical whip was introduced and the gag law enforced, which is: "Say nothing about it."[133] While official correspondence has not yet been discovered between Horner and McAlister and despite their disagreements over the new wave of revival, there were close connections between the McAlister family and Horner's ministry as evident through census records and early photographs.[134]

Ironically, both the break of the Canadian Holiness Movement from Methodism and the separation of the early Pentecostal movement from its Holiness roots started in ambiguity but eventually became unmistakable. Beneath the surface, their basic theological positions and particularly their pneumatological perspectives remained strikingly similar, but certainly not distinct enough one might argue for such distancing to have taken place. But family feuds are not easily resolved. Fear and mistrust associated with new approaches to orthodoxy and orthopraxy tend to result in entrenchment of the majority view that sees itself as the guardian of true doctrine. The fear of the Methodist leaders was not renewed emphasis on the Wesleyan doctrine of Christian perfection but the fear that it might become the specialization of one group and so result in divisiveness and de-emphasis on other Christian doctrines. Similar angst was to be manifested in the later classical Pentecostalism as the Charismatic Movement would be accused of elevating the *charismata* above other more central doctrines of Christian faith.

Fuller rightly concludes that the very first generation of Pentecostal leaders was of Holiness preparation. By the 1920s, that source had all but dried up as more and more leadership came from individuals with non-Holiness backgrounds. Pentecostal churches had achieved a separate identity, the PAOC in particular, having received its charter in 1919, and were rapidly outstripping Holiness groups across the country in growth.¹³⁵ Theology had also shifted by the second and third decades so that the Holiness view of sanctification as a crisis experience had been dropped and sanctification as a progressive work of grace had taken a firm foothold along with Spirit baptism as the source of empowerment for service with tongues as evidence.

The emergence of the PAOC as a distinct entity was due not only to the ripple of a new wave of renewal sweeping the globe but also was the product of a group of Christians within the Holiness Movement who had clearly become less than completely fulfilled with their progress in the Christian life. Fuller concludes:

> These people worked hard to fulfill the conditions for receiving the experience of speaking in unknown tongues, and were rewarded, often modifying their theology to fit the new understanding. This change was a direct alteration of the distinctive doctrine of the Holiness movement…which identified baptism of or in the Holy Spirit as the same as sanctification or anointing for service, and earned these people expulsion from their churches, and an immediate need for a new identity… there are indications that the demonstrations of the Spirit once associated with the holiness churches were emphasized less as the reputation of the Pentecostals spread.¹³⁶

While Fuller's assessment may not be universally accurate for all individuals and groups who became part of the early PAOC, its distinctive theological development is the story of an adaptation of Holiness emphasis on personal experience of the Spirit rather than a rejection of it. Disputes over the nature of Spirit encounters, sanctification, and empowerment created the same distancing that would occur decades later when a new wave of global renewal would make itself felt in Canada. By that time, similar dissatisfaction, in this case, with the growing institutionalization of the PAOC and its perceived loss of the spiritual vigor that had fuelled its inception would attract some to ride the new wave of spiritual renewal.

A New Latter Rain

The first real doctrinal threat to the original revival came for the PAOC in the late 1940s and early 1950s with the theological controversy called the "New Order of the Latter Rain," originating at North Battleford, Saskatchewan in 1948. Early inheritors of the first global revival often referred to the phenomenon as "The Latter Rain Outpouring" and to themselves as "Latter Rain" people. Despite the rapid growth of PAOC churches during and following the Great Depression, the original fervency and prominence of the spiritual gifts had begun to wane and so created the vacuum needed for a renewed emphasis on what was considered to have been lost. *The Pentecostal Testimony* in the 1940s printed numerous articles about the need for revival because of the "settling down" of the movement.¹³⁷ It is intriguing that a general perception of the need for spiritual renewal had developed barely more than three decades following the movement's beginning. That reality found its parallel in the 1960s, or arguably its continuation in the spiritual hunger that was widespread around the time of the outbreak of the Charismatic Movement. The later "Toronto Blessing" was likewise seen by many within the

PAOC to be the answer to the contemporary malaise within Pentecostalism under the notion not of the movement having been afflicted by a "settling down" but having "plateaued."

New twists on old orthodoxy frequently become catalysts for deep division within renewal. The New Order was the agent of a significant such crisis for a still relatively young, fledging denomination. Associated with the rise of healing evangelists like William Branham and Oral Roberts and their salvation-healing campaigns, the movement created challenges for the PAOC along the lines of its accepted orthodoxy and orthopraxy. Branham's claim to personal visions, for instance, and reports of mass healings made many Pentecostals uncomfortable even though divine healing was one of their distinctive doctrines. Extreme manifestations, doctrinal aberrations, lack of accountability, and the ever-present potential for autocratic leadership have often met with caution from PAOC leaders and more traditional members and constituted the basis of its concern with the New Order. Essentially, the Latter Rain revival was not a rejection of long-held doctrinal positions, but from the viewpoint of the PAOC, it was an attempt by a group of disgruntled Pentecostals to sabotage the growth of Pentecostalism in Canada by infusing those doctrines with different meanings.

An organizational schism was also intertwined with the Latter Rain controversy. A small Bible school that operated independently but drew financial support from PAOC churches found itself in dispute with the PAOC over the school's teachings on demonology and fasting, with fasting being taught as the route to greater spiritual powers over demons. Miller recalls, "Canadian Pentecostal leaders drew back in dismay from some of the practices associated with the 'Latter Rain Movement' as it expanded throughout the country."[138] There was fear that exaggerated importance was being given so much to the *charismata* that the gifts appeared to be viewed as approaching equal status with Scripture.[139] This was alarming to Pentecostal leaders, many of whom had longtime Holiness sensibilities where public exhibition of the gifts had been largely foreign. It would elicit a similar reaction two decades later when it became clear that a major emphasis of the Charismatic Movement was the restoration of the *charismata*. Many who remembered the Latter Rain controversy would associate one with the other which undoubtedly contributed to shaping the response of the PAOC in the 1970s and 1980s. What leadership seems to have missed, however, is that the second wave of renewal originated from within mainline churches rather than from within the older Pentecostal tradition.

A major difference between the Latter Rain controversy and the Charismatic Movement was that the former viewed itself as a group of Christians who were seeking a new fullness of the Spirit and open to all its accompanying manifestations but were being misunderstood and persecuted by other Pentecostals. The later movement, conversely, arose largely independent of classical Pentecostal expectations or out of a desire to restore what was believed to have been lost from early twentieth century Pentecostal revivals. It was this self-understanding of the Latter Rain that created problems for PAOC leadership in that "the radical movement found considerable sympathy among Pentecostals because it presented itself as a persecuted body of spiritual people who were interested in reviving moribund Pentecostalism" whereas leadership saw the sect as actively involved in the "exploitation of zealous Christians"[140] and encouraging entire congregations to join with them.

In addition to an acute emphasis on spiritual gifts, a heightened view especially of the role of "prophets" and "apostles" opened the door for disagreement and division among Pentecostals in the1950s. Miller observes that many initially were attracted because of what appeared to be a "fresh surge of power and vitality."[141] Apostolic authority, private prophecy, and the impartation of spiritual gifts seem to have been the new definition of a fresh working of the Spirit. Further, not only had the PAOC ironically been exhorting its followers through its official publication to seek spiritual renewal, its language carried overtones of a global vision. In his 1946 New Year's editorial, A. G. Ward called for a new awakening: "Thus far we have only touched the outer circle of this great maelstrom of Pentecostal power; God is challenging us to launch out upon His liberality until we see how near we can come to bankrupting heaven. The world is greatly in need of another old-fashioned revival of old-fashioned religion...."[142]

The movement along with its controversial theological emphases expanded beyond Canadian borders into the United States. From the American perspective, Edith Blumhofer proposes:

> Some first-generation Pentecostals had begun within a decade to bemoan the movement's waning power and had pointed to future, more copious showers of the latter rain...while many Pentecostals looked contentedly on their growing, stabilizing movement, a few here and there, uncomfortable with acculturation sought to fulfill a prophetic role. In doing so, they recalled a radically separatist part of their Pentecostal heritage most Pentecostals had gladly neglected. As outsiders calling a movement to task, however, they helped reveal dimensions of self-understanding that had seldom been so clearly targeted.[143]

In their indictment of fellow believers, they sent a clear message that this was a full restoration of apostolic power, the PAOC/AG being the 'former' rain and the New Order as the 'latter' rain.

The effects of the Latter Rain were felt worldwide in the post-World War II evangelical awakening.[144] While tongues as initial evidence of Spirit baptism was held to firmly, caution and even doubt about the practice of spiritual gifts would be pervasive in much of the PAOC in subsequent years, making the soil hard for the Charismatic Movement to take initial root. Proving that it had a direct impact on the later movement is a formidable task but similarities in the emphasis on the spiritual gifts are striking. The practice of the laying on of hands for their impartation and emphasis on private prophecy was a significant shift away from the older Pentecostal practice of "tarrying" for the Holy Spirit.[145] Praying for the Spirit to sovereignly impart *charismata* was the traditional comfort zone outside of which anything else would have been deemed as human manipulation. Fear of human beings controlling what many Pentecostals saw as the prerogative only of the Spirit made for an uncomfortable response to the later renewal. In the post-Charismatic Movement era of the PAOC, the practice of tarrying for Spirit Baptism and spiritual gifts has all but disappeared.

In the end, the tendency toward authoritarianism and sectarianism within The New Order of the Latter Rain would produce a fluidity that soon turned the revival into a phenomenon that had little to do with its place of origin: "The Latter Rain movement rapidly fused with the North American healing revival and its global extensions...."[146] Hutchinson makes the case that the Latter Rain movement as "a renewer of renewal" had a global reach as far as Southeast Asia, Australia and New Zealand and eventually made its way back into Canada via such influences as Hillsong Australia. In mapping out those connections, he argues that "in all of these churches, contemporary worship music, a theology of Presence, and liturgical acts such as laying on hands, provide clues for those who know where to look for the historical influence of the Latter Rain."[147] The stress on local church autonomy, a culture of sectarianism and independence, claims of special insight into mysteries contained in the Bible as well as the "unveiling of peoples' lives and hearts through the agency of the Spirit of God"[148] led to confusion when prophecy did not come true.

The discrediting of the movement by the PAOC left the denomination with more than a dark chapter in its history. The residual fallout was a climate of conservative pneumatological expression that would set the stage for ambivalence at best in its response to the Charismatic Movement. The majority view, in this case the PAOC, was experiencing the same reality in its dealings with the new fringe group that it had experienced itself in its relationship with the Holiness Movement. For example, McAlister who found himself previously having to defend a third work of grace as a tongues experience now was compelled to defend the original revival. He wrote a short booklet designed to dispel what he saw as error. "The Manifestation of the Spirit" argued that gifts are resident in the triune God, and are neither received, imparted, nor confirmed in humans, but are manifested and are conferred by the Spirit and not by self-appointed prophets.[149]

Many pastors became familiar with the British preacher Donald Gee's writings on the misunderstandings and extravagances[150] within the Pentecostal movement worldwide and found in him a close ally. Common ground notwithstanding however, Donald Gee's strong ecumenical outlook would not have resonated easily with the PAOC and the conservative ecclesiastical culture in which it operated. He was clearly opposed to the practices and direction of the Latter Rain revival:

> The whole passage in James has been cheapened by being used far too promiscuously. It does not teach an appeal by the Elders to the sick to come and be prayed for; it does teach an appeal by the sick to the Elders. And it means those who are seriously ill, not those with trivial and minor complaints that have not hindered them attending the meeting of the local church.... Anointing with oil...ought to be exercised with gravity in cases of serious need, and it would seem more suited for the privacy of the home and sick-chamber than the parading in public of prayer for the minor or intimate complaints of the bodies of believers, sometimes to our embarrassment.[151]

Gee was intent on maintaining what he saw as scriptural order regarding the *charismata*, so demonstrating his concern over what he saw happening with the extreme autonomy of the Latter Rain movement that by then was spreading well beyond denominational boundaries.

While Richard M. Riss claims that many of those involved in the Latter Rain revival continued to hold and develop ideas that had arisen in the 1940s and who eventually became part of the Charismatic Movement of the 1960s and 1970s,[152] direct connection between the two in Canada is not so easy to establish. Yet, it is almost certain that Latter Rain ideas filtered back into Canada along with the later movement. The practice of setting psalms to music which became a core part of Charismatic worship, emphasis on the "foundational ministries" of Ephesians 4:11, Old Testament tabernacle teaching, and the continuity of some institutions such as *Logos Journal* which was the outgrowth of a previous publication associated with Latter Rain and edited in part during those years by Gerald Derstine[153] is when taken together significant evidence that the reach of the 1940s revival went as far as the Charismatic Movement, though certainly in a less than direct way on the Canadian side of the border.

Blumhofer's assessment of the links between classical Pentecostalism and the Charismatic Movement in the United States are also valid for Canada in that the soft religious border between the two countries made what was to some degree true of one also true of the other largely because key figures in both movements travelled and preached in each other's space. First, the Latter Rain movement despite its elitism and extremism energized expectations that would fuel motivation for later Charismatic leaders. Second, it was the popularity of salvation/healing revivals during the 1950s that introduced masses of non-Pentecostals to Pentecostal practices and expectations and so helped sustain and fuel interest in charismatic worship and reception of spiritual gifts. Third, it was David du Plessis, a classical Pentecostal leader best known for his ecumenical activities among mainstream denominations and Catholics, who was the key international connection between both movements.[154]

Early in 1961, shortly after the beginning of the Charismatic Movement sparked by Dennis Bennett's experience of Spirit baptism, Du Plessis visited Calgary, Alberta and Vancouver, British Columbia's Broadway Tabernacle (PAOC) and "ministered...with much blessings."[155] At this early point, "the Pentecostal ecumenicalist"[156] was well received and his meetings reported in glowing terms. Nevertheless, hidden beneath this initial endorsement of what appeared to be Pentecostalism having finally reached into institutional Protestantism was the notion that those who had experienced Spirit baptism would not be able to stay in their own churches any more than those who had experienced it in the first wave of renewal did. Time was to prove that ripples from the second wave would indeed profoundly impact the PAOC but no mass exodus of neo-Pentecostals from mainstream churches would take place. Yet, the long-term effect was in many ways to radically transform the PAOC.

While there were perhaps as many dissimilarities as similarities between Latter Rain phenomenon and the Charismatic Movement, both insisted that the new work of the Spirit was a renewal movement that should not be confined to specific denominations but was meant to empower and unify the church. The golden age of the Spirit was not in the past but in the present and the future. Latter Rain emphasized a new day of divine activity, not a return to prior power, meaning the former rain. Healing evangelists associated with that movement had a broad interdenominational appeal without calling for denominational loyalties,[157] and in doing so at least prepared the ecclesiastical atmosphere for the outbreak of the Charismatic Movement. Openness to new revelations with only a loose commitment to Scripture as final authority was the major point of divergence as the PAOC saw it, a concern that was to keep dogging the denomination throughout the era of the Charismatic Movement and into the later Toronto Blessing. Deferring to new revelation as new authority has always alarmed PAOC leaders and many of its members, especially those whose roots go back to the early Pentecostal revival. The Latter Rain position that new insights and teachings could not be questioned since they originated with the Spirit recalls the ministry of Nelson Burns who ran into trouble with his fellow Holiness leaders when he claimed private guidance of the Spirit. Teaching the restoration of apostles and prophets was viewed as leading to abuse of authority as 'apostles' and 'prophets' claimed to receive new insights that were not open to question, thus becoming the means of exercising autocratic control over followers.

Nevertheless as Miller correctly points out, a positive result of the New Order controversy was

> ...a fresh realization of the widespread hunger among believers for a genuine move of the Spirit and fresh awakening of love and joy in the church services. The laity wanted a continued emphasis on the *charismata*, but one that was properly balanced with correct practice and sound theology...—it reminded the Fellowship throughout Canada that Pentecostalism could survive only by perpetuating both its biblical and charismatic distinctives.[158]

For the most part, that sentiment continued within the PAOC during the Charismatic Movement and beyond. The impulse to recover the original fervor of the first generation of twentieth century Pentecostals as well as to romanticize the Azusa revival have never really gotten lost. It would guide many rank and file members of the PAOC in their response to news of the outbreak of a new movement that had every initial sign of a renewed Pentecostalism for a new generation. Individuals would move freely back and forth between Charismatic Movement events and PAOC local churches while PAOC leadership struggled to respond appropriately without unnecessarily ostracizing those attracted to a deeper spiritual experience.

Notes

1. Mark A. Noll, *A History of Christianity in the United States and Canada* (Grand Rapids, MI: Eerdman's, 1992): 126-127.

2. Ibid., 127-128, 129.

3. Neil Semple, *The Lord's Dominion: A History of Canadian Methodism* (McGill-Queen's University Press, 1996): 31.

4. G.A. Rawlyk, *Ravished by the Spirit: Religious Revivals, Baptists, and Henry Alline* (Kingston & Montreal: McGill-Queen's University Press, 1985): 3.

5. Ibid., 5.

6. Rawlyk argues that Alline as a transmitter of the "Whitefieldian sound" also gave shape and substance to what has been more recently called the 'New Light Stir'—a broader religious revival that swept much of New England between 1779 and 1781. Furthermore, the "Alline neo-Whitefieldian evangelical tradition" rejecting predestination and embracing the responsibility of the individual in conversion directly impinged upon the Maritime religious climate, in particular, the Free Will Baptist tradition.

7. Noll, *History of Christianity*, 169.

8. Playter, George F., *The History of Methodism in Canada: With an Account of the Rise and Progress of the Work of God Among the Canadian Indian Tribes* (Toronto: The Wesleyan Printing Establishment, 1862): 9-10.

9. John Wesley, "The Signs of the Times" (*The Sermons of John Wesley, Sermon 66*, August 25, 1787, Wesley Center Online) http://wesley.nnu.edu/john-wesley/the-sermons-of-john-wesley-1872-edition/sermon-66-the-signs-of-the-times/ (accessed December 22, 2013).

10. Laurence W. Wood, *The Meaning of Pentecost in Early Methodism: Rediscovering John Fletcher as John Wesley's Vindicator and Designated Successor* (Lanham, MD: Scarecrow Press, 2002): 177-178. Meanwhile, Laurence Coughlan, a lay Methodist minister arrived in 1766 and began preaching in what was then the Newfoundland colony. Five years later, William Black, born in England but raised in Nova Scotia started evangelizing the Maritimes. Another early preacher, John Hoskins, left London, England in March 1774, arriving at Trinity, Newfoundland a little over a month later. He recounted his experiences in a letter to Rev. Wesley in 1781. John Hoskins, "An Account of Mr. John Hoskins: in a Letter to the Rev. John Wesley," Old Perlican, 15 October 1781, *ARMINIAN MAGAZINE* 8 (1785): 24-27, 85-88, 143-44, 194-96. http://www.mun.ca/rels/meth/texts/hoskins/hoskins2.html (accessed April 4, 2013).

11. Semple argues that New England expatriates in the Maritimes were too closely tied to their Calvinist Congregational roots and Anglicans too loyal and attached economically and politically to the British Empire for Methodism to take deep long-lasting root. Semple, *The Lord's Dominion*, 37.

12. Ibid., 54.

13. Ibid.

14. Phyllis D. Airhart, *Serving The Present Age: Revivalism, Progressivism, and the Methodist Tradition in Canada* (Montreal: McGill-Queen's University Press, 1992): 12-13. Yet, Airhart observes that when Canadian Methodism reached its centennial in 1891, Wesley was celebrated as "the foremost of all revivalists whom the church has ever witnessed." Even by then, stories of the early days of revival were being chronicled and colorful tradition woven of personalities and

the zeal of early converts. "In the century after Wesley's death, Methodist lore cast him from high-Anglican to revivalist par excellence."

15. While Noll notes in passing that Asbury made several trips into Canada, the evidence suggests that Asbury only visited Canada once. See John Wigger, *American Saint: Francis Asbury & the Methodists* (Oxford University Press, 2009): 375. But since it was late in his life, it is likely that Asbury's profile and influence still had a significant impact upon the fledgling Methodist revival movement in eastern Ontario.

16. Henry Boehm, *Reminiscences: Historical And Biographical of Sixty-Four Years in the Ministry,* ed. Joseph B. Wakeley (New York: Carlton & Porter, 1865): Nelson & Phillips Cincinnati: Hitchcock & Walden, 1875): 355-356. http://books.google.ca/books/about/Reminiscences_historical_and_biographica.html?id=QR0RAAAAIAAJ&redir_esc=y (accessed May 4, 2013).

17. Ibid., 353,356.

18. Ibid., 348.

19. Ibid.

20. *The Journal and Letters of Francis Asbury, Volume 2*, Chapter 12, Sept. 1, 1811, The Wesley Center Online. http://wesley.nnu.edu/other-theologians/francis-asbury/the-journal-and-letters-of-francis-asbury-volume-ii/francis-asbury-the-letters-vol-2-chapter-12/ (accessed May 8, 2013) Asbury's opening words to this entry indicate the long reach of the Second Great Awakening:

> Oh what manner of men we ought to be in labor, in patience, in courage, 6000 miles a year to ride, we to meet 8 conferences, you to hold camp meetings, quarter meetings, give me the number, and nomination, number of people upon probability that attended, preachers present; and guess at the number connected. I rejoice that camp meetings still prevail more or less, in all the states, provinces of Upper Canada, Tennessee, New York, Jersey, and Pennsylvania.

21. Clara McLeister, *Men and Women of Deep Piety*, ed. E.E. Shelhamer (Syracuse, NY: Wesleyan Methodist Publishing Association, 1920): 14.

22. Louise A. Mussio, "The Origins and Nature of the Holiness Movement Church: A Study in Religious Populism," *Journal of the Canadian Historical Association/Revue de la Societe historique du Canada* 7, no.1 (1996): 81.

23. Airhart, *Serving the Present Age*, 22.

24. *Dictionary of Canadian Biography Online*, s.v. "CAUGHEY, JAMES," (by Peter Bush), http://www.biographi.ca/EN/009004-119.01-e.php?id_nbr=6021 (accessed May 14, 2013).

25. Charles Edwin Jones, *Perfectionist Persuasion: The Holiness Movement and American Methodism*, 1867-1936 (Metuchen, 1974): xiv in Mussio, "Origins and Nature," 81.

26. Richard Wheatley, *The Life and Letters of Mrs. Phoebe Palmer* (New York: W.C. Palmer Publisher, 1881): 300.

27. Ibid.

28. Ibid., 300-301.

29. "The Time for Prayer: The Third Great Awakening." *Christian History*

(Summer 1989): 32-33. (no author listed)

30. Wheatley, *Life and Letters*, 331.

31. Ibid., 332.

32. Cited in Melvin Easterday Dieter, *The Holiness Revival of the Nineteenth Century* (Metuchen, N.J.& London: The Scarecrow Press, 1980): 59.

33. See *Christian History* (Summer 1989): 32-33.

34. J. Edwin Orr, *The Event of the Century: The 1857-1858 Awakening* (Pennsylvania State University: International Awakening Press, 1989). See also, J. Edwin Orr, The Awakening of 1858 in America (audio lecture), 28 min. 14 sec. http://archive.org/details/TheAwakeningOf1858InAmerica-ByJEdwinOrr-BroughtBy-Peter-john_658 (accessed August 16, 2013).

35. Daina Doucet, "The Day When Hamilton Changed the World" http://www.christianity.ca/page.aspx?pid=11878 (accessed August 21, 2013). http://query.nytimes.com/mem/archive-free/pdf?res=F40B1FFF3E581B-7493C2AB1788D85F4C8584F9

36. Ibid.

37. http://query.nytimes.com/mem/archive-free/pdf?res=F40B1FFF3E581B-7493C2AB1788D85F4C8584F9 (accessed August 22, 2013).

38. D. William Faupel, *The Everlasting Gospel: The Significance of Eschatology in the Development of Pentecostal Thought*, Journal of Pentecostal Theology, Supplement Series 10 (Sheffield, England: Academic Press 1996): 70.

39. "The Time for Prayer: The Third Great Awakening." *Christian History* (Summer 1989): 32-33 (no author listed).

40. Wheatley, *The Life and Letters*, 340.

41. Ibid., 445.

42. Ibid., 465-466.

43. Ibid., 471-472.

44. "The Holiness Movement Timeline 1824-1923," *Christian History* 82 (2004). http://www.christianitytoday.com/ch/2004/issue82/6.26.html (accessed September 27, 2014). "Phoebe Palmer: Mother of the Holiness Movement," *Christian History*. http://www.christianitytoday.com/ch/131christians/moversandshakers/palmer.html (accessed September 27, 2014).

45. Dieter, *Holiness Revival*, 63.

46. Clifford Roy Fortune, "Ralph Cecil Horner: Product of the Ottawa Valley" (unpublished master's thesis, Carleton University, 1999): 85.

47. *The Canadian Encyclopedia*, s.v. "Holiness Churches."(R. Gerald and Helen Hobbs) http://www.thecanadianencyclopedia.com/articles/holiness-churches (accessed August 28, 2013).

48. Marilyn Fardig Whiteley, "Sailing for the Shore: The Canadian Holiness Tradition" in George A. Rawlyk (ed.), *Aspects of the Canadian Evangelical Experience* (McGill-Queen's University Press, 1997): 257.

49. Nelson Burns, *Divine Guidance, or the Holy Guest* (Brantford, ON: The Book and Bible House, 1889): 261 in David W. Bebbington, "The Holiness Movements in British and Canadian Methodism in the late Nineteenth Century"

(The Wesley Historical Society Lecture in E. Alan Rose (ed.), *Proceedings of the Wesley Historical Society*, 50: October, 1996): 204.

50. Bebbington, "Holiness Movements," *Proceedings of the Wesley Historical Society*, 204.

51. Albert Truax (ed.), *Autobiography of the Late Nelson Burns* (Toronto: The Christian Association, n.d.): 8.

52. Burns, *Divine Guidance*, 261. The vibrancy of the Canadian Holiness Movement is also evident from the ministry of Ernest Crossley, one of Canadian Methodism's chief evangelists during the closing years of the nineteenth century. Under his ministry there might be over three hundred seekers of salvation during a three-week mission, teaching perfect love in every town where he preached. *Christian Guardian*, 30 Sept 1891, 612 in Kevin B. Kee, "The Heavenly Railroad: Ernest Crossley, Johm Hunter and Canadian Methodist Revivalism, 1884-1910," (master's thesis, Queen's University, Kingston, 1994): 9, 115 in Bebbington, "Holiness Movements," *Proceedings of the Wesley Historical Society*, 205.

53. Truax, *Autobiography*, 87.

54. Ibid.

55. Ibid., 88.

56. Ibid.

57. Bebbington, "Holiness Movements," *Proceedings of the Wesley Historical Society*, 208.

58. *Christian Guardian*, 11 Feb 1880, p. 47; J. W. Totten to editor, 16 Sept 1891, p. 579 in Bebbington, "Holiness Movements," *Proceedings of the Wesley Historical Society*, 208.

59. Bebbington, "Holiness Movements," *Proceedings of the Wesley Historical Society*, 212, 214.

60. Burns, *Divine Guidance*, 33.

61. Whitely, "Sailing for the Shore," in Rawlyk, *Aspects*, 259-260.

62. Bebbington, "Holiness Movements," *Proceedings of the Wesley Historical Society*, 204.

63. Mussio, "Origins and Nature," 81-82.

64. Glenn Lockwood, *Smiths Falls: A Social History of the Men and Women in a Rideau Canal Community, 1794-1994*. (Corporation of the Town of Smith's Falls, 1994): 454.

65. Fortune, "Ralph Cecil Horner,"131.

66. Mussio,"Origins and Nature," 82.

67. *Dictionary of Canadian Biography Online*, s.v. "Horner, Ralph Cecil," (by Neil Semple) http://www.biographi.ca/009004-119.01-e.php?BioId=41953 (accessed September 27, 2014).

68. Donald Dayton, "The Doctrine of the Baptism of the Holy Spirit: It's Emergence and Significance." http://www.freerevivalcd.com/cdlive/2/holyspirit.htm (accessed September 27, 2014). Although there is no known contact between Horner and Irwin, the latter apparently did visit Canada on at least a couple of occasions in 1899 and conducted revival services in Manitoba and Ontario. http://

www.seeking4truth.com/bh_irwin.htm#47 (accessed September 27, 2014). See also: Vinson Synan, *Fire Baptized: The Many Lives and Works of Benjamin Hardin Irwin: A Biography and a Reader* (Asbury, KY: Emeth Press, 2017): 58-59, 71-72.

69. Thomas Waugh, Twenty-Three Years a Missioner, (n.d.), p.142; Burns, *Divine Guidance*, p. 116. Horner, p. 107 in Bebbington, "Holiness Movements," *Proceedings of the Wesley Historical Society*, 206.

70. Ralph C. Horner, *Reminiscences From His Own Pen* (Brockville, n.d.): 10-11 in Mussio,"Origins and Nature," 85.

71. *Dictionary of Canadian Biography Online*, s.v. "Horner, Ralph Cecil."

72. Ralph C. Horner, *Pentecost* (Toronto: William Briggs, 1891).

73. Brian Ross, "Ralph Cecil Horner: A Methodist Sectarian Deposed 1187-1895" *Journal of the Canadian Church Historical Society* 19, no. 2 (1977): 101.

74. Ibid.

75. *Christian Guardian*, September 30, 1891, 612.

76. Ralph Horner, *Evangelist* (Brockville, Ontario, 1926?): 82, 137, 40, 139, 51 in Bebbington, "Holiness Movements," *Proceedings of the Wesley Historical Society*, 216.

77. *Minutes of the Proceedings of the 10th Session of the Montreal Annual Conference of the Methodist Church*, Toronto, 1893, p. 72.

78. *Dictionary of Canadian Biography Online*, s.v. "Horner, Ralph Cecil."

79. Fourth Census of Canada 1901, Vol 1, Population. Prepared by S. E. Dawson, Printer to the King's Most Excellent Majesty, 1902, 144. http://archive.org/stream/fourthcensusofca01canauoft#page/144/mode/2up (accessed September 4, 2013).

80. Mussio,"Origins and Nature," 82.

81. Ibid, 83.

82. Fortune, "Ralph Cecil Horner," 115.

83. Ibid.

84. Ibid., 99-100.

85. *Dictionary of Canadian Biography Online*, s.v. "Horner, Ralph Cecil." See also, Fortune, "Ralph Cecil Horner," 192, 195.

86. Mussio,"Origins and Nature," 82-84.

87. Separation from worldly practices was interpreted in most holiness circles as relating not only to dress and abstinence from alcohol but abstention from secret societies as well as from life insurance societies that Burns saw as symptomatic of lack of faith in divine provision. *Divine Guidance*, 156.

88. Nelson Burns to editor, *Christian Guardian*, 25 Jan 1893, p.51. Ron Sawatsky, 'Unholy Contentions about Holiness': the Canada Holiness Association and the Methodist Church; *Canadian Society of Church History Papers*, 1982, pp. 13, 2. Burns, *Divine Guidance*, pp. 284-6 in Bebbington, "Holiness Movements," *Proceedings of the Wesley Historical Society*, 211.

89. One speaker remarked, 'I am a Baptist, but I have got the water out of my eyes'! J. Ferguson to editor, CG, 7 Dec 1892, p. 771. J. Ferguson to editor,

Christian Guardian, 7 Feb 1894, p.84. J. Ferguson to editor, 16 Jan 1895, p. 36 in Bebbington, "Holiness Movements," *Proceedings of the Wesley Historical Society*, 211.

90. Douglas A. Foster, Anthony L. Dunnavant, Paul M. Blowers, and D. Newell Williams (eds.) *The Encyclopedia of the Stone-Campbell Movement* (Wm. B. Eerdmans, Publishing Co., 2004): s.v. "The Movement in Canada."

91. Ibid.

92. Leroy Garrett, *The Stone-Campbell Movement: The Story of the American Restorationist Movement* (Joplin, MO: College Press Publishing Company 1981): 292-296.

93. Ibid., 296.

94. John Carroll, *Canadian Methodists for the Last Forty Years* (Toronto: Alfred Dredge Publishing, 1860): 65.

95. Bebbington, "Holiness Movements," *Proceedings of the Wesley Historical Society*, 222.

96. Ibid.

97. Burns, *Autobiography*, 116-117.

98. Ibid., 113.

99. Ibid., 106.

100. *Christian Guardian*, October 12, 1892, 644 in Bebbington, "Holiness Movements," *Proceedings of the Wesley Historical Society*, 222, 225.

101. Whitely, "Sailing for the Shore," in Rawlyk, *Aspects*, 259.

102. Fortune, "Ralph Cecil Horner," 74.

103. Hugh T. Crossley, *Practical Talks on Important Themes* (Toronto: Wm. Briggs, 1895): 14-15.

104. Adam Stewart, ed., *Handbook of Pentecostal Christianity* (DeKalb, Illinois: Northern Illinois University Press, 2012), 105.

105. Ibid,.

106. Ibid., 106.

107. Gloria Grace Kulbeck, *What God Hath Wrought*, eds. Walter E. McAlister and George R.Upton (Toronto: The Pentecostal Assemblies of Canada, 1958): 34.

108. *The Promise*, no. 12 (February 1909): 3.

109. Thomas William Miller, *Canadian Pentecostals: A History of the Pentecostal Assemblies of Canada*, ed. William A. Griffin (Mississauga, ON: Full Gospel Publishing House, 1994): 44.

110. Stewart, *Handbook*, 107.

111. Miller, *Canadian Pentecostals*, 39-40.

112. Frank Bartleman, *Azusa Street: the Roots of Modern-day Pentecost* (Plainfield, NJ: Logos International): 120-121.

113. Miller, *Canadian Pentecostalism*, 41-42.

114. Ibid., 40-41.

115. Ibid., 44.

116. Kulbeck, *What God Hath Wrought*, 36.

117. A.H. Argue, "Azusa Street Revival Reaches Winnipeg," *The Pentecostal*

Testimony (May 1956): 9.

118. Miller, *Canadian Pentecostals*, 78.

119. Ibid., 62-63.

120. Ibid., 65-66.

121. Kulbeck, *What God Hath Wrought*, 37-38.

122. Douglas Rudd, *When the Spirit Came Upon Them: Highlights from the Early Years of the Pentecostal Movement in Canada,* ed. William A. Griffin (Mississauga, ON: The Pentecostal Assemblies of Canada, 2002): 135.

123. Fortune, "Ralph Cecil Horner," 202.

124. Ibid. See also *Dictionary of Canadian Biography Online*, s.v. "Horner, Ralph Cecil."

125. Ibid.

126. Clare Fuller, "The Effect of the Pentecostal Movement on Canadian Methodist and Holiness Churches, 1906-1930," (Unpublished Paper, Ontario Theological Seminary, May 1986).

127. Melvin E. Dieter, "Wesleyan-Holiness Aspects of Pentecostal Origins" in *Aspects of Pentecostal-Charismatic Origins*, ed. Vinson Synan (Plainfield, NJ: Logos International, 1975): 3-12.

128. A. H. Argue, "After Twenty-Five Years," *The Pentecostal Testimony* (June 1932): 13.

129. "The Comforter Has Come to Herbert E. Randall," *The Promise*, no.2 (June 1907): 1.

130. "Have Ye Received the Holy Ghost Since Ye Believed," *The Good Report*, no.1 (May 2011): 2.

131. Fuller, "The Effect of the Pentecostal Movement on Canadian Methodist and Holiness Churches, 1906-1930." See also, Gordon A. Atter, *The Third Force* (Peterborough, ON: The College Press, 1962): 67-79.

132. Ibid.

133. Ibid.

134. McAlister's oldest brother James and his family are listed in the 1901 national census as Hornerites. Fortune notes that an early photograph of *the Apostolic Faith* Mission Conference of 1911 shows Horner's first missionary, Herbert Randall with his arms around the shoulders of McAlister and two other early PAOC leaders. Fortunate, "Ralph Cecil Horner," 203-204.

135. Fuller, "The Effect of the Pentecostal Movement on Canadian Methodist and Holiness Churches, 1906-1930."

136. Ibid.

137. Miller, *Canadian Pentecostals*, 259.

138. Ibid., 261.

139. Ibid.

140. Ibid.

141. Ibid, 262.

142. "A New Year," *The Pentecostal Testimony* 27, no.1 (January 1, 1946): 2.

143. Edith L. Blumhofer, *The Assemblies of God: A Chapter in the Story of*

American Pentecostalism, vol.2, Since 1941 (Springfield, MO: Gospel Publishing House): 57.

144. T*he New International Dictionary of Pentecostal and Charismatic Movements,* rev. ed., eds. Stanley M. Burgess and Eduard M. Van Der Maas (Zondervan, 2003), s.v. "Latter Rain Movement." (by Richard M. Riss).

145. Ibid.

146. Mark Hutchinson, "The Latter Rain Movement and the Phenomenon of Global Return," in *Winds From the North: Canadian Contributions to the Pentecostal Movement,* eds. Michael Wilkinson and Peter Althouse (Leiden, Boston: BRILL, 2010): 266.

147. Ibid., 276.

148. Ibid.

149. L. Thomas Holdcroft, "Strange Fire: The New Order of the Latter Rain" http://www.spiritwatch.org/firelatter2.htm (accessed May 24, 2014). See also Miller, *Canadian Pentecostalism,* 264.

150. Walter J. Hollenweger, *The Pentecostals* (Peabody, MA: Hendrikson Publishers): 212.

151. Donald Gee, T*rophimus I Left Sick: Our Problems of Divine Healing* (London: Elim Publishers Co. and Springfield, MO: Gospel Publishing house, 1952): 17. http://www.sermonindex.net/modules/articles/index.php?view=article&aid=13678 (accessed May 24, 2014).

152. *NIDPCM,* s.v. "Latter Rain Movement" (by Richard M. Riss).

153. Ibid.

154. Blumhofer, *The Assemblies of God,* 86.

155. "Pentecostal Pioneer," *The Pentecostal Testimony* 42, no. 4 (April 1961): 9.

156. Ibid.

157. Blumhofer, *The Assemblies of God,* 87.

158. Miller, *Canadian Pentecostals,* 265-266.

3

Neo-Pentecostalism Threatens a Near Monopoly

More Winds from the South

Within months of the outbreak of what was first known as Neo-Pentecostalism in the United States, its effects soon began to be felt within Canadian mainline denominations. The religious and general cultural and political environment of the 1960s became the context of a desire for deeper personal spiritual experiences, particularly for Roman Catholics following Vatican II, and provided fertile ground for a fresh wave of the Spirit. Its emergence in Canada had a profound and lasting impact not only upon Canadian Protestant and Roman Catholic churches but the PAOC as well. Although much research still awaits especially on the comparative response of different regions of the country and thus the acquisition of a more accurate scientific picture of the interplay between classical Pentecostal churches and Charismatic Christians at the grassroots, evidence is available to sketch some broad strokes about the Charismatic Movement's certain and lasting impact upon the PAOC.

In 1967, Canadian Catholics gathered in Toronto, Ontario for a Congress on the Theology of the Renewal of the Church, an event designed to bring the message of Vatican II home. Although the emphasis was on renewal of the church's social mission to humanity, there were hints that some speakers were ready for a new day. The larger community was invited to participate with a many non-Catholics sharing in the planning, speaking from the platform, sitting on panels, and helping form the lively and attentive audiences. Meanwhile, Bernard Lonegan, a Jesuit from Toronto, became introspective and presented theology as a reflection on the experience of conversion. Catholic theologian Yves Congar, discussing the challenge of theological reconstruction, expressed dissatisfaction with the conventional theology of the Counter-Reformation, seeing it as useless for interpreting the gospel to modern man. He, along with others, rejected a return to the older scholastic theology as an adequate solution and found in contemporary thought some direction toward a new theological method.[1]

A direct link has yet to be demonstrated between this event and the Charismatic Renewal[2] that followed but there was a spirit of renewal in the Canadian ecclesiastical environment. The stage was being set and fresh winds of the Spirit were about to blow through the Catholic Church and other mainline churches in Canada. This was the Renewal that for some time had already begun to influence the Anglican Church. Canadian Catholic bishops, reflecting in 2003 on the occasion of the thirty-fifth anniversary of the Renewal among Canadian Catholics, refer to it as a "spontaneous emergence...in 1968 from coast to coast and in places far removed from one another" resulting in a "great upsurge of spiritual vitality and renewal."[3] In this way, the Renewal was being interpreted in much the same way as many leaders had interpreted the classical pentecostal revival.[4] Prayer groups sprang up in almost every diocese across the nation with diocesan committees set up to unite and assist them. They note also that the Catholic Renewal recognized early on that healing was an integral part of Jesus' ministry and that he empowered his followers to heal as well.[5] What the bishops believe to be remarkable about its history and rapid growth is the way it arose so spontaneously, not from the hierarchy but from the grassroots of the faithful to become very quickly such a nation-wide spiritual phenomenon.[6] Interestingly, now three decades from the events, the bishops appear to recognize little if any connection between the Renewal in Canada and the events that had occurred in the United States.

The Charismatic Movement emerged first among Anglicans in Canada at Prince Rupert, British Columbia where a young Anglican priest returned from California in 1961 with news of a Pentecostal outpouring among Episcopalians. Soon thereafter the dean of the cathedral, George Pattison, and some local clergy were baptized in the Spirit. Controversy erupted and glossolalia was forbidden in public resulting in the clergy involved feeling pressure to leave the area. However, among Anglicans, the movement that would result in greater longevity began in Ontario in 1962 under the leadership of Ron and June Armstrong who had both received the Spirit without direct contact with Charismatics. Ron, an Anglican priest, began to hold praise meetings in his parish in Toronto. Other Anglicans received the Holy Spirit following contacts made at the International Anglican Congress in Toronto in 1963.[7] However, Anglican renewal really took root after the annual synod of the Diocese of British Columbia passed a resolution in 1972 inviting Dennis Bennett to visit the diocese.[8]

Although there were individual Catholics who had experienced the Holy Spirit before the Renewal began to spread in Quebec and the rest of Canada, the actual incident that sparked its outbreak within the Catholic Church following neo-Pentecostal phenomena in mainline Protestant churches is believed to have taken place in Combermore, Ontario on August 20-21, 1968. James Hanrahan, professor at St. Thomas More College, Saskatoon, Saskatchewan recalls that during those two days, people from Ann Arbor, Michigan visited Madonna House and spoke about the move of the Spirit in the United Sates as they had experienced it since 1967. Hanrahan observes that there were Canadians attending Notre Dame some of whom joined the Charismatic Renewal as early as 1967, one of them being Sister Flore Crete. Also, one of the first members of a prayer group in June 1969 had been involved with prayer groups in Ann Arbor and East Lansing.⁹ Catherine Doherty, the principal foundress of Madonna House had long been concerned about the lack of awareness of the role of the Holy Spirit in the Latin Church compared with the deep sense of the Spirit's presence in the Eastern tradition where she grew up. After hearing reports of renewal in May 1967, she initiated contacts in early 1968 with some of the leaders with the aim of inviting them to Combermore. Hanarahan describes the result of the visit later that summer:

> Those who were present in Combermore for those days of teaching agree that it was a wonderful experience. They felt the power of the Spirit and the presence of Christ in a new way. They prayed in tongues and rejoiced to receive the Holy Spirit's gifts. And this was not just an experience of a couple of days; it stayed with them and became a normal and accepted part of their life.¹⁰

A fresh sense of unity, new openness, and the exercise of ministries and gifts were the result in a way not known before. From the experience at Madonna House, a movement was put in motion that eventually resulted in the development of Catholic charismatic prayer groups in other parts of Canada. Father James Duffy was sent to the Marian Centre in Regina, Saskatchewan where, after several months, he was successful in conducting the first open prayer meeting and later that same week prayed with one of those in attendance who then received the gift of tongues. Other groups followed soon after in Edmonton, Vancouver, and Calgary.¹¹

Whether through curiosity or a genuine sense that God was doing a new thing that classical Pentecostals could not afford to overlook, there is evidence of initial cooperation between some within the PAOC and mainline charismatic influences. Late 1967 in Vancouver, British Columbia, a local interdenominational committee comprised of Anglican, United, Lutheran, and Pentecostal lay and clergy representatives came together to pray and plan for an upcoming visit by Kevin Ranaghan, one of the early leaders of the Catholic Charismatic Renewal.¹² Ranaghan spoke at the University of British Columbia (UBC) and described the Renewal as one of returning to basic, simple, and uncluttered Christianity.¹³ Bernice Gerard, PAOC chaplain to UBC, had a leading role in planning the activities, an event viewed as a means of precipitating western Canadian participation in the spiritual renewal to the south that was by then spreading rapidly. More than a hundred claimed to have received the Holy Spirit¹⁴ including at least twenty-five on the university campus.¹⁵ A banquet was attended by an exceptionally diverse group of guests including university and theological college professors, prominent ministers from various denominations including liberal Protestant leaders, priests, nuns and classical Pentecostals.¹⁶ Gerard expressed the general sentiment of many within her classical Pentecostal tradition at the time by noting that the breakthrough was encouraging but that a much greater stirring of the Holy Spirit was being expected.¹⁷ The importance of Gerard as instrumental in the interface between the youth of the PAOC and the Charismatic Movement will be explored further in Chapter Six.

Although the Charismatic Movement sprang up somewhat independently across the spectrum of Protestant and Catholic churches in Canada, without any single outstanding leader, there is little doubt that news of renewal events in the United States had a significant inspirational impact upon what was taking place. The charismatic experience and subsequent notoriety of Dennis Bennett along with stories coming out of the university scene, particularly the 1966 retreat at Duquesne University at which students and faculty claimed to have received the Holy Spirit and tongues as well as the similar event at the University of Notre Dame in 1967 where the first Catholic Charismatic Renewal Conference was held served as catalysts for what happened in Canada.[18] Although the time had already become ripe for renewal, Peter Prosser's argument perhaps has some merit as well that "no Pentecostal renewal could have developed in Canada without the far-reaching consequences of Vatican II" whose documents contained fifty-three pronouncements on the Holy Spirit.[19] At any rate, it is also difficult to imagine the Charismatic Movement in Canada not being quickly influenced, if not accelerated, by the events at Duquesne and Notre Dame universities, at least for Canadian Catholics.

The increasing liberalization of some Canadian denominations, particularly the United Church of Canada (UCC), the conservatism of some other traditions such as the Anglican and Presbyterian churches, and the secularization of French-Canadian culture in Quebec with the consequent declining influence of the Roman Catholic Church in that province, provided the environment in which the Renewal could flourish. At the time, Canadian scholars Fr. Joseph Bistyzo and Dr. John Thompson of the University of Saskatchewan pointed to the increasing rationalizing of theology and the institutionalizing of the Church due to a widening acceptance of humanistic principles in the 1960s. The outcome was the creation of a religious and social "malaise and disorientation... among many Catholics" resulting in a "...vacuum providing a context in which profound emotional and spiritual needs could be met."[20] A similar openness to the winds of renewal was evident across the country though few, if any, appeared to be giving priority to formal organization.

New Associations and Denominational Accommodation

The new renewal movement in Canada was slower to develop national structures than in the United States although an association of evangelical/charismatic Christians called Renewal Fellowship was established in the UCC as early as 1965 with some of their renewal groups continuing to flourish today.[21] However, the real focal point of national interdenominational renewal developed with the PAOC minister David Mainse, who with deep Holiness roots founded an organization that led the way for ecumenical cooperation during the Charismatic Movement and became symbolic of Canadian evangelical and Pentecostal/Charismatic ecumenicity under its corporate name, *Crossroads Christian Communications In-*

corporated (CCC). The importance of Mainse's initiative as a public vehicle for Spirit-filled Christianity will be explored further in Chapter Five.

Canadian Anglicans who were experiencing the same renewal as was occurring to individuals and small groups in non-traditional church settings on a global scale were also eventually successful in organizing, although it occurred some time later. The International Anglican Conference on Spiritual Renewal held in 1978 in Canterbury, England sparked two attempts to establish a network for renewal but neither materialized until 1983 when sixty-six Canadian Anglicans attended an Episcopal Renewal Ministries Clergy Conference where through prayer, they heard words of encouragement and prophecy and a sense of God's call for "oneness" of the ministries of renewal in Canada.[22] They proceeded to form a committee, chose the name "Anglican Renewal Ministries," and held their first conference in Ottawa July 1985. With almost no money, the organizers proceeded in faith and watched as unsolicited donations arrived in time for each financial obligation. The conference was an exceptional success with over a thousand delegates, some of whom reported that they had a strong sense of being sent forth from the conference to minister in their churches and the world.[23]

The shape of the Canadian Catholic Renewal is believed to have begun at Regina as early as 1969 with the formation of what its members saw as a 'structureless' prayer group led by Father James Duffy. By 1972, the group of fifty or sixty Catholics, the majority of them in their twenties and thirties and calling themselves 'The House of Emmanuel', were meeting regularly. It had begun on the eve of Pentecost with a group of seven Catholics led by Duffy and with the blessing of Regina's archbishop. One of the leaders, Adrian Popovici, explained, "The participants didn't come together to pray a rosary, to participate in a novena, or to recite a Divine Office....They came to pray in their own words as each was inspired by the Holy Spirit."[24] Their commitment to the fellowship was evident by group members speaking "about what the Lord has done for them, or of their desire to discover what the Lord wants them to do.... After experiencing the reticence most liberal Protestants have about revealing their motivation or expressing the deep convictions of their faith, one is startled to hear such unabashed testimony from 'mod' young men and women."[25] Meetings were characterized by informality with folk songs, spontaneous prayer, thanksgiving, brief periods of silence interspersed by murmured prayers, chanting, and glossolalia. At various intervals, someone would read a Scripture passage and comment on it. Following this, members would ask for prayer for specific people or for themselves. The most striking aspect was the warmth, not the 'glad-handling' variety but one of 'acceptedness.'[26]

At this early stage in the Charismatic Movement, a surprising level of maturity is evident in Popovici's own assessment, in which he stressed that the charismatic experience is not purely for the sake of personal comfort but so that the Holy Spirit's gifts can result in Christian behavior in the world. He acknowledged that the group needed to be constantly on guard against emotional excesses and urged the participation of theologians and priests to help keep it on course.[27] It seems that this attitude would have contributed much to the positive relationship that existed between many Catholic charismatic groups and the established Roman Catholic Church itself.

There were hundreds of prayer meetings taking place right across Canada by 1973. In the province of Quebec, thirty-two French-speaking prayer meetings were being held each week.[28] Miller points out that the so-called "living room revolt against the clergy" in the 1970s was further exacerbated by the impact of television carrying gospel and charismatic programs, helping to expose Quebecois more to the outside world.[29] By this time, salvation and healing evangelists had managed to cross the language barrier to bring their crusades to Quebec using television as the primary medium with French translation. Miller continues, "The emphases of the Charismatic Movement that swept through Roman Catholicism …had a powerful impact on spiritually hungry souls."[30] It should be noted that it was a time of unprecedented change in Quebec culture when Catholicism as an institution was in serious decline. Although not without opposition from some aspects of both church and laity, the growing Renewal among Catholics flourished for a time in the spiritual vacuum created alongside major progress made by the PAOC resulting from such evangelistic efforts as providing French language training for Anglophone pastors.

In analyzing the Canadian version of the Charismatic Movement, Kydd has identified the development of three branches: denominational, nondenominational, and the "Jesus People."[31] The first consisted of those who welcomed the new winds of the Spirit but wished to remain within their own denominations; the second was made up of those who had distanced themselves from any existing Christian group, many of whom had been Pentecostals; and the third consisted largely of those converted out of the drug culture.[32] These interacted with each other and with older Pentecostal groups, particularly the PAOC.[33]

It is reasonable to assume that the first group was the largest and most significant in terms of its potential influence on classical Pentecostalism mainly because its emergence within the nation's mainline churches created dissonance for many Pentecostals who struggled to reconcile what was happening with the doctrine and praxis of those denominations. William A. Griffin, a PAOC leader and scholar, observes that the Charismatic Movement also created dissonance within the PAOC caused by effectively taking away a unified message that originally linked Spirit baptism with other evangelical doctrines of faith and service and in its place projected a message that the latter foci are of little consequence in a thorough-going Spirit emphasis.[34] The thought of Catholics continuing to hold to their doctrines of Mariology, transubstantiation, and prayers for the saints while practicing glossolalia was seen to have created confusion within Pentecostal theology. Peter Prosser was also a PAOC minister, who had prepared himself for French Canadian outreach and pastored the French congregation during the early 1970s that was part of Montreal's Evangel Pentecostal Church, a largely English-speaking church in downtown Montreal. He attended and observed many Catholic Charismatic retreats, prayer meetings and other events and believed at that time that classical Pentecostals "need[ed] to be both warned and informed."[35]

The second group would have been those who had largely become dissatisfied with the perceived loss of the Spirit's power in their own context due to the growing institutionalization of the PAOC and so opted for a non-denominational, if not anti-denominational setting, while the third and much smaller group became a ready-made catalyst for renewal on some university campuses through their music and teaching ministries. Nevertheless, in some places, Catholic and Anglican priests were invited to speak in Pentecostal churches to share their experiences. Pentecostals were initially intrigued but soon bewildered in that the prayer groups that quickly began to form comprised primarily of Catholics were gathering to worship like Pentecostals but were not leaving their parishes as many Pentecostals had expected. Some applauded what was happening and attempted support while others criticized and questioned authenticity with the emotional excesses and doctrinal differences.[36]

In March 1964, *The Pentecostal Testimony* reprinted the entire newspaper item from the Saturday, March 7, 1964 issue of the *Toronto Daily Star* covering the visit of Dennis Bennett to Toronto. Interestingly, the newspaper reported that Father Bennett preached in Pentecostal churches and in a number of Anglican congregations and informed the newspaper that many bishops of the church were sympathetic to the experience of glossolalia.[37] Although the volatile 1970's saw the movement of some individuals from mainline churches to independent charismatic congregations and older Pentecostal groups, with the passage of time, Anglicans who identified with the experience and practice of charismatics also elected to stay and remain active within the institutional church.[38]

None of the mainline denominations made official mention of the Charismatic Movement prior to 1971 suggesting that it had minimal impact on them before that date.[39] Relationships between those denominations and participants in the new renewal improved significantly over time, while in the earliest days the environment was characterized by tension. Generally, Protestant opposition came more from traditionalist than liberal circles. Although small charismatic groups emerged in the Anglican Church of Canada, for instance, few whole parishes were led into renewal.[40] Al Reimers, Anglican writer and frequent host on *100 Huntley Street*, refers to a number of cases including those where the dean of an Anglican Cathedral, another Anglican priest, and three UCC ministers had to be terminated at a diocesan or parish ministry as a result of their involvement in the Charismatic Movement.[41] This tension may have been moderated eventually by the teaching emphasis of some of the early leaders such as Bennett and Ranaghan who stressed that those who had come into the renewal movement should also remain in their churches.

The official response of the older Protestant denominations was positive but cautious. In 1973, the General Synod of the Anglican Church passed a resolution requesting bishops and delegates to do everything possible to "enable and support it."[42] The UCC with its deep Methodist roots quickly embraced the Charismatic Movement seen by many of its adherents as the answer to the growing liberal philosophical and theological positions being adopted by the denomination's leadership.

The Presbyterian Church was the first to officially respond to the renewal wave by commissioning a study in 1972. The results of the Special Committee to Study the Charismatic Movement were brought to the 101st General Assembly in 1975 and then referred to the Committee on Church Doctrine, which released its final report at their 1976 General Assembly.[43] Indicative of the seriousness with which the Presbyterian Church viewed the new movement is the fact that three interim reports had been submitted in 1972, 1973, and 1974 as well as several study papers made available to the Church. The study committee admitted that the religious environment in which the Charismatic Movement arose was one ready for freshness and vitality, insightfully pointing within its ranks to a "...lack of a sense of reality in matters of faith, an absence of the awareness of the presence of Christ in worship and daily life, lack of joy, of peace, of love, and of hope. They spell an emptiness in the church's life, which imparts itself to the daily life of its members."[44]

The 1975 report was incisive in its assertion that ministers were preaching the same message and no lives were being changed while the hunger for God remained unsatisfied. The church's message was seen as more implicit than explicit and that standards of conduct and belief had weakened or disappeared resulting in alienation from the church. The way forward was declared to be accepting and recognizing that the new renewal should be included in the life of the church and likewise, that those involved in it avoid isolation by meeting only among themselves cut off from the teaching of the church. The chief concern, however, seems to have been more over the exercise of any one or just a few of the spiritual gifts instead of the use of all the gifts, especially those in Scripture considered to be the most valuable such as wisdom, teaching, and ministry.[45] There was a tendency to point out the dangers of the new movement, to adopt a wait-and-see attitude and remain hopeful.

Presbyterian leadership sensed the need to give counsel to neo-Pentecostals within its ranks by suggesting that neo-Pentecostal teaching was in danger of losing sight of the all-sufficiency of Jesus and that therefore, care must be taken that by the interpretation of the experience of the work of the Spirit, a wedge was not driven between Jesus and the Holy Spirit. It wanted to guard against ignoring the insight and wisdom gathered throughout the church's history and usage of the Bible that becomes arbitrary and individualistic. Meanwhile, it pled for an attitude on the part of the whole church that neo-Pentecostals not be isolated but be given room to express their gifts under patient and understanding leadership. The church leadership also made it explicit that no particular one of the gifts, be it tongues or any other should become the touchstone of a person's being filled with the Holy Spirit. Instead, the genuineness of the gifts lies in the evidence of the fruit of the Spirit.[46]

At the time of the Committee on Church Doctrine's final report in 1976, the Presbyterians had become concerned that Spirit baptism not be interpreted as a "second blessing" but as a "release" of what was already possessed, declaring specifically that "no interpretation of Pentecost is allowable that attempts to discover a Spirit-baptism that is dissociated from water-baptism in the name of Jesus."[47] Yet, they felt that identifying those in the Charismatic Movement with the "enthusiasts" of the Reformation was unwarranted and that hasty rejection militated against the love and patience that ought to characterize the church. Rather, there was a need to listen both to the experience of the church and the experience of contemporaries. If the Spirit is sovereign, the manifestation of certain of his gifts should be available today as much as in apostolic times. Given that the essence of the life of faith itself is charismatic, fellowships ought not to develop into either "a church-within-the-church" or "a church-away-from-church."[48] Its conclusion was that "theological self-examination is something in which leaders of the charismatic renewal should engage, and it is up to the whole church to provide ways and means to this end."[49] It appears that the onus was left to Presbyterian renewal groups to stay within the boundaries of the teaching church with the expectation that they would be accepted.

The single most difficult challenge for the PAOC when it became clear that the Charismatic Movement was not the same phenomenon as the first wave of Pentecostalism was explicit in the Presbyterian response. For classical Pentecostals, the work of the Spirit in Spirit baptism was seen precisely as a second blessing (though rarely stated in those terms) and also viewed as subsequent to water baptism rather than bound up with it as one experience. The latter position would have alarmed PAOC leadership and pastors and confirmed their worst fears. While the Presbyterian Church in Canada was small in relation to Catholic and Anglican constituencies, Pentecostals, if they had knowledge of this most likely would have understood the stance adopted by the Presbyterians as representative of the theological shape of the wider Charismatic Movement.

The notion of avoiding the development of church apart from church would have caused further consternation when the badge of honor of many Pentecostals was that they had come out or were forced out of the older denominations. They had inherited from their denomination's early history a residual fear of trans-denominational interaction and the expectation that a Spirit-baptized individual should not be surprised but expect to inevitably run counter to the orthodoxy and orthopraxy of any mainline church. Kulbeck, representing the general view of Pentecostalism at the earliest days, noted succinctly, "The Pentecostal revival has been criticized, ridiculed and denounced." Opposition was "the attitude of many who did not look kindly on any evangelical faith." She continues, "However, many evangelicals looked askance at Pentecost for other reasons. For example, many of the outstanding evangelists, missionaries, teachers, and pastors of the Pentecostal Assemblies of Canada have been women. Such dedicated Christian ladies…have been active in pulpit ministry. Some in other denominations have held that this is unscriptural.[50] Miller agrees, "The persecution and opposition faced by the first group of Pentecostals is a common denominator in the histories of most of the early assemblies." [51]

Decades later, Douglas Rudd, historian and former archivist, recalling the history of Pentecostalism in Canada observed:

> Because pioneer Pentecostals were forced out of their churches when they embraced the baptism in the Spirit and the accompanying tongues, they developed separate denominational identities of their own statements of faith. Many Charismatics became hyphenated Charismatics by continuing to worship with their home churches and denominations (i.e. Charismatic-Catholics, Charismatic-Lutherans) and generally held the faith statements of the non-Pentecostal denominations.[52]

Although most religious animosity toward Pentecostals has long ago dissipated, a misunderstanding and fear on both sides is sometimes still evident and was at the time of the outbreak of the Charismatic Movement when two distinct perspectives were at play—Pentecostals believing that it would not be possible for individuals having received Spirit baptism to stay within their own church and mainstream Christians believing that experiencing the Spirit enhanced their spiritual life within their church.

Nevertheless, the Catholic Church's response was warm and anticipatory of spiritual newness within the Church. The Canadian bishops issued a document in 1975 characterizing the Renewal as "a hymn of whole-hearted trust in the all-powerful presence of the Spirit in the world" and called for the best possible communications to be maintained between charismatics and their home dioceses.[53] The statement was addressed to all Canadian Catholics because the bishops believed that the Renewal being "within the Church and part of the Church... serves as a new witness proclaiming that Pentecost continues."[54] They recognized that its rapid expansion among Canadian Catholics had caused a variety of reactions ranging from enthusiasm to caution, misgivings and even mistrust. Admitting also that there was aptness to stand apart from the Renewal, the bishops intentionally chose to dispense with that "protective space" and endorse and promote it while honestly facing the problem areas. The bishops commended the Renewal for "the factual indications in Canada that it is 'centered on the presence of the Holy Spirit in the Church community and its members' and on Jesus who draws the believer into intimacy with the Father"[55] and furthermore, that in the theological suppositions of the Renewal, they saw the Trinitarian structure of the Christian faith. They applauded charismatic groups for the joy they experience as Christians when they come together in the name of Christ.[56]

The bishops, meanwhile, also discussed at length the "negative aspects" but claimed to speak as from within the Renewal. They indicted as false "any seeking after exclusively extraordinary manifestations of the Spirit."[57] They believed that any emphasis that centered on the need of belonging to the new movement was excess and an expression of elitism. Other concerns included an exaggerated importance placed on the emotional experience of God, the presence of fundamentalism, and the apparent indifference of some groups to participation in the Church's involvement in the world, choosing rather to escape into a kind of Christian ghetto.[58]

Comparing their position on leadership in the Renewal to the 1975 statement by bishops in the United States, they strongly recommended theological and biblical formation for leaders[59] and called for cooperation, collaboration, and communication between the Renewal and the church. Their conclusion was succinct and simple: "Remain attentive to the Spirit. He alone can bring to completion, in ways no human hand can trace in advance, our common efforts to build tomorrow's church."[60] This is significant in that it reveals clearly the positive sentiment of the bishops, setting the tone for the future attitude of the Catholic Church in Canada toward the Renewal.

Success of Canadian Renewal

It can be concluded with reasonable accuracy that the reticence and misunderstanding that was initially present in some circles between charismatic groups and Catholic and Protestant churches has long since disappeared. From a global perspective, unlike the Pentecostals who were largely forced out of their churches at the turn of the century, 75 percent remained in their churches during the 1960s, which increased to 86 percent in the 1970s.[61] In 2003, the Canadian Conference of Catholic Bishops in looking back at the thirty-five years that had elapsed, declared at the very outset of their celebratory statement: "With deep gratitude and a renewed sense of hope in our hearts, we invite everyone to join us in celebrating the many blessings and gifts that the Charismatic Renewal has brought to the life of our Church in Canada.... If we needed a tangible sign that the risen Lord has kept his promise...the presence of the Charismatic renewal in our Canadian Catholic Church is certainly one telling sign."[62] The Renewal was still described as having no membership lists, unbound by internal structures or rules, a diverse collection of individuals, prayer groups, communities, and activities, yet all sharing and espousing the same goals:

> ...to foster a personal and continuous conversion to Jesus Christ, receptivity to the presence, power, and gifts of the Holy Spirit, a deep love for the Church and its work of evangelization, a strong fellowship, and a joyful zeal for the Gospel... the Charismatic Renewal has been and continues to be the sovereign work of God, realized through the Holy Spirit. It touches the lives of men and women in every walk of life, renews their faith, and enkindles in them a joyful love and zeal to serve God and his People. These lay faithful, priests and religious have allowed themselves to be surprised by God, surprised at the experience of the presence and action of the Holy Spirit in their lives.[63]

After more than three decades, those sentiments reveal a deep relationship that had developed over time between Catholic charismatics and Canadian Catholic Church leadership. It is likely that early acceptance of the Renewal by the Catholic Church in the United States was quickly able to find its counter-part in Canada. That fact would not have been lost on either charismatic groups or church leaders.

The PAOC at the time was generally applauding the events to the south. It is noteworthy given later concerns over its inability to reconcile Catholic theology with glossolalia that *The Pentecostal Testimony* reported on the 7th annual international conference of the Catholic Charismatic Renewal Movement held at Notre Dame University in 1973. Twice the number of delegates from the previous year attended and two high ranking prelates praised the delegates for participating in a growing movement that promises to "revitalize the church around the world."[64] The denomination from that point on, however, began to give spread of the Charismatic Movement into Canada a cool and cautious reception. Yet, in retrospect, many grassroots members of the PAOC, if not its leaders, would be inclined to agree with the bishops who in their anniversary statement enumerate some of the spiritual fruits of renewal, including the impact of personal experience of the Holy Spirit, the high premium placed on prayer, praise and thanksgiving, a new desire for evangelization, service to others, and the emphasis on healing for the whole person.[65] Similarly, the PAOC named the 1990s as its "Decade of Destiny" and launched this initiative in the January 1990 issue of *The Pentecostal Testimony*, in which all the articles call for a return to Spirit empowerment, holiness, prayer, humility, evangelism, and service to others.

As part of a larger movement that Reimers estimates eventually grew to two thousand prayer groups involving over one hundred thousand people with the majority of them being in Catholic Quebec,[66] the Catholic Church seems to have been the most active in the Renewal of all Canadian denominations. According to Peter Thompson, Canadian International Catholic Charismatic Renewal Services representative to the Vatican, in the 1970s Canadian Catholic renewal grew quickly with some prayer groups reaching into the thousands. Interestingly, Thompson observes, "There was a great enthusiasm but a distinct lack of maturity, which did cause problems...problems of misunderstanding between the hierarchy and those involved. Some were disillusioned and left the church for Pentecostalism."[67] While participating in the July 1976 Summer Olympics outreach in Montreal the author observed that there was a considerable fusing of the atmospheres of both the Charismatic Movement in Quebec and the energetic evangelism of the PAOC. However, they still appeared to be separate tracks with the PAOC experiencing considerable uneasiness with the Catholic Charismatic Renewal that was then flourishing among many Quebecers.

Likely the largest Charismatic conference ever held in Canada drew fifty thousand francophones to Montreal in 1977.[68] In June 1979, 24,000 people again attended a charismatic conference at the Olympic Stadium in that city. [69] By 2003, the bishops reported that over one million Catholic Canadians had been touched or in some way influenced by the Charismatic Renewal in Canada with still some 862 prayer groups in roughly sixteen percent of all Catholic parishes.[70]

It was becoming increasingly clear to those conditioned to the classical Pentecostal world of the PAOC with its hybrid fundamentalist-Wesleyan heritage that Catholics active in the Renewal were continuing to be actively involved in parish activities and organizations and had no plans for departure. Rather, they were becoming the backbone of regular congregational activities in many parts of the country and attracting others to the Renewal. Archbishop James Hayes of Halifax, for instance, was drawn into the Renewal partially as a result of the faithfulness of the participants in attending the Eucharist.[71] The positive and affirming environment surrounding charismatics and local Catholic parishes and dioceses is likely due also in part to the early teaching of Catholic leaders such as Kilian McDonnell who continued to stress that those who came into the Renewal should remain within their own denominations.[72]

The reason it took several years for the Charismatic Movement among Anglicans to organize is unclear but it appears that in the beginning, the level of acceptance by the Anglican Church of Canada was substantially less than that of the Catholic Church. It is difficult to assess with any degree of certainty the impact that Dennis Bennett's experience of the Spirit as an Episcopalian priest had upon the Anglican Church of Canada but response to the Movement in general was mixed. *The Anglican Journal*, an official publication of the church, reported in 1974 following a decade into renewal that a recent survey showed no part of Canada "untouched by the waves of the charismatic movement" and stated that some bishops had established centers for renewal, giving "the charismatic movement a respectable presence within the worshipping life of the diocese."[73] On the other hand, it stated:

> As early as 1963 the charismatic spirit reached into Canada, but it brought with it strife and discord. Some bishops declared that there would be no speaking in tongues in their diocese and forbade their clergy to discuss the baptism in the spirit. It took nearly a decade before the church in Canada recognized the movement by permitting and encouraging discussion of the movement and its gifts.[74]

It is probable that views expressed by the wider Anglican Communion helped to foster a growing understanding and appreciation for what was happening in the Charismatic Movement. In 1973, Robert Runcie, an Anglican bishop in the Church of England wrote in his diocesan newsletter that movements like the new renewal and the Jesus People can help the church and the church can help them and argued that, for some people, these movements have an appeal that formal church life often lacks.[75] One might well speculate that such expressions would have helped to soften any tension or mistrust between charismatics and the Anglican Church.

The ready acceptance of the Charismatic Movement by the Anglican Church despite its slow formalization was made clear at the Anglican General Synod in May 1973 when a motion was passed recognizing the need for spiritual renewal and requesting the House of Bishops and each delegate to the Synod, "to take steps to challenge our people to use all available resources to enable and support the charismatic renewal in the Church, and to discover and share our personal commitment to Jesus Christ and our relationships with each other, in order that we can minister sacrificially to the community at large."[76] An attempt to integrate the Movement into the larger church seems to have been the intent of the Anglicans by this time. The church never lost sight of the contribution that it did and could continue to make. In 1981, its Consultative Council recommended that the Secretary General "request all member Churches to report on the incidence, progress, and significance of spiritual renewal, including the Charismatic Movement, within their life...."[77]

As late as 1984, the House of Bishops reported that a task force recommended encouragement be given to the Cursillo[78] and other renewal movements. In cautioning against divisions and elitism, it recommended that movements within any Diocese be accountable to the Bishop or someone designated by him. The depth of support that had grown for the Charismatic Movement is further illustrated by the recommendation that the National Executive Council make provision for national staff personnel and time to provide the support necessary for renewal movements and evangelical strategies that had arisen in the church. The Anglican Church was openly recognizing the richness of the Spirit's activity within its overall life.[79]

David Reed proposes that the renewal of the 1960s and 1970s within the Anglican Church of Canada was an expression of the oscillating periods of weakness and vitality within the history of the church and represented the outward swing of that pendulum. The church had entered new territory of spiritual experience but throughout the 1980s, the pendulum was swinging back into the institution. In other words, there occurred a shift among Anglican charismatics from an emphasis on experience to ministry within the established church.[80] The phenomenon appears to be part of a broader evolving tendency within both the PAOC and charismatic groups to move away from spiritual encounter and crisis experience toward deeper societal involvement and social justice. The deep religious roots of Anglican charismatics (as well as Catholic charismatics) would have been a definite deterrent in any thought of leaving, given that the actual renewal had occurred within their own theological tradition rather than from outside.

Reed's survey found that thirty percent of Anglican parishes in Canada had been influenced by renewal.[81] He further discovered significant sociological stability with lifelong Anglicans making up the majority of charismatics and that the 'to'ing' and 'fro'ing' of some charismatics is a memory of the 1970s, and thus he concludes, "Although the charismatic experience may have once been exclusively Pentecostal, the renewal is clearly a movement within its own mainline church tradition."[82] The evidence clearly points in the direction of most Anglican charismatics having become fully integrated into their denominational tradition rather than shunning, being shunned or rejected by it.

Meanwhile, most classical Pentecostals have tended to be dismissive of the authenticity of such a spiritual experience that can flourish with any degree of freedom and spontaneity within the confines of a liturgical tradition. In any case, the Charismatic Movement that began over four decades ago continues to have a positive impact on the participants' faith, lifestyle and the relationship with their church. It has translated into increased Christian motivation, commitment and activity such as Bible study, prayer and praise services, outreach, and increased giving. Reed also found that of those who claimed to have had a charismatic experience, more had received it within the five years previous to the study (1990) than during any five year period since 1970. It seems that the incidence of the experience of renewal continues to be strong among the laity but not so much among the clergy.[83] The majority of charismatics who chose to remain and make the Anglican Church their spiritual home have felt supported by the Church and its hierarchy. A significant proportion of Canadian Anglicans have come to identify with the experience and practice of charismatics resulting in a revitalization of their spirituality.

Intersection of Charismatic Movement and PAOC

As Canadians in the early 1960s began to hear about the experiences of Dennis Bennett, James Brown, Kevin Ranaghan and other mainline leaders who were beginning to act like Pentecostals, it soon caught the attention of the media and for established Pentecostal denominations like the PAOC, it provided social validation for what they had already been experiencing for over fifty years.[84] When the Charismatic Movement began to make news in Canada, the largest classical Pentecostal denomination, the PAOC, reacted initially with significant enthusiasm. This is clearly evident from news items about the Movement that began to appear in *The Pentecostal Testimony*. The "Whitsunday Edition" of June 1963 was dedicated entirely to celebrating the ongoing work of the Spirit and appropriately anticipated further growth of renewal with its promotion of David Wilkinson's *The Cross and the Switchblade* on the back cover. The publication featured a detailed item on a revival among students at Yale University stating that the campus had become the site of the same Pentecostal-type "speaking in tongues" phenomenon that had been reported in some traditional denominations with twenty members of the Inter-Varsity Christian Fellowship having experienced "tongues."[85] Its full-page reproduction of the *Toronto Daily Star*'s coverage of the visit of Dennis Bennett in March 1964 is another example of the excitement created by the news of a clergyman from a traditional Protestant denomination receiving the baptism in the Holy Spirit.[86]

The PAOC's report in April 1968 on the beginnings of the Charismatic Movement in Vancouver and its first specific mention of charismatic influence in Canada indicates that it looked with some favor on cooperation with older denominations in what appears to have been a sense that finally, this was the spread of the same Pentecostal revival that it had experienced decades earlier.[87] In the same year, the PAOC also printed an abridged version of a paper by Kilian McDonnell, "The Ecumenical Significance of the Pentecostal Movement" in which McDonnell, although noting that glossolalia decreases as Pentecostalism grows, nevertheless highlighted the rapid growth of Pentecostalism around the world.[88]

By 1970, Pentecostal writers were beginning to comment on the new movement and to see the PAOC as being in a position of potentially significant influence. Writings from both inside and outside the denomination were encouraged and articles were reprinted from other Pentecostal/Charismatic sources. In August, it reprinted an article, "The Spirit is Moving," from *Unction,* the official publication of the Union of the Assemblies of God in Argentina by Amaro Rodriquez, a former Catholic priest converted to classical Pentecostalism.[89] Rodriquez was exhorting Pentecostals to take advantage of the "favourable atmosphere" within Catholic charismatic circles to teach the truth of the Scripture to "hungry and thirsty Roman Catholics." He stated explicitly what was at that time still very much the sentiment among many classical Pentecostals, namely, that Catholics who receive the Holy Spirit would likely have to "go out of the church of Rome, whose very essence would have to change to be in accordance with the Word of God."[90] The sentiment of the PAOC at this juncture is no better represented than in this call for true Christians not to miss the current opportunity:

> ...where there is a mutual coming together of various groups, to reach those who are seeking the truth. Today, more than ever we must have dialogue with Roman Catholics, talk with them, pray with them where possible, and offer them the impact of our own lives transformed by the power of the gospel. We must show to them Jesus Christ who prayed, lived, and died on the cross for the unity of all men, bringing down the wall of separation.[91]

E. A. Hornby's assessment as superintendent of the denomination's British Columbia District indicates how some Pentecostals saw its role at that point: "The established Pentecostal church must encourage those in the denominational churches who are experiencing modern charismatic renewal. As the ecumenical world church takes shape, influencing the religious trend of the whole world, the Pentecostal church is given of God a place of power and influence in proclaiming the gospel of personal salvation until Jesus comes."[92] The self-understanding of the classical Pentecostal movement as the final revival and as the arbiter of sound doctrine was still deeply embedded. In this case, however, Hornby seems to leave the door open enough to allow that those experiencing renewal be "encouraged," perhaps in their faith as they continued to live it out within their respective denominations.

C.H. Bronsdon, then president of the PAOC's Eastern Pentecostal Bible College, wrote in 1973 that in an age of church growth and charismatic renewal, there is a great need for sound doctrine, that someone must train Spirit-filled young people for "this great move of God's Holy Spirit," making a Pentecostal Bible college concerned with charismatic ministries essential.[93] The denomination's magazine continued to carry positive news reports throughout that year of the Charismatic Movement around the world including an endorsement by Percy Brewster, well-known British Pentecostal pastor and secretary of the World Pentecostal Fellowship.[94] These continued to appear occasionally until 1977 after when reference to charismatics disappeared. By that time, it had become clear that the denomination was not about to have significant impact upon a movement that had emerged within the traditional churches and seemed to all but dismiss its impact and value to the global church. The excitement had died down; nevertheless the PAOC was to benefit not so much from its corporate impact upon the Charismatic Movement through direct involvement but upon its reception of many people who eventually came to the conclusion that they would be better served in a classical Pentecostal-type environment. This trend would manifest itself in those with charismatic backgrounds attending PAOC churches, Bible colleges and involvement in missions work.

As the Charismatic Movement in Canada continued and changed its shape, Pentecostals became more cautious as they perceived excesses and aberrations of classical Pentecostal doctrine. Many PAOC adherents seemed to expect those within the Movement, especially those in the Catholic Renewal, to eventually 'see the light' and to realize that the way to be free in Christ and be taught the truth was to cut ties with their former denomination and become part of the PAOC fellowship.[95] This break did occur frequently though there was no mass exodus from those mainline churches. But with the influx of new Spirit-filled, non-traditional Pentecostal believers came religious and cultural baggage that did not entirely fit older Pentecostal church culture.

Kydd argues that the Charismatic Movement had a negative impact on classical Pentecostalism through worship, for example, that tended to become more privatized and self-gratifying and through the reinforcing of its emphasis on experience rather than reflection and engagement. He points out that this phenomenon nevertheless needs to be understood in terms of the factors within Pentecostalism itself versus the Charismatic Movement that shaped its responses such as its very different histories, differences in its natures as "corporate entities" and the inevitable institutionalization of the PAOC as the "reduction of tension" between itself and the larger society.[96] Although Pentecostalism in Canada, including the PAOC, was evolving into something quite different from what it was at its inception decades earlier, Canadian Pentecostals viewed what the charismatics were experiencing as being significant.[97] Some saw experience of the supernatural accompanied by glossolalia by others with no connection to the PAOC initially as a vindication of decades of teaching and experiencing Spirit baptism all the while enduring misunderstanding and rejection by the mainline churches. With their history, Pentecostals tended "to assume that they would be able to provide teaching for the charismatics, but generally, they were not asking questions or showing any inclination to be taught by the established Pentecostal church."[98] This unfolding of events contributed to the PAOC eventually seeing both movements as widely divergent.

But yet, PAOC people, especially the Boomer generation gradually began to connect with the Charismatic Movement—buying tapes, singing the songs, attending the conferences and listening to the speakers—and tended to read into it a return to what Pentecostalism once was and should be. The PAOC attracted those charismatics only loosely attached to denominational structures. Into the classical PAOC milieu came the high energy of youth and the beginnings of a radical shift in musical styles that was to change the ethos of classical Pentecostal worship forever. Kydd suggests, "The words of choruses sung and the atmosphere created by leaders emphasized what one 'got out of' the experience of worship."[99] This would eventually replace church choirs and congregational song leaders with worship bands and traditional hymnody with praise music.

The revolution in musical styles that began in the 1960s, associated with the

Charismatic Movement and the Jesus era, and that continued well beyond has contributed to a permanent transformation of the PAOC. Right from its beginnings, Pentecostalism had been characterized by lively church services with a worship style unencumbered with the rituals of former liturgical traditions. Emphasis on the baptism in the Holy Spirit, openness to the charismatic gifts and the joyous expression of praise made Pentecostals receptive to new choruses, with their biblically-based lyrics that some, especially the younger generation, saw as more "spiritual" than many of the older songs. This newfound freedom in worship and the renewed emphasis in the 1960s and 1970s on spiritual gifts was nowhere more evident than in PAOC camp meetings,[100] as well as at weekend retreats and conventions. It appears that the environment created by the Charismatic Movement compelled the PAOC not to become 'Charismatic' but to attempt to reconsider its raison d'être and so rediscover a new vitality of the Spirit.

Finally, Canadian Pentecostals began to realize that there were doctrinal issues that had to be addressed. They rejected the Catholic Church's claim that the gift of the Spirit was an actualization of what was conferred at baptism. They also expected dramatic changes in lifestyle among those who professed to have received the Holy Spirit: "Pentecostals were not quite sure about some Charismatic practices and Charismatics were not totally comfortable with Pentecostal mores."[101] The PAOC, with its roots in Wesleyanism and the Holiness Movement and its consequent emphasis on holiness of life and separation from the world, was bewildered at the indifference with which Charismatics viewed such practices as smoking and alcohol and why Bible studies did not prompt them to modify their theology. In essence, as Miller notes, Canadian Pentecostals moved from enthusiastic approval of the Movement in the 1960s to a more wary assessment of it by the end of the 1970s.[102] The reality is, in fact, borne out by the explicit attempt of PAOC leadership toward the end of the decade to ensure that 'Pentecostal' was retained in the actual name of each of the local churches citing "the current Pentecostal and charismatic emphasis in the world" as the primary reason.[103] The trend toward retreat and re-entrenchment was well underway.

At the national level, it appears that the PAOC much like classical Pentecostal denominations elsewhere had become so concerned with theological issues surrounding the Charismatic Movement that it saw the need to reiterate and reaffirm its doctrinal position on some points. Similarly, the Church of God, Cleveland, Tennessee very early recognized that a response regarding Spirit baptism and glossolalia was in order in the wake of increased widespread interest in the subject. Wade H. Horton, a former General Overseer of the Church of God, strongly restated his denomination's traditional stance on tongues as evidence of baptism in the Spirit:

> ...in recent years the vast majority of Christians, as well as the news media, religious and secular, have principally heard from those who know little about glossolalia theologically and nothing about it experientially; or those who know little about it experientially and almost nothing about it theologically. Those persons have gained much attention either because of opposition to it or because of the

supposed uniqueness of receiving the experience in non-Pentecostal churches. This has inadvertently and inappropriately thrust upon them the role of the voice of authority on the subject.... It seems a little inappropriate for them to almost immediately assume the position of authoritative teachers pointing out what they claim is an easier, quieter, and more respectable way to receive the Holy Ghost;.... Would it not be more charitable for them to re-examine the total Pentecostal picture and seek to be taught rather than to teach, at least until they are familiar with spiritual manifestations and have reached a degree of maturity in the Spirit-filled life.[104]

Evidence suggests that the Assemblies of God, however, adopted a significantly more open position than did either the PAOC or the Church of God, perhaps in an effort not to overlook the potential of the Charismatic Movement. Although the PAOC approved verbatim the text of the Charismatic Study Report passed by the 35th General Council of the Assemblies of God, Minneapolis Minnesota in 1972, it was one of the few places where the PAOC officially expressed some openness to the Charismatic Movement. Meanwhile, the Assemblies of God in 1977 adopted a resolution regarding the Charismatic Movement, part of which stated, "We have maintained a posture of appreciation and openness to what God is doing in the outpouring of the Holy Spirit," at the same time expressing concern that the denomination not inadvertently degenerate into "a quasi-experience-oriented position" and that it "not assume an 'elder-brother' complex."[105]

Renewed interest in demonology prompted response as well as the need to clarify the purpose of spiritual gifts in the face what the PAOC deemed to be excessive and unwise use in some circles. In replying to the charismatic pneumatological tendency to believe that a sign of having received the Holy Spirit was not limited to tongues but could involve any gift of the Spirit, the PAOC re-affirmed its position. It seems that this was an attempt at an apologetic for the Pentecostal distinctive of Spirit-baptism with the initial evidence of speaking in tongues as distinct from the purpose and place of the other spiritual gifts.

In the final analysis, arising as a result of several factors, there was a spiritual hunger in the 1960s and 1970s that invited a fresh wind of the Spirit. In Canada, as in the United States and elsewhere, the new renewal that took place was very different from the Pentecostal revival at the turn of the century in that those members of mainline Protestant as well as of Catholic parishes who claimed to have experienced the Spirit largely remained attached to their own denominations. Those churches, though cautious at the outset, generally grew to accept and affirm the Charismatic Movement and to recognize that their traditions had been enriched by the freshness of the Spirit's activity. For classical Pentecostals, there was somewhat of the opposite effect in that the initial exuberance over the Movement gradually gave way to caution and sometimes even dismay over doctrinal differences and lifestyle issues.

The renewal of spiritual vitality within many local mainline congregations was welcomed albeit with some caution, but as time progressed, those churches saw the eventual integration of charismatic groups into the mainstream of church life. What is most significant is that the Charismatic Movement of those decades had a profound and lasting impact on the PAOC, as many Charismatics did finally drift into PAOC churches bringing with them a different piety that helped to spark a transformation particularly in worship style and content that continues to this day.

Notes

1. Eugene R. Fairweather, "Canadian Catholics Offer Milestone Conference on Renewal," *The Christian Century*, (October 4, 1967): 1261-1265.

2. The choice of "Charismatic Renewal" over "Charismatic Movement" here is because of its more general usage within Catholic circles.

3. Canadian Bishops Statement on the Catholic Charismatic Renewal, "The Charismatic Renewal in Canada 2003," *Catholic Charismatic Renewal Services of Canada*, (Pentecost, 2003):1.

4. The bishops here are using language that appears to suggest a providential approach to renewal as suggested by Augustus Cerillo and Grant Wacker in their analysis of the rise of early Pentecostalism in United States. This interpretive model is the perspective reflected by many early Pentecostal leaders including Charles Conn of the Church of God, Cleveland, Tennessee and Carl Brumback of the Assemblies of God who wrote histories of their respective denominations. (Conn, *Like A Mighty Army: A History of the Church of God, 1886-1976*, [rev. ed.,1977]; Brumback, *Suddenly... From Heaven: A History of the Assemblies of God* [1961]). The emergence of Pentecostalism is defined, for instance, by Conn as appearing "spontaneously and simultaneously in many far-flung regions of the world." *NIDPCM*, s.v. "Bibliography and Historiography of Pentecostalism in the United States."

5. Canadian Bishops Statement, 1-2.

6. Ibid., 2.

7. *NIDPCM*, s.v. "Charismatic Movement" (by P. D. Hocken).

8. David Reed, "From Movement to Institution: A Case Study of Charismatic Renewal in the Anglican Church of Canada," *American Theological Library Association Summary of Proceedings* 45 (1991): 178.

9. James Hanrahan, "The Nature and History of the Catholic Charismatic Renewal in Canada," *CCHA Study Sessions* 50 (1983): 309.

10. Ibid., 309.

11. Ibid., 310-314.

12. Bernice Gerard, "Charismatic Renewal in Vancouver," *The Pentecostal Testimony* (April 1968): 8.

13. Ibid.

14. Miller, *Canadian Pentecostals*, 302.

15. Gerard, "Charismatic Renewal in Vancouver," 8.

16. Ibid.

17. Miller, *Canadian Pentecostals*, 302. Miller also argues that a considerable number of charismatics left Catholicism as well as some from the Protestant charismatic groups and joined Classical Pentecostalism. While no known statis-

tics exist to measure the extent of this phenomenon, there was ease of movement back and forth, but mainly to and from PAOC churches and Protestant Charismatic groups.

18. Presbyterian Church, Canada, 1976, "The Work of the Spirit," in Kilian McDonnell (ed), *Presence, Power, Praise* Vol II, Continental, National, Regional Documents, (Collegeville, MN: The Liturgical Press, 1980): 227. This final report of the Presbyterian Church of Canada's Committee on Church Doctrine appointed to study the Charismatic Renewal distinguished between Catholic Pentecostalism and Neo-Pentecostalism, associating the latter with the Protestant churches. In the first four years of the movement, there were an estimated 50,000 followers in the United States and Canada.

19. Peter Prosser, "Roman Catholic Charismatic Impact Increases," *The Pentecostal Testimony* (September, 1973): 5.

20. Ronald A. Kydd, "Pentecostals, Charismatics, and Canadian Denominations," *Eglise et Theologie* 13.2 (May, 1982): 229.

21. With the increasing liberalization of the UCC, more and more of its members have turned toward the renewal wing of the church to uphold what they deem to be traditional biblical standards.

22. Anglican Renewal Ministries of Canada, "History of Anglican Renewal Ministries," http://armcanada.org/history.htm (accessed June 9, 2014).

23. Ibid.

24. Grace Lane, "Catholic Charismatic Movement Flourishes in Western Canada," *The Christian Century* (May 24, 1972): 618.

25. Ibid., 617-618.

26. Ibid., 618.

27. Lane, "Catholic Charismatic Movement Flourishes in Western Canada," 618.

28. Prosser, "Roman Catholic Charismatic Impact Increases," 5. Prosser reports also that it was a French Canadian priest who spread the movement in Rome itself.

29. Miller, *Canadian Pentecostals*, 311.

30. Ibid.

31. *NIDPCM*, s.v. "Canada" (by Ronald A. Kydd).

32. Ibid.

33. Until her death in 2013, PAOC archivist Marilyn Stroude was a product of a 1970s UCC prayer group but who eventually became a long-time member of a large Toronto area PAOC church.

34. William A. Griffin, personal conversation with the author, May 1, 2014.

35. Peter Prosser, *The Pentecostal Testimony*, (September, 1973): 5.

36. *NIDPCM*, s.v. "Canada" (Kydd).

37. "Priest 'speaks in tongues' now everyone's doing it," *TORONTO DAILY STAR* (March 7,1964): 55 in *The Pentecostal Testimony*, (June 1964): 7.

38. David Reed, "From Movement to Institution: A Case Study of Charismatic Renewal in the Anglican Church of Canada," *American Theological Library Association Summary of Proceedings* 45 (1991): 192.

39. Kydd, "Pentecostals, Charismatics, and Canadian Denominations," 223.

40. *NIDPCM*, s.v. "Charismatic Movement" (Hocken).

41. Al Reimers, *God's Country: Charismatic Renewal* (Toronto: Welch, 1979): 11ff, 42, 76, 91 and 140.

42. Official Record, General Synod of the Anglican Church of Canada, May 1973, Act 42/43.

43. Kilian McDonnell (ed), *Presence, Power, Praise,* Vol. II, Continental, National, Regional Documents, (Collegeville, MN: The Liturgical Press, 1980): 221.

44. Acts and Proceedings of the 101st General Assembly of the Presbyterian Church of Canada in Canada (Montreal, Quebec, June 4-13, 1975): 320-329, "Report of the Committee to Study the Charismatic Movement, " in Kilian McDonnell (ed), *Presence, Power, Praise* Vol II, Continental, National, Regional Documents, (Collegeville, MN: The Liturgical Press, 1980): 57.

45. McDonnell, *Presence, Power, Praise*, 53-54.

46. Acts and Proceedings of the 101st General Assembly, "Report of the Committee to Study the Charismatic Movement," in McDonnell, *Presence, Power, Power,* 62-65.

47. "Minutes of the 101st General Assembly of the Presbyterian Church of Canada," 375-393, reprinted in Presbyterian Church, Canada, 1976, "The Work of the Spirit," (introduction by McDonnell), *Presence, Power, Praise*, 221-222.

48. Ibid., 222.

49. Ibid.

50. Kulbeck, *What God Hath Wrought*, 13.

51. Miller, *Canadian Pentecostals, 51.*

52. Rudd, *When the Spirit Came Upon Them*, 364.

53. *NIDPCM*, s.v. "Canada" (Kydd).

54. Roman Catholic Church, Canada 1975, "Charismatic Renewal: Message of the Canadian Bishops Addressed to all Canadian Catholics" (introduction by McDonnell), *Presence, Power, Praise,* 84.

55. Ibid.

56. Ibid., 84-85.

57. Ibid., 85.

58. Ibid., 85, 92-96.

59. Ibid., 85.

60. Ibid., 97.

61. David Barrett, "Statistics, Global." *Dictionary of Pentecostal and Charismatic Movements*, ed. Stanley Burgess and Gary McGee (Grand Rapids, Mich.: Zondervan Publishing House, 1988): 819 cited in Reed, "From Movement to Institution: A Case Study of Charismatic Renewal in the Anglican Church of Canada," 173.

62. "Canadian Bishops Statement on the Catholic Charismatic Renewal," 3. http://www.catholiccharismatic.ca/index_files/BishopsofCanadaStatementBooklet.pdf (accessed June 10, 2014).

63. Ibid., 5.

64. *The Pentecostal Testimony* 54:8 (August 1973): 10.

65. "Canadian Bishops Statement," 5-16.

66. Reimers, *God's Country: Charismatic Renewal,* 18.

67. Catholic Register Staff, "Charismatics Gifted by the Holy Spirit for 40 Years," *The Catholic Register* (October 5, 2007). http://www.catholicregister.org/item/8376-charismatics-gifted-by-the-holy-spirit-for-40-years (accessed September 20, 2014).

68. Ibid.

69. Roland Chagnon, *Les charismatiques au Quebec* (Montreal: Que/Amerique, 1979): 10 in Kydd, "Pentecostals, Charismatics, and Canadian Denominations," *Eglise et Theologie* 13.2 (May 1982): 229.

70. "Canadian Bishops Statement," 4.

71. Reimers, *God's Country: Charismatic Renewal,* 22, 135f.

72. Kydd, "Pentecostals, Charismatics, and Canadian Denominations," 222.

73. "25 years ago: December 1974," *The Anglican Journal* (December 1999) http://www.anglicanjournal.com/articles/100-years-ago-december-1899-377 (accessed June 11, 2014).

74. Ibid.

75. "Dateline: World of Religion," *The Pentecostal Testimony* 54:9 (September 1973): 11.

76. Official Record of the Anglican Church of Canada, General Synod, May 1973, Act 42/43.

77. Text of resolutions taken from "ACC-5: Anglican Consultative Council: Report of Fifth Meeting: Newcastle upon Tyne, England 8-18 September, 1981." London: Published by the Anglican Consultative Council, c1981.

78. The Cursillo Movement (CM) is an apostolic movement recognized by the Roman Catholic Church but which has spread to other Christian churches. Its goal is to share with the community the essence of Christianity and Christian values and so to gradually transform the community from within. It uses the expression "leavening society with the gospel" through the testimony of friendship and the deepening of the personal conversion of its members. "French-Speaking Cursillo Movement of Canada," http://www.cursillos.ca/en/cursillo.htm (accessed June 11, 2014).

79. Official Record, "House of Bishops," February 1984, Resolution 15-2-84.

80. Reed, "From Movement to Institution," 177-178.

81. Anglican Church...Confirmation Questionnaire, 3 in Reed, "From Movement to Institution," 182.

82. Reed, "From Movement to Institution," 182-183.

83. Ibid.,188-189.

84. *NIDPCM,* s.v. "Canada" (Kydd).

85. "The Holy Spirit Falls on Yale Students," *The Pentecostal Testimony* (June 1963): 6.

86. "Priest 'speaks in tongues' now everyone's doing it," *The Pentecostal Testimony* (June 1964): 7.

87. Gerard, "Charismatic Renewal in Vancouver," *The Pentecostal Testimony* (April 1968): 8.

88. Kilian McDonnell, "The Ecumenical Significance of the Pentecostal Movement," *The Pentecostal Testimony* (June 1968): 8.

89. *The Pentecostal Testimony* (August 1970): 8-9. A few months earlier in its April issue, it had featured similar writing by Rodriguez, "What is Happening in the Roman Catholic Church?"

90. Ibid.

91. Ibid.

92. E. A. Hornby, "The Word of God is Relevant," *The Pentecostal Testimony* (December 1970): 8. *The Pentecostal Testimony* (August 1970): 9.

93. C. H. Bronsdon, "Why a Pentecostal Bible College?" *The Pentecostal Testimony* (January 1973): 11.

94. "Dateline: World of Religion," *The Pentecostal Testimony* (November 1973): 18.

95. Miller, *Canadian Pentecostals,* 300, 302.

96. Ronald Kydd, "The Impact of the Charismatic Renewal on Classical Pentecostalism in Canada." *PNEUMA* 18.1 (Spring 1996): 55, 63-65.

97. Ibid., 62.

98. Ibid., 63.

99. Ibid.

100. Miller, *Canadian Pentecostals,* 314.

101. Kydd, "Impact of the Charismatic Renewal," 62-63.

102. Miller, *Canadian Pentecostals,* 301.

103. The General Executive in August, 1978 received a report from its Standing Committee on Home Missions that recommended a resolution for the next PAOC General Conference: "WHEREAS we believe that in the light of the current Pentecostal and charismatic emphasis in the world today, it is of great importance to identity our assemblies as being "Pentecostal", and WHEREAS in view of the growing favour with which we are regarded, and the increasing number of people looking for a Pentecostal church home, and to assist tourist and other visitors in locating a Pentecostal assembly, BE IT RESOLVED that we encourage that the name "Pentecostal" be displayed prominently, either in the specific name of the assembly or in the use of the phrase "affiliated with The Pentecostal Assemblies of Canada (not abbreviated) in connection with the actual name,...."

104. Wade H. Horton (ed.), *The Glossolalia Phenomenon* (Cleveland TN: Pathway Press, 1966): 14-15.

105. Resolution 7: Charismatic Movement, General Council of the Assemblies of God, 1977. PAOC Archives.

4

Quebec Revision, Charismatic Renewal and the PAOC

Societal and Ecclesial Transformation

A distinctive language, religion, and culture from the rest of North America had for centuries defined Quebec until the last half of the twentieth century when radical social, political, and religious change began to occur. Hundreds of rural farming towns scattered across a vast expanse of countryside and dominated by Catholicism had until then existed in relative isolation from the outside world. The church had been responsible for most facets of the life of Quebecers including education, health, and the administration of social services: "No provincial government prior to 1960 would have introduced legislation of any significance without first seeking the approval of the Quebec hierarchy [of the Catholic Church]."[1] The urbanization trend that followed World War II was largely the cause of the massive transformation that was to take place during the ensuing years. Whereas the Catholic Church had provided society's reference point, the newly urbanized and educated were to pose an unprecedented challenge to its control as the latter criticized Quebec Catholicism as being "excessively conformist, quasi-superstitious, and militantly anti-intellectual...."[2] The forces at work opened the way for a radical change in spirituality and church life that has been of deep and lasting consequence.

What transpired has become known among Quebecers as "la Revolution tranquille," defined as a period of rapid and profound transformation beginning around 1960. The religion that had been the lifeblood of Quebec since the founding of New France in the sixteenth century was rapidly pushed into the background as provincial governments expanded bureaucratic control and regulation and began a reformation of education that effectively made public a system that had been the exclusive domain of the Catholic Church. The glue that had held together Quebec society deteriorated as Quebecers rapidly entered the modern world. With modernity came materialism, education, and the impulse to cast off religious tradition perceived as being confining and coercive. The Church that had mothered them now became an embarrassment as it condemned their materialism and social mores.³ The result was what Charles Doran, a leading American observer of Canada calls "a persistent anxiety over identity."⁴ As a new generation of Quebec Catholics rejected the Church's control over society and its resistance of the modern world, in retrospect, the question is whether the younger generation was rejecting Christianity and spirituality outright. For some at least, such did not appear to be true. In any case, the days ahead were to give evidence that the secularization of society had resulted in a loss of roots, a spiritual vacuum and a state of restlessness.

As with many Catholics worldwide, the reforms of Vatican II were eagerly received in Quebec and had, in fact, been influenced by the powerful Quebec clergy. Kevin J. Christiano argues that the roots of the Quiet Revolution were deep within the Church itself as well as within the broader society and go back long before 1960.⁵ It is a fact that the thrust of the reforms coming out of Vatican II were of deep interest to Catholics in Quebec as they were elsewhere. The thinking of the archbishop of Montreal, Cardinal Paul-Emile Leger, had a major impact upon these events. Initially, he had been traditional in his approach following his appointment in 1950, but by the end of the decade, he had become more open to new values and with Montreal being the largest diocese, he assumed a decisive leadership role.⁶

The pressure for Quebec society to open itself up and embrace the modern world was latent and needed little to make itself manifest. The PAOC itself would ride the crest of that wave in its own evangelism efforts in the province during the 1960s, 1970s and into the 1980s with initiatives that capitalized on a culture in transition with an apparent spiritual vacuum especially among a younger generation of francophones. Michael Di Giacomo outlines and analyzes these efforts, seeing them as part of a larger awakening going on in French Canada. In his account he notes that Robert M. Argue, son of PAOC pioneer A.H. Argue, following his appointment as Executive Director of Home Missions and Bible Colleges in 1966 became aggressive in mobilizing all the resources he could in a new evangelism thrust among francophones in Quebec: "At end of the sixties, during a period of extremely slow growth for French Pentecostal churches, [he] desire[d] to stimulate spiritual vitality within the French Pentecostal movement and committed the full force of his department with the major part of its resources to the churches and in the initiation of the FLITE program" (this author's translation).⁷ The creation of FLITE as PAOC's means of training anglophone missionaries in the French language and the founding of Formation Timothée as a ministerial training institution for francophones were significant steps forward for the PAOC in an environment of general, social, spiritual, and political awakening.

As early as 1952, another trend that had helped to lay the groundwork for the Charismatic Renewal was the rise of ecumenism in Quebec under the leadership of a Jesuit priest, Father Irenee Beaubien, who organized interdenominational meetings calling them the Catholic Inquiry Forum with the aim of improving Protestants' understanding of Catholicism. Upon the tenth anniversary in 1962, Cardinal Leger went so far as to acknowledge that the Catholic Church had not had a monopoly on the truth of the Gospel in the past and in that same year authorized a diocesan commission on ecumenism and published a pastoral letter *Chrétiens disunis* (disunited Christians), obviously a radical departure from traditional Quebec Catholicism.[8]

Despite the reality that the Church was moving in the direction of ecclesial reform and so was instrumental in accelerating if not precipitating the massive societal changes that transpired, these same efforts had the "ironic effect of ushering into Quebec society the very trends whose results the faithful remnant and their leaders now lament."[9] The tension that existed in Quebec throughout the twentieth century was between the desire for change and the impulse to maintain the distinctiveness of its culture with the former eventually gaining the upper hand. The result was a rapid decline in the Catholic Church's influence in all aspects of life. Although the majority of Quebecers would still today identify themselves as Catholic and view the Church with a certain amount of respect, church membership, worship attendance, and numbers entering the priesthood have become only a fraction of what they were previous to 1960. By the early 1970s, the slide was rapidly underway with clergy recruitment at a standstill and priests leaving the priesthood. To compensate for the loss of a spiritual reference point, some found comfort in small group settings where groups of people lived their faith collectively in a particular location.[10]

The loss of spiritual roots that many Quebecers were experiencing coupled with the increased emphasis on and encouragement of lay involvement within church and society undoubtedly ripened the environment for spiritual renewal in the 1960s and 1970s. As the Church tried to come to terms with its future, the Dumont report commissioned by the Catholic bishops of Quebec in 1968 recommended that instead of "hauling into the future the dead weight of a sprawling network of bricks-and-mortar institutions,"[11] it move less in the direction of renewed stress on the traditions and structures of the past and more toward an increasingly flexible Catholicism characterized by individual awakening and social justice.

It needs further study but in the individualism of the modern era, while many devout Quebec Catholics began to see their mission as a social or political calling, the loss of past certainties drove many to the search for new spiritual meaning. Just as the Renewal met the need of those who had become weary of the formalism of their denominational institutions in other parts of the world including English Canada, so in Quebec, the Renewal blossomed as prayer groups, healing ministries, and retreats became attractive spiritual exercises in an environment not so much of anti-Catholicism but in one of growing indifference. Whereas in 1961, fewer than 6,500 Quebecers or less than 1 per cent declared themselves to be unbelievers and church attendance was at 61 per cent, by 1971, church attendance had dropped to 30 per cent with only 12 to 15 per cent being young adults aged twenty to twenty-four.[12] Essentially, the emerging individualism and pluralism in Canada seems to have been reflected quite early following the 1968 encyclical *Humanae vitae* officially condemning the use of artificial birth control when Canadian bishops "emphasized the primacy of the individual in regard to

Vatican teaching."[13]

Thus, the creativity, openness, and spirit of self-determination following World War II and the changes of Vatican II created a mentality conducive to new spiritual experiences apart from the traditional worship practices of the Church though not necessarily in opposition to them. The rapid secularization and modernization of Catholic Quebec issuing from a variety of sources including the widespread availability of the media of television was leading Quebecers to see the need to think for themselves and to chart their own spiritual journey.

The Charismatic Renewal Reaches Quebec

The waning influence of the Catholic Church in Quebec opened the door to the influence of the worldwide Charismatic Renewal. Together with the ministries particularly of American television evangelists whose sermons were broadcast each Sunday and the Full Gospel Business Men Fellowship International (FGBMFI), a new way of expressing faith emerged not so closely tied to traditional institutions.[14] In 1971, there were only a few isolated Charismatic prayer groups known in Canada as a whole but two years later, there were over five thousand people meeting weekly in more than a hundred groups across the country.[15] By that time, there had been several prayer groups serving English-speaking Canadians in Montreal but the impact upon the French-speaking population of the province had been slight.[16] The situation appeared bleak in the eyes of some as indicated in a sentiment expressed by Father Eugene Cullinane, a priest with strong socialist leanings. The people from Quebec visiting Madonna House[17] in Ontario were reporting a mass exodus from the Church. Cullinane laments:

> Quebec is going through a cultural revolution, and it's a very deep and complex thing. Their evolution into the modern world has been delayed by sociological and economic factors. It's hit them within the last ten years and there's very strong movement in Quebec province to become independent from the rest of Canada. A similar reaction is occurring in the Church in Quebec.... There's a revolt and an anticlericism in many places...a disdain for the priests and the Church structure, considering them as antiquated and finished. And there's a great crisis of faith at the bottom of all this. Quebec is going through fantastic turmoil and is in a revolution touching every area of their life: political, economic, cultural, and spiritual. The charismatic renewal in Quebec has hardly begun.[18]

The perception at least was that the rising nationalism in Quebec itself had some relationship to the revolt that was occurring within the Church.

The language barrier too played a significant role in the slow pace of the Charismatic Renewal in Quebec in the early years. Leaders of prayer groups in the Montreal area, recognizing that clergy were reluctant to accept the Renewal because of a lack of information in the French language, organized a day of orientation in September 1972 for clergy and other religious leaders. Well-known personalities within the wider Catholic Renewal, Edward O'Connor and Kevin

Ranaghan addressed the meeting with their talks being translated into French. This effort to cross the language line into Quebec culture was considered to be a major breakthrough for the Charismatic Renewal among Quebecers.[19]

The contribution of Catholic Quebec to the Renewal is evident in the formation of the Catholic Charismatic Church of Canada (CCCC), a body independent of the Roman Catholic Church. While still holding to the teachings of Catholicism, it was founded by a Quebecer, Patriarch Andre Barbeau, in 1968. Barbeau was ordained as a Catholic priest in 1940 and after serving for twenty-eight years in the Archdiocese of Montreal, he left the Church and was consecrated a bishop, the first autonomously appointed patriarch of the new CCCC by the pro-uniate Old Catholic bishops in Europe. Faith churches and communities were soon established in Canada and in several northeastern states in the United States. The CCCC still exists and believes that the manifestations of the Holy Spirit including spiritual gifts such as speaking in tongues, prophecy, healing, and miracles are for today just as in the first century Christian Church.[20]

In Quebec, there was a direct link between what had occurred at Notre Dame and the first French-speaking charismatic group. Sister Flore Crete was studying there in 1967 when the Renewal started and upon returning home wanted to start a group, which she did in her family home after being refused by her superiors to start it in the motherhouse.[21] The Renewal among Catholics, however, began to attract much greater attention the following year under the leadership of Father Jean-Paul Régimbal who had been introduced to the Renewal and had experienced the outpouring of the Spirit in Phoenix, Arizona where he had gone for health rehabilitation. Hermann Giguere, associate professor in the Faculty of Theology at Université Laval recalls that while Régimbal was there,

> Sandy Winters, an Episcopalian lady in the course of a meeting, herself received her experience of the 'baptism in the Spirit.' Father Régimbal who had never heard of this experience remained skeptical. However, he went through the Acts of the Apostles, the epistles of Paul and the texts of Vatican II. He went to see the lady in question, got on his knees and asked her to lay her hands upon him. He received the outpouring of the Spirit after which he was led to preach in California, Denmark, Spain, France, and Italy.[22] (This author's translation)

Régimbal was called home to Canada in 1970 to become director of a retreat house in Granby, Quebec where he immediately began to bring a charismatic influence to the retreats being held there[23] and where the first charismatic meetings took place in October of that year.[24]

The following March, Régimbal along with some Anglican charismatics organized a "Rally for Christ" at the Forum hockey stadium and another gathering at St. Joseph's Oratory in Montreal at which David du Plessis was the guest speaker. The result of these initial efforts was that Renewal was planted in six Francophone areas of Montreal and in the city of Granby. The spread of the Renewal among Quebec Catholics was well underway by 1973.[25] Régimbal's influence at "la Maison de retraite de Montplaisant" resulted in people being healed and hundreds coming to see and experience what was going on, in turn precipitating the startup of new groups. Each Monday in Granby, the evening of prayer attracted over a thousand people with many coming by bus from as far away as Ottawa, Ontario and Vermont.[26] Richard Dubé, a former Catholic charismatic parishioner and current pastor of an independent charismatic church near Granby recalls that Régimbal was in a sense viewed as the leader and father of the movement. Dubé remembers that the early days were very powerful with the crowds gradually increasing each night from one to two hundred and on to a thousand.

The rapid spread of the Renewal with the reports of miracles and glossolalia apparently resulted in initial resistance from the Catholic community. According to Dubé, Régimbal was sent to France where he was placed in isolation and forced to submit to Catholic discipline, resulting in health problems that remained with him upon his return to Canada. He was given a "hard time by the community" because the healings and his "disturbing religious spirits" earned him the reputation of being "too Pentecostal, too much alive."[27] Dubé recalls how one night when he himself was present, there was such a large number (in the vicinity of 80 percent) who raised their hands requesting prayer ministry that Régimbal prayed that the Lord would help him do the ministry because he would not be able to get to pray with everyone. Immediately, those who had raised their hands which was the majority of those present, fell on the floor, overwhelmed by the Spirit. He is adamant that Régimbal retained his zeal and conviction until his death, a claim substantiated by the establishment of the Centre Jean-Paul Régimbal and the esteem in which he is still held. He is viewed by Catholic charismatics as a man of "great religious faith, apostle heart of fire and God's mercy but unfortunately remains an unknown figure and his message sometimes misinterpreted"[28] (this author's translation).

The first English language charismatic meetings among Catholics in Montreal began under the leadership of Father Joseph Kane OMI, a missionary from Peru who returned to Montreal in 1970 through Seattle, Washington where he had seen the Renewal firsthand. His work in the predominantly French city quickly led to other diocesan priests becoming involved and several new groups beginning.[29] On Labor Day weekend 1972, Kevin Ranaghan met with several leaders at Le Grand Séminaire de Montréal and a charismatic conference took place in the summer of 1973 at Loyola University. From there, the development of Renewal gained significant momentum. A central service was organized for Renewal groups with the leaders expressing a desire to hold a Francophone conference that subsequently took place in June 1974 at Université Laval. The event was touted as a great success with six to eight thousand people attending.[30]

The French Canadian Assembly of Catholic Charismatic Renewal was founded in August 1975 with the responsibility of organizing a second national French charismatic conference at the Olympic Stadium in the summer of 1977, an event that Giguere claims brought together fifty thousand people. It was preceded by the first diocesan convention in the Quebec City diocese in October 1976 which five thousand people attended, revealing the escalating momentum of Charismatic Renewal groups in the area at the time. A third French conference was held at the Olympic Stadium in 1979, after which the French Canadian Assembly of Catholic

Charismatic Renewal decided to favor diocesan conferences in place of national conferences. These continued to take place at the initiative of the Canadian Council of Charismatic Renewal (CCCR), established in 1985 under the leadership of Hermann Giguère, then priest responsible for the Charismatic Renewal in the Quebec City diocese.[31]

Two features of the Renewal in Quebec are evident in these developments. The first, being unique to that province, was the very significant role played by priests[32] which perhaps more than any place else created controversy. After all, in the minds of conservative Catholics, priests having been influenced by outside forces now appeared to be the ones leading the new movement. In a province that had been all but closed to the rest of North America and in a sense oriented more toward Europe than America, the "cultural forms of Pentecostal piety"[33] so foreign to Catholics everywhere were doubly puzzling and even threatening to a society that was becoming increasingly sensitive to the dominant English speaking majority within the rest of Canada and the United States.[34] This angst was undoubtedly due in part to the exploding media culture including the stream of evangelistic and Pentecostal type television programs making their way into a hitherto predominantly rural French-Canadian society. Despite the welcomed change in Quebec vis-à-vis control of the Catholic Church over its society and culture, there was a growing fear of the continual intrusion of English culture that threatened to assimilate Quebec and in doing so destroy its distinctiveness expressed in its own language, culture, and religion. The Renewal could certainly be seen as part of that threat since priests were involved and often leading it from the outset. Hanrahan proposes that "…many in the Church were very much aware of the dangers of new doctrines and forms of worship in the Church. For some, Jean-Paul Régimbal embodied these dangers."[35] Although Régimbal was denounced to the Archbishop of Sherbrooke and the matter was settled, it was apparently not enough to avert some long-term damage.[36] The validity of such charismatic experiences continued to meet with criticism from some aspects of Church authority.

Nevertheless, those involved in the leadership of the Renewal worked within the environment of the Catholic Church in Quebec rather thinking they needed to separate because they felt threatened or that the expression of their newfound experience was being stifled. Their response was an ecclesial one. They requested and received permission from the Archbishop of Montreal to be able to hold a seminar especially for priests and religious leaders to provide them with information regarding the history of the Charismatic Renewal, the experience of the Spirit and the developing theology.[37] This proved to be what might be called the turning point in the Renewal in Quebec. Their intense loyalty to the Church was in a sense the driving force behind the effort to bring understanding and to encourage the priests to take leadership of the Renewal. The priests responded positively and within six months following those meetings in 1972, the numbers of people involved in the Renewal doubled.[38]

The direct involvement of priests with the Quebec Renewal was somewhat unique compared with the widespread lay leadership that emerged in other regions of Canada. Outside Quebec, there were often priests unwilling to become involved which effectively separated those in the Renewal from the Church, leaving them without a voice to speak to them. In this way, a gap was sometimes created between the charismatic experience of prayer, emphasis on the Word of God, and pastoral concern of leaders for their groups and the sacramental life of the Church.[39] In Quebec, this problem seems to have been largely avoided as priests were called upon to accept what was happening and to assume leadership. The effect was strong unity and trust between the charismatic leaders and the Church's leadership.

When the development of the Renewal began to really accelerate in Quebec, the second feature that Hanrahan notes was the explosive growth. At the beginning of 1973, there were only eighteen prayer groups known to exist in Quebec.[40] Ronald Chagnon outlines the growth: "One year later an entirely French-speaking conference in Quebec City drew 6,500 and 400 groups existed. In 1977 about 40,000 gathered in the Olympic Stadium in Montreal for the closing of a conference, with about half of them probably to be counted as actively involved in the renewal. By 1979, there were some 822 groups in the province with a membership of over 38,000."[41] A study conducted by Paul Reny and Jean-Paul Rouleau (1978) confirms those figures but also that by 1977, there were as many as seven hundred charismatic groups with an estimated membership of sixty thousand comprised mainly of lower middle class, middle-aged women, and men and women in religious orders.[42]

Renewal among French Catholics in Quebec had come a long way since the return of Regimbal from Arizona and the first charismatic retreat in Granby. Meanwhile, Catholic bishops while applauding the good results of the Renewal, tempered it with caution. In an attempt to keep relationships healthy with the Charismatic Movement in1974, the Bishops of Western Quebec issued a statement suggesting the necessary appointment of priests as liaison persons between bishops and the many prayer groups.[43]

With Quebec's movement away from its social isolation and clerical domination on the one hand and its attempt to retain its distinctiveness on the other, the Charismatic Renewal seems to have steered those associated with it in a direction away from either of those major issues. Individual spiritual hunger largely supplanted concern over either the changing role of the Catholic Church as the fundamental institution of Quebec society or any fear of cultural assimilation. There was a tendency for Charismatics not to be involved in any political way with the growing restlessness in Quebec. Thomas Csordas observes that while seventy per cent of Charismatics voted in elections, only just over twelve per cent chose the nationalist Parti Québecois, a party dedicated to an independent Quebec. He refers to a study by Zylberberg and Montminy (1980) in which the authors suggest that the Quebec nationalistic spirit with its emphasis on French monolingualism stood in symbolic contradiction to the universal spiritual language of speaking in tongues.[44] It appears that the Renewal in Quebec aided Quebecers in refocusing on a spirituality that seemed to be threatened by the massive cultural upheaval of the 1960s and the erosion of their traditional way of life with its emphasis on religion and the clergy as well as on the simple rural, communitarian life.[45] For many, the sense of displacement and loss of identity would have provided fertile ground for spiritual renewal.

The rapid growth of the Charismatic Renewal, therefore, paralleled the rapid changes taking place in the society and church of Quebec during the 1960s and 1970s. The Quiet Revolution had been underway before Vatican II but both worked in tandem. Schools, hospitals, and other social services became democratized and secularized: "A clear pattern of life characteristic of a rural and religious society shifted and changed; the clerically dominated cultural monolith that had been perceived as Quebec gave way to a sort of secular pluralism. Then came the renewal...."[46] Chagnon likely comes closest to the truth about the quickness of the Renewal's expansion in Quebec when he states, "the charismatic conversion, working within a framework in which the Church has lost a major part of its power to control and to constrain, enabled a body, which had been held down, to pull itself together, recognize its own reality and become free."[47] Underneath the rigidity of religious and cultural traditionalism lay the impulse for spiritual renewal and, by extension, spiritual freedom.

With the Church having all but lost its grip on the minds of Quebecers, the spiritual fervor of many continued but took on non-traditional forms. Di Giacomo notes "almost every ideology—religious, political, or otherwise—could get a hearing somewhere."[48] Non-Catholic groups including French-speaking evangelicals were winning converts everywhere. Almost all French Protestant churches grew in the 1970s, particularly classical Pentecostal ones that saw astounding growth through conversion and church planting.[49]

PAOC Accelerated Evangelism

The strengthened efforts of the PAOC to penetrate what was perceived as the Catholic stronghold in Quebec began in the late 1960s under the leadership of Robert Argue. Following his election as Executive Director of the National Home Missions and Bible Colleges Department in 1966, Argue soon discovered when working with the French PAOC Conference that the movement was stagnant in both finances and church planting and he was determined to see the situation change. Under his leadership, the now well-known FLITE program was implemented to recruit English Bible college graduates, give them one-year scholarships to learn French and then deploy them as missionaries and church planters. This strategy of church planters and evangelism was implemented but not without resistance from many French Pentecostals who felt threatened by the cultural forces foreign to Quebec thinking. Di Giacomo describes the sharp controversy that erupted at the May 1974 annual Quebec PAOC conference when a resolution was presented that attempted to ensure that a French Canadian would always hold each major leadership position, including that of superintendent. Opposition to the resolution was swift, hinging on the notion that it was not consistent with the General Constitution of the PAOC that did not provide for leadership on the basis of ethnicity: "Ultimately, the meeting contributed to a dysfunctional relationship between the administrations of the French Conference and the National Home Missions Department that engulfed adjacent administrative Districts and all of the top leaders of the national headquarters of the denomination." Such administrative wrangling over responsibility for the evangelization of French Canada continued until 2000 when a complete restructuring took place that resulted in the creation of the Quebec District of the PAOC.[50]

Di Giacomo further proposes that the cultural divide was so deep and complex that the Pentecostal theology of the Spirit as crossing ethnic lines "was not sufficient to break the historic and cultural patterns that led to conflict between the English majority and the French minority."[51] He also suggests that Pentecostal leaders in Quebec in the 1970s were called upon to deal with the same issues that previous generations had to deal with at the political level, which in essence was the perceived threat to the preservation of the cultural and linguistic characteristics of Quebec and the issue of authority over finances and manpower. His position is that "they reacted in ways similar to their historical counterparts, consistent with historical patterns in French-English, federal-provincial relations."[52] Notwithstanding left wing, progressive attitudes toward social issues, the defense of Quebec nationalistic aspirations has continued. Nevertheless, Pentecostal churches grew along with the Catholic Renewal in an environment that was hungry for deeper spiritual meaning regardless of broader ongoing political and ethnic tensions. Ironically, with both movements originating from outside the culturally sensitive milieu, great spiritual strides were made.

Toward the end of the 1960s, the trend of the PAOC's evangelistic efforts within Quebec turned toward the use of literature, the distribution of Bibles, and emphasis on education including language courses. *The Pentecostal Testimony* reported in 1969 that a massive distribution of literature by Youth With a Mission (YWAM) during the previous summer had reached seven-eighths of the homes outside Montreal as well as much of the city with a gospel witness. The PAOC in this article suggested that in support of this effort, funds should be sent to their national office in Toronto. They continued to cooperate with YWAM in its Quebec outreach, particularly at the 1976 Montreal Summer Olympics.[53] By this time, the changes in Quebec society associated with the Quiet Revolution had taken firm grip on the psyche of Quebecers. Although Argue lamented that after fifty years, there were still only nineteen French-speaking Pentecostal churches, he was also optimistic that the environment was now different and open doors were everywhere just waiting for those who would be willing to learn French and go to Quebec as missionaries.[54] Nevertheless, a weekly French television program called *Message De Vie*, apparently the only French Pentecostal telecast in the world at the time, was already celebrating its tenth anniversary in 1971.[55]

Quebec summer outreaches continued into the 1970s with increasing numbers of conversions, enrollments in correspondence courses and increased interest in French language study for evangelism purposes. In 1972 the PAOC as a result of the programs of the previous four or five years which included the combined thrust of Institut Biblique Berée and French language study, was able to report that sufficient numbers of Pentecostal ministers were being trained to pastor the churches already established and to pioneer unreached areas. There were thirty-six locations where French language church services were being conducted, making the PAOC the largest evangelical voice in French Canada. The spirit of the denomination's momentum was no better expressed at this point than by Argue in his report to the 1972 General Conference: "By television, by radio, by literature, by crusades, by correspondence courses, by visitation, by AIM programs in conjunction with the Quebec and Gaspe outreaches, we are doing all in our power to take advantage of the open doors in French Canada...."[56] The Pentecostal church in Quebec was seen as being on the move with new buildings needed in several places and meetings and intensive evangelism being conducted in many other locations throughout the province.[57] One pastor, a recent graduate of the French language study program, was sent to Drummondville, a town well known for its strong Catholic influence. Within five months, he had conducted his first water baptism service with seventeen believers being baptized, others being healed, and attendance steadily increasing.[58]

The evangelism efforts of the PAOC in the province of Quebec have always faced culture and language challenges, but in the 1970s the same social and cultural forces that made the environment conducive to renewal paved the way for the PAOC to expand its ministry there. Miller posits that Pentecostalism in the province no doubt benefited from the so-called "living room revolt against the clergy" of the 1970s. Gospel and charismatic programming being telecast at that time was "a powerful force in opening the eyes of the Quebecois to the outside world." The Charismatic Renewal had a "powerful impact on spiritually hungry souls." With the Catholic hierarchy complaining that only about 25 per cent were regularly attending mass and many turning away from the traditional church, the people of Quebec were open to other groups entering the province.[59]

Although not easy to prove with any significant degree of certainty, the PAOC appears to have been riding the crest of a wave of a renewal that was rolling quickly through Quebec by the early part of the decade. The pinnacle, it seems, was the 1976 Olympic Games in Montreal which saw about two hundred youth evangelize the Olympic sites as well as work with local PAOC churches, many of which had already taken on a more charismatic flavor. Youth from across Canada, including the author, were privileged to participate in that outreach for the month of July. There was a definite sense of renewal, particularly among French-speaking PAOC churches where the influence of the wider Charismatic Movement was evident in the frequency of the operation of the *charismata*, in the use of its songs as well as those of the Jesus Movement, and singing and chanting in the Spirit.

The growth that the PAOC experienced in Quebec was by any account phenomenal in both church plants and adherents during the 1970s and into the 1980s, more than at any time in the history of the Pentecostal movement in that province. The FLITE program served as an integral part, a revitalization effort to get a stagnant Pentecostalism moving again and working effectively. Di Giacomo summarizes its success:

> ...language-training was but the portal through which anglophone missionaries passed to become the major participants in that renewal process, a missionary thrust into French Canada that spurred Pentecostal growth in numbers of adherents and churches. FLITE was the motor that drove spiritual change in the Québécois Pentecostal community in the 1970s and 1980s....[the]work of anglophone missionaries in Quebec dislodged the French-Canadian Pentecostal church from its inertia and stimulated it to growth...Pentecostals would make the greatest contribution to expanding the francophone Protestant presence in Quebec. The Pentecostal Assemblies of Canada (PAOC), the largest of the Pentecostal groups, would plant four times as many churches in the next thirty years as in the previous fifty. By the end of the 1970s the number of Pentecostal adherents in Quebec had tripled, especially among francophones. Many factors - political, sociological, and historical, as well as religious - originating both from within and from outside the province, led to explosive growth for the PAOC in the 1970s as well as for other religious groups. [60]

During the mid-1970s, reports of growth and revival in Quebec became well known within PAOC circles. Anglophone missionaries from a classical Pentecostal tradition were making unprecedented progress in penetrating what had been a very traditional Catholic way of life.

The Pentecostal Testimony continually updated its readers with exciting news of the revival in Quebec as evidenced in the numerous conversions, growth in church attendance, number of churches planted, churches built and increasing enrolment of Bible school students.[61] Yet, it continually kept before its readers the depth of the spiritual need in the province: "There is the need, much of which has been described before. Questionnaires show that more than 30 per cent of Quebec's 6,000,000 has, in practice, severed religious ties in the last fifteen years!"[62] The publication celebrated the launching of the Quebec Literature Crusade as the answer to the dearth of biblical knowledge and looked to the upcoming Olympics as the catalyst for a revival in Quebec.[63] It looked back at the Olympic outreach as a great success in partnering with local churches in the greater Montreal area: "A most telling effect was the moving of the Spirit of God, Pentecostal emphasis with gifts of the Spirit in operation did something very special for the young people that no amount of programming genius could ever accomplish. Unabashedly, they prayed openly for people with results."[64] Donald Martin, academic director at FLITE, expressed the excitement of many within the denomination over what they perceived to be happening:

> There seems to be no end in sight to the rapid growth which The Pentecostal Assemblies of Canada churches are experiencing in French Canada. A revival is in progress. This encourages the hearts of all those who minister in the various areas of PAOC outreach. Indeed, it is felt that this move of God has no counterpart in the history of the Church, that it will continue to augment to the point when it will spill over the borders of French Canada to bless the entire world.[65]

Not only pastors, but lay people were being encouraged to enroll in language training to prepare for possible teaching in Quebec and so to be in a place to assist in local church planting and evangelism.

The Charismatic Renewal in La Belle Province and a re-vitalized classical Pentecostalism might be called a double track work of the Spirit that often blended with each other in a context of rapid and unprecedented social change. In many cases, there were Catholic Charismatics who ended up gravitating toward Pentecostal churches many of which began slowly but surely to adopt charismatic worship styles (including chanting) with common songs borrowed from the Jesus Movement and charismatic circles across North America.

The stagnation within PAOC churches in Quebec that had become common in the mid-1960s had also become a sensitive point for French pastors such as Bernard Sigouin who believed that English pastors had perceived them as falling asleep at the leadership wheel. His response was that he and his fellow pastors had for years worked under a 'leaden sky' but that times had now changed and were continuing to change for the better. Being able to submit articles freely to newspapers, renting halls for special meetings, and not having to endure the same misunderstanding and even mistreatment from family members was seen as evidence that it was a new day with "almost unlimited possibilities and even such a thing as the Charismatic Renewal.... Our Pentecostal pastors are invited to go and speak in Catholic churches, as some of you have been invited to do."[66] The largest of the French–speaking Protestant groups in Quebec became PAOC affiliated churches and Quebec City, the provincial capital, became the hub of Pentecostal expansion in French Canada. One of the most influential and best-known churches was Église évangelique de Pentecôte (now called Carrefour Chrétien de la Capitale) located at Sainte-Foy near that city.[67] It became a flagship church with both French and English worship services being conducted with a blend of traditional Pentecostal and Charismatic elements. The church also had an exceptionally effective small group ministry for that time.

Assessing PAOC Involvement

While the success of the PAOC in Quebec's renewal climate during the 1970s and well into the 1980s is difficult to attribute to any one factor, the new freedom of the Jesus Movement and the wider Charismatic Movement was occurring at a time when Quebec society was beginning to open up. The loss of influence of the Catholic Church and the popularizing impact of Vatican II were all converging strands. The contrast between what took place in those years and the sluggish spread of Pentecostalism in Quebec prior to then, is stark indeed. In preparation for the 24th biennial national General Conference of the PAOC to be held in Montreal in 1964, there had been reflection on the successes in Quebec. Yet by all standards, the gains had been very modest. Although Montreal had been the site of the first formal meeting in 1917 consisting of thirteen early Pentecostal leaders who formed the organization and succeeded in getting its federal charter granted by the Canadian Parliament in 1919,[68] in the Canadian census of 1921, there were only 374 Pentecostal believers in Quebec and 7012 in the rest of Canada. In the 1941 census, the number had only risen to 1,158 in Quebec and 57,742 throughout the remainder of the country. Forty years after 1921 (1961), there were still a mere 5,730 Pentecostals in the province compared to 143,877 nationally.[69] It is clear that up to the time of the Quiet Revolution, Quebec's culture, including the dominance of the Catholic Church, had been all but impervious to renewal. But a permanent social and religious transformation was now in the making.

Quebec began to be seen and referred to by the PAOC from the mid-1960s onward as a mission field requiring the same attention as any other mission location in the world. Only a few years before the Catholic Charismatic Renewal, Samuel Buick in reporting on home missions for the PAOC expressed the sentiment of so many Pentecostals in English Canada:

> The challenge of Quebec as a mission-field is brought home to us by the importance and power of the Roman Catholic Church. The population is 82% French Canadian and Roman Catholic... There are more than 100 towns with a population exceeding 5,000; many of these, not to speak of numerous villages, are without any evangelical witness.... The Pentecostal Assemblies of Canada have not turned a blind eye to this great mission-field on their doorstep. Since the first meetings in the French language were held in Montreal in 1919, great efforts have been made to claim Quebec for Christ.[70]

It is indeed true that although by 1963, there were only twenty-two full-time PAOC workers in Quebec, it was still at that time the second largest Protestant group. In relative terms, there had been some success considering that most other groups had a history going back more than a century compared with the PAOC French-speaking work, said to have begun in 1919 when Rev. Louis Dutuad received the "Pentecostal Baptism in the Holy Spirit."[71]

As in other parts of North America and the world where the earlier wave of renewal had spread, there were various pockets of the same in Quebec. On the Gaspé Peninsula, for example, miraculous healings from cancer, heart disease, and injuries sustained in military combat had been reported as well as baptisms in the Holy Spirit.[72] There was a sense by 1965 that the religious climate was beginning to loosen with less dependence on the clergy by the laity and more tolerance toward non-Catholic groups. A revealing ministry update at the time reported, "Many Catholics are sincere and buying Bibles, but few are willing to pay the price of leaving the church in which they were born. Although they are now permitted to visit other churches, few dare to do so."[73] The emphasis of the earlier revival upon conversion with subsequent water baptism and Spirit baptism created the same kind of misunderstanding and tension that had occurred in other areas, except that in Quebec with its mostly monolithic religious culture, it would have been so much more pronounced.

The two tracks of renewal in Quebec during the 1970s were by no means totally separate. This was at least partly a result of the influence of Christian television personalities, such as David Mainse. In March 1972, Mainse who was rapidly gaining the reputation of becoming a Pentecostal ecumenist was invited by Allan Bowen, pastor of l'Église évangélique de Pentecôte to conduct an evangelistic campaign. While in Quebec City, he addressed a Catholic ecumenical class at

Montmartre Canadien, a Catholic ecumenical institute, on the new Holy Spirit outpouring at which two people, Bowen reported, "were filled with the Spirit." He continued excitedly: "The final statistics for the seven days are: 38 events; 2,800 - total attendance; 1,100 - total rally attendance. This is remarkable in a city where total Sunday morning attendance in Protestant churches is less than 600. Signs of revival are becoming apparent."[74] This event would have been only the beginning of Mainse's national ministry as a PAOC evangelist and television talk show host to the Charismatic community. Meanwhile, Bowen's ministry in the city was well known among Catholics as he attempted to build a rapport with them:

> ...he found them fascinated by the arrival of English Canadians at a time of Quebec nationalism. Quebecers were awakening to the outside world. Pastor Bowen visited and spoke with Catholic priests who did not see this English Protestant evangelizing of French Canadians as a threat but rather saw it from the perspective of Vatican II, that is to say that "separated brethren" were coming to pray with Catholics, and thus was an answer to the prayer of Pope John XXIII inviting the Holy Spirit to do a new work.[75] (The author's translation).

When Bowen became pastor of the church in 1971, only ten people made up the congregation. Within five years, it grew to 350. The ripples of the Jesus Movement infiltrated Quebec especially through some anglophone young people who had been converted in Florida and returned to Quebec, witnessing to their friends and provoking a revival in the mostly English-speaking church at Sainte-Foy. French Canadian youth were equally affected as young hippies, drug addicts, and prostitutes came and were accepted as they were. Seventy-five to eighty-five percent of those converts were under the age of twenty-five. Bowen spoke of it as "a Jesus People explosion in Quebec."[76]

There were many within Bowen's congregation who could be called the Quebec version of the "come-outers." They were Catholic but had left their Catholic backgrounds and became uncomfortable with anything in the Ste-Foy church that they associated with Catholicism as they understood it. Some resisted even the positioning of a cross anywhere inside or outside the building, causing the church to be quite unadorned.[77] This seems to indicate that whereas Bowen had developed great rapport and understanding with the Catholic clergy, most of his congregation was basking in the freedom of being out from under the domination of the Church. It is likely a reflection of the times when Quebec was opening to the outside world and there was a desire among youth to shake off anything that smacked of rigidity and control. By 1984, the church had attracted over five hundred French people[78] resulting in the need for services in both French and English.

For the PAOC, the 1970's in Quebec was a decade of obvious renewal that retired ministers still speak of with fond recollection. Enhanced outreach efforts continued throughout those years with English-speaking Bible College graduates being recruited and trained. The challenge was always framed (and still is) under the notion that Quebec is a big mission field, "the least evangelized area on the North American continent... [with] less than 10,000 evangelical Christians in a population of 6,000,000."[79] The denomination reported that some surveys were showing more than thirty per cent having severed religious ties within the previous fifteen years.[80]

By 1980, the challenge was still being put forth that thirty-five cities of over five thousand population had never been evangelized. At the same time, however, the PAOC was able to rejoice in the fact that "an unprecedented move of God in this province has increased the Church of Jesus Christ by nearly ten times in the last ten years."[81] While the success of the Pentecostal movement in Quebec was widely celebrated, there was still so much more that needed to be done in such a large geographical and uneven demographical region of the country. The call was to continue to push forward in the decade ahead, an appeal that focused continually on the spiritual need but one that was always balanced with anticipation. With growing political upheaval and the real threat of separation from the rest of Canada, optimism for revival was high and the challenge was not to give up but to use "every means, every modern tool, every resource which exists in the world of today if needed. These are not dreary days of defeat but days of glorious victory."[82] The outlook of most PAOC churches in Quebec during this time of uncertainty was perhaps best expressed in a news item in the June 1980 issue of *The Pentecostal Testimony* on the growth of the church at Dorion just outside Montreal: "The uncertainty felt in Quebec in so many areas is not felt in the spiritual vision of the congregation. They have seen the first signs of the showers of blessing, and eagerly await an unprecedented move of God in the area."[83]

Donald Martin reflecting on the nine years of the FLITE program stated that it seemed as if the need for workers was greater than at the beginning of the program in 1971. Yet, he stated optimistically:

> There seems to be no way we can keep up with the growth we are experiencing.... There seems to be no end in sight to the rapid growth which the Pentecostal Assemblies of Canada are experiencing in French Canada. *A revival is in progress.... Indeed it is felt that this move of God has no counterpart in the history of the Church, that it will continue to augment to the point when it will spill over the borders of French Canada to bless the entire world.*"[84] (emphasis added)

The enthusiasm expressed here seems to expect that the PAOC would be at the leading edge of such a global awakening. The Lausanne Committee for World Evangelization in 1982 also reported that there was an unprecedented evangelism and growth of French-speaking evangelical congregations in Quebec of which the PAOC had the largest contingent with over a hundred organized churches and many more study groups and outreach points: a total of seven thousand members and adherents.[85] From 1967 to 1982, French congregations had grown from nineteen to 170.[86] A 1983 report spoke of Good Friday services in Montreal in French-speaking assemblies being "indicative of the spirit of revival that is sweeping over French Canada. As never before, French-speaking Quebecers are coming to the Lord and being filled with the Holy Spirit."[87] For example, Le Temple de l'Évangile in St. Hubért had grown from a small cell group seven years earlier to a congregation of 500.[88]

Despite declining church attendance of around twenty percent per year and only two out of every one thousand people in Quebec considered evangelical and furthermore, given that the forty years of PAOC history in the province had resulted in less than twenty churches, now just four years into the decade, *The Pentecostal Testimony* reported that the years 1974-1984 alone had seen the establishment of eighty new churches.[89] David Boyd, a pastor and educator in Quebec, noted that forty churches were now being pastored by graduates from the FLITE program. In his view, "the opposition of the past has diminished...the doors are open."[90]

The impact of Christian television upon Quebec during the early 1980s is also clear as David Mainse and his *Crossroads* ministry program, *100 Huntley Street*, conducted rallies in Sherbrooke and Montreal and drew such large crowds unheard of before in the province for such events, many of whom had already been exposed to Mainse's French program, *Au Cent Tuple*.[91] By this time, almost a third of all evangelical churches and believers in Quebec were affiliated with PAOC churches.[92] In 1985, David Wilkerson was invited to conduct a ten-day crusade in four locations during which two thousand people became believers and resulted also in some PAOC churches doubling, tripling, and in one or two cases, quadrupling overnight. Le Carrefour Chrétien de la Capitale (formerly l'Église évangélique de Pentecôte) increased to eight hundred from only thirty in the congregation thirteen years earlier. The PAOC believed the 1980s were "Quebec's day for a Holy Ghost visitation" and that the denomination was "on the cutting edge in 'La Belle Province.'"[93]

Renewal Begins to Wane

On the thirty-fifth anniversary of the Charismatic Renewal in Canada in 2003 when the Canadian Conference of Catholic Bishops took time to reflect on its current status, it re-affirmed its position that the emergence of the Renewal in 1968 had resulted in "a great upsurge of spiritual vitality and renewal" from coast to coast.[94] In the French sector, it recognized that organization had taken place early with the formation of the Assemblée canadienne francophone du Renouveau charismatique catholique (ACFRCC) in 1974-75, later becoming the Conseil canadien due Renouveau charismatique (CCRC) as it is today.[95] The bishops were just as supportive of the on-going work of the Spirit in renewal as they had been more than three decades earlier and repeated the same pastoral exhortation addressed to the faithful in 1970 on the Charismatic Renewal: "Remain attentive to the Spirit. He alone can bring to completion, in ways no human hand can trace in advance, our common efforts to build tomorrow's Church."[96] The bishops believed that the words were just as relevant and in fact, took on an even greater urgency as the Church launched out on the uncertain waters of the new millennium.

The Fourth National Congress of the Catholic Renewal was held at Université Laval in 1990 at which Archbishop Paul Cordes, the representative of Pope John Paul II for the Charismatic Renewal, participated. That event attracted more than seven thousand people but groups and communities within the Renewal began to experience a decline in the 1990s. Other national conventions followed with the eighth taking place in 2002 in Verdun near Montreal with around three thousand in attendance.[97] Meanwhile, isolated pockets of charismatic renewal continued to take place even in remote areas of the province.

Christianity Today reported in 2000 of a "church-based charismatic renewal" among the Inuit of northern Quebec in 1999 that had resulted in the lives of thousands of people being affected and many communities being completely transformed. Some church leaders reported that the renewal had quite visible results: "...People give more of themselves, they make major changes in their lifestyles, and they influence their communities for the better."[98] In some cases, mayors and council members became active believers with mayors sometimes doubling as local pastors. Concern was expressed, however, from traditional leaders within both the Anglican and Roman Catholic Churches, regarding the value of charismatic worship and teaching as well as such issues as a second baptism for Christians already baptized as infants, the exploitation of emotions, and the "health and wealth" gospel. They were wary of evangelists claiming that "native people are hearing the gospel story for the first time."[99] Consistent with the pattern of renewal in the past characterized by fear and faith, opposition and acceptance, there emerged positive changes including more emphasis on Bible study, grace, and biblical morality. One Innu man declared, "The Lord calls me to be filled with the Holy Spirit and introduce [others] to the Lord and fill them up with the Holy Spirit."[100]

Meanwhile, the PAOC continued its work in Quebec within the context of a self-governing district (District Quebec des Assembliées de la Pentecôte du Canada). One of the many thriving churches resulting from the years of active evangelism is Église Nouvelle Vie in suburban Montreal. Though now independent, it is in a sense the product of both the presence of classical Pentecostalism and the Charismatic Renewal in Quebec. As of 2006, it had grown in its initial thirteen years from forty adults to about three thousand regular Sunday attenders. With no direct emphasis on traditional evangelism, it focuses on prayer and meeting the needs of people within the community, thus "bringing the message of Jesus' love to the secular, cynical people of Montreal."[101] Highly charismatic in nature, its ministries range from programs for disadvantaged children, pregnant teenagers, depression, addictions, and the elderly. The effects of the Charismatic Renewal long after its growth had peaked and the parallel evangelism efforts of an early twentieth century Pentecostal denomination resulted in the establishment of urban and suburban churches, many of which have developed a hybrid form of classical Pentecostal and charismatic expression.

In summary, renewal in Quebec during the 1960s, especially the 1970s and well into the 1980s was taking place on two fronts against the backdrop of profound social and cultural changes. The Catholic Charismatic Renewal with its roots at Duquesne and Notre Dame universities made its way into the province through the influence of Quebecers who had experienced the Holy Spirit themselves while in the United States. Classical Pentecostalism represented largely by the PAOC was spreading into previously almost exclusive Catholic urban and rural areas spurred on by increased emphasis on Quebec as a mission field requiring both solid biblical training as well as language preparation. These cannot be viewed as two distinct movements but two strands of the one season of renewal among Canadian francophones. They did not move forward in isolation but instead influenced each other within the common environment of spiritual hunger.

As Quebecers became aware of the wider world and their consequent criticism of a "suffocating cultural environment,"[102] the result was a fundamental social and cultural transformation in the 1960s that created the right moment for both tracks of renewal. The current PAOC Quebec District website puts it into clear perspective:

> The Quiet Revolution did not spare the religious landscape but left in its wake a plethora of new religious groups and ideologies replacing the former omnipresent and socially powerful Roman Catholic Church which had been the de facto state religion of Quebec. The Pentecostal work was one of the major beneficiaries of the French Canadian cultural revolution. In terms of numbers of souls saved and churches planted it was in the 1970s and 1980s that the Quebecois Pentecostal church enjoyed its finest hour. From approximately 1,000 francophone Pentecostals in the 1960s the movement grew to about 15,000 by 1991. From about 18 churches in Quebec in 1960, at the end of the century there were 82 francophone churches in Quebec....[103]

Ronald Chagnon's position is essentially the same with respect to the Renewal among Catholics:

> The Charismatic Renewal must be understood, it seems as a response to the profound upheaval that has marked the social and religious life in Quebec for the last twenty years. In the face of the process of social and ecclesial change and the insecurity that it produced for citizens and Christians, the Charismatic Renewal constituted a vibrant call to a new social and ecclesial leadership that would be a source of peace, tranquility, and stability.[104] (author's translation)

Both tracks were furthermore strikingly similar. PAOC leaders claimed tight reins on the mission to Quebec sometimes at the price of significant misunderstanding with their French brothers and sisters. Likewise, the Catholic Charismatic Renewal quickly came under the control of the bishops, which in turn essentially insured that it would remain Catholic. The result is that the Renewal became largely routinized in the form of the Conseil Canadien du Renouveau Charismatique. Still, the common ground shared by both trajectories with the latter having emerged at least indirectly from the former, and then their intersection in a common environment of crumbling Catholic culture are realities that ought not to be lost. Rather, they can be recognized and built upon, providing opportunity for greater understanding and renewal.

Finally, the picture of renewal in Quebec might not be complete if the mission work of classical Pentecostalism and the Catholic Charismatic Renewal are viewed solely as products of social and cultural transformation. Such would be a thoroughly naturalistic approach ignoring the possibility of providential timing and circumstances. The right conditions had converged in Quebec with the decisions of Vatican II and the Quiet Revolution. The picture needs to recognize what cannot be empirically substantiated: the sovereignty of the Spirit as the agent of renewal whereby the broader structures of society and the human agents associated with them were conditioned by spiritual forces beyond our grasp and ability to totally explain.[105]

Notes

1. Leslie Woodcock Tentler, ed., *The Church Confronts Modernity: Catholicism Since 1950 in the United States, Ireland, and Quebec* (Washington, D.C.: The Catholic University of America Press, 2007): 4.

2. Susan Mann Trofimenkoff, *The Dream of Nation: A Social and Intellectual History of Quebec,* (Toronto: Gage Publishing, 1983): 286-87, 291, 293-94 in Tentler, ed., *The Church Confronts Modernity,* 5.

3. Kevin J. Christiano, "The Trajectory of Catholicism in Twentieth Century Quebec" in Tentler, *The Church Confronts Modernity,* 22-23.

4. Charles F. Doran, *Why Canadian Unity Matters and Why Americans Care: Democratic Pluralism at Risk* (Toronto: University of Toronto Press, 2001): 78-79 cited in Kevin J.Christiano, "The Trajectory of Catholicism in Twentieth Century Quebec" in Tentler, *The Church Confronts Modernity,* 23.

5. Christiano, "The Trajectory of Catholicism in Twentieth Century Quebec" in Tentler, *The Church Confronts Modernity,* 24.

6. Paul-Andre Linteau, Jean-Claude Robert, Rene Durocher, & Francois Ricard,*Quebec Since 1930* (Les Editions du Boreal Express. 1986), trans. Robert Chodos & Ellen Garmaise (Toronto: James Lorimer & Company Publishers, 1991): 477.

7. Michael Di Giacomo, "Les Pentecôtistes Québécois, 1966-1995: Historie d'un Réveil" (PhD Diss. Université Laval, October, 1999): 238-239.

8. Ibid.

9. Christiano, "The Trajectory of Catholicism in Twentieth Century Quebec" in Tentler, ed.,*The Church Confronts Modernity,* 24. The trends suggested here refer particularly to the crumbling family tradition revealed in plummeting fertility rates and skyrocketing abortions and divorce rates.

10. Linteau, Robert, Durocher, and Ricard, *Quebec Since 1930,* 480.

11. Christiano, "The Trajectory of Catholicism in Twentieth Century Quebec" in Tentler, *The Church Confronts Modernity,* 56.

12. Michael Gaureau, "They are not of our generation," in Tentler, ed., *The Church Confronts Modernity,* 63.

13. Michael Cuneo, *Catholics Against the Church: Anti-Abortion Protest in Toronto, 1969-1985* (Toronto: University of Toronto Press, 1989), 26-27 cited in Michele Dillon, "Decline and Continuity," in Tentler, ed., *The Church Confronts Modernity,* 254.

14. Linteau, Robert, Durocher, & Ricard. *Quebec Since 1930*, 481.
15. Opening caption, "The Canadian Renewal," *New Covenant*, 1:7 (January 1973): 11.
16. Edward O'Connor, "The Canadian Renewal," *New Covenant*, 1:7 (January 1973): 12.
17. Madonna House, now called Madonna House Apostolate, was founded in 1947 and is located in Combermere, Ontario. It describes itself as "a community of consecrated lay men, women, and priests…a family within the Roman Catholic Church, dedicated to loving and serving Christ in one another and in all men and women." www.madonnahouse.org (accessed June 16, 2014).
18. O'Connor, "The Canadian Renewal," *New Covenant*, 12-13.
19. Ibid.,13.
20. "History of the Catholic Charismatic Church of Canada," http://bethanycc.org/CCCChistory.htm (accessed June 16, 2014).
21. Peter E. Prosser, "An Historical and Theological Evaluation of the Charismatic Renewal" (unpublished Master's thesis, University of Montreal, 1978), cited in Al Reimer, *God's Country: Charismatic Renewal* (Toronto: G.R. Welch, 1979), 122-123.
22. Hermann, Giguère, "Notes Historiques sur les Debuts du Renouveau Charismatique," *Selon sa Parole* 25:6 (June-July, 1999). http://selonsaparole.tripod.com/gig996.htm (accessed June 17, 2014). Peter Prosser noted in 1973 that "a French Canadian priest spread the movement in Rome itself." Peter Prosser, "Roman Catholic Charismatic Impact Increases," *The Pentecostal Testimony*, (September, 1973): 5. Whether Prosser's claim can be substantiated with any reasonable degree of certainty is unclear but Jean-Paul Régimbal is likely the priest referred to here.
23. Prosser, "Historical and Theological Evaluation," in Reimers, *God's Country*, 123-124, and Jean-Paul Régimbal's own account, ibid., 125-126 in Hanrahan, "Nature and History," 318.
24. Giguère, "Notes Historiques," http://selonsaparole.tripod.com/gig996.htm (accessed June 17, 2014).
25. Ibid.
26. Ibid.
27. Personal interview with Richard Dubé, charismatic pastor near Granby, Quebec, November, 2008.
28. Sentiers de la spiritualité chrétienne, http://www.michel-lafontaine.com/sentiersspirituels_christ_jeanpaulregimbal.html (accessed June 17, 2014).
29. Giguère, "Notes Historiques," http://selonsaparole.tripod.com/gig996.htm (accessed June 17, 2014).
30. Ibid.
31. Ibid.
32. Hanrahan, "Nature and History," 318.
33. Ibid., 318.
34. Ibid., 318-319.

35. Ibid., 319.

36. In the author's conversation with Dubé, he confirmed that Régimbal was the target of huge misunderstanding of the Renewal on the part of some.

37. Hanrahan, "Nature and History," 319.

38. Ibid.

39. Ibid., 319-320.

40. In May 1973, *The Pentecostal Testimony* reported that the "Catholic-Pentecostal" movement in the US was spilling over into Canada and that five thousand Roman Catholics were meeting from coast to coast in more than a hundred "Pentecostal prayer groups." The phenomenon appears to have been viewed at this point as a continuation of classical Pentecostalism and so should be applauded even if numbers were somewhat inaccurate. Whether the figures are precise is a matter of conjecture.

41. Ronald Chagnon, *Les charismatiques au Quebec* (Montreal: Quebec/Amerique, 1979): 11 in Hanrahan, "Nature and History," 320.

42. Thomas J. Csordas, *Language, Charisma, and Creativity: The Ritual Life of a Religious Movement* (Berkeley, Los Angeles, Oxford: University of California Press, 1997): 23.

43. Message of the Bishops of the Western Province of Quebec [sic] on the Catholic Charismatic Renewal," in *Presence, Power, Praise: Documents on the Charismatic Renewal*, ed., Kilian McDonnell (Collegeville, Minnesota: Liturgical Press, 1980), Vol. 1: 582 f, in Ronald N. Kydd, "Pentecostals, Charismatics, and the Canadian Denominations," *eglise et theologie*, 13.2 (May 1982): 228.

44. *Language, Charisma, and Creativity*, 23-24.

45. Ibid., 24.

46. Hanrahan, "Nature and History," 320.

47. Chagnon, *Les charismatiques*, 103 in Hanrahan, "Nature and History," 320-321.

48. Michael Di Giacomo, "Pentecostalism, Nationalism, and Quebec Culture," *PNEUMA* 28:1 (Spring, 2006): 33.

49. Ibid.

50. Di Giacomo, "Pentecostalism, Nationalism, and Quebec Culture," 35.

51. Ibid.,56.

52. Ibid.

53. Ruth E. Wilson, "Are You With Us?" *The Pentecostal Testimony* (July 1969): 11.

54. Robert M. Argue, "The Answer—French Scholarships," *The Pentecostal Testimony* (February 1970): 10.

55. Mlle. Marie-Paule Gagnon, "Tenth Anniversary for French Telecast," *The Pentecostal Testimony* (February 1971): 10.

56. Robert M. Argue, " HOME MISSIONS from Report to General Conference," *The Pentecostal Testimony* (October 1972): 10.

57. Robert M. Argue, "A Bomb Bursts in Quebec," *The Pentecostal Testimony* (December 1972): 10.

58. Kennneth Birch, "From Lennoxville to Drummondville," *The Pentecostal Testimony* (March 1972): 10.

59. Miller, *Canadian Pentecostals*, 311.

60. Michael Di Giacomo, "FLITE: Religious Entrepreneurship in Quebec in the 1970s and 1980s," *Journal of the Canadian Church Historical Society* 46:1 (Spring 2004): 50-51.

61. Ibid., 73.

62. W. H. K. MacGowan, "Quebec's Greatest Need," *The Pentecostal Testimony* (April 1976): 18-19.

63. Ibid.

64. Editor's Observations, "Olympic Outreach," *The Pentecostal Testimony* (October 1976): 18-19.

65. Donald R. Martin, "FLITE Celebrates Anniversary," *Pentecostal Testimony* (June 1980): 24.

66. *Transcription/Translation of the Proceedings of Twenty-sixth Annual Business Conference of the French Conference of the PAOC,* Institut biblique Bérée, May 15-17, 1974, 7, in Giacomo, "FLITE," 78.

67. Michael Di Giacomo, "La Vieille Capitale: son importance pour le pentecôtisme au Canada français dans les années 1970," *SCHEC, Études Historie Religieuse,* 70 (2004): 81. https://www.researchgate.net/publication/216168969_La_vieille_capitale_son_importance_pour_la_croissance_du_pentectisme_canadien-franais?ev=prf_pub (accessed June 24, 2014).

68. Salome Cressman, "A Half Century of Pentecost in Quebec," *The Pentecostal Testimony* (September 1964): 4.

69. Earl N.O. Kulbeck, "What God Hath Wrought in Quebec," *The Pentecostal Testimony* (September 1964): 2.

70. Samuel Buick, "Challenge of Quebec," *The Pentecostal Testimony* (July 1967): 11.

71. Earl N.O. Kulbeck, "Canada's National Birthday," *The Pentecostal Testimony* (July 1963): 2.

72. Reg and Doris Solmes, "Gaspe Calls," *The Pentecostal Testimony* (March 1962): 10.

73. Rev. and Mrs. Carl Verhulst, "Quebec's Hour," *The Pentecostal Testimony* (June 1965: 10.

74. Allan D. Bowen, "Quebec City at the Crossroads," *The Pentecostal Testimony* (July, 1972): 9.

75. Di Giacomo, "Les Pentecôtistes Quebecois, 1966-1995," 104-105.

76. Ibid., 105.

77. Randall Holm, a history professor at Providence College and Seminary, Manitoba, and former associate pastor with Al Bowen; telephone interview Dec. 2, 2008.

78. David P. Boyd, "Quebec: Canada's Samaria," *The Pentecostal Testimony* (September 1984): 24.

79. Donald R. Martin, "Aboard!...Calling for Quebec Flite," *The Pentecostal*

Testimony (May 1975): 16-17.

80. W. H. Ken MacGowan, "Quebec's Greatest Need," *The Pentecostal Testimony* (April 1976): 18-19.

81. Donald Martin, "Formation Timothée," *The Pentecostal Testimony* (August 1980): 10.

82. Ibid., 12.

83. "Church Growth, Bilingual Style," *The Pentecostal Testimony* (June 1980): 13.

84. Donald R Martin, "FLITE Celebrates Anniversary," *The Pentecostal Testimony* (June 1980): 24.

85. Gordon Upton, "A Race Against Time," *The Pentecostal Testimony* (January 1983): 21.

86. Robert M. Argue, "General Conference Reports: Executive Director of Home Missions, Bible Colleges and Men's Fellowship Departments," *The Pentecostal Testimony* (October 1982): 21.

87. Marguerite Clarke, "Revival in French Canada," *The Pentecostal Testimony* (June 1983): 23.

88. Ibid., 23.

89. Boyd, "Quebec: Canada's Samaria": 24.

90. Ibid., 25.

91. NEWSLINES, "100 Huntley Street-French," *The Pentecostal Testimony* (September 1984): 26.

92. Gordon R. Upton, "Mission Canada," *The Pentecostal Testimony* (April 1984): 17.

93. Stewart Hunter, "QUEBEC—Canada's Sleeping Giant Awakens," *The Pentecostal Testimony* (November 1987): 6.

94. Canadian Council of Catholic Bishops, "The Charismatic Renewal in Canada 2003," Commission of Theology (June 2003): 1.

95. Ibid., 2.

96. Ibid., 20.

97. Giguere, "Notes Historiques," http://selonsaparole.tripod.com/gig996.htm (accessed June 17, 2014).

98. Debra Fieguth, "Fire and Ice," *Christianity Today* (October 23, 2000): 20. It is difficult to determine whether these events by CT were more directly connected with the earlier Charismatic Renewal in Quebec or with the neo-Charismatic Third Wave development. It seems to have occurred separate from the established churches rather than within them.

99. Ibid.

100. Ibid., 20-21.

101. Debra Fieguth, "A Church You Should Know: Eglise Nouvelle Vie, Longueuil, Quebec," *Faith Today* (November-December 2006). http://www.evangelicalfellowship.ca/NetCommunity/Page.aspx?pid=761&srcid=384 (accessed June 25, 2014).

102. Ron Rust and Michael Di Giacomo, "Quebec: Mission not Impossi-

ble,"http://dqpaoc.org/?s=QUEBEC%2C+MISSION+IS+NOT+IMPOSSIBLE (accessed June 25, 2014).

103. Ibid.

104. Chagnon, *Les charismatiques au Quebec*, 205-206.

105. The approaches to renewal history referred to here are those outlined by Augustus Cerillo, Jr. and Grant Wacker in "Bibliography and Historiography of Pentecostalism in the United States," Burgess and Van Der Maas, eds. *NIDPCM*, 397-405.

5

David Mainse: The Bridge Between Two Movements

Catalyst for Greater Understanding

The thought that there could be much common ground between an older Pentecostal group and non-Holiness, ultra-traditional mainline Canadian denominations, especially with respect to Spirit-baptism and tongues, was exceedingly remote for most adherents of the PAOC. Little did people within the denomination realize that one of their own ministers would be instrumental as both a renewal visionary and an ecumenical link with the other denominations. David Mainse's foray into the world of the Charismatic Movement was a risk that he did not seem to be seeing as severe enough to prevent him from the mission to which he believed he was being called. Some Pentecostals of his own generation were not, at least initially, entirely comfortable with the direction he was going, seeing in his approach the danger of compromise. In retrospect, Mainse's humble demeanor, tenacious commitment and integrity maintain his place and reputation within the history of the PAOC and provided a base from which to launch further endeavors to cooperate with and promote ongoing renewal.

Mainse's roots reach deep into the Holiness Movement. He is perhaps the single figure within the PAOC with the most direct line to Ralph C. Horner's Holiness Movement Church. Roy Lake Mainse, his father, was a HMC missionary who spent two lengthy terms working with the denomination's mission program in Egypt and was present when the HMC finally merged with the Free Methodists in 1959.[1] Fifth Avenue Holiness Church in Ottawa, the church where as a boy Mainse and his family attended, was pastored by his mother's brother, Manley Pritchard, a well-known Hornerite preacher. He had stayed with the HMC in 1916 when Horner was dismissed and formed the Standard Church of America. Mainse discovered later that his uncle had experienced the Holy Spirit and spoken in tongues during the early part of the century but had kept quiet about it. He concludes that his mother would have known about it which was the reason she was more accepting of the Pentecostal Movement, sometimes taking her son to PAOC meetings.[2]

Although somewhat vague, Mainse's earliest religious recollection is that of the HMC as a denomination with strict external standards:

> We belonged to a denomination called "The Holiness Movement," with about 50 congregations in eastern Ontario and Quebec which had sprung out of the Methodist tradition during the previous century... We were like some of the old Mennonite groups in some ways, though we were not quite as severe as they were about outward adornment. We did take our worship seriously and had prayer and family altar after each meal and again kneeling by our beds at night. And there was Bible-reading once a day usually after supper.[3]

Holiness experiential piety minus the trappings of external legalism would follow Mainse from his early days including his education at Brockville Bible College, a training institution founded by Horner. On the occasion of the school's dedication in January 1921, Horner had referred to it as "a place in which preachers, evangelists and missionaries were to be trained and baptized with fire to go and rescue the perishing masses."[4] Mainse further training was in the Pentecostal tradition at Eastern Pentecostal Bible College (EPBC), Peterborough, Ontario. The deep passion that he inherited and assimilated for Spirit empowerment and the salvation of others regardless of their church affiliation would drive him to push the boundaries of established denominational expectations as far as necessary.

Mainse's passionate spirituality never waned but continued throughout his early ministry years and beyond. The interwoven nature of Holiness, Pentecostal and Christian and Missionary Alliance influences were brought to bear upon his maturing spiritual awareness. Reuben Sternall, one of the signees of the original PAOC charter in 1920, became a mentor to younger pastors including Mainse during the 1950s. Sternall had experienced the Spirit not from direct contact with the Azusa Revival or the Hebden mission but while a student at the CMA Bible College in Nyack, New York. When the early revival began to have an impact on the college, the leadership looked upon it with some disfavor and forbade the formation of groups to pray for the Pentecostal experience. Meanwhile, Sternall received the Spirit in 1910 while visiting in New Rochelle, New York.[5] However, Gordon Atter adds that the school itself became "the centre of numerous great outpourings of the Spirit on Pentecostal lines for several years, especially from 1901 to 1906. It was in the visitation in 1901 that R. E. Sternall of Canada received the baptism of the Holy Spirit."[6] Many years later Mainse recognized in Sternall a similar spiritual passion, simplicity, and faith. While he and his wife, Norma Jean were pastoring in Hamilton, Ontario, Mainse had been fasting and praying for his children to receive Spirit baptism. On one occasion, he returned home to find Sternall praying for four of his children all of whom then experienced the Spirit with tongues, with one even being delivered from stuttering.[7] Such was Mainse's spontaneity and openness to the work of the Spirit enabling him to look well beyond denominational lines.

With a lack of historical attachment to any specific mainline denomination, Mainse was not limited by the frequent "came out of" mentality that often conditioned the attitude of many early Pentecostals who looked back to the undesirable formalism of their parent churches and who subsequently now attached themselves firmly to the PAOC. His relationship with those churches was much more fluid and thus, his ecumenical inclination more natural. This ecumenism was conditioned early on following his father's return from his second term in Egypt, having left his family at home for six years. Roy Mainse worked for an influential member of the UCC in exchange for caring for his family while he was away. Mainse recalls, "That was the beginning of the broadening of my ecumenical outlook,...."[8] The apparent lack of a deeply entrenched denominational consciousness within his family background made him the ideal candidate for the ecumenical leadership role that he would take on. His parents allowed him to attend Sunday School at the local CMA church as well as sometimes at the Salvation Army. His father and other Holiness preachers in his denomination had felt "a kindred spirit with other holiness churches in our area,"[9] a truly revealing statement from a developing Pentecostal ecumenist. He was able to forge a union between two Holiness schools, Brockville Bible School in Brockville and Annesley College in Ottawa, representing two denominations. The younger Mainse regrets church divisions and schisms and applauds the era when "there were such things as church unions."[10] Yet, when he came into contact with the Pentecostal Movement among some high school friends in Pembroke, Ontario, his father wrote to him from Egypt: "I want you to stay away from Pentecostal churches. There are plenty of churches within our own denomination where you can find fellowship." Nevertheless, shortly thereafter, he received the baptism of the Spirit.[11] Mainse's passion for cooperation and mutual understanding has remained prominent throughout his entire life.

Ironically, in spite of the lack of mainline church loyalty in his personal history, when it came to the issue of tongues, the group closest to the PAOC's own doctrine and piety refused to recognize tongues as the indication of having experienced baptism in the Spirit. His father, as a preacher in the HMC, arranged for one of his senior ministers to speak with his son. The preacher adamantly advised, "If you are ever going to be a Holiness minister, you're going to have to remain absolutely silent about the tongues experience...you will never be able to preach or share about it, and will have to regard it as if it never happened."[12] Sensing a call to ministry, he assumed he would follow the tradition of his family in the Holiness denomination. It had never occurred to him that he would be associated with the PAOC even though he had experienced the Spirit in one of its churches.[13]

Mainse's experience prepared him to become the key figure in the intersection of classical Pentecostalism with the Charismatic Movement as well as interdenominational cooperation. Ian Rennie, professor emeritus of Tyndale University College, Toronto submits: "The constant emergence of new pulsations of the Pentecostal movement suggest that this great renewal was nowhere near completion, and as a result it began to produce leaders for the wider evangelical Protestant domain...."[14]

Rennie goes on to assert that Mainse became one of the two most recognized and respected evangelical leaders in Canada, the other being Brian Stiller.[15] He was able to maintain his ministerial credentials with the PAOC in excellent standing while striving to set up a non-denominational television and evangelism ministry. Adherents of the older Pentecostal movement initially were often ambivalent towards his ministry, unsure if what appeared to be a familiar and genuine Pentecostal approach would end up being an initiative that would compromise Pentecostalism itself. Yet, Mainse received considerable financial and moral support from Pentecostals with whom, as Miller concludes, his ministry "enjoys a unique relationship."[16]

Community to National Television Pastor

From humble church plants in rural Ontario, always characterized by aggressive community evangelism and testimonies of divine intervention, to larger established urban churches and through a chain of extraordinary events, Mainse came to the realization of the power of television as a tool for wider influence. In 1964, he began a partnership-based, pre-recorded program called *Crossroads* that soon grew to become the first Canadian gospel television program carried on the CTV network in major Canadian cities. The relationship between his early television ministry and the PAOC developed because the ministry was expanding beyond his ability to manage alone as the leader, developer, and host while still pastoring a PAOC local church. General Superintendent Tom Johnstone appointed a committee to work in cooperation with Mainse and his deacon board to take responsibility for the oversight of finances and administration. A national board of directors was formed to which two of his deacons were appointed, an arrangement that continued until *Crossroads* became incorporated in 1977, at which time, it launched its daily Christian television program, *100 Huntley Street*.[17] Mainse maintains that it was the PAOC that gave *Crossroads* its start: "It could only have been birthed out of the PAOC...There is no other movement or denomination where it could have been birthed."[18] Although he is perhaps overstating his case, no denomination in Canada would have likely been as strong in both its support for active evangelism and in its sympathy for a non-cessationist approach to the work of the Spirit.

The beginnings of *Crossroads* had the warm support of the PAOC—a phase in its development when it was no threat to administrative leadership or its reputation as guardian of Pentecostal orthodoxy. Some of its leaders such as Homer Cantelon who had succeeded Mainse in his Sudbury pastorate and eventually became his district superintendent were keen supporters from the outset. Mainse recalls, "I would have no qualms about saying that Homer is the biggest fan Crossroads has in Canada." Meanwhile, it seems that not everyone within the PAOC's top leadership felt the same way. Two realities always appeared to be in tension for Mainse: the tendency for PAOC culture to be suspicious of any one person achieving undue notoriety, on the one hand, and the necessity for prudence on the other. He observes, "The PAOC resists personalities coming forward and yet God uses personalities. But I can understand it. They should." For him, his situation was not unlike that of David Wilkerson and his tenuous relationship with the Assemblies of God as his Teen Challenge ministry experienced explosive growth.[19]

His denomination began to see Mainse's growing ministry initiative as belonging to the evangelism arm of the organization in addition to a few other locally produced television programs that Johnstone believed should become part of a larger effort "to put the gospel on national television." It is clear in retrospect that Johnstone was doing everything in his power to affirm Mainse's vision and to harness his enthusiasm and energy. This seems to have been a mixed blessing in that, inadvertently or otherwise, *Crossroads* would have become denominationally controlled while being granted full permission to solicit from and minister in PAOC churches. It is perhaps safe to conclude that the "huge support" offered by Johnstone and a few other key individuals, such as his successor as general superintendent Robert Taitinger, helped to reinforce long-term loyalty to the PAOC. Mainse argues, "…what the PAOC General Executive did was they opened the door to our churches."[20]

It is not at all clear whether Johnstone was caught in the unenviable position of both wanting and needing to maintain Mainse's loyalty and ministry affiliation while knowing that pressure might be building at the executive table, as well as at the grassroots, if it had not already begun. Johnstone is remembered as one of those "wide open" guys who had said to Mainse, "pure evangelism must not in any way, shape or form be denominational."[21] The statement appears to be strikingly uncharacteristic of a senior denominational leader, leaving the reader wondering whether some political patronizing may be in the mix by unequivocally asserting that evangelism by its very nature must be inter-denominational. Meanwhile, Johnstone had asked a fellow PAOC minister, Keith Parks, who had developed follow-up curriculum for *Crossroads* "to keep an eye on me," Mainse recalls. The expansion of the ministry was getting beyond Johnstone's ability to monitor. Parks was asked to keep watch because "this thing is coming into such prominence." [22]

A resolution presented at the 1968 General Conference called for *Crossroads* to be a "national public service telecast" of the denomination with "the production cost being covered by the churches of the viewing area" though not to "involve underwriting by the Fellowship." It also asked the General Conference give to the evangelism department "authority to promote the telecast, *Crossroads*, as a National Television Voice of The Pentecostal Assemblies of Canada."[23] The initial freedom afforded *Crossroads* seems to have pleased Mainse in that the Conference did not mandate that it was *the* official television evangelistic tool but rather, simply one of them.[24] The relationship continued to be amicable but not without some discomfort as Mainse slowly began to reach out to individuals within the Charismatic Movement who, while they might be sympathetic and similar in their spirituality to PAOC adherents, were not inclined to come under its banner.

While his gentle personality and impeccable integrity endeared him to both adherents and the leadership of his denomination, the emerging and transitioning period of a PAOC-administered national television ministry into an independent, inter-denominational initiative was not entirely smooth. Its original constitution was drafted with the assumption that any such program would be "subject to the approval and direction of the Standing National Evangelism Committee of the Pentecostal Assemblies of Canada [and] its objects and purposes shall conform to the general stated objects and purpose of the Pentecostal Assemblies of Canada *and shall subscribe to its Statement of Fundamental and Essential Truths*."[25](Emphasis added). Concern over potential for aberrations of doctrine and practice was evident as it further articulated: "In order to avail itself of the opportunity of greater outreach and support, *Crossroads* personnel may become involved with non-P.A.O.C. opportunities, provided such activity does not contravene the initial and ultimate purpose of the telecast."[26]

From the outset, the impulse of Mainse's mission was clearly national and ecumenical. The Charismatic Movement, then at its height, provided that opportunity for him to reach across to other denominations. Thus, it became increasingly clear that the reach of *Crossroads* was creating the angst of potential compromise that the PAOC would find unmanageable and would be obligated either to counter or ignore. Even the perception of any ministry within its jurisdiction not to be in line with its stated positions would have caused alarm. Early on, not only was it recommended that production costs be covered by PAOC churches within their specific viewing areas but that follow-up "shall endeavor to channel all contacts into area churches."[27] Established Pentecostal churches were seen to be the only appropriate worship venues where new believers ought to be directed.

Years before Mainse had perhaps even considered the hiring of staff and having guests on his program from within the Charismatic Movement, he had been comfortable associating with leading figures in other denominations. It was a UCC minister in Sudbury who suggested to him the idea of setting up a telephone call-in centre that he eventually incorporated into his daily television program.[28] It was in the same city on the occasion of Canada's centennial anniversary in 1967 that his interdenominational leadership began to flourish. Mainse had become president of the city's ministerial association and had "prayed over many buildings and pronounced many invocations and benedictions."[29] He actually had involvement in so many civic projects that the mayor awarded him with a certificate of lifetime honorary citizenship.

On Pentecost Sunday 1967, Mainse led a combined service at the main intersection of the downtown area with participation from all denominations, both Protestant and Catholic, carrying torches through the streets:

> [It was] a great parade of Christian unity. This was the first time to my knowledge that the Protestants and Catholics had joined together in a religious observance of this nature. The torches symbolized the tongues of fire on the day of Pentecost; but to me the morning symbolized God's promise to pour out His Spirit upon all flesh. All who love Jesus Christ are truly one in Him, regardless of their denominational differences.... It was going to happen in Canada. In fact, we bore witness to the events of that very day, it had already begun.[30]

The event was covered by the local Protestant periodical, *Protestant Action*, in a report associating Mainse with lighting candles in the Catholic Church. A fellow

PAOC minister that summer confronted him with the accusation that he was compromising and demanded that Mainse repent. His response was characteristic of his view that fear ought not be the *modus operandi* among Christians: "Instead of being angry at me, you should be making full proof of your ministry. And you don't [do that] inside the walls of your church.... You should be out there making contact with Roman Catholics and seeing them born again and filled with the Holy Ghost."[31] Mainse felt vindicated when three months later, the pastor baptized five nuns.

The courage of such an ecumenical perspective positioned Mainse for national influence and would help to transform or at least moderate the outlook of the PAOC from its "intra-dependence"[32] mode of self-confidence and autonomous activity to a more outward oriented consciousness as well as penetrate the Canadian evangelical world. He would continue to move freely among evangelicals and, to a large degree, also mainline Protestants and Catholics in the following decades.

While the PAOC was an active member of the larger Pentecostal world including the Pentecostal Fellowship of North America (PFNA) and the World Pentecostal Conference, ecumenical involvement on any level was minimal except for a few parachurch organizations such as the Canadian Bible Society and the Gideons, Pentecostal ministers generally avoided any more than a loose connection with local ministerial associations. Mainse was, in effect, leading the charge in opening doors for a new generation of ministers and leaders to achieve more healthy mutual understanding among people of all Canadian denominations. His passion for evangelism superseded any thought that misunderstanding at best or offense at worst might result from his energetic initiatives. In honoring and reflecting on his ministry at the 2012 PAOC General Conference, Superintendent David Wells noted that Mainse pushed the boundaries.[33]

He was uniquely gifted in his ability to discern what opportunities he should capitalize on in order to make the most of them for evangelistic purposes. While Mainse was tenaciously loyal to his denomination, it was neither his distinctive Pentecostalism nor any expressed desire to be identified with the Charismatic Movement that drove him, rather, it was his passion for people regardless of denominational affiliation.[34] On-air conversation focused neither exclusively on the PAOC and its churches nor on the unfolding events of the Charismatic Movement as much as on individual transformation. Mainse was impatient with all Protestantism that "couldn't see the forest for the trees" but was so entrenched in its various traditions that evangelism was no longer priority, even with pastors in his own denomination who were not "soul winners." In defense of his vision, Mainse continued to hold that "soul winners had understood what God had led us to do because you've got to break down barriers."[35]

The major reach beyond his PAOC environment took place in the early 1970s following resignation from his Hamilton, Ontario pastorate. In 1972, Mainse organized and led a highly successful Grey Cup Christian Celebration and had it recorded for national television, a significant financial feat at the time. The following year, a pre-teen children's program, *Circle Square*, was launched as what

Mainse saw as a needed response to increasing youth crime and the breakdown of the family.[36] By 1976, *Crossroads* television was being carried on more than one hundred fifty main and satellite stations in Canada. It was positioned for a whole new chapter that Mainse believed he was being called to write.

The Pastor-Evangelist Embraces New Wave of Renewal

A passionate spirituality, evangelistic fervor, loyalty to his classical Pentecostalism and openness to those associated with the Charismatic Movement equipped Mainse to be the ideal candidate for the mission that he was to carry out. He became a role model for a new generation of Pentecostal leaders to reach beyond their traditional boundaries in the interest of corporate evangelism. As time progressed, he was able to garner respect across most denominational groups as the authenticity of his character and ministry became widely evident.

Although the concept of daily Christian television was embraced by the PAOC, the denomination was reluctant to become involved in some aspects of overseeing a ministry with which it had no reference points or experience from which to work. In early 1977, Mainse was pushing forward with his vision, having been influenced by the excellence in communications technology and production that he had witnessed in the United States and saw no reason why Canada should not have the same. David Manual maintains, "It was a tremendously risky undertaking, fraught with pitfalls, but David pressed toward the mark never taking his eyes off what he could see so clearly on the horizon. He was a natural leader. Others caught his vision and joined his team."[37]

Mainse was driven in part at this juncture by his conviction that in ministry delivery, as well as in all aspects of social and economic life, the "national inferiority complex among Canadians" must be overcome.[38] Still under governance by the PAOC, the *Crossroads* Committee went to work on a revision of its constitution to reflect the new reality and to draw up guidelines for operation of the follow-up program. PAOC leadership seems to have been concerned especially about the latter, given the growing concern over the lack of follow-up often associated with mass evangelism and they were undoubtedly anxious that new believers be directed to their local churches.

As time passed, the denomination was having difficulty keeping up with Mainse. Just two weeks before his daily television program was launched in June 1977, the Committee drafted a resolution that clearly indicated its concern that follow-up be the prerogative of its churches and asked the General Secretary of the PAOC to notify the General Executive of the changes and new guidelines and that the same be shared with district superintendents who would then disseminate them to their pastors. The aim was that "encouragement be given to the pastors to use to the maximum the new opportunity afforded them in Evangelism through this TV ministry."[39] The shape that the growing ministry would take was still unknown which in itself seemed to cause some uneasiness, but since it had begun within the PAOC and was the vision of one of its loyal pastors, it was hoped and perhaps assumed that local churches would be able to reap maximum benefit from its evangelistic effort. There was little reason to believe that Mainse's audience would be inclined to connect with any but a PAOC congregation. Nevertheless, in time, as more non-PAOC lay individuals and clergy became involved in *Crossroads* leadership following its incorporation in 1977, consternation began to be expressed to the denominational leadership by many adherents at the grass-roots level.

In celebration of the first daily program televised live in Ontario in mid-June 1977, *The Pentecostal Testimony* featured a lengthy news item by the editor that stated: "Underscoring the gigantic venture is a sense of mission to our nation."[40] It was rapidly becoming clear that Mainse's intention was the provision of a national platform where a classical Pentecostal ethos could be projected but not at the exclusion of other traditions. His simple sincerity caused him to believe that no reason existed for denominations not to work together for the common good of God's Kingdom, to respect each other, and worship together. His national vision was evident with his very first guest, Robert N. Thompson, a Christian politician and former leader of the federal Social Credit party, touting a line that would be repeated many times in succeeding years, namely, "Canada's need to remember its beginning as a nation under God—'a dominion from sea to sea.'"[41]

It is noteworthy that the other two guests on the launch also seemed to anticipate the road ahead. William Prankard, another PAOC minister, was venturing as well into non-Pentecostal territory and would eventually become a well-known faith-healing evangelist to many remote parts of the nation. The third guest was none other than David du Plessis who had surrendered his credentials with the PAOC's sister organization, the Assemblies of God in 1962 under pressure from the denomination's leadership over his ecumenical engagement. To complete the eclectic lineup of participants, the program was co-hosted by Brandt Gillespie, an American Charismatic evangelist and Christian TV producer. The report applauded the ministry as "a platform to God-called ministries in our country" and as "a wholesome counteracting alternative to programming which many are condemning as unhealthy..." and affirmed that "the Holy Spirit is evidently motivating those concerned and giving desired anointing for ministry with innovations and potential."[42] Yet, it is doubtful that the interdenominational breadth that developed was at all anticipated. The report, it seems, was careful to include only members of his full-time staff who were PAOC personnel with an accompanying photograph which shows just three other PAOC minsters and wives. Two of them were involved full-time with counseling and follow-up—a strategy that was considered essential by PAOC leadership. However, according to Mainse's later recollection, several figures representing various Canadian denominations had already joined him in 1977 including Al Reimers (Anglican Church of Canada), Father Bob MacDougall (Roman Catholic) and later in 1983, Gordon Williams (UCC).[43]

Mainse's vision of reaching beyond the PAOC was evident when he suggested that the evolving ministry was like "an electronic roof over a huge congregation" or like building a church the size of a huge stadium.[44] As he invited those from other traditions with whom he had previous association, and in whom he had acquired confidence, to join in the new venture, he gradually moved away from direct contact with PAOC leadership. He remained convinced that divine guidance was at work as each person who came with the ministry in 1977 "had the direction of his or her life suddenly altered by God, to allow them to come on board."[45] While few, if any, would have accused Mainse of intentionally misleading or creating confusion within the ranks of his own denomination, concern and tension developed over the next few months. It was unprecedented at the time for a PAOC minister to be working in such close cooperation with representatives from the three major Canadian denominations and within an organization whose vision was active evangelism within a renewal context. In short order in 1977, Mainse had invited three charismatic representatives to partner with him full-time.

The first of the three was Al Reimers, an Anglican priest whom Mainse had come to know while both were ministers in Sudbury and involved with the local ministerial association. Reimers had experienced baptism in the Spirit in 1965, having come into contact with it for the first time in 1963 at an Anglican Congress in Toronto just as the Charismatic Movement was beginning to impact mainline denominations across Canada.[46] Interestingly, Reimers' Pentecostalism reached way back in his childhood in New York City where his parents attended a German-speaking congregation of the Irvingites whom he saw as the first charismatics of the modern era who wanted to stay within their respective denominations but, unfortunately, were "pushed out." As a result, they started their own liturgical denomination, one that was not meant to perpetuate itself but to fulfill its mission and then cease.[47]

A report given by the principal of the Anglican theological college in Seoul, Korea about Koreans getting up at five o'clock in the morning for prayer and Bible study as a consequence of something called "the baptism of the Holy Spirit" had captivated Reimers' interest. Years earlier in 1954, he had also been impacted while working with the World Council of Churches General Assembly where he had been assigned to work with du Plessis who was just beginning to recognize the work of the Spirit in the older churches.[48] It was equally uncharacteristic for a local PAOC pastor to have invited an Anglican priest (even a tongue-speaking priest!) to his church, but Mainse pushed the boundaries very early by inviting Reimers to do just that. Reimers would frequently attend Mainse's church when he was not conducting services in his own parish.[49]

Upon reconnecting with Reimers in 1977 when he was doing research for his book, *God's Country: Studies of Charismatic Renewal*, the only documented account of first-person experiences of the Charismatic Movement in Canada, Mainse invited him to join the staff of *Crossroads*. With deep respect for Reimers' wisdom as a Charismatic leader and valuing his involvement in difficult telephone counseling situations, Mainse was confident he should be part of the *Crossroads* team. In Reimers' previous contact with du Plessis at the 1954 WCC conference, the latter had reminded him, "God has no grandsons," a statement that strongly influenced Reimers to seek a personal relationship with God because "none of us become Christians involuntarily or by inheritance."[50] The evangelical call to be "born-again" thus equipped Reimers for the task that Mainse assigned him but at the same time confused some PAOC adherents who wondered why Reimers would not want to become one of them.

But Reimers was a staunch supporter of people who had experienced the Spirit in the Charismatic Movement staying within their own church traditions, a position that adherents of the PAOC in general had difficulty comprehending. Representative of the position held by many other Canadian Charismatic leaders, Reimers argues: "…until now there has never been a spiritual movement that has touched the whole nation…. The Holiness movement of a hundred years ago affected several denominations. The Pentecostal movement of 1900 to 1925 touched individuals of many denominations, but the only visible effect was the transfer of members from the 'historic' churches to the new Pentecostal assemblies."[51]

The distance between his perspective and that of the PAOC whose self-understanding was its mission to get people saved and released from formalism and dead orthodoxy and to experience the Spirit could not be starker. It was this perhaps unexpected development soon after the Charismatic Movement began that caused some within the denomination to be concerned, if not alarmed. Reimers, however, delights in recalling that within a year following Dennis Bennett's announcement in April 1960 that he had spoken in tongues, Anglicans, Presbyterians, and others in Canada were acknowledging that they had experienced the same:

> …but they did not leave their "respectable" denominations and join the Pentecostals. They felt called to stay and pray within their own traditions in spite of being misunderstood. The loyalty has borne fruits, so that now, instead of new Pentecostal denominations being born (as happened when charismatics were forced out of their churches in the first part of the century), new life has come to the old churches including the Roman Catholic.[52]

Mainse's fearless affirmation of renewal wherever he saw it, regardless of denominational label, endeared him to people like Reimers who claimed they had experienced the Spirit.

Mutual conviction regarding the necessity for unity if evangelism and social service are to be effective led both Reimers and Mainse to decry long-term disunity and suspicion among Canadian denominations. Reimers was fully aware of the relative uniquenesss of Mainse's perspective as a Pentecostal minister that evangelism could only make use of and succeed in the new electronic age if there was cooperation among Christians. Reimers and likely most of the *Crossroads* interdenominational staff were also cognizant of the courageous stand that Mainse was taking. Reimers stated at the time, "Because of his ecumenical approach, David Mainse is taking criticism from some members of his own denomination but God has honored his insistence on cooperation" and reiterated that God had drawn the staff together in love for one another and prompted nation-wide support for the program. Mainse's ecumenical bent clearly resonated with Reimers: "If God can do so much through these few workers who have agreed to be Christians first and denominationalists second, imagine what He can do as many other Christians adopt this attitude."[53] Not every classical Pentecostal was inclined to frame the issue that way.

If there was a level of discomfort with an Anglican priest collaborating in a full-time evangelism venture with a PAOC credential holder, it was magnified with the hiring of a Jesuit priest, Bob MacDougall. A vibrant, buoyant individual, MacDougall saw himself as a Catholic Pentecostal. After being shot down during World War II and surviving a Nazi prison camp, he sought for a way to overcome the resulting fear and depression. In 1972, a fellow priest attended a charismatic prayer meeting in Toronto and claimed he was told to go home and lay hands on MacDougall. That night, MacDougall experienced a radical transformation, inner healing, spoke in tongues, and eventually claimed he was divinely directed to work at *Crossroads*.[54] Mainse had met him for the first time in Winnipeg through a professional football player friend whose priest he was at the time and where he asked Mainse to join him on an exorcism. MacDougall's loyalty to his Catholic faith was unmistakable. His obituary notice in 2004 reported: "From 1977 to 2000, he worked in the Charismatic Apostolate, first on the *100 Huntley Street* television show, then after 1984 as the Director and Host of the *Food for Life* TV ministry for six years."[55] The last venture was a separate Catholic charismatic ministry launched with support from Mainse.[56]

Few things seem to bother Mainse since his retirement from *Crossroads* as much as the memory of complaints from some of his detractors who happened to be former Roman Catholics and yet who strongly opposed the presence of MacDougall on the daily television program. The irony of their argument, Mainse claims, was that while they insisted they still would not be "saved" had they stayed in the Catholic Church, neither would they have watched his *100 Huntley Street* program had not MacDougall been on with him as a co-host in the first place. He maintains that MacDougall gave him the platform for reaching out to Roman Catholics, a strategy that created openness that would otherwise have been impossible. He speaks of having "reached out through Father Bob MacDougall."[57] Although MacDougall rarely wore his Jesuit dress, when he did, he was assuming his "ministry garb" so that he would not be isolated from his own people. He quipped, "Really, I'm a Pentecostal but this is how we get them to listen" and was often heard to weep, "O, my dear precious Catholic people are not saved."[58] MacDougall did not wear his clerical collar on the daily television program, but this was not done at Mainse request. As Mainse recalls, "That was his idea. I had to talk him into putting it back on for a couple of formal occasions!"[59] Furthermore, he believes that thousands of Catholics became followers of Christ and were Spirit-baptized because MacDougall had decided to join his ministry.[60] In fact, French language television in Quebec expressed interest early in having a French version of *100 Huntley Street*, resulting in the launch of *Au Cent Tuple* likely possible, at least in part, Mainse believes because of the presence of MacDougall at *Crossroads*.[61]

Mainse insists that the long-held view by some that those who become believers and experience the Spirit will automatically leave their traditional denominational home would be unfair and unreasonable.[62] His high view of the sovereignty of the Spirit allowed him to welcome people like Reimers and McDougall and to downplay lines of demarcation between church traditions. For him, people just do not establish their theology quickly and to become unduly concerned, for example, when a person has not left her Catholic faith immediately after becoming a believer and experiencing the Spirit within a Pentecostal context is to be blind to the gentleness required to nurture those newly born into the kingdom of God. He is impatient with longtime Pentecostals thinking and acting in ways that demonstrate their willingness to keep denominational walls thick and protective.

If any mainline church representative were easier for classical Pentecostals to accept than another, it would have been Gordon Williams. With more immediate connection to the Wesleyan roots of Pentecostalism, Williams' presence with *Crossroads* beginning in 1983 would have brought at least some comfort to older Pentecostals who now saw an exuberant pastor with an evangelistic fervor in the tradition of an old time Methodist minister. PAOC people had been aware for years that the UCC had been in steady decline since the 1960s while their own movement had grown significantly.[63] Williams was one with Mainse in his view that the proper use of television provided new hope for Christian churches, not in replacing them but in enhancing them.[64]

Williams started out at *Crossroads* as the Toronto Area Director and later became assistant to the president, responsible for a biblical overview at the end of each telecast as well as frequently co-hosting the program.[65] He brought with him a mixture of a pleasant demeanour, youthful energy and old-fashioned evangelism. Personalities like Williams attracted many Pentecostals who saw in them the same spiritual vitality that they remembered from a previous era of Pentecostal revival. But far from being a fundamentalist evangelist, Williams appears to have seen renewal as a potential bridge over the growing ideological divide within the UCC. He was alarmed that "answers for many now seem to lie in extremism. Conservatives provide simplistic answers to complex questions and liberals follow cultural mores with pious overtones."[66] It was belief in the sovereignty of the Spirit over doctrinal and ecclesiastical differences of many within the Charismatic Movement that bewildered Pentecostals and compelled them to question, if not reject, what could not fit into their theological framework. Richard Quebedeaux had observed a few years earlier, "Protestants and Catholics, conservatives and liberals, do not automatically discard their own theological and ecclesiastical differences when they come together in this movement."[67] Mainse's passion for the evangelistic enterprise and the experience of the Spirit impelled him to dispense with debate over any of these issues, thus making Willliams and other charismatic figures ideal partners.[68] The self-understanding of PAOC leadership and most of the rank and file, however, involves the responsibility to protect its distinctive doctrinal tenets including its stated position on the Spirit's operation against any such theological reductionism.

Ambivalence Towards *Crossroads*

Mainse was and continues to be a highly respected minister within PAOC ranks. It was precisely his impeccable integrity and deep spirituality that made it difficult for his denomination to know how to manage his vision. While there was concern over financial liability with *Crossroads* continuing as a ministry under PAOC governance, it is not too far-fetched to conjecture that the greater fear was the inability to foresee where his vision was going and whether or not doctrinal compromise might eventually become an issue.

By 1979, slightly less than two years following the incorporation of *Crossroads* and the launch of the daily television program, it had become clear that Mainse was spreading the net far beyond the comfort level of many within his own denominational circle. In April, a joint meeting of the PAOC national officers and the *Crossroads* Board of Directors was convened in an effort to address some of the growing concerns. The general superintendent as chair was quick to express appreciation and support for *Crossroads* as "one of the miracles of our lifetime" and his personal satisfaction at the "excellent brotherly relationships" which had always persisted between both bodies.[69] But the purpose of the meeting was also clear: "A few comments concerning the *Crossroads* ministry had recently reached the P.A.O.C. National Office from various P.A.O.C. ministers, etc., and it had therefore been judged expedient to discuss these as between P.A.O.C. officers and the Crossroads' Directors."[70] The intent was to deal with any such misunderstanding or dispute within the circle of long-time friends.

The matters that PAOC leadership believed needed clarification reveal the angst over potential loss of leadership influence and accountability as well as possible doctrinal error. First, lay community councils had been established in various parts of the country for the purpose of promoting the television ministry in an effort to increase viewing audiences, and as a mean of increasing prayer and financial support. These councils were not to be comprised of members of any one denomination but each one was "to serve as a convenient vehicle for occasional fellowship among local Christians of all denominations, along similar lines to the trans-denominational 'image' portrayed through 100 Huntley Street;...."[71] Measures were being taken to ensure that these councils would not end up becoming churches themselves nor holding meetings that would compete with local congregations but instead would guide new converts from the *Crossroads* ministry into a local church. Such precautions would have been seen as essential by local PAOC pastors some of whom would have felt somewhat threatened by a potential rival congregation. *Crossroads* wanted to assure the PAOC that these councils were designed to act in a supportive, serving role to local congregations in any way they would be welcomed. While Mainse and his team were celebrating the possibility of ministering to individuals and their families from local churches by video teaching, for example, local PAOC pastors were less than enthusiastic about the possible intrusion into their ministry, including the probable siphoning of funds that might have ended up in the church offering plate, a concern that had already become reality in some of the preliminary meetings. Concern over these councils continued for some months as the record of a later meeting indicates in which consideration was still being given to the necessity that local PAOC ministers be advised of the establishment of any Local Community Council in a given community.[72]

Fear of a ministry that had no historical reference points was unusually obvious according to the record of a meeting where one suggestion was that local PAOC pastors and people should not only be advised of developments but should perhaps assume leadership as far as possible in the formation of the councils. The General Superintendent was concerned that "there might be a danger that some independent charismatic group might 'take over' an L.C.C. and might perhaps use it as a 'quasi-church' vehicle."[73] *Crossroads* responded appropriately that the function and organization of the councils was still in a fluid and experimental stage with appropriate guidelines still needing to be formalized regarding the composition of a local ministerial advisory board. Time was to prove that such trepidation was largely unwarranted. Meanwhile, cooperation carried the day with both groups agreeing that the purpose and organization of the councils needed clarification and with *Crossroads* welcoming any input from the PAOC including the formation of a joint committee with representatives from both groups to assist the *Crossroads* Board of Directors in that process.

Nevertheless, the most sensitive and potentially divisive issue centered on doctrine. Seeing itself as the guardian of correct Pentecostal orthodoxy, the PAOC was always worried should any minister or ministry affiliated with it begin to be seen as accommodating divergent viewpoints. By 1979, PAOC leadership had received several representations, especially from Quebec, concerning "possible doctrinal confusion that might be arising from the Roman Catholic presence on the *100 Huntley Street* program, including some questionable statements made by Catholic guests from time to time alleged to have gone uncorrected."[74] However, Mainse's response in retrospect to this controversy was strongly evangelical, quite typical of his outlook on ministry amidst the complexity of denominational constraints. He argues, "The point is that we can work together in winning souls to Jesus on the very most elementary step, simply believing in Jesus as your Savior Lord before we get into the doctrinal issues."[75]

The degree of concern among the various leaders was undoubtedly anything but monolithic and so would have determined their response. It is not clear, however, whether some PAOC constituents were more concerned than the leadership and therefore whether the leadership was simply carrying out what it believed its duty to be in such matters. Moreover, it would be presumptuous to assume the relationship between both bodies turned into a conflict. On the contrary, it seems that a spirit of grace and mutual understanding undergirded the discussions. It is also not unlikely that such a climate was largely instrumental in future good relationships between both bodies, especially between Mainse and his credentialing denomination.

Members of the *Crossroads* board did not adopt a defensive stance as much as try to understand what was being questioned and whether the presence of other denominational figures on the daily telecasts was causing concern as well. Interestingly, one of the PAOC leaders drew attention to the Lausanne Occasional Papers and suggested that the other members make a study of them, drawing specific attention to the matter of syncretism and "the desirable balance to be achieved between grace and truth."[76] The reference was quite sincere but in looking at the appropriate LOP paper, it does not appear that the paper was in any way intended to apply to the issue at hand. It instead deals with the danger of syncretism in its purest sense, where the church is trying to express its life within cultural forms that may be inherently evil or have evil associations.[77] While care to maintain doctrinal purity was fundamental, understanding and the willingness to consider other perspectives was paramount. For many PAOC constituents, particularly the theologically educated segment, real tension was emerging and would continue to grow between the need to maintain classical Pentecostal orthodoxy, including especially initial evidence, and the necessity to understand and appreciate the different theological conception of the Spirit's activity within the Charismatic Movement. The same kind of tension was soon to manifest itself as well between classical Pentecostalism on the one hand and the broader evangelical world on the other. Congregations within the PAOC would find themselves pulled in one direction or the other and so would change the face of the denomination.

Although *Crossroads* had been already incorporated for two years by 1979, it still maintained strong ties with the PAOC. But the nature of that relationship going forward was not at all clear. Discussion arose in the April meeting on the technical issue of whether the General Superintendent should act as an "ex officio" member of the *Crossroads* board or as an honorary director, presumably with the former title holding more weight with voting privileges being afforded. While *Crossroads* was in agreement with either arrangement, the PAOC officers considered the issue important enough to merit discussion at their upcoming General Executive meeting a few days later. The result was that the PAOC leadership's wish was to retain the original clause in the *Crossroads* Constitution providing for the General Superintendent to be an ex officio member of the *Crossroads* board.[78] The obvious implication is that the denomination still wished to have input, if not some potential control, over an organization in which it still did not have complete confidence doctrinally or methodologically.

In the September meeting of the two bodies, concern over "potential doctrinal confusion" continued to surface. Tension was evident. Correspondence from the Quebec district to the PAOC executive was read indicating to the denomination's leadership that it was "apparent that the 'Roman Catholic presence' on the program of *100 Huntley Street* had caused distress."[79] Meanwhile, *Crossroads* was quick to point out that a thousand conversions had occurred in the first four months that the English language version was being aired in Quebec. Release of the French version, *Au Cent Tuple* seemed to relieve some of the pushback from Quebec, at least for a time. Presumably in an attempt to retain some sense of doctrinal accountability, there was agreement that "acceptance" by ministerial staff at *Crossroads* of an evangelical statement of faith be required. Though not explicitly stated, this action seems to have been viewed as a minimum requirement even if some staff were unable to give full assent to the PAOC *Statement of Fundamental and Essential Truths*. By this time, PAOC officers had other concerns as well such as the potential that one of their credential holders might get hired to the staff of *Crossroads* while under disciplinary action, a scenario that would necessitate that communication be initiated by the PAOC national office.[80]

While Mainse would have been happy continuing to work with the initial arrangement as a ministry similar to a local church under the auspices of the PAOC, the incorporation of *Crossroads* in 1977 was very timely. The denominational executive requested that it become a separate corporation so that the PAOC would not be liable in any potential financial crisis such as a bankruptcy. In retrospect, Mainse believes it was divine ordering in that it was the point at which Reimers, MacDougall and others from a variety of denominations were joining the *Crossroads* staff. The General Superintendent eventually removed himself from the board in the early 1990s, even as a member, when the current facility was being considered, for fear that his presence there might have the potential consequence of dragging the PAOC into a debilitating financial situation.[81]

Philosophy of Ministry as Bridge to the Charismatic Movement

The intersection of a PAOC minister with the Charismatic Movement in such a manner was both timely and appropriate. Mainse's openness to the Spirit and his ability to see beyond sectarian differences surfaced at the opportune time for him to participate in the burgeoning renewal. Few of any denominational label would accuse him of being unbalanced or fanatical as he was able to earn credibility with intellectuals, top political and religious leaders, and ordinary Canadians. Leaders of most denominations came to respect and welcome him into their ranks. Needless to say, it was these very developments that for years engendered a mixture of concern, respect and admiration among PAOC clergy and laity in spite of tenuous confidence over doctrinal concerns.

Mainse was fond of quoting Paul the Apostle's exhortation to Timothy to "make full proof of your ministry"(2 Tim. 4:5 KJV). For him, it meant that the weight of responsibility lay heavily with the person in leadership to determine the most effective way to give the ministry gifts imparted by God to others.[82] Even a cursory observation of Mainse's speech, personality, and leadership style reveals a dual emphasis—a relentless passion for evangelism and the promotion of the Charismatic-Pentecostal movement. His exceptional energy for the cause of evangelism regardless of denominational structure or organization has continued unabated and has overshadowed his conversations and reflections on his work.[83] It is perhaps reasonably safe to conclude that the charismatic wave of renewal that had swept in from the United States and was by then at its height in Canada provided the fuel for the evangelistic vision that Mainse brought with him to a national audience.

For a large gathering of PAOC pastors and constituents in 1987, he was asked to prepare a paper exploring classical Pentecostals and Charismatics with special reference to barriers and bridges. In his address, he admitted that he had elected to talk less about barriers and more about building bridges and was concerned about the reactions of classical Pentecostals. He noted, "We've been hit by reactionary forces I believe in the last couple of years in connection with the outreach from the Pentecostals to the Charismatics and I am not convinced that these reactionary forces are healthy. In fact, I believe they are counterproductive to the winning of lost souls to Jesus Christ."[84] With ten years having elapsed since the launch of *100 Huntley Street* and the incorporation of *Crossroads,* these "reactionary forces" would seem to have been going on much longer than two years.

It was one of few opportunities for Mainse to be transparent with so many of his fellow ministers, confessing to them that just prior to the June 15, 1977 launch of *100 Huntley Street*, he had become convinced that God was directing him "to have clergy of various non-Pentecostal denominations right upfront with us. We were to work together."[85] He believed he had received a prophetic word to that effect that at the time he had recorded in writing. Mainse was unashamedly providing for his PAOC parent body an apologetic for the ministry he had undertaken that by then was approaching three decades since its inception with the first *Crossroads* telecast, June 6, 1962.[86] Admitting his reluctance to write such things down lest some person end up giving it undue prominence, he nevertheless used the occasion to read it to his audience:

> Denominational lines must remain for a little while yet for the work of perfecting my body. There is a love that transcends the groupings within my body but d o e s not organize the groupings into one. From the mind of Christ in the divine head of the body flow impulses along many messenger systems.... But by loving as one organism and by caring for each other as members of the same body we will show that we are one to the world around and they will believe that the Father sent his Son, Jesus Christ.
> ...Do not run beyond me enforcing a premature oneness.... Should you proceed in forcing a unity that is untimely you will unseat my plan in human strength,...even as one would force on one of my beautiful creatures, the butterfly from its cocoon before the metamorphosis is complete. I have allowed the Pentecostal Movement to come because the rest of my followers turned aside for a time my personal visitation by the Holy Spirit. I took the Pentecostal Movement in its early days and by molding together a diverse group of my followers....
> Today as a result of a falling away in many groupings of my followers there has been a looking at the success of the Pentecostals. As a result, many of them have opened themselves to my Spirit but are developing within their own tradition only, not gaining the wealth that comes from a truly free fellowship within the body unencumbered with those traditions.... Do not become entangled with traditions that have bound my followers for centuries.... Hold fast the principles given to the vast majority of those in the Pentecostal Movement.... Let your practices be as you have received in the past and conduct the work over which I have made you overseer in accordance with those principles and practices.[87]

The statement seems to reflect the essence of Mainse as a charismatic and inter-denominational leader before it conditioned, if not provided the catalyst for, the direction of his leadership of *Crossroads* from that point on. In any case, several points are noteworthy. First, the influence of charismatic-style prophecy is more evident here than would have been the norm among most of his classical Pentecostal contemporaries. Prophetic revelation in the PAOC environment has often been traditionally associated with fringe groups hardly labeled as "Pentecostal," particularly in the Latter Rain controversy. Second, it demonstrates that Mainse, far from being an iconoclast, believed that denominational structures were in themselves beneficial as long as they did not inhibit the progress of the Spirit. Third, there is deep respect here for his classical Pentecostal tradition while at the same time having no scruples about self-evaluation and further, no reluctance to put words into action. Finally it reveals Mainse's concern that those who have become open to the Spirit not confine themselves to their own traditions but seek fellowship on a broader level. He falls short of recommending that they join the PAOC but instead, it seems, he is advocating that those who have experienced the new work of the Spirit network with like-minded Christians all across the denominational spectrum.

This unorthodox approach to Pentecostal ministry resulted in a unique expression of ecumenical cooperation without any apparent loss of the original vision of total evangelism. The *100 Huntley Street* on-air staff was comprised in the early days by no less than seven "born again and Spirit-filled, ordained ministers"[88] representing as many as six different denominations—PAOC, Roman Catholic, Anglican, United Church of Canada, Baptist, and Free Methodist. As late as 1999, the tenor of the prophetic word Mainse claimed to have received seemed to be as strong as ever, as he believed that the ministry was perhaps the most visible expression of the "unity of the Body of Christ" in the nation. For him, it was a "working demonstration" of their corporate "call to build up the whole body of Christ" which he emphasizes was not a singular vision of his but of the whole enterprise. His philosophy, though perhaps unwittingly stated, he expresses thus: "The truth is, we all feel that *100 Huntley Street* is a window to the Body of Christ, and that God intends his children to work together in harmony, to the glory of His Son."[89]

The acceptance and affirmation of the Charismatic Movement by Mainse and the participation of his staff in renewal continued throughout the years of his ministry at *Crossroads*. One of the pivotal events was the attendance of three of his ministers at the historic 1977 Kansas City Charismatic Conference, an occasion that had a far-reaching impact upon an already motivated Canadian delegation. For them, it too became as Vinson Synan observes, "the climatic ecumenical event in the history of the movement."[90] Mainse recalls: "Our men brought the spirit of Kansas City home with them, and it coincided with the way the Holy Spirit had been leading us all along. He was not calling us to forgo our denominational identities or to merge our denominations in one; He was calling us to merge our hearts in one, and be one in Him."[91]

Another significant turning point that same year for Mainse was a potent gesture he initiated, one that was as symbolic as it was real. He took the interdenominational staff that had already joined his ministry on a retreat where he led a foot-washing ceremony and asked forgiveness for attitudes and hurts that he may have caused them because they happened to be from other Christian traditions.[92] Unity in diversity not for its own sake but for the greater cause of the Church nationally and globally was the guiding principle for all of Mainse's ministry and one that he championed with amazing consistency.

Whether or not he was fully cognizant of it, his ecumenical sense was strikingly similar to Pentecostal stalwarts of the mid-twentieth century such as Donald Gee, Walter Hollenweger, and particularly David du Plessis. The latter he deeply respected and admired as the pioneer of the attempt by a classical Pentecostal to reach across to Charismatics on the one hand, and then to bridge the ecclesiastical chasm to mainline Christians, especially Roman Catholics on the other. Evangelistic passion intersected with ecumenical endeavor for Mainse in such a way that theological differences were secondary. He argues: "I am convinced that the greatest enemy of soul-winning is polarization without bridges....[that] building and crossing bridges between our classical Pentecostal Movement and the Charismatics presents the greatest opportunity to win nominal Christians to a genuine heart conversion to Jesus Christ that we have. The Apostles had favor with all the people. They built bridges."[93] Mainse saw himself as a traditional evangelist-pastor, called not primarily to his own denomination but to the wider church and the Charismatic Movement was the environment that made his bridge building possible.

Although few of his PAOC colleagues would have been comfortable as yet with his line of argumentation, he did not hesitate to defer to biblical precedent, declaring that the apostle Peter had no reluctance in stepping over the barrier of Jewish animosity towards the Jesus sect by preaching Christ to those in the temple shortly after Pentecost. Mainse was always careful to point out that theological disagreements and any previous mistreatment of classical Pentecostals by mainline churches was never reason enough to be "separatists." His philosophy of ministry was clear: "Peter did not avoid the matter of the guilt of the leaders of the Jews in the crucifixion of Jesus but he did not dwell on that. Rather he proclaimed boldly the message of Jesus Christ, that great harvest of precious souls would have never happened without bridge building."[94] He concluded that there would already have been secret believers in the temple who were "waiting for someone to come to their place of prayer not shouting at them from the outside but showing them respect and praying for them."[95] In a more recent current affairs program interview, when asked to summarize the success of his ministry, Mainse responded that it was due to the God who was more interested in people and communications than he could ever be—a response that essentially defined him in his obsession both with his faith and the use of modern media to convey the Christian message, at the core of which he believed there was no "doctrinal divide."[96]

A Canadian Incarnation of
Billy Graham and David du Plessis

The fundamentalist-evangelical fabric of the PAOC along with its Methodist Wesleyan roots have always fostered enormous respect for Billy Graham, not so much for his ability to cross denominational boundaries but for his evangelistic focus and altar calls with which older Pentecostals could readily identify. Mainse applauded the same, but more than most Pentecostals of his time, he fully associated himself with Graham's broader ecumenical appeal. He recalls with fondness the early PAOC Sunday evening evangelistic services that were "essentially a Billy Graham type evangelistic service that most of our churches had every Sunday night."[97] In assessing Graham's impact on Canada, Mainse contends, "Billy Graham broke down a lot of barriers between the denominations. He never compromised in any way the straight preaching of the gospel."[98] These two criteria were seen as essential for him to make "full proof" of his ministry. Ironically, it seems that it was the ability of a non-Pentecostal to preach cross-denominationally within a traditional Canadian Catholic and Protestant context that was inspiring him to do the same.

It is reasonably safe to conclude that Mainse's self-understanding was that he was more than anything the Canadian counterpart of David du Plessis. He had met du Plessis at a World Pentecostal Conference and became convinced he was a leader that the Pentecostal movement could not ignore. Mainse argued, "We must answer some very serious questions about this man, one of our own…who in my judgment embodies the bridge builder between classical Pentecostals and Charismatics."[99] Mainse is perhaps alluding to the removal of du Plessis' credentials with the Assemblies of God in 1962 and their restoration in 1979. He was aware that his adventure outside his own denomination and into other traditions was not at all new. He took delight in referring to Smith Wigglesworth's prophecy to du Plessis that through the old line churches would come a revival that would eclipse anything known throughout history, including the earlier Pentecostal revival that had engendered strong opposition from the established churches. He believed that history had shown the prophecy to be true with as many as 175 million having "come into a personal experience of the new birth and of the baptism of the Holy Ghost."[100] It is somewhat ironic as well that most PAOC pastors came to hold in high regard the writings of both Wigglesworth and Gee, both of whom were sympathetic ecumenists.

Du Plessis's approach to the historic denominations resonated soundly with Mainse and was likely, intentionally or otherwise, behind his action of seeking forgiveness from representatives of each of the Canadian denominations at the time of the launch of *100 Huntley Street*. By the early 1960s when du Plessis had already attended three WCC gatherings, his once sectarian attitudes had changed dramatically: "Instead of the old harsh spirit of criticism condemnation in my heart, I now felt such love and compassion for these ecclesiastical leaders that I would have rather have died for them than pass sentence upon them."[101] Mainse emulated du Plessis' spirit of forgiveness toward Catholics, Protestants, as well as his fellow Pentecostals who did not discern the need for ecumenical cooperation as he did. He held to the notion that effective evangelism could not take place unless the strong Canadian denominational barriers were penetrated with love and unconditional forgiveness. He adopted du Plessis' belief that love and forgiveness always go together and that "we will not do anything to stop the move of God by our lack of love or harsh criticism of those who have hurt us in the past."[102]

A spirit of openness to Roman Catholics was especially uncharacteristic for a PAOC minister. Nevertheless, the backlash that Mainse received for having a Jesuit priest on his full-time staff was ironic and unexpected coming from Catholics themselves who had left their own tradition after having had a transformational experience through watching *100 Huntley Street*. Many of them appear to have in time assumed some of the characteristics of classical Pentecostalism, in particular, rejection of religious formality and doctrines such as purgatory and the veneration of Mary. Mainse contends that many thousands of people moved from formal religion to a personal relationship with God because of the presence of McDougall and that such criticism was unjustified in that many of those same individuals would never have been interested in viewing his program in the first place had a priest not been there.[103] There are no detailed studies of conversions as a result of the *Crossroads* ministry but Mainse theorizes that many who experienced salvation and Spirit baptism, joined a Charismatic group first for prayer and Bible study but eventually believed they should attend an evangelical or Pentecostal church where the Bible was being preached.

Ecumenical and Charismatic Legacy

A robust evangelical faith, a non-cessationist position on the Spirit and the *charismata* and a keen sense of the power of electronic media provided the ideal mix for Mainse to be able to reach across denominational lines while maintaining exceptional relationships with PAOC leaders and pastors. Moreover, Mainse's personal reputation of integrity, simplicity, and fairness endeared him to a wide spectrum of denominational leadership. David Manuel again echoes the sentiment of many Canadian Pentecostals who have come to look at his stellar record with utmost respect: "David has maintained the highest standards of broadcasting excellence… matched by an equally high level of moral integrity—to the extent that he literally has no naysayers among his fellow clergy. Even the few who were initially hostile, now regarded him warmly; they have seen their own congregations enlarged with new members whose lives have been touched or converted by his ministry."[104]

During the late 1980s when widespread negativism toward televangelism began to develop as a result of the Jim Bakker and Jimmy Swaggart scandals, he had already established major credibility not only with mainline churches but also with political and social leaders. His nationwide profile garnered from his interest in the national political scene and his concern for national unity resulted in commendation from figures such as Charles Templeton, broadcaster and former evangelist, as well as the primate of the Anglican Church, Michael Geoffrey Peers. Such confidence in one of their own could not but help increase Mainse's popularity and admiration among his PAOC peers even if they were still uneasy, if not bewildered by his apparent lack of caution in mingling with other denominations. Inter-denominational cooperation and understanding had some precedent in the PAOC as far was Mainse was concerned. He saw his work with other denominations reflected in the person of James Eustace Purdie (1880-1977), an Anglican priest in Winnipeg who had experienced Spirit-baptism, had become friends with Walter McAlister and was eventually asked to become the founder and principal of the first PAOC Bible college in Winnipeg in 1925. Purdie maintained his ordination as an Anglican while at the same time being ordained in the PAOC, preaching in its church and wearing his clerical collar.[105]

In the final analysis, Mainse was not primarily attempting to promote the Charismatic Movement per se. Conversely, he would have likely preferred for those who became converted through the *Crossroads* ministry to find their way into a local PAOC church, or at least an evangelical one. Essentially, the timing of his vision to provide daily Christian television was pivotal as *Crossroads* became tethered to the Charismatic Movement during the era of the 1970s into the 1980s. His embracing of the Movement helped to give the necessary impetus to *Crossroads* in those years.[106] Not only were fear and sometimes even animosity between church traditions beginning to ease, but a PAOC evangelist was helping to accelerate it. While some PAOC leadership at all levels would remain reticent for years based largely on fears of doctrinal compromise, adherents began to lend increasing support to Mainse and the *Crossroads* vision.

Although there are several other touchpoints between the Charismatic movement and the PAOC, including the Full Gospel Businessmen's Fellowship (FGBMFI)[107] and various prayer groups attended by Pentecostals, Mainse essentially opened the field, giving wide legitimacy to classical Pentecostals in participating and feeling comfortable in other denominational environments where any number of doctrinal points might not be in line with their own. The traditional sectarianism of the PAOC was slowly beginning to break down, and though likely not due exclusively to Mainse's influence, was certainly assisted by it. The Charismatic Movement made it easier than ever for many classical Pentecostal people anxious for renewal to mingle with those from the historic churches and feel liberated by it, if not proud they were able to do so while others would not. Quebedeaux points out the inevitable breakdown of such separation when the experience of Spirit baptism is such common ground: "And since the advent of Charismatic Renewal in 1960, it has become increasingly difficult for classical Pentecostals as a whole to continue separating themselves altogether from the historic denominations, many of which include large numbers of Neo-Pentecostals within their ranks who also share of the same experience."[108]

As late as 1987 when Mainse spoke at the Congress on Pentecostal Leadership (COPL) in Toronto, the line of questioning from leaders still demonstrated extreme reluctance with his approach. Concerns revolved around how to balance the coming "world church system" with his call to forgiveness and the acceptance of "idolatrous activities" with repentance and his position that Charismatics might remain in their own churches.[109]

For a younger generation, Mainse's determination to build bridges or perhaps even better to become a bridge to the Charismatic Movement, other denominations and to the national scene helped to advance the 'evangelicalization' of the PAOC. Both the Charismatic Movement and the growing evangelical movement, however, contributed to blurring the denomination's traditional distinctives. *Crossroads* too has blended into the evangelical landscape in much the same way that many pockets of classical Pentecostalism within the PAOC have, with each entity quite comfortable with the other. The denomination's discomfort with any one personality attaining national profile, with television as a medium for good, and working side by side with ecclesiastical leadership of other denominations has all but disappeared, with the exception perhaps of some more remote areas of the country. It has witnessed Mainse become a nationally recognized figure with significant international influence, and his legacy continue through evangelism, communications training programs, and humanitarian efforts.

Notes

1. Fortune, "Ralph Cecil Horner," 202-205.

2. David Mainse, *100* (Burlington, ON: Crossroads Christian Communications, 1999): 61. See also Dr. Roy Lake Mainse, *A Happy Heart: One Man's Inspiring Story of God's Fulfillment in His Life* (Crossroads Christian Communications, 1988): 29-58.

3. Ibid.,18.

4. Glen Lockwood, *The Story of Brockville* (Henderson printing, Inc. n.d.): 371.

5. Aleta A. Piper, "Sternall Biographical Notes," November 1987, PAOC Archives in Rudd, *When The Spirit Came Upon Them,* 182.

6. Gordon F. Atter, *The Third Force*, (Peterborough, ON: The College Press, 1962): 32.

7. Mainse, *100*, 137-138.

8. Ibid., 22.

9. Ibid., 39.

10. Ibid.

11. Ibid., 51, 53.

12. Mainse, *100*, 60.

13. Ibid.

14. Ian Rennie, "Pentecostalism and Christianity," *The Testimony* (June 2001): 7-8.

David Mainse: The Bridge Between Two Movements 121

15. Ibid. Stiller became influential through his leadership of the Evangelical Fellowship of Canada and was arguably more of a thoroughgoing evangelical than a Pentecostal or Charismatic leader.

16. Miller, *Canadian Pentecostals*, 305

17. Mainse, *100*, 127.

18. David Mainse, in discussion with the author, Battersea, ON; August 8, 2012.

19. Ibid.

20. Ibid.

21. Ibid.

22. Ibid.

23. Minutes of the 26th General Conference of the Pentecostal Assemblies of Canada, Windsor, Ontario, August 22-26, 1968. PAOC Archives.

24. Mainse discussion, August 8, 2012.

25. CONSTITUTION-*Crossroads*, PAOC Archives.

26. Ibid.

27. Ibid.

28. Mainse, *100*, 126.

29. Ibid., 131.

30. Ibid., 131-132.

31. Mainse discussion, August 8, 2012.

32. "Intra-dependence" and "extra-dependence" are terms used by Bruce Reed in an analysis of human behavior involving oscillations between independence and dependence, both individually and corporately. Bruce Reed, *Dynamics of Religion: Process and Movement in Christian Churches* (London: Darton. Longman and Todd, 1978). Both Ronald Kydd and David Reed apply the theory to the PAOC and the Anglican Church of Canada respectively. See Ronald A. N. Kydd, "The Impact of the Charismatic Renewal on Classical Pentecostalism in Canada" *PNEUMA* 18:1 (Spring 1996): 55-67 and David Reed, "From Movement to Institution: A Case Study of Charismatic Renewal in the Anglican Church of Canada," *American Theological Library Association Summary of Proceedings* 45 (1991): 178.

33. Mainse discussion, August 8, 2012.

34. This fact was clearly and easily detectable through the constant, passionate reference to the importance of evangelism beyond all denominational barriers during the lengthy interview that the author conducted with him.

35. Mainse discussion, August 8, 2012.

36. Mainse, *100,* 155-160.

37. David Manuel, "Templeton Prize Nomination of David Mainse" in Mainse, *100*, 207.

38. Mainse, *100*,163.

39. Official correspondence from the PAOC General Secretary, Charles Yates, to the General Executive, June 1, 1977. PAOC Archives.

40. "100 Huntley Street," *The Pentecostal Testimony* (August 1977): 16.

41. Ibid.
42. Ibid., 17, 30.
43. Mainse, *100*, 173-190.
44. "100 Huntley Street," *The Pentecostal Testimony*, 17.
45. Mainse, *100,* 173.
46. Ibid., 176.
47. Reimers, *God's Country*, Kindle edition.
48. Ibid.
49. Mainse discussion, August 8, 2012.
50. Reimers, *God's Country*, Kindle edition.
51. Ibid.
52. Ibid.
53. Ibid.
54. Mainse, *100,* 177-180.
55. http://passages.winnipegfreepress.com/passage-details/id-91315/name-Robert_Macdougall/ (accessed July 15, 2014).
56. *NIDPCM,* s.v., "Charismatic Movement: Development in North America," (by Peter D. Hocken).
57. Mainse discussion, August 8, 2012.
58. Ibid.
59. *Context with Lorna Dueck,* http://www.contextwithlornadueck.com/episodes/david-mainse-crossroads-cts-tv (accessed August 12, 2014).
60. Mainse discussion, August 8, 2012.
61. Ibid.
62. Ibid.
63. *Macleans,* a national weekly magazine, reported in its April 28,1980 edition that UCC decline had been taking place since the 1960s when liberal attitudes had begun to take root in the church. Since 1965, its membership had dropped by 157,000, Sunday School attendance to 236,000 from 702,000 and that 254 churches had closed whereas Pentecostals had doubled their membership in the 1970s to 300,000. By 2001, UC congregations had dropped forty percent to 3,650. Denyse O'Leary, "A Velvet Oppression," *Christianity Today* (April 2, 2001). http://www.ctlibrary.com/ct/2001/april2/7.75.html (accessed July 16, 2014).
64. *Macleans* (April 28, 1980): 47.
65. http://gordwilliams.comvgordonwilliamsc242.php (accessed July 16, 2014).
66. *Macleans* (April 28, 1980): 47.
67. Richard Quebedeaux, *The New Charismatics: The Origins, Development, and Significance of Neo-Pentecostalism* (New York: Doubleday and Company, 1976): 8.
68. Mainse referred to them as 100 Huntley Street "irregulars." Mainse, *100,* 188.
69. Minutes of the joint meeting of the PAOC General Superintendent and

National Officers with Crossroads Christian Communications Incorporated Board of Directors, 100 Huntley Street, Toronto, Ontario, April 6, 1979. PAOC Archives.

70. Ibid.

71. Ibid.

72. Minutes of Joint Meeting of the PAOC and the Crossroads Christian Communications Incorporated Board of Directors, PAOC National Office, September 16, 1979. PAOC Archives.

73. Minutes, April 6, 1979, PAOC Archives.

74. Ibid.

75. Mainse discussion, August 8, 2012.

76. Ibid.

77. http://www.lausanne.org/en/documents/lops/73-lop-2.html (accessed July 21, 2014).

78. Minutes, April 6, 1979, PAOC Archives.

79. Minutes, September 16, 1979, PAOC Archives.

80. Minutes, September 16, 1979. PAOC Archives.

81. Mainse, *100,* 127 and interview with Mainse, August 8, 2012.

82. Paper given at the Congress on Pentecostal Leadership (COPL), Fall 1987, Toronto, Ontario.

83. In addition to the release of *Au Cent Tuple* as the French version of *100 Huntley Street*, *Crossroads* also developed a wide range of programming for children, youth, the hearing-impaired as well as Christian television for sixteen languages represented in Canada.

84. Paper given at COPL, Fall 1987.

85. Ibid.

86. Mainse, *100,* 116.

87. Paper given at COPL, Fall 1987.

88. Mainse, *100,* 194.

89. Ibid.

90. Vinson Synan, *The Holiness-Pentecostal Tradition: Charismatic Movements in the Twentieth Century* (Grand Rapids, MI: Eerdmans's, 1971,1997): 261.

91. Mainse, *100,* 195.

92. Paper given at COPL, Fall 1987.

93. Ibid.

94. Ibid.

95. Ibid.

96. *Context with Lorna Dueck: Life Beyond the Headlines*, episode #1139, http://www.contextwithlornadueck.com/episodes/david-mainse-crossroads-cts-tv (accessed August 12, 2014).

97. Mainse, discussion, August 8, 2012.

98. Karen Stiller, "The Man Next Door: Billy Graham's Impact on Canada," *Faith Today* (July-August 2009): 20.

99. Paper given at COPL, Fall 1987.

100. Ibid.

101. David du Plessis, *The Spirit Bade Me Go* (Plainfield, NJ; Logos International, 1970): 16.

102. du Plessis quoted in Jamie Buckingham, "Breakthrough in Unity," *Logos Journal* (September-October, 1972): 39 in Quebeceaux, *New Charismatics*, 125.

103. Interview, August 8, 2012 and Paper given at COPL, Fall 1987. *Crossroads* began publishing a Bible study guide, *New Direction*, as a way of getting new converts from all denominations into Bible study. However, there was never any indication nor encouragement that those from historic churches should leave and become part of the PAOC.

104. Manuel, "Templeton Prize Nomination" in Mainse, *100*, 207-208.

105. Rudd, *When the Spirit Came upon Them*, 163-166 and paper given at COPL, Fall 1987.

106. Ibid.

107. For a time, the FGBMFI in Canada, whose members and frequently its leadership included numerous PAOC lay and business people, served as bridge between the PAOC and the Charismatic Movement. The FGBMFI though not a child of the Charismatic Movement, nevertheless became a conduit of it. In Canada, some Charismatic people who made their way to PAOC churches found the style of worship and testimony similar to what they were experiencing at the FGBMFI. The music and ethos of the Charismatic Movement quickly took root in the organization as speakers from many walks of life openly emphasized and practiced the use of the charismatic gifts. There exists very little printed material on its growth in Canada.

108. Quebeceaux, *New Charismatics*, 153.

109. Paper given at COPL, Fall 1987.

6

Youth of the PAOC—Another Bridge Between Two Movements

In most renewal movements, youth have always been involved as the catalysts, the beneficiaries or both. Of the First Great Awakening, Jonathan Edwards wrote, "In the spring of 1740, there was a perceptible alteration for the better; and the influence of the Spirit of God was most obvious on the minds of the people, particularly on those of the young...."[1] Similarly, it was a young generation of spiritual seekers in an age of uncertainty about the future politically, economically and environmentally that precipitated a fresh wave of renewal that became global in the 1960s and 1970s. The generation of PAOC youth of those decades was able to capture the momentum and many of them did so, moving on to be educated as ministers and lay people who would occupy positions of leadership in their local churches as well as in para-church organizations.

The Toronto Catacombs:
A Jesus Movement-Charismatic Phenomenon

As Quebedeaux argues, the rise of the Charismatic Movement took place in an era when there was already a growing dissatisfaction with modernity and a desire for spiritual experience.[2] For many PAOC youth in particular, there was an accompanying weariness with the "cultural baggage"[3] and sameness of Pentecostal orthopraxy. Adherents of all age groups, however, had at least one thing in common—an inherited curiosity about Spirit baptisms, healings and miracles, if not an attraction to and desire to experience them. The younger generation of the 1960s and 1970s, already conditioned by widespread cultural rebellion to institutional authority, was easily attracted to the music and worship of the Jesus Movement and the tongues-speaking of Charismatic prayer groups. Though still loyal, they had no qualms about visiting, observing, and participating in prayer groups alongside other people interested in spiritual experience regardless of denominational affiliation.

Students, in particular, were open to the wave of new spiritual interest that was sweeping the continent and Christian clubs on high school and university campuses were thriving. One that was attended by several PAOC youth, some of whom eventually became leaders and pastors in the denomination was known as The Toronto Catacombs. In 1968, two students at Birchmount Collegiate in Scarborough approached their band teacher, Merv Watson, about the possibility of beginning a Christian club at their high school. Watson suggested the name "Catacombs" because he saw Christians as an underground presence in society, hence resulting in "The Catacombs Club."[4] When school reconvened in fall 1969 and the group met again, many of its members had experienced Spirit baptism as a result of contact with the Charismatic Movement. In this way, The Catacombs clearly became a hybrid development of the Jesus Movement and the Charismatic Movement. As with Charismatics everywhere who gravitated to fellowship groups for Bible study, prayer, and worship regardless of their denominational affiliation and whether they left or stayed, The Catacombs provided just such a forum.[5]

By 1972, the group had experienced exceptional growth and would continue to thrive for the next few years. This weekly gathering had expanded from the original six members of a high school fellowship club to over two thousand counter-cultural youth ranging from fifteen to thirty years of age. One of the most notable converts at The Catacombs was Benny Hinn, who later became an international televangelist.[6] The Thursday night meetings had started in Merv and Merla Watson's home, then moved to Bathurst Street United Church in 1970, and to Cody Hall at St. Paul's Anglican Church in 1971 when attendance grew to over 800. In early 1972, the meetings finally moved to the sanctuary of that building, the largest church in the Toronto diocese. While estimates vary, the Thursday night 'Praise and Worship Celebration' at its peak between 1972 and 1974 drew many hundreds of enthusiastic young people. Apparently no formal attendance records were kept. Structure and administration were at a bare minimum, a reality that helped to make the Catacombs attractive to a generation repelled by stuffy institutionalism. However, the Watsons recall fondly, "It grew to be 2500 kids a week for four years, every week."[7]

In reflection, Watson is quick to point out the opposition that he encountered during the early days of the group: "The Canadian Pentecostals reacted a bit against the Charismatics like we were invading their territory. [They were] a little bit suspicious...critical, you know....They felt they had [the Holy Spirit] wrapped up."[8] Yet, it was common knowledge among local PAOC pastors in the Toronto area that each week many of their young people were looking forward to The Catacombs Thursday night meeting.[9] While pastors from all over the region would come to observe and bring people with them, the Watsons intentionally did not involve them in the meetings because they believed it was "really important that it stay young and fresh and moving."[10] Furthermore, no formalized networking apparently took place between The Catacombs and PAOC churches or other churches.[11] They would have seen such arrangements as restrictive and counterproductive.

It is clear that the Watsons perceived a substantial gap between established Pentecostal churches and what they believed was happening at The Catacombs. They saw little common ground and no need at all for any kind of formal relationship. Clearly displaying an attitude of annoyance with the PAOC, they sensed that they were being expected to be in connection with PAOC constituents. Merv Watson recounts that they did not mingle much with PAOC people but instead attended an evangelical Anglican parish. He says, "We didn't really mix a lot.... That kind of stuck in their throat. And then they had Jim McAlister who was not a good representative.... In one sense they didn't like us because we didn't need them. It's not that we didn't like them but we were so busy, so involved. I got eight elders appointed and it took all their time to keep things going." [12] In fact, any intentional tie may have been perceived as a detriment as the traditional holiness ethos of the PAOC was considered much too restrictive for the kind of ministry needed for countercultural youth. Watson argues further in this regard:

> And [the PAOC was] also quite straight-laced. With our group, they were counter-culture kids, you know, who would spill their drugs out all over the chancel very often. They didn't come to the Lord through the Four Spiritual Laws or through any formula. The worship was just so intense that they would just crumble to their knees and receive the Lord on the spot. We saw that fifty times over every week.[13]

The phenomenon unfolding there was seen as an authentic work of the Spirit that did not need input or interference from any denominational hierarchy.

Although The Catacombs was sparked by Charismatic renewal, it soon became identified with the Jesus Movement presumably in part because of the predominance of counter-cultural youth. Bruce Douville observes: "More importantly, the Jesus People attracted a growing number of mainstream evangelical youth who had never been hippies. For many of these young people, the movement offered a more authentic, vibrant expression of Christianity than they could find in their churches."[14] This would be true for PAOC youth who attended. Their denomination had come of age and the vibrancy of the earlier revival had long begun to wane in many local contexts. Coupled with heightened interest in spiritual experience, they were attracted to any venue where the familiar musical style of the hippie movement was flavored with a genuine sense of worship and piety. Pentecostal youth who attended would not have been aware, nor would it have likely mattered, whether the group was Charismatic or associated with the Jesus People. Those who did attend still refer to the phenomenon as part of the Charismatic Movement most certainly because the message conveyed focused on the Spirit with a new freshness for them. Much like Mainse was doing at *Crossroads*, the ethos here was both evangelical and charismatic, a comfortably legitimate combination for PAOC young people.

As with other religious movements originating south of the border, it took some time for the Jesus Movement to make its presence felt in Canada. Although the beginning of the Jesus People can be traced back to 1967 in southern California, it is estimated that by late 1971, there were 30,000 to 50,000 Jesus People in Canada "with more and more youth converting every day." There were Jesus People ministries in all of Canada's major cities with Toronto being the largest center and the Catacombs being the most visible entity.[15] Douville notes that Tasler provides neither source nor explanation for this figure. As an estimate of active participants at the time, he suspects this figure to be exaggerated. Nevertheless, as an estimate of those who identified as Jesus People at some point between 1969 and 1974, he believes 30,000 to 50,000 is quite plausible.[16] It is fair to say that accurate figures of Canadian participation in both the Charismatic and the Jesus Movements are practically impossible to obtain due to each ones' fluidity and lack of clear theological and organizational structures.

While the Watsons had become aware of the Jesus Movement in California, and the fact that people were associating their group with it, Merla Watson suggests that they did not consciously choose that label, but rather, it was imposed upon them by the Toronto media:

> I don't think it was consciously thought by anybody. We just did it. And then suddenly we found people writing about the Jesus People Movement and including us. So we thought, "Oh! I guess we're part of it!" It just grew and, of course, it attracted a lot of the counterculture people; it just emerged. But we didn't identify with the Jesus People movement... people thought that's what we were.[17]

Any confusion as to The Catacombs' identity was due to its composition, a mixture of youth both from the drug culture and from various church backgrounds. For a short time in the history of Christianity in Canada, denominational and cultural identification seemed to matter little as Pentecostal youth worshipped and listened to teaching side-by-side with a wide cross-section of others in a historic Anglican church building. Local journalist and religion editor Tom Harpur referred to The Catacombs ministry and this venue as "throbbing with a new beat" with services lasting more than three hours each Thursday evening. The composition of the audience from across denominations was recognized and welcomed by the Catacombs' leaders. Merv Watson reported at that time: "Between 30 and 40 per cent of the kids are Jesus People, with the kind of mixed background—often including the drug scene.... [Others] are straight kids from every church and from every part of town.... The group's basic aim is to create a bridge between young people and the churches—to give them a kind of worship experience in teaching that hits them where they are."[18] Catacombs leadership was essentially unconcerned about labels being assigned to them. However, they were intent on not being confined to rigid denominational or Movement paradigms.

Artistic Worship Environment

Any ambiguity as to whether The Catacombs was largely a Jesus Movement phenomenon or an expression of the Charismatic Movement was eclipsed for Pentecostals in particular by the nature of the meetings themselves. Many PAOC youth felt entirely comfortable in an environment where there were echoes of the familiar but accompanied by a freshness and vibrancy they so much craved. Having grown weary of the heavy concentration on Methodist and Holiness hymnody, they were easily attracted to the simplicity of style and substance, spontaneity and exuberance. Juanita Craig, a life-long Canadian Pentecostal recalls her experience at The Catacombs:

> And I remember the first time I walked up, I was standing with [my] mouth hanging open, looking at what was going on. There were people dancing on the stairs. And the whole time I didn't even really participate. I just sat there and just watched, because...it was everything I'd ever heard church was supposed to be like, and I'd never seen it before in my life, I only heard about it, you know.[19]

As Harpur wrote in *The Toronto Star*, "The Thursday night sessions are a mixture of the old-time revival meeting, a modern hootenanny and a classical concert."[20] Such a combination of style as well as substance appealed to a new PAOC generation, who were not so much disconnected from their past or unappreciative of it, rather, they were attracted to the musical style of the era that was Christianized in the Jesus Movement and now being used to convey the same message and experience of their PAOC heritage.

However, there was at least one major departure from the classical PAOC worship climate. Younger Pentecostals were captivated by a quieter, more contemplative approach to worship, in addition to contemporary upbeat music, and in reaction to the revivalistic camp-meeting style inherited from their Holiness and Methodist roots. The meetings at The Catacombs would gravitate from the reflective to the exuberant and back again:

> When Merv and Merla perform—usually their own compositions—there is a hushed and reverent silence; many of the youngsters have their eyes closed in prayer. When they all join in, however, the whole place rocks with handclapping, body-swaying exuberance.... They join hands, hold them high and sing: "A new commandment I give unto you, that you love one another as I have loved you..." They stand in silence, some with tears in their eyes, and then, as Merla chants softly in a strange language, a growing whisper sweeps up and you realize that dozens around you are "praying in tongues."[21]

While it is true that traditional Pentecostal worship flourished when led by common folk with a rudimentary musical sense at best, and in many cases absolutely no training, it is also true that trained musicianship and lifelong involvement in musical performance when linked with a passion for the presence of the Spirit is a winning combination. The Catacombs would not have been nearly as successful and attracted so many youth from both church and counterculture if the Watsons had been amateurs in their music leadership.

Merv was born in Penticton, British Columbia, of Irish/Scottish Plymouth Brethren heritage and studied piano, voice, art, and pre-medicine in Vancouver, before attending the University of Toronto Faculty of Music where in summers he wrote music for a popular resort, acted, and sang for holiday productions. He taught bands and orchestras in high schools and at a Jewish Talmud Torah school. It was in Toronto during those years that he met his future wife, Merla.[22] She was of a Swiss Mennonite background. Her father started The People's Church in Toronto with Oswald J. Smith, after whose daughter she claims she is named.[23] She received training in piano, violin, composition, and voice, and by the time she was 15 had become a competent and recognized musician, having amassed 150 scholarships and awards with her stringed quartet performing weekly on the CBC. After their marriage, they began to perform classical concerts and in time Merv became the director of the Christian Performing Arts of Canada. It was in 1967 after a life-changing experience of the Spirit that they launched into a full-time faith music ministry.[24] It was this professional background and Charismatic experience that the Watsons brought to The Catacombs, a ministry it seems that they had not envisioned. Merla Watson wrote most of the songs they sang and played, the bulk of which had a rich Jewish flavor and leaned heavily on the Psalter. Of her almost 500 worship songs, "Jehovah Jireh", "Awake, O Israel", and "Then Shall the Virgin Rejoice" are three that became popular at The Catacombs.

It ought to be noted though that it was not just a blending of excellent musicianship and experience of the Spirit that allowed the Watsons to connect with so many youth of that era. They began to actively self-identify with the counterculture itself in dress and in their overall presentation. Their refusal to condemn the anti-establishment culture of the time by embracing its ethos and yet their faithfulness to biblical and theological orthodoxy combined with their ease of public performance and their sincerity garnered widespread respect even from those of the older Pentecostal tradition. The Watsons were church-based professional performers with a Pentecostal flavor, the likes of which few had ever experienced. The openness, freshness of expression, and lack of denominational baggage was a breath of fresh air for countercultural youth who frequently viewed church as stale and uninviting as well as for some Pentecostals who were attracted to a venue where spirited worship (or Spirit-filled worship) was happening in the most unlikely context.

Venue, Style and Substance

Because the Watsons were young and respected as musicians themselves, they were able to attract a lot of other musicians, singers and dancers. With profound fondness, they recall:

> Many, many people found the Lord. During worship, in fact sometimes the worship would go on so long that the preacher wouldn't get on to preach. It would be three hours of worship. We used the 5-manual Casavant pipe organ. We had two loads of dancers; some were athletic and others were more folk and we had real instruments in the choir loft, not just rang-a-tang guitars. We had clarinets, oboes, trumpets and all kinds of stuff. We had singers up there as well. It was the most glorious praise you would ever want to hear in your whole life before, during or since. We have been all over the world and heard every conceivable denomination but never have we heard worship like that. It was fabulous.[25]

Whereas the original meetings in the Watsons' home and then the Bathurst

Street United Church continued to be a somewhat intimate group setting due to the structure of the church that was conducive to the folk-style Jesus music and praise songs, more personal yet performance-based weekly meetings began to draw hundreds into a sense of community without any formal structures but where an atmosphere of warmth and welcome was pervasive. For some, this seems to have been the heyday of The Catacombs phenomenon. Regarding the height of spiritual renewal in many traditional churches and the trickle-down effect of the Jesus Movement, reflections are positive if not nostalgic with hints of a current yearning to return to simpler worship and sense of community. Paul Bramer, a non-Pentecostal regular attendee and current professor at Tyndale University College Toronto, remembers it as worship as he had never seen it.[26]

The direction of The Catacombs worship and atmosphere, however, began to shift noticeably when it relocated to St. Paul's Anglican Church—a very different venue than the previous one with traditional seating and a large pipe organ. In hindsight, this more historic church context seems to have been a most unlikely choice to have any promise of success in an era of significant retreat from institutional religious forms. Yet, the Watson's musical skill, variety of instrumentation, and introduction of choreographic dance blended with their passion for worship and deeper spirituality to become key factors in attracting hundreds more than at the previous location from a wide range of interests and age groups. Notably though, with the move to St. Paul's Church there was also loss of intimacy as the meetings became more formal, attracting more church people. It appears that it corresponded roughly to a shift of emphasis from the Jesus culture to the Charismatic Movement both of which were at play in the culture of The Catacombs. It became a Christian tourist destination of which people would ask the question, "Have you been to The Catacombs?" much like they would ask years later in the mid-1990's, "Have you been to the Toronto Airport Vineyard?" Surprisingly, there were more people flocking to this large cathedral seemingly to observe the unique phenomenon but who had no connection with the original group.[27]

The Watsons were by no means oblivious to the mêlée of religious and sociological crosscurrents in which they were ministering. Young people with connections to the Catholic tradition and a range of mainstream Protestant denominational backgrounds were able to function comfortably in the traditional church venue but with a radically different outlook on contemporary life, its institutions and social mores than their parents and grandparents. Added to the mosaic was a Pentecostal climate attractive enough to draw some PAOC young people and to create inquisitiveness about Pentecostalism among those with no such background.

As the crowd's composition shifted with the relocation to St. Paul's Church there also occurred some backlash over style. The previous close Charismatic worship environment became all but lost and the plethora of new songs and the singing of the Psalms tended to dry up. The little club had lost its simplicity and coziness. There occurred an indiscriminate appropriation of any musical genre from almost any source. Southern gospel, Charismatic and Jesus People music all converged and along with it a concern over whether the Pentecostal narrative would eventually win out. In any case, the musical variety seemed to have the Spirit's blessing and was magnetic in continuing to draw hundreds of people on a weekly basis.

Included with this evolution in worship at The Catacombs was a significant move towards singing hymns. Until this point, Bramer believes that the Watsons had been making an ecclesial statement by not singing hymns, that is to say, distancing themselves from the institutional church. Nevertheless, a feeling was emerging that the worship was light on theology.[28] Driven by the musical talents, leadership style, and awe-inspiring location, the focus on Scripture put to simple tunes common in Charismatic circles gave the initial impetus to the worship environment. However, as helpful as Scripture songs were for teaching the Bible to youth, many of whom had little biblical knowledge, a shift began to take place with the singing of hymns in the large St. Paul's Anglican Cathedral filled mainly with teenagers and young adults. The Watsons recall:

> And then we started to say, "Look, never mind the choruses. Let's get into the big stuff." ...so we decided to get into the hymns...Just the gospel hymns, l i k e "Since Jesus Came Into My Heart", and "Praise to the Lord, the Almighty, the King of Creation", the liturgical ones.... We had fourteen instruments playing at the same time... a wonderful sound so the kids started to sing like a choir, like a 2,500 voice choir.[29]

This concern for theological depth would have been a significant drawing point for classical Pentecostals, helping to reduce their fears of shallow spirituality. Merla Watson also recalls this development as being somewhat ironic:

> One thing that was very new in the music part of it was [that] it wasn't just the guitar-slingers...We had musicians who were trained...The fact that we used hymns a lot...if somebody would have said this is the way to reach young people, that would be the last thing you'd even think of. Because they're antiquated (to their knowledge), and the music wouldn't be like the Beatles generation, and there was a lot of that going on in the Jesus People movement...And [the young people] would say, 'I've never heard this kind of stuff,' or 'I usually wouldn't like this kind of stuff.' ... [But] that's what they would request: "Please, can we sing a hymn? Please, we want a hymn" – because it had meaning.[30]

There is little evidence that the return to traditional hymnody, however, survived past the time of The Catacombs as Charismatic type groups later defaulted to worship patterns that were clearly postmodern and frequently shallow theologically, not to mention poorly performed. The Watsons' perspective on older Pentecostal piety was obvious in the selection of music for their worship. Merla Watson declared, "It certainly wasn't the old Pentecostal songs.... If we used them it would be sparingly because we used a complete kaleidoscope of music and it was good music, not this drivel."[31]

The Charismatic Movement, arising as it did mainly among a younger generation, spiritually and intellectually motivated seekers of truth, seems to have opened the door for a wider variety of expressions of worship and faith. Students who had experienced the Spirit preferred discipleship teaching to evangelistic sermons and often enjoyed classical music in addition to traditional Protestant hymns as part of their worship, all of which were part of the mix at The Catacombs.

The inclusion of traditional hymns with pipe organ accompaniment is mentioned repeatedly by those involved: "Such worship sprang forth as to cause world famous preachers and teachers to emotionally claim it was the finest worship they had ever heard."[32] It appears that the traditional venue helped to shape the unique style and atmosphere of The Catacombs meetings. For many, experience of the Spirit within the context of the Charismatic Movement was giving new meaning to mainstream church worship that had previously become cold and formal. A cathedral-type sanctuary with a large organ, which was unusual to PAOC people as most of their buildings were simpler, more recently constructed halls, also made the singing of hymns a majestic and unifying activity. Steve Sture, a current PAOC pastor, at that time associated with an apostolic denomination, claims he personally attended The Catacombs every Thursday night for two years, and recalls that the organ, ironically, became a treasured instrument. He says: "The organist would get that pipe organ rumbling so much the building would almost shake. But the praise that would arise within the building while he was playing that organ was absolutely beautiful.... He would do old hymns, 'Great is Thy Faithfulness' and 'Guide Me O Thou Great Jehovah'.... The kids wanted it all."[33]

Hundreds of countercultural and Charismatic youth doing traditional worship together was not only appealing because it had meaning but also because of its theatrical qualities. The Watsons' training and artistic style was a perfect fit that appealed to the senses and a meeting became what Merv Watson fittingly refers to as a "three-hour spectacle."[34] Bramer recalls that the hippies' high value placed on self-expression made the Watsons "high sense of drama fit right in with the hippies or with the Jesus people and of course the music they were singing and playing, that went along with it."[35]

Impact on PAOC Worship Style

The musical style represented at The Catacombs signaled the beginning of a permanent shift in the worship ambience of much of central Canadian PAOC church culture, though admittedly, it was only one piece of a set of influences being brought to bear on classical Pentecostal worship. When questioned about the changes inspired by The Catacombs, the Watsons state, "The instrumentation changed and there were more guitars and less Hammond organs and less pianos, less male quartets. Even four-part harmony wasn't used so much. So there was this infusion of contemporary instruments."[36] In time, organ, brass, and woodwind instruments almost totally disappeared and were replaced with guitars, drums and eventually electronic keyboards. At the time, this was a major innovation in Christian music and indeed an attraction for most PAOC youth who attended. This pattern has continued throughout the era of praise music within the denomination and elsewhere. Sture observes that some of the music certainly made its way into PAOC churches and finds it intriguing that, while there is a tendency within Pentecostal ranks to avoid publicly identifying with either the Charismatic or Vineyard movements, yet the music of each is freely embraced.[37]

Sture recalls the unforgettable worship atmosphere with drums, guitars, violins, and cellos making a "beautiful sound." But, in particular, he claims he was impacted by the dance teams, one of which included Benny Hinn. Sture became well acquainted with Hinn through his father, David Sture, a local Pentecostal pastor who eventually became Hinn's own pastor for a short period before the latter launched his evangelistic and deliverance ministry. The Jewish style songs such as "Awake, O Israel," were performed with choreographed dance and streamers down the huge center aisle of the sanctuary. He reminisces: "From that day on I have loved the idea of that kind of dancing before the Lord. I have seen much of the other kind of dancing before the Lord, where of course you dance in the Spirit and there's nothing wrong with that. It would be glorious, victorious, too…not something that was…. sensual…or out there. It just fitted in perfectly with the worship service."[38]

As a young Pentecostal having grown up in a church that primarily made use of a piano and organ, Sture was captivated by the inclusion of multiple guitars and drums, both rare instruments in traditional Pentecostal environments. Typical of many youth exposed to the music of the Jesus and Charismatic Movements, he then found himself wanting to play drums in his own church. He remembers, "I was asked not to play during any slow songs, just in fast songs only. It was very strict back then in most churches, of course, with even drums being played [at all]."[39] Through the influence of The Catacombs, he became a passionate worship leader beginning at the PAOC church in Islington, where his father became pastor during the mid-1970s. He states, "The Catacombs really did affect me with regard to that because I saw how beautiful worship could be. I had a hunger for the Word, too, because the Word was being taught and taught well."[40] He believes that the Watsons had so many international contacts that they were able to introduce the music of the era in addition to their own compositions and so had a far-reaching influence on the Pentecostal youth of his generation.

Yet, developments in worship music within Pentecostal-Charismatic contexts since then seem to be cause for some frustration for the Watsons who themselves now fear excess in worship expression. They convey a distinct impression of having adopted a more conservative, maybe even a more 'holiness' approach to music and ministry. They lament the passing of the good old days when the music they created was simple and uncluttered. Just as older classical Pentecostals tend to look back with a longing for what they perceive to have been genuine, so these charismatic leaders look back at what they see as having been the real thing. They seem to believe that there has been a distortion of the Charismatic Movement that they knew. Merla Watson argues:

> The Charismatic Renewal as such has grown. [But] I think that people are trying to put cosmetics on it. They are trying to beat it to death to put new life into it. And we're getting a lot of conjuring up of the Holy Spirit. It's not the Holy Spirit. It's something else, and calling it by names that are not even vaguely biblical. So we are terribly concerned. That doesn't mean everybody in it.... What we're saying is there is an incredible...inroad of the enemy into the charismatic.[41]

The Watsons still consider themselves very much charismatic people with a strong belief in miracles, but Charismatics who have come of age through a "reappraisal" of their faith, meaning a return to the "historic roots" of their faith rather than focusing too much on the "fruit and blossoms" which they believe has led into "extremities... abnormalities... a perversion kind of thing that is not godly." Yet they retain some optimism— "we just want to be pure before the Lord and be ready for the next move of God."[42]

Those who followed them, the Watsons believe, took what they created and did with it what was not intended. Merla Watson poignantly articulates her feelings about what she believes has happened to corporate worship expression:

> ...a lot of the things that the Lord laid upon our hearts to instigate as an expression of our worship to Him, other people have gotten a hold of it, run with it and did not have either the training or the anointing or the knowledge of it and did some pretty weird things to it. Especially did it come out in the area of the dance where there would be groups dancing with inappropriate gestures that were not godly. We never would have stood for that, or even what they wore....
> Back then scripture was the big thing, you know, and that's how we all learned scripture, as a group. Now it's just absolute drivel. It is bad musically. It's bad theologically. It's bad poetry. Sometimes we just have to walk out and say this is not our God. Who are you worshipping? This is not our God. This is not worthy and it's not holy.[43]

There was a sense at the time when The Catacombs was flourishing that this was a new music genre that was more spiritually meaningful, both personally and corporately. It was a blending of classical with both the old and new in the Christian tradition and, furthermore, it was meant to become a means of teaching the Bible. In the PAOC, the debate still goes on as to the correct balance between traditional and contemporary as the denomination has found itself caught up in the 'worship wars.'

Pentecostal youth from the Greater Toronto Area who frequented The Catacombs were exposed to the music of the Jesus Movement, the emphasis on Spirit baptism, and somewhat to the operation of the *charismata* of the Charismatic Movement as both Movements became intertwined. The Watsons certainly saw what they believed God was doing through them as being fundamentally a part of the Charismatic Movement. They recall conducting a retreat near Kingston, Ontario where a former ballerina dancer and wife of the director of the national Inter-Varsity Christian Fellowship received the Holy Spirit while giving her testimony.[44]

Singing, which was so central to both the movements and a comfort zone for classical Pentecostals, characterized a typical service at the Catacombs with an hour or more of songs, some originating from Calvary Chapel in California. The Catacombs also began holding an annual Maranatha Festival in May 1971, featuring music and guest speakers including Larry Norman, the well-known Jesus People rock musician.[45] Similarly to what many Pentecostals could readily identify with from their own churches, singing was then followed by a time of "impromptu 'witnessing.'"[46] Harpur reported, "Members stand up and recount 'what the Lord has been doing in my life this week.' The mood is relaxed—the majority are sitting cross-legged on the floor—and there is a lot of laughter."[47] Integral to the initial success of The Catacombs was the strong, talented leadership of the Watsons who were able to effectively keep the group from extremism. During Harpur's visit, one youth told how "two cavities in his teeth had been miraculously healed through prayer" followed by one of the elders publically cautioning against "coming just to get 'painless dentistry' but then added 'God can surely heal you as you believe.'"[48] Leadership discernment of this kind would have been comforting to PAOC youth who, though accustomed to the doctrine and practice of divine healing, would generally not have been at home with excess or trivialities.

Charismatic Worship in the Spirit

A major attraction of The Catacombs for PAOC youth was the practice of singing in tongues and chanting. Though most would not have been accustomed to this, it had not been entirely unknown within PAOC circles in previous years.[49] As classically trained musicians who played several instruments and composed many of the songs, along with a team of talented singers and instrumentalists whom they had gathered around them, Merv and Merla Watson were quite capable of guiding the group into 'worship in the Spirit.' After they moved into St. Paul's church sanctuary "rather than shying away from using the [huge] pipe organ, they used it to support the Israeli-style folk music and ballet dancers in the chancel, the various solo instruments in the choir area, and the vast intense congregation."[50] Two attendees, Bob and Lorraine Tadman, recall further that people were "singing full out, full heart, just total expression" and that "your eyes could be closed, and nobody was looking at you or paying any attention to you, so in a sense you could have your individual worship time in a community…because there was an anonymity, and at the same time, a sense of community."[51] The Watsons emphasize that experiencing the Spirit, singing in tongues and deliverance were central to what was happening at The Catacombs. They remember a lot of singing in the Spirit, sometimes going on for hours with a single song being sung many times over.[52] The common memory of those who experienced The Catacombs is the exceptional worship atmosphere that most claimed they had never known before and have not experienced since. This is substantiated in Douville's research when he writes: "It is striking that most of my interviewees emphasized the vitality of the collective singing and worship, and several indicated that they have not experienced anything comparable since then, even though they remained active in charismatic churches over the decades."⁵³

Environment was, in fact, the major attraction at The Catacombs. Sture notes that there was no organized welcome with greeters or ushers and argues unequivocally:

> The love of the Lord was there every Thursday, not just the first time I went but every Thursday. You walked in and felt right at home.... You walked in and just met people and just talked to people.... Total strangers were talking to each other.... I sensed that special love that I haven't sensed in a lot of churches since then.... I could only call it a move of God to have that kind of love with, at times, well over two thousand people.⁵⁴

For teenagers like Sture, "every service was exciting" with "a sense of expectation [because] you knew God would show up."⁵⁵ Although it bore little resemblance to a Pentecostal revival service, PAOC youth would have found a vibrant worship environment, altar times, and public conversions familiar and compelling. Remembering the 'altar call' being very common and unintimidating, he notes: "There was not a problem with regard to people coming to the altar. They didn't shun that. People that I talked to there, and myself as well, had a true hunger to know God more."⁵⁶

Sture now views his experience of The Catacombs as transformational in his perspective on ministry: "I could imagine my ministry as not really expecting a whole lot more from the Lord with regard to [the Spirit's] moving in church...."⁵⁷ While he believes that the Charismatic Movement in the form that he knew was specific to that period and is now history thus making a new wave of renewal necessary, he nevertheless maintains that he would likely not be ministering in the vein of renewal today had it not been for the Charismatic Movement of the 1970s, specifically The Catacombs. Increased openness to charismatic gifts, worship with a new dimension, and a new desire for unity where people "absolutely love each other and have each other's backs"⁵⁸ constitute the motivational factors behind Sture's current ministry with the PAOC.

For youth from classical Pentecostal churches, the worship and practice of the *charismata* at The Catacombs would have been a mixture of the familiar and unfamiliar. Singing in tongues was not unheard of, yet not at all widespread in PAOC churches in the form that Charismatics were practicing. Some older Pentecostals refer to singing in tongues as "singing in the Spirit" but as a personally unplanned and uninitiated event occurring as a spontaneous phenomenon resulting from the Spirit's presence in a moment of intense spiritual ecstasy. Known to have happened to specific individuals and seen as something quite special and extraordinary, to witness corporate singing in tongues at The Catacombs or in any other Charismatic event was something quite new for PAOC participants. Within a short time, however, the same practice of singing in the Spirit became quite common in many PAOC churches as the Charismatic flavor spread to mainstream Pentecostalism.

Furthermore, while prayer for deliverance from evil influences was also not at all unknown in PAOC churches, it too was not nearly as common and, in that sense, would have been an eye-opener for younger Pentecostals. It seems that many older Pentecostals saw both the Charismatic practices of singing in tongues corporately and regular prayer for deliverance as somewhat extreme, maybe even diluting their mystique and showing some irreverence towards the supernatural nature of both.

Where Pentecostals and Jesus People-Charismatics Converged

In familiar evangelical style, preaching occupied a core part of The Catacombs meetings with prolonged time given for ministry at the end. People would be invited forward to receive Christ, Spirit-baptism, healing, or for other needs.[59] In addition to the Watsons and other local speakers such as Jim McAllister, a former PAOC minister who would eventually take over leadership of the Catacombs, there were influential speakers from the United States, notably Bob Mumford, Don Basham, and Derek Prince, three of the five leaders of the Shepherding Movement. Prince had served as a PAOC missionary in Kenya as well as a Bible college teacher in Western Canada before emigrating to the United States. He had come to North America from the United Kingdom through the PAOC, having been appointed a missionary to Kenya by the denomination in 1958 followed by a brief teaching stint. Although his arrival preceded the outbreak of the Charismatic Movement, many Pentecostals followed his teachings long after he became a popular teacher and author in the United States and one of the famous Florida Five. The Shepherding Movement was a phenomenon that developed as a result of the structureless nature the Charismatic Movement. S. David Moore describes it as

> ...an influential and controversial expression of the charismatic renewal that emerged as a distinct nondenominational movement in 1974. The shepherding movement, also known as the discipleship movement, developed in response to the increasing independence among many charismatic Christians who were leaving their denominational churches and joining independent churches and prayer groups. It also grew in response to the highly individualistic and subjective nature of spirituality of many charismatics.[60]

Reflecting on this phenomenon, Sture emphasizes that preaching and teaching was always a core component of The Catacombs worship along with lots of testimonies and interviews which would inevidently be celebratory proclamations. While it was once being high on drugs that was a source of excitement, now it was being high on Jesus that became the experience that would never stop.

He draws a definite distinction between his experience there and that of a later renewal movement in the 1990s, presumably referring to the Toronto Blessing, where he found that the preaching of the Word was not always given prominence. The pervading appetite among Pentecostal youth at the time for substantial biblical teaching rather than revival-style evangelistic preaching was met at The Catacombs where those invited to speak were profoundly effective and taught discipleship concepts with much talk of "the love of the Father." They would speak for an hour or longer receiving exceptional attention from the audience. The preaching was "bathed in love; otherwise, it wouldn't have worked in that atmosphere."[61] Sture fondly recalls his father frequenting The Catacombs shortly after he started attending and being quite impressed with the balanced teaching. In fact, it was common for parents of the youth to attend from time to time. He reminisces:

> But I remember a lot of grandmothers and grandfathers being there. They loved the balance of it. They loved the fact that kids were having such a good time in the Lord's presence. They approved. I thought that was pretty cool. We kids were having an awesome time but so were they in that sense. It was really striking to me.... They were checking it out. [But] they just loved it...there was no generational gap.[62]

Undoubtedly, it was an exceptionally rare trans-generational worship experience.

In the late 1960s, the Watsons had been exposed to the teaching of leaders of the Charismatic Movement while in Ohio and were captivated by the activity of spiritual deliverance and their teaching on spiritual warfare.[63] Their Charismatic experience expanded quickly, and spread within the group. Merla had received baptism in the Spirit as the result of the testimony of a ballerina at a retreat near Kingston, Ontario. Later in Ohio, Merv had likewise experience the Spirit as a result of seeing a girl receiving deliverance after being prayed for by Derek Prince and others.[64] For the Watsons, it was a spiritual revolution and the opening of a new chapter as they left their jobs and went into full-time ministry at The Catacombs.

Ministry involvement extended well beyond the Thursday evening meetings as evangelism and social action also took place. The Jesus People were known for their passion to take the good news to the streets; thus, the members of The Catacombs, empowered by their Charismatic excitement did just that. They held street services, staged music and drama presentations in hospitals and prisons, and travelled in teams around the Toronto area telling the news of what was happening.[65] The Watsons themselves became known around PAOC churches in the Toronto region, speaking and conducting concerts in some of them.

There was at least one striking similarity between the Watsons and many Pentecostals: they were in harmony in their emphasis on Christ's imminent return, with apocalyptic language and end-time expectation in evidence at The Catacombs, as was common elsewhere among the Jesus People. The Watsons' fascination with Israel's reestablishment as a nation and its reclamation of Old Jerusalem holy sites in 1967 reinforced a dispensational approach to eschatology. At the annual Maranatha Festival a song written by Merla Watson was sung: "Maranatha, Jesus is Coming; Maranatha, come Lord Jesus soon."[66]

Douville reports that most of his interviewees acknowledged that there was an elevated interest in the end times and an anticipation that led some Jesus People to believe predictions about the date of Christ's return. A rather bizarre incident took place in late 1973 or 1974 when Jan Willem van der Hoeven, at the time custodian of the Garden Tomb in Jerusalem and later the founder of the International Christian Embassy in Jerusalem spoke at The Catacombs. At the conclusion of his talk on the centrality of Israel to the events of the last days, he gave an "altar call" inviting people forward to commit to go to Jerusalem in 1975 for Christ's return! The chancel was filled with hundreds of people committing themselves to go. While it did not result in a mass exodus of young people to Israel, it indicates the intensity of eschatological concerns among Jesus people and Charismatics at the time.[67]

Intersections with PAOC Leadership

Notwithstanding indications of the close contact of Pentecostal youth with The Catacombs, Douville's wider research on the Jesus People in Toronto, 1965 to 1975, found that the relationship between them and the PAOC as a denomination was paradoxical. Toronto PAOC ministers and laity did not have the same central role as they did in other cities. He observes, "At first glance, it seems strange that Toronto's PAOC clergy were not the Jesus Movement's key supporters, and it is equally puzzling that Jesus People did not automatically gravitate to PAOC churches."[68] Leadership was certainly aware of the Jesus People and gave favorable coverage in *The Pentecostal Testimony* suggesting there was agreement on core doctrines such as being born again and adult baptism.[69]

Ken Birch, a PAOC national executive leader, reporting in the denomination's magazine on his visit in 1971 to the Jesus People on the Sunset Strip in Hollywood was accordingly sympathetic: "But neither should we write this phenomenon off as something which is suspect or at least entirely irrelevant to our style of Christianity. The Jesus People Movement, I believe, is essentially a work of God's Holy Spirit."[70] Birch saw major strengths amongst the Jesus People with their simple lifestyle, lack of reservation in sharing their faith with others, their love of worship, and the obvious sense of "brotherly love" among them.[71] Other positive allusions to the Jesus movement were made in subsequent issues, such as a reprint of *Christianity Today* report applauding the involvement of the Jesus People at the 1972 Munich Olympics.[72] Another was part of a news item regarding David Wilkerson who severely criticized established Pentecostal churches for their inability to look beyond the physical appearance of Jesus people and see the miracles that happened to them, accusing churches of saying in effect: "If those kids are really Jesus people, let them prove it. Get them into the barbershop. That's the only way I'll believe it . . . And how about all those Catholics who claim Holy Ghost miracles in their lives? Why don't they leave the Catholic church like we did? How can they still be Catholic and charismatic at the same time?"[73]

Yet, this kind of affirmation of the Jesus People had not been uniform across Canada either. Alvin Schindel, President of Canadian Pentecostal College, Saskatoon, Saskatchewan in giving an appraisal of progress at his school, reported:

> An assessment is not easy to make, partly because it involves me in a judgment of intangibles and some are going to be disappointed. On the one hand, there is still a disturbing amount of evidence, as I told you last year, "that in dress, entertainment, patterns of speech, styles of music and standards of life, Bible college students, along with many of our young people, are allowing themselves to be unduly in-

fluenced by the secular world." From my association with those who are the most deeply involved, I must confess with the utmost solemnity that I find very little reason to hope for a reversal; that is, apart from a sovereign, divine intervention of the Holy Spirit.

That such an intervention is possible and desirable, none will deny, but how probable it is as long as our desire for it remains as irresolute and trifling as it is now is a question for ALL of us to ask ourselves. *There is, I should add, one place where a reversal is taking place and that is among some of the "Jesus People," a group as a whole upon whom many of us still look with more than a few misgivings and no little suspicion.*[74] (emphasis added)

Deep reticence characterized the attitude of classical Pentecostals toward both the Charismatic and Jesus Movements.

Albert Vaters, PAOC pastor at The Stone Church in downtown Toronto, attended meetings of The Catacombs and reflects a sentiment toward the newer waves of spiritual vitality that would have been common among many of his young minister contemporaries: "[I] came from a Pentecostal church that was more ordered.... They were dancing freely... It was amazing, and God was in the place. But it's just not my style of worship."[75] Merv Watson confirms that some of the members of Vaters' church, particularly young people, would come over to the meetings and recognizes this church as having had a prominent role in the spiritual climate of the time.[76] Vaters reflects on the days of The Catacombs and the Charismatic Movement as a time of extreme excitement and busyness as he and his church engaged in multiple cooperative initiatives with other denominations.[77] There was also a direct connection between Vaters and David Mainse; Vaters was a member of the original *Crossroads* subcommittee of the PAOC. As close personal friends and former Bible college classmates, both carried the same rare propensity toward interdenominational cooperation within the context of the Spirit's larger working.

Warmer acceptance of the Jesus People (and specifically The Catacombs participants) would have taken place when they showed signs of lifestyle modification more in line with traditional holiness-type Pentecostal expectations and interest in participating in local churches. However, it is also quite likely that the PAOC would not have used its official publication to advertise The Catacombs nor to appear to be encouraging attendance at a non-PAOC event that was unknown, if not suspect. Paul Bramar, a non-PAOC adherent and member of the Toronto Jesus Movement recalls PAOC youth in Oakville being discouraged from attending The Catacombs: "The kids in the Pentecostal church were kind of warned about us. We weren't quite kosher as far as the Pentecostals were concerned.... At that time, there was a fairly big discrimination that was being made between charismatic and Pentecostal. And the sort of traditional Pentecostals did not see the charismatics as a fully developed, legitimate expression of the Christian faith."[78] Clearly, the aim would have been to protect PAOC doctrine and practice as well as its local pastors from having to deal with possible fallout, whereas any good that it perceived in the wider Jesus Movement was more general, therefore more benign and less prone to negative feedback from the grassroots.

Yet, perhaps more than anything, it appears that the main ingredient uniting for a time the youth of all three movements was the emphasis on emotion and experience, again an obvious comfort zone for PAOC youth. Along with the artistic approach to worship at The Catacombs, the Watsons clearly believed that feeling must be a part of worship. As an external reporter, Harpur's immediate assessment was that the emphasis was on "personal experience, on a free-flowing emotionalism—'If you can't get emotional I feel sorry for you,' Merla says—on music and teaching in tune with young people, and on direct, authoritative answers to life's problems."[79] However, Harpur was also quick to point out, not without some validity, that "in its appeal lies also its dangers" and that the temptation may prove strong to become its own church, another splinter group.[80] This, in reality, proved entirely prophetic. The Catacombs eventually became known as "A Christian Church on a Hill," a fellowship that would last only a short time and eventually disband.

In retrospect, while Harpur's criticism of emotionalism in religion is a typical evaluation by the media elite, it still seems unwarranted in its dismissal of the place of an emotional encounter with the Spirit in favor of an intellectual approach to spirituality. His assessment, nevertheless, would seem to have contained some truth, at least for critical observers of The Catacombs and of the broader Jesus and Charismatic Movements. He asserted, "The emotionalism and the tendency to get simple answers to complex issues could result in just another 'trip' destined to end in a rude shock once the initial 'high' is over."[81]

Likewise complex are the reasons for the demise of The Catacombs and other groups associated with that era. Almost a decade later, many PAOC people would eventually be attracted to another wave of renewal in the Toronto Blessing. Overall though, there would be a gradual move toward a more evangelical approach to religion that would be at the same time intensely practical and cautious of emotion, not so much as it relates to physical and verbal expressiveness in the context of concert-style worship, but to the reception of Spirit-baptism and the operation of the *charismata*.

Many young Pentecostals of the era were enamoured with what appeared to be the breakdown of denominational barriers, particularly as individual members of mainline churches were reported to have received the Pentecostal experience. While it is true that older PAOC adherents may have fully expected Charismatics to eventually leave their own churches or be forced out, as they were, and join PAOC ranks, it is not at all clear whether younger Pentecostals felt the same way, or even if they cared. There was unmistakable excitement whenever a priest, minister, or layperson showed interest in experiences of the Spirit. A new day of spiritual renewal was dawning with an anticipation that the best was yet to come.

The climate of interdenominational acceptance is exemplified by the extraordinary offering of St. Paul's Church by the Anglican leaders of the Corporation of Parish to such a diverse Charismatic group as The Catacombs. In fact, some Anglicans attended and participated. Andy Leroux, who would later become an Anglican priest in that diocese, recalls a memorable evening there when David Ward, an Anglican priest, celebrated the Eucharist from the Book of Common

Prayer, an unusual experience for youth who had become accustomed mainly to extemporaneous prayer. The Watsons also recall a two-hour Eucharist service, held early on a Sunday morning at St. Paul's, in which five priests assisted in the celebration. When the celebrant invited the 1,500 youth in attendance to come forward and receive communion, "a horde of these kids [rushed] forward, nearly pushed the priests over... It was just amazing... It was just a surge of 'yes, I want this.'"[82]

Another example of the cross-denominational character of The Catacombs phenomenon was the Maranatha Festival, a multi-day gathering that began under The Catacombs' leadership in 1971. It involved a variety of speakers and Christian rock musicians with no known denominational ties, thus conveying a clear message that traditional church lines mattered little within this spirit of renewal. According to Merv Watson, it drew about 3600 young people, filling St. Paul's Anglican Church. This was where their use of banners, choruses in minor keys and the choreographed dance began, which he is quick to point out was not "waltzing up and down the aisle and not hitting anybody."[83]

It was in this environment that Benny Hinn was converted, later becoming connected for a short time with a local Pentecostal congregation and preaching in a few Ontario PAOC churches. The Watsons had a special fondness for Benny Hinn's Christian witness. They remember his early days when he was "really, really empowered by the Holy Spirit." Merla Watson says, "He had a beautiful way. That's not to say that the things he's involved with now that we entirely go along with, but his heart was pure at that point." They regret that his ministry passed into a business under the weight of pressure from public performance.[84]

It would not be entirely accurate to conclude that PAOC youth were either anti-church or generally anti-institutional. However, rebellion against the perceived legalism of an older generation of Pentecostals was common. Youth were looking for relevance, warmth, and authenticity, all of which those who attended seem to have found at The Catacombs. There was little in the evangelical ethos of the Jesus Movement that did not appeal to them and when combined with the Spirit-focus of the Charismatic Movement, it felt like a safe place to be. The message of love as the true expression of spirituality, rather than preoccupation with adherence to traditional doctrines, was to become the hallmark of community life within many PAOC churches in the years to come. The Catacombs was part of a larger environment that ensured future PAOC worship would be largely existential, heartfelt, and exuberant, where community life would be paramount, and statements of doctrine would be all but ignored.

It was the comfort of a venue such as The Catacombs, where the trappings of institutional control and theological rigidity appeared to be shed, that attracted both Charismatics and youth from the counterculture as well as some from the PAOC. The thirst for freedom in worship and an experience of radical spirituality was common to all three. As Preston Shires contends, "The flexible ecclesiology of the charismatic movement had definite ties to the counterculture."[85] In this regard, he correctly observes, "The main difference between the charismatic Christian and the traditional Pentecostal was the charismatic's greater measure of tolerance for Christian doctrines and practices that did not specifically emanate from the initial turn-of-the-century Pentecostal movement."[86] Although arguably not to the same degree in Canada as elsewhere, flexibility and openness were hallmarks of the day and the Charismatic Movement offered a new world-view that ministered to the "anti-technocratic spiritual aspirations"[87] of youth without abandoning popular culture. In reality, PAOC youth were drawn to the music of both the Charismatic Movement and the Jesus People but also to the stardom of popular Christian artists such as Larry Norman, Chuck Girard, and Keith Green. This trend has not diminished but instead, has accelerated over time.

While the Jesus music resonated with the experience of young people, inspiring and motivating them, they also "wanted not only to bask in their light, they wanted to be stars themselves."[88] Long hair, hippie-style dress, and Christian rock music slowly gained acceptance from pastors and youth pastors "though such acceptance was sometimes grudging, and hardly universal."[89] For the first time in the history of the denomination, a younger generation was able to have the best of both worlds—the warmth of an immanent spirituality including the operation of the charismatic gifts consistent with Pentecostal tradition, and the 'cool' contemporary culture that older Pentecostals had castigated as worldly.[90] PAOC youth groups became active, inviting places and participation in them fashionable. Through school connections, they attracted numbers of youth from mainline churches where there might not be a youth group or where the program might not be as energetic and appealing.

Fracturing of the Catacombs

The growing thirst for theological and spiritual depth and perhaps by extension an impulse for more structure, was not lost on the Watsons. The increasing authoritarian trend was unknown and not entirely welcomed by those who attended. One converted speed freak was heard to ask, "What happened to dear sweet Jesus?!" The simplicity of a spiritual phenomenon within the life of hundreds of Canadian youth in the Toronto area was beginning to fade as pressure for The Catacombs to become more church-like increased. The Watsons did not see themselves qualified to lead in that direction nor do they appear to have wanted to be.

The Catacombs eventually began to run into trouble with a change of leadership. Its eventual demise would itself become a tragedy of history and a potential case study in the social transformation of a renewal movement. As a teenager, Sture recalls a distinct change in atmosphere as "a [different] couple on the platform" began to take over with more "speaking" and "interrupting." He notes, "I would sense a colder presence there. It was almost like the Spirit of God left that corporate worship.... The numbers started to drop and then I finally left.... [It] became for all intents and purposes a cult.... It just died out."[91] He remembers sensing that something strange was taking place: "So I'm a kid back there, not knowing what was going on but something was going on behind the scenes that we didn't know about... So these people obviously did it and it wasn't the same.... It's so easy to quench the Spirit,... I think about that quite often, as a minister now."[92]

The church that emerged from it was pastored by Jim McAlister, who had begun his ministry with the PAOC and had direct roots to the denomination's founders. He had previously served on the pastoral staff at the PAOC Stone Church in Toronto while his father Hugh McAllister was pastor but his hope to be elected as his father's successor did not materialize.[93] McAlister began to adopt more conservative views on gender roles and was not sympathetic to gender inclusion in ministry. A young couple recalled how they approached McAlister seeking guidance on whether they should proceed to attend university after being accepted on a university scholarship. The wife related, "...he came back saying [my husband] should go, but I shouldn't – that a woman should not be smarter than her husband, i.e. that a woman should not outshine her husband." Meanwhile, she is a self-described "born academic" who later went on to graduate-level university studies but she and her husband submitted to the decision at the time.[94]

The Jesus People-Charismatic ethos of The Catacombs slowly gave way to greater social conservatism (though arguably not so much political) in line, it seems, with what counterculture scholars like Shires argue happened to the Jesus Movement south of the border.[95] Former attendee, Paul Bramer, reflects on the shift:

> As we started to integrate with the establishment, we found that our positions on some moral issues were much more conservative, ironically, than other people's were. It was a little bit of a surprise perhaps to some of us.... The experience we had prior to being Jesus People, which was in the hippie drug culture, we saw the damage that was done, and we became fairly moralistic in a number of areas.... By the late seventies and early eighties, I and a whole lot of other people had really moved; I think the abortion issue was one of the big ones.... I don't think we thought of it initially as a right-wing issue; we thought of it as an issue of conscience and life and things like that, but it got framed as a right-wing issue, and that's where we ended up.[96]

Although those who attended The Catacombs had been impacted by the anti-establishment influence from the left and although they had embraced openness and freedom in lifestyle expression and beliefs, they eventually gravitated to the right. Rather than continuing to confront the dominant culture, they blended with it and its social structures.[97] Bramer's assessment of The Catacombs group as part of the wider Jesus Movement was that it had "a sense of undergrounded-ness" similar to the secular counterculture but that, ...one of the major issues that the Jesus People started to face...was whether they could continue to be underground... separated from the normal establishment... I would say that it began to dawn on us around 1974 that somehow this movement was not sustainable."[98] As the Catacombs youth matured, the trend toward returning to mainstream and evangelical churches was underway.

Meanwhile, although Douville's sweeping analysis of the wider Jesus Movement may not be an exact template for The Catacombs, there are some parallels. In retrospect one thing is certain: its members did become absorbed into the surrounding culture including that of the evangelical church. Some youth who attended became PAOC pastors and others became involved in music and the arts, carrying with them not only their memories of The Catacombs but also the atmosphere of its music and spiritual expression. There were those both originally from within and without the PAOC who ended up in its churches, evangelical churches or other charismatic-type ministries. Furthermore, PAOC youth and youth pastors from that point on would continue to follow the development of an exploding plethora of charismatic musical styles and artists and to embrace them fully. Taking Douville's argument regarding the broad outcome of the Jesus Movement in a slightly different direction, it was that very phenomenon in combination with the Charismatic Movement that helped reshape PAOC churches mostly in their worship style but also in other areas such as their view of the work of the Spirit.

By 1974, exactly as Harpur had predicted, The Catacombs' Thursday night fellowship and worship had evolved into a church. The Watsons had appointed McAlister as pastor but were now no longer connected with The Catacombs. They had needed experienced workers and because the ministry had increasingly begun to resemble a church with, for example, young people requesting to be married there, they saw the necessity of having permanent pastoral leadership. Ironically, therein lay a serious weakness with The Catacombs and its lack of strong organizational structure. McAllister was not apparently carefully vetted resulting in the later revelation of deep differences in eschatological perspective, particularly with the Watsons' preoccupation with Israel. McAlister had come under the influence of the teachings of Myrtle Dorothea Beall,[99] sometimes referred to as the mother of the Latter Rain Movement,[100] and had embraced amillennialism and replacement theology. Merv Watson remembers:

> Anyway, we didn't realize that he was very much against our involvement in the Zionistic approach to life with Israel being very, very important.... We did not know. And he finally brought the whole thing to a halt, just from his activity.... He came in, first of all, to kind of help when people would come forward to the altar to get saved. We needed a lot of workers in there.... But eventually he started to take over and then we realized the guy was totally anti-Semitic. So we couldn't bear that.[101]

Under McAlister's leadership, it first took the name, "The Church of the Toronto Catacombs," later changing to "A Christian Church on a Hill" (CCOH) to signify that they were no longer an underground presence but were, in fact, a light set on a hill. The Watsons' preoccupation with Israel and messianic Judaism that began in the early days of the group eventually provoked contention distancing them from McAllister and led to a parting of ways.

The Watsons had by then formed an evangelistic performing arts group called "Shekinah," traveling with them across Europe and Israel.[102] They recall the summer of 1973 when they held a summer school and 95 people enrolled in preparation for their tour a year later: "From that we took a group to Europe in 1974 and 65 musicians came, including Benny [Hinn] and various others. We toured there for three months, through all the big cathedrals in England and ...in Holland."[103]

Their vision to have people reflect God's creativity in their worship was closely linked with their Judaic interests. The name chosen was intentional as Watson explained: "And this is part of the concept... taking the presence of the God of Israel into the marketplace, wherever people are.... At the same time we want to awaken believers in the God of Israel, Christians included, to their whole tradition—the color, spontaneity, artistry, involvement, enthusiasm and enjoyment of Davidic praise and worship... as depicted in the Psalms."[104] As they moved farther from the Catacombs, the Watsons became increasingly convinced that "comforting Zion" was to be a major part of their responsibility—"to arouse an awareness among believers as to our responsibility toward the House of Israel, that is to provoke the Jew to jealousy [and]... to express the richness of the 5600-year tradition of God's dealings with mankind."[105]

In the new group, the Watsons infused the same focus on instrumental music and dance as a more meaningful way of praise and worship that they had introduced previously. The ambiance that they were able to create with the group lends some further insight into the attraction that their meetings had at The Catacombs. In 1973 when they spent most of the summer on a farm just north of Toronto rehearsing for upcoming concerts in different parts of Canada and Europe, the local newspaper reported, "All of the people involved are dedicated to the praise of the Lord and all have a warm inner glow toward each other."[106] Watson made it clear that this initiative was an alternative to the music and art of the pop-culture where the intent was commercial success and to cast Jesus in a very different light than he was presented in the movie, *Jesus Christ Superstar*.[107] The object was "to lead people to a new dimension" and "to stir up the artistic gifts into an active praise of God."[108] The Watsons contribution became a trailblazer for some of the members of The Catacombs who became involved in music and dance careers or who at least desired to replicate the same atmosphere elsewhere.

This approach to worship as reported by that local newspaper is revealing in terms of its long-range impact: "God inhabits the praises of his people, and this very act of worship can be powerfully evangelistic as unbelievers are struck by the reality of the presence of God."[109] In more traditional-style PAOC churches, the act of singing hymns was not viewed as much an evangelistic activity as a worship and exhortation one. The Watsons and others were setting the stage for a new view of worship that placed emphasis not only on the content/theology but also on the atmosphere created by the music and choreographed dance that would appeal to unbelievers as a conduit of the presence of God.

Dancing as a planned act of worship would have been new to most, if not all, PAOC people who frequented The Catacombs. Viewed as distracting, if not irreverent, unless done "in the Spirit," it would have caused some to be initially uncomfortable. Nevertheless, it did not take long before dancing as a possibility in regular worship went mainstream in some PAOC churches and even more so in independent charismatic churches. Watson noted at the time that different aspects of the worship were being criticized, with dance being the most difficult for people to understand: "People just cannot get used to the idea of dancing in church and perhaps do not see the religious aspect to it. There must be something in it though as we have had more supporters than detractors and at present about 30 people or more a week have been joining Catacombs."[110] A British newspaper, The Surrey Daily Advertiser, also reported: "One felt the challenge this must prove to many with the totally new concept of dancing to the glory of God."[111] Interestingly, Watson claims that after Lorne Cunningham, international director of YWAM, saw the effectiveness of what The Catacombs was doing with banners and dance movements, YWAM incorporated it into their street presentations.[112] While dance as a form of worship art is still not widespread in the PAOC, it is accepted in some circles and no longer an issue of notable contention.

The positive memories and long-term outcome of The Catacombs ministry for both PAOC youth who attended and others from the counterculture is matched by the tragedy of its demise. Attendance continued to drop until the congregation had only about 200 members and was no longer the gathering point for Charismatic youth in the Toronto area. In early 1980, St. Paul's Anglican church decided to evict the congregation after seven years of using its buildings, fearing that it was becoming a cult. Former members made charges and in the *Toronto Star*, Harpur reported:

> ...the charismatic-type 'church' idolizes the leader, Rev. Jim McAllister 'as if he were God,' that he, his wife Mae, and a group of 17 elders control members to such a degree that 'nobody is allowed to think for himself;' that there is a heavy emphasis on possession by "evil spirits" and that physical force is used to prevent suspect or excommunicated members from attending meetings.... The watchmen, about eight in number, are said by critics to be 'elite bouncers' who control discipline...ejecting or barring undesirables and monitoring conversations of those considered to be wavering.[113]

McAlister's ministerial status with the Independent Assemblies of God (Canada) was withdrawn after he failed to meet with its leaders to discuss questions that had arisen regarding his relationship with the church and his tight control. Concerns about his leadership revolved around his teaching about his role as "shepherd" and that of its members as "sheep."[114] In his booklet, *The Shepherd-Pastor*, McAlister stated:

> Shepherds must lead. They can never be prodded by the sheep... If sheep presume to prod them, they presume to do the wrong thing. Shepherds must provide. Sheep are not ingenious enough to make do. Shepherds must protect. Sheep have no weapons to ward off attack. Sheep should know that and remember it, and be reminded of it constantly.[115]

While McAllister was apparently not connected directly with The Shepherding Movement, he exhibited many of the characteristics attributed to its leaders. The same tension, for instance, between charismatic and institutional impulses in the Charismatic Movement that David Moore describes was very much in evidence in the final days of the CCOH as McAlister tried to bring shape to a free and celebratory worship and Word phenomenon.[116] He was clearly trying to create some organizational control for a group that had not been accustomed to it. He refused to support at least one proposed marriage because it did not come under his oversight, the couple having arranged to be married elsewhere rather than by him at St. Paul's.

Yet, McAllister's authoritarian leadership seems to have been more extreme than that in the Shepherding Movement. Regarding that movement, Moore suggests that no ill intent or ulterior motive is evident:

> While freedom of conscience was always taught, followers knew that obedience to one's pastor was very important. Followers were not encouraged to an unquestioning, blind obedience to their shepherd but to an informal trusting obedience that was an outflow of a close caring relationship. The exercise of spiritual authority was well intentioned and seen as a means to be health and maturity to the people.[117]

McAlister's strict pastoral style is evidenced again in his document that says a shepherd has to "rule" and must never be caught in a position of letting the "sheep" initiate any action on their own. He held that in order to see ahead the shepherd must also possess "the voice of a prophet."[118]

Paul Pynkoski, a former deacon with the church stated that at the time under the prophetic utterances of the director of worship, Mae McAlister, the shepherd-sheep concept was pushed to the point of total "mind control" and alleged that the McAlisters' and their church elders' demand for unquestioning allegiance smacked of Jonestown. Pynkoski had been excommunicated for writing a letter to the McAlisters questioning their terminology regarding evil spirits.[119] Meanwhile, those who continued to support the CCOH downplayed such accusations by arguing that there should be unity in the church and that McAllister was neither viewed as a super-saint nor worshipped. Concerns continued to escalate over leadership and in the early 1980s, the McAlisters were asked to leave. By the middle of the decade, the church joined the Christian and Missionary Alliance and as Douville, concludes, "The Catacombs had been absorbed into the mainstream of evangelicalism."[120]

For the PAOC, Douville's optimism regarding the overall lasting impact of the Jesus Movement, specifically The Catacombs with its Charismatic flavour rings true:

> ...the movement's long-term successes would outweigh its short-term failures. It would take several years – even decades – before they could see the full extent of the profound changes that the Jesus People had initiated in North American evangelicalism. The Jesus Movement imbued evangelical churches with new energy, by bringing in new, youthful members, and perhaps more importantly, by helping to retain and energize those youth already present. The same energy infected evangelical youth organizations; while campus groups such as the Student Christian Movement dwindled in numbers.... Campus Crusade for Christ and Inter-Varsity Christian Fellowship continued to thrive throughout the seventies and beyond. Moreover, the Jesus Movement had a far-reaching effect on evangelical style – on the way that they worshipped, the music they sang, and many other aspects of evangelical Christian culture and identity.[121]

Freedom, energy and spontaneity in worship and praise became the heritage of the next generation of PAOC constituents, albeit a development constantly analyzed for its depth of theological substance and the appropriateness of ever-changing music styles. Unprecedented advances in technology have only aided this trend and the energy of youth group activities continues unabated.

Enduring Implications

As for any long-term effects upon the PAOC through the conditioning of young people who eventually would become pastors or parishioners within the denomination, it would have taken place in the earlier days of The Catacombs when it was a vibrant place to worship for Pentecostals who understood what was happening but yet felt a newness there that was compelling. If the Jesus and Charismatic Movements, as manifested in The Catacombs, resulted in a disproportionate number of youth entering ministry as Douville suggests, it is likely true as well of PAOC youth who attended while others became committed members of local churches. There is evidence within the current PAOC national leadership and among a few local pastors and evangelists of positive impact through their experience at The Catacombs. Yet, it would not be a balanced assessment to overlook those who also became disillusioned and struggled with their faith, whether through falling into disfavor with the leadership or defending the leadership until the end only to see their church disappear. McAlister himself disappeared from active ministry involvement but maintained some connection with Queensway Cathedral, a large Toronto PAOC church, and its then pastor, Ralph Rutledge.[122]

Most ex-members maintain that while control gradually tightened to the point where McAllister and the elders were directing every detail of members' lives, in the early days, the gathering was a helpful, attractive place to be, "so 'alive' compared to other churches."[123] What would have attracted PAOC youth of the 1970s was the excitement of denominational diversity worshiping in common space and the adventure of stepping outside their own boundaries. Carrying a tinge of the anti-institutionalism of the era, they joined with converted hippies and others from the evangelical subculture. As Douville suggests: "They occupied a space where previous norms did not apply, where young people in their twenties (without theological training) could be 'elders' and evangelists, and where speed freaks and lifelong church members were seen to be in equal need of redemption."[124]

Those who frequented the meetings never seemed to view The Catacombs so much as a tightly knit community or family church but as a place of unparalleled worship, love, and acceptance. As part of a wider climate of renewal, it played a part in energizing some PAOC youth in the Toronto area to experience more of the Spirit, to become more deeply involved in their local churches and for some to study theology and prepare for a life of service. In that sense the next generation of PAOC constituents are beneficiaries.

Douville suggests that just as the radical Christian activists of the 1960s helped to push the liberal church to the left, the Jesus People caused evangelicals to adopt a style similar to the hip youth culture.[125] Pentecostal youth would have tended to veer in that direction due to their non-liturgical heritage and inclination toward spontaneity. It was all part of a set of influences that transformed PAOC style from a fundamentalist-oriented and hymn singing consortium of churches where in most contexts, dress and appearance were often linked to moral values into churches constantly open to and embracing new trends in popular culture.

It also should be noted that given the denomination's history of women preachers and missionaries, PAOC people would generally not have had the same level of concern over the wider participation of women in preaching/teaching functions and leadership roles as would have been more common in the Baptist, Anglican, and Catholic traditions. The relatively egalitarian character of The Catacombs where Merla Watson shared leadership along with her husband would perhaps have been a minor adjustment for PAOC youth who attended. Women were often invited as speakers to the group including Corrie ten Boom,[126] the famous Dutch woman who helped Jews escape the Holocaust.

New Renewal and University Ministry

The scope of the Charismatic Movement further extended to encompass student ministry on university campuses, the most visible of which for the PAOC was led by a woman, Bernice Gerard, well-known PAOC minister and university chaplain who had been appointed to the University of British Columbia (UBC) in 1963. She also became chaplain at Simon Fraser University (SFU) all the while serving as co-pastor of the Fraserview Pentecostal Assembly in Vancouver when she became involved in the Charismatic Movement. Gerard was well known both within her own denomination and wider Canadian evangelical circles. In 2000, *The Vancouver Sun* named her as the most influential religious figure in British Columbia in the twentieth century.[127]

Gerard also had a connection with The Catacombs, having been invited by the Watsons to speak there. Although only a small proportion of PAOC youth frequented the Catacombs, many encounters with the new renewal were occurring on university and college campuses across Canada. As David Mainse stepped forward and turned new soil by cooperating with Charismatic figures in media evangelism, Bernice Gerard too ventured fearlessly into the Charismatic world, convinced that genuine renewal was essential and was spreading on university campuses. She was one of the first leaders to promote the Charismatic Movement in Canada, and in particular within the university culture. While the Watsons maintained a distance between The Catacombs and the PAOC, in the years immediately following, they developed a close relationship with Gerard who befriended them while they were living in western Canada. Merla says: "She got behind us 1000%. She loved us dearly and just really helped us in so many ways." [128]

Along with several other ministers including Anglican priest George Pattison and Ken Gaglardi, a doctoral student in physics at UBC, she led in the arrangements for Kevin Ranaghan to spend four days on campus in January 1968 to relate what had happened at the University of Notre Dame a year earlier. Interestingly, Ranaghan arrived in Vancouver precisely on the day that students, clergy, and laity were gathering at Notre Dame to celebrate the outbreak of the renewal the year before.[129] It is striking that Gerard referred to it as a "Pentecostal move," an assessment that at this early stage would have been cause for optimism on the part of PAOC leaders. The segment that she selected from Ranaghan's comments would also have caused PAOC people to applaud what they were reading. He had described the renewal as essentially one of "trying to get back to the basics of Christianity and clear out all the nonsense, all medieval, baroque and imperial accretions - an attempt to get back to the pure Gospel."[130] Gerard clearly used language that would resonate well with PAOC general readership and reassure its leaders. She referred to the five hundred Catholic students, clergy and lay people in Indiana as having received "the Pentecostal baptism with speaking in tongues." Nevertheless, Ranaghan's visit was undoubtedly nothing short of "dramatic" as Gerard notes, and even more so, given that a PAOC minister was leading the event with a team from a variety of denominational and educational backgrounds. She had become involved in an inter-church committee in the fall of 1967 chaired by Robert Birch of St. Margaret's Reformed Episcopal Church and comprised of Anglican, United Church, Lutheran, and Pentecostal lay and clergy representatives. They had met to plan and pray for Ranaghan's visit to the Greater Vancouver Area. At least two of the United Church members had already experienced baptism in the Spirit.[131]

The visit of Ranaghan and his Catholic Charismatic team apparently had the support of John Watts, PAOC pastor of Broadway Tabernacle who encouraged his people to support generously, pray fervently, and "work quietly" for the outreach. It is fair to say that at least in some initiatives such as this one, PAOC churches did not view themselves as collaborating with Charismatics for the cause of spreading renewal, but rather participating in a local trans-denominational initiative for evangelism much as they were accustomed to doing for evangelistic crusades. Nevertheless, the prayer for Vancouver was the well-known Charismatic prayer, "Come, Holy Spirit." Gerard's enthusiastic anticipation of what great things might be happening through the new wave of renewal regardless of denominational reticence, is evident in her report that the prayer was answered and "in such a way that it seemed also to promise better things to come." [132]

The event was unique by any standard as four hundred clergy and laypersons comprised of university and theological college professors, prominent ministers, priests and several nuns, gathered for a seminar dinner. Undoubtedly, curiosity was high at a time when the Charismatic Movement was still growing and, by then, with the widely known event of Dennis Bennett's experience of the Spirit to the south, it had become a subject of interest for most denominations. Gerard reported, "One visitor commented that the gathering which had strong representation from the liberal Protestant, Roman Catholic, and fundamentalist leaders was the most interesting he had ever seen." It is not so clear whether such response was an indication of the level of genuine support from those who had never seen similar interdenominational cooperation but were receptive to renewal or that of curious onlookers. She also noted that the series of meetings "had not been highly advertised in the Pentecostal Church" and added that "perhaps to many of them it sounded like something they already knew about." It is not impossible at that stage that the local PAOC pastor would have felt some pressure from his church board and /or district to exercise caution in enthusiastically advertising the event and risk venturing into uncharted territory. In any case, the multi-day event drew capacity audiences, two-thirds being people from the Anglican, Presbyterian, Baptist, Mennonite, and United Churches, with at least one hundred receiving the Spirit and twenty-five on the university campus.[133]

The argument so widely used at the time that all renewal must be firmly anchored in Biblical revelation is evident here as well. Gerard had to cope with her detractors, those who claimed that the "charismatic renewal is dead," or that there never really was one. But the major challenge seemed to be those who insisted, "when renewal comes, it will be through a return to Biblical theology." Mainline Protestant denominations were generally wary of groups that put too much emphasis on the subjectivity and prominence of a strong Spirit theology. Gerard seemed to have been aware of people who did not look with favor on any movement that "overtly calls attention to the need for dependence upon the Holy Spirit." Her response was tacit affirmation of both Spirit and scripture and that, in fact, what was happening in Vancouver was evidence that one was not taking place without the other: "Hundreds of people in the churches of Vancouver, including Catholics and Pentecostals, have been made aware that when the Holy Spirit quickens the believer, he is at the same time impelled to return to Scripture." In this way, Gerard firmly stood within the Charismatic perspective that an experience of the Spirit compels a person to delve into the Bible in order to be a more effective disciple. She also shared the same optimism for the future that any progress celebrated now anticipated "a much greater stirring by the Holy Spirit."[134]

Until recently, the PAOC had no clearly articulated national campus ministry strategy. Gerard's work at UBC and SFU was one of the few, if not the only, intentionally organized effort to bring a Pentecostal-Charismatic presence to the university environment. Another Pentecostal campus ministry in Canada had been initiated by the PAOC's sister organization, the Pentecostal Assemblies of Newfoundland (PAON) in 1959, in cooperation with the Assemblies of God (AG). This ministry still ongoing, known as Chi Alpha, became an annually chartered student society of the American AG campus ministries. In a sense, both initiatives became vehicles through which classical Pentecostal students became exposed to the Charismatic Movement. Gerard's important contribution to the spiritual development of university students on Canada's west coast was recognized and extended to the eastern extremities of the nation as she was invited by PAON leadership to address the students, the provincial executive, and a large local church.

The nature of a university with its academic and social freedom combined with the spiritual openness of students provided an ideal environment for the Charismatic Movement to easily impact classical Pentecostal students. Gerard wrote, "Today Christians and non-Christians alike are more open than they have ever been to the Jesus Revolution."[135] She believed that Pentecostal students could have high impact on a university campus because of their reliance on the power of the Spirit to give them direction. What Gerard was able to accomplish on the university campus would have been much more difficult at the local church level where defending Pentecostal doctrine likely would have been given greater priority. She argued poignantly: "... it must be born in mind that the 'brick-and-mortar' mentality (how many churches have you built?), "the denominational drive" (how many new members this year?) and the competitive, often schismatic spirit (my church against your church) that has pulled down so many spiritual endeavors has no part in our unique heritage."[136] Gerard was concerned that denominational or other structures had contributed to prejudice and robbed Pentecostals of their calling to communicate the gospel to everyone. When the Charismatic Movement first became evident, she was surprised to discover the scores of people from old-line denominational traditions who were very open to personal Christian faith but whom classical Pentecostals had stereotyped and effectively written off.[137] This she saw as applying to the university scene as well.

The same freedom characteristic of the time also allowed PAON students at Memorial University of Newfoundland (MUN) to experience the dynamics of the new renewal. Ripples from the Charismatic Movement reached Pentecostal students there in at least two direct ways. The first was the influence of renewal in the UCC that had emerged in the early 1970s largely as a reaction to the liberalization of that denomination brought on by the introduction of the New Curriculum in 1964, a Sunday School program with a liberal perspective on the Bible shaped by historical criticism.[138] Many old-line Methodists felt disenfranchised and were already open to a return to Wesleyan piety by the time of the spread of the Charismatic Movement. A handful of PAON students occasionally attended United Church renewal events and at least on one occasion in 1972, a UCC renewal minister, Mervyn Skey, was invited to speak and share his experience at the Chi Alpha group. The approach to Spirit baptism with its non-'waiting' and non-'seeking' method to reception was radically different from that to which classical Pentecostal students would have been accustomed. While it did not pull them directly into the new Charismatic approach, it ignited a general desire to experience the Holy Spirit at a deeper level leading to the emergence of several weekly prayer groups among the Pentecostal student population at which several Spirit baptisms took place. Special revival services conducted at one of the local churches, Elim Pentecostal Tabernacle, helped to bring all the strands together resulting in a genuine environment of renewal with many Pentecostal students receiving Spirit baptism.

The second avenue was through affiliation with the AG campus ministries. PAON Chi Alpha leaders at the time, through AG publications, became aware of an atmosphere of renewal on American college campuses. In the fall of 1974, the AG national student ministries director, Dave Gable, visited the MUN Chi Alpha group bringing with him some of the songs of the Charismatic Movement that had already become popular to the south. As much as this development is hardly directly traceable to the Charismatic Movement, the echo was clearly detectable in Gable's teaching approach and demeanor. Furthermore, although it was not immediately connected to the existing style of classical Pentecostal church life and worship, it had a far-reaching impact on the future direction of campus ministry and the worldview of the next PAON generation. Subsequently, it affected the PAOC, as many PAON young people became future minsters and laity across the nation due to the frequent out migration of Newfoundlanders to other provinces and territories of Canada and the ease of transfer of credentials from the PAON to the PAOC. Recognition of the Spirit's workings across traditional church boundaries would become more widespread, though few actual initiatives toward ecumenical understanding would ensue within either the PAOC or PAON. However, in the 21st century, campus missions have become a key initiative with the PAOC and Chi Alpha, with the PAON, continues to flourish with the same tone and appeal of the Charismatic Movement.

Meanwhile, at UBC and SFU, Gerard was not hesitant in celebrating the work of PAOC students and neo-Pentecostals as having common goals—the salvation of students and their experience of the Spirit.[139] She fearlessly developed relationships with people whom she met on those campuses who had no connection with the PAOC but who had shown interest in the Spirit or had identified themselves as being Pentecostal-Charismatic. She recalls one encounter in which she was introduced to a guest speaker, Norman Stevens, member of Parliament for New Westminster, England; when she told him she was Pentecostal, he had no idea what she meant. Gerard was surprised when his response was, "I think I'm Pentecostal, only I didn't know there were others like me."[140] Later that evening when she introduced him to a gathering of priests, nuns, and the Catholic archbishop, he noted that he had experienced a most remarkable day by discovering that he was Pentecostal and wanted to be put in touch with the movement in Britain.

Nonetheless, Gerard was far from reckless in her view of the operation of the *charismata*. In 1974, just six years following Ranaghan's visit to Vancouver she seems to have become slightly more guarded. She indicated her awareness that sometimes the charismatic gifts tend to be misused; prophecy, for example, must not be used as a replacement for ministries of church government, as a means of revealing and judging individual sin, or as isolated guidance from one person to another. She had full appreciation for prophetic utterances but believed that there exists an obligation to call a prophetic utterance into question, always submitting it humbly to Scripture and the consensus of the group.[141] While embracing the ongoing renewal, Gerard observed: "But I also see people getting off into what I consider to be rank fanaticism totally disengaged from the realities of the Christian life. We are always kept in a tension and that forces us to keep our balance." [142]

In the spirit of the times though, Gerard emphasized genuineness among Pentecostal-Charismatic people and gentleness in allowing space for prophetic utterances to occur albeit with imperfections and openness to correction. In some segments of Canadian Pentecostalism, operation of the *charismata* was rare and sometimes almost non-existent while there was at the same time strong emphasis on receiving the baptism of the Holy Spirit as part of the *ordu salutis* with the initial evidence of speaking in tongues. In some cases, it seems that the Charismatic Movement has resulted in greater understanding of the charismatic gifts and ease in their usage.

Other Charismatic-related events took place in the early 1970s that were planned by, or in which, the PAOC had direct involvement. One of the best known was Charisma'73. *The Pentecostal Testimony* reported in glowing terms on the "Charismatic revolution" sweeping student campuses: "The Charismatic revolution has spilled over onto college and university campuses. In many schools, charismatic groups are the fastest growing student organizations and in other places an increasing percentage of members of the older established Christian groups such as I.V.C.F. and Campus Crusade are reported to have received this Pentecostal experience."[143] The PAOC had become aware of the spread of the Movement as the result of a series of Charismatic student meetings in the Toronto area and in spite of any reservation regarding the renewal, it was attempting to capitalize on the momentum. The Charisma '73 event was spearheaded by the Stone Church (PAOC) and its pastor, Albert Vaters who, as noted earlier, frequented The Catacombs and by Ken Birch, PAOC national office representative, with the express purpose of "establishing a base of fellowship among students who share this experience."[144]

Still, it was a combined evangelistic thrust into the Toronto student culture and a Charismatic event that appears to have been designed to provide what the organizers deemed to be balanced teaching "concerning the operation of the Holy Spirit within the lives of individuals and groups."[145] In retrospect, the lineup of speakers was also very revealing for their Charismatic sympathies. One was David Argue, son of Robert Argue, a prominent PAOC pastor, executive member and grandson to A.H. Argue, one of the PAOC founders. As Director of Campus Ministries for the Nebraska District of the AG, David Argue reported on the rapid growth of the Charismatic group, Prayer and Praise, at the University of the Nebraska, extolling the renewal that was happening there where 100 to 300 students were meeting twice a week for an extended period of Bible study and prayer, with frequent singing and speaking in tongues.[146] The other was Geoffrey Shaw, a PAON pastor and executive secretary of its province-wide education system who had strong Charismatic leanings, he having been a close personal friend of Derek Prince and instrumental in having Prince invited to work as a PAOC missionary before the latter's emigration to the United States.[147]

It is not at all clear whether much follow-up was done to events such as Charisma'73 except that interest was shown in continuing further meetings regarding the charismatic dimension to Christian living. The common thread seems to have been that interest was piqued and spiritual hunger precipitated by efforts such as these to engage with the Charismatic climate prevalent at the time. Birch summarized it best by noting, "Others said that the door had been opened and they wanted to find out more."[148] Shaw expressed his own excitement about the event, reporting in the PAON's official publication, *Good Tidings,* that both students and faculty from three major university campuses and one college attended with there being "a manifestation of spiritual gifts, tongues, interpretation and prophecy."[149]

Yet, it seems that the major drawback of such initiatives was the common tendency among Pentecostals to try to gain ground in Charismatic circles by sponsoring events based in PAOC venues. The ambivalence toward the new renewal appears evident from the desire to participate in it but yet not to risk venturing into unknown territory. It was deemed essential to resist changes to the formalized structure and belief system of the PAOC where possibly loss of influence and control might be the result. There is some evidence that PAOC leaders and writers attempted to adopt the terminology, "charismatic" and "charisma" and to infuse them with classical Pentecostal meaning, leaving the impression perhaps that classical Pentecostals were the original Charismatics. The January 1970 issue of *The Pentecostal Testimony* carried a prayer proclamation resolution, the preamble of which read, "WHEREAS - It has enjoyed *the charismatic renewal in apostolic fashion,* and has contended for Pentecostal relevance in this present age, and..." (emphasis added).[150]

Long Term Consequences of Youth Involvement

Widespread tentativeness within the organization towards the Charismatic Movement likely would not have been commonly known among Charismatic youth who attended The Catacombs. In this regard, Douville perhaps overstates the case that the PAOC's hesitation to recognize the Charismatic Movement as a legitimate phenomenon resulted in Charismatics and Jesus People not automatically flocking to their churches. Such a hypothesis is difficult, if not impossible to prove. Though no known statistics are available, there are numerous stories of people who had either direct or indirect ties to the Charismatic Movement eventually ending up in PAOC churches. Admittedly the prevalence of such caution would not have been a positive factor in redirecting them even had they been so inclined. The core of David Mainse's argument regarding Pentecostal-Charismatic relations was precisely that such connections were unsustainable if Pentecostals continually criticized the church traditions of those they wished to attract. Regarding evangelism, he said, "You can't say nasty things about somebody's mother and expect to lead them to Christ."[151]

In any case, the PAOC grew phenomenally in the years 1970-1981. At the beginning of the decade, it had 743 churches, 1933 credentialed ministers, and 220,390 who claimed affiliation. By 1981, the number of churches had risen to 959 with 2580 credentialed minsters and 338,790 adherents[152] while other denominations experienced only modest growth or declined.[153] There is merit in Douville's observation that while Charismatic youth did not immediately stream into its churches in the 1970s, the phenomenal growth in the PAOC during those years, especially among youth can be attributed directly to the influence of the Jesus Movement. It was not so much due to an influx of new converts from the counterculture as through the impact of the Jesus People culture in a more general way upon church youth.

Yet, Douville does not take his argument far enough. It would be impossible to separate the culture created by the Jesus Movement from that of the Charismatic Movement. The period was characterized by a thorough-going renewalist ethos. Ripples from the intertwining of both in places like university and college campuses, special Charismatic events, and groups like The Catacombs resulted in the replication of similar spiritual environments in many PAOC contexts across the country. As he correctly notes: "the Jesus Movement gained in visibility throughout North America, teenagers in 'straight' evangelical churches began to identify as 'Jesus People,' and adopted the symbolic performances of the movement. And in Canada, because the Pentecostals shared a common theology and practice with the Jesus People, teenagers in the PAOC were quick to adopt this identity."[154] The "One Way" symbol[155] was everywhere in PAOC youth publications such as its AIM (Ambassadors in Mission) magazine which attempted to reflect the new youth culture and so to attract more youth to PAOC churches. The spiritual hunger and vitality of both movements, whether or not PAOC youth attached themselves to The Catacombs, infiltrated the Pentecostal youth scene with a new brand of appearance, dress and music style.

In spiritual awakenings, such as that of the 1960s to 1980s decades, the edges are fuzzy, cause-and-effect is exceedingly difficult to nail down and the wind of the Spirit keeps blowing indiscriminately. Denominational structures with their longevity and success become rigid and leadership can tend to lapse into a pattern of thinking that their world is ultimate renewal. Furthermore, leadership can also easily stifle fresh spontaneity either out of fear of excess, desire for influence or both.

A renewal phenomenon nevertheless is rarely without some positive impact as subsequent years often reveal significant individual contributions to the wider church. While it is difficult to measure, members of The Catacombs of many denominational roots eventually found their way into various evangelical and independent Charismatic-type groups. The effects trickled well beyond a traditional Anglican Church in the heart of Toronto.

Finally, the power of the arts, especially music and dance minus the trappings of technology that too often camouflage the absence of real musical acuity ought not to be underestimated in its ability to facilitate an environment where the Spirit and human beings can meet. The Watsons were musical artists connected to the creative arts community and their introduction of liturgical dance broke down walls between the old and the new, particularly with those who had seen art as unholy. They had an effortless demeanor, confident and flamboyant. They had the ability to draw people into worship while worshipping along with the participants too. Reflecting on the environment of the Catacombs after 40 years, Bramer fondly carries the memory of a corporate palpable presence of the Spirit in a most unusual life-changing time. Though not initiated by the PAOC, it was this wave of renewal that Pentecostalism was riding and on which it was being refreshed.

Ultimately, the spiritual outlook of youth of the PAOC boomer generation was conditioned if not transformed by a new environment of renewal. Like their parents, they were loyal to their history but rarely at the expense of stifling the winds of the Spirit. They carried with them the mantle of Charismatic-Jesus People style worship, discipleship-oriented preaching and teaching rather than revivalistic evangelism, and a less defined view of tongues as initial evidence of Spirit baptism. For many, this would all translate into a reduced classical Pentecostal climate and more of a combined charismatic-evangelical mood. In spite of the well-intentioned efforts of older Pentecostal leaders, the PAOC was forever changed.

Notes

1. "Memoirs of Jonathan Edwards," in *The Works of Jonathan Edwards*, ed. Edward Hickman (Edinburgh: Banner Of Truth Trust, 1974): 2:lii.

2. Quebedeaux, *New Charismatics*, 181-190.

3. Ibid., 134.

4. There was another group called the Catacombs in California associated with the Jesus Movement, a coffeehouse, opened in 1969 near the Space Needle built for the 1962 World's Fair. It is not clear whether there was any connection or whether this was mere coincidence. http://www.hollywoodfreepaper.org/portal.php?id=2 (accessed August 19, 2014).

5. Bruce Douville, "The Uncomfortable Pew: Christianity, the New Left, and the Hip Counterculture in Toronto, 1965-1975" (PhD diss., York University, August 2011): 446-447.

6. Merv and Merla Watson, *Toronto Catacombs: St. Paul's Cathedral, Toronto, 1974, Maranatha & Sunday Morning Communion* (Abbotsford, B.C.: Catacombs Productions Ltd., 1998): compact disc jacket information.

7. Merv and Merla Watson, in discussion with the author, Toronto, ON, August 23, 2012. See also David di Sabatino, "History of the Jesus Movement," http://streetlevelconsulting.ca/www.streetlevelconsulting.ca/newsArticlesStats/Jesus_Movement.htm (accessed August 14, 2014).

8. Ibid.

9. Robert Skinner, in discussion with the author, Cobourg, ON, September 8, 2014. Robert Skinner is a retired PAOC missionary, Toronto pastor, and former editor of *The Pentecostal Testimony*.

10. Merv and Merla Watson, discussion, August 23, 2012.

11. Ibid.

12. Merv and Merla Watson, discussion, August 23, 2012.

13. Ibid.

14. Bruce Douville, "The Uncomfortable Pew: Christianity, the New Left, and the Hip Counterculture in Toronto, 1965-1975," 444.

15. Peter Tasler, "'It Was Simple. I Just Gave My Heart To The Lord,'" *Weekend Magazine*, January 1, 1972 in Douville, "The Uncomfortable Pew," 445-446.
16. Ibid.
17. Ibid., 448.
18. Tom Harpur, "Fervent teenagers say: Isn't Jesus Wonderful?" *The Toronto Star* (Saturday, February 19, 1972): 85.
19. Douville, "The Uncomfortable Pew," 487.
20. Harpur, "Fervent teenagers," 85.
21. Ibid.
22. http://www.mervandmerla.com/home (accessed December 28, 2015)
23. Watsons, discussion, August 23, 2012.
24. http://www.mervandmerla.com/home (accessed December 28, 2015)
25. Watsons, discussion, August 23, 2012.
26. Paul Bramer, December 11, 2015.
27. Ibid.
28. Ibid.
29. Watsons, August 23, 2012.
30. Douville, "The Uncomfortable Pew," 451.
31. Ibid.
32. Merv and Merla Watson, *Toronto Catacombs,* compact disc jacket information.
33. Steve Sture, discussion with the author, Cobourg, ON, June 2, 2014.
34. Ibid.
35. Douville, "The Uncomfortable Pew," 452.
36. Watsons, discussion, August 23, 2012.
37. Steve Sture, discussion, June 2, 2014.
38. Ibid.
39. Ibid.
40. Ibid.
41. Watsons, discussion, August 23, 2012.
42. Ibid.
43. Ibid.
44. Ibid.
45. Douville, "The Uncomfortable Pew," 449.
46. Harpur, "Fervent teenagers."
47. Ibid.
48. Ibid.
49. James Craig, Telephone conversation, August 19, 2014. Craig, a former PAOC Bible College student and attendee of the Catacombs, is currently Archivist at the PAOC International Office, Mississauga, Ontario.
50. Merv and Merla Watson, *Toronto Catacombs,* compact disc jacket information.
51. Douville, "The Uncomfortable Pew," 450-451.
52. Watsons, discussion, August 23, 2012.
53. Douville, "The Uncomfortable Pew," 451.

54. Sture, discussion, June 2, 2014.
55. Ibid.
56. Ibid.
57. Ibid.
58. Ibid.
59. Douville, "The Uncomfortable Pew," 450.
60. *NIDPCM*, s.v. "Shepherding Movement."
61. Sture, discussion, June 2, 2014.
62. Ibid.
63. Watsons, discussion, August 23, 2012.
64. Ibid.
65. Douville, "The Uncomfortable Pew," 452.
66. Merv and Merla Watson, *Toronto Catacombs* (Abbotsford, B.C.: Catacombs Productions Ltd., 1998), compact disc.
67. Douville, "The Uncomfortable Pew," 471.
68. Ibid., 487.
69. Ibid.
70. Ken Birch, "Can We Learn From The Jesus People?" *The Pentecostal Testimony* (December 1971): 25.
71. Ibid.
72. Jesus People at the Olympics," *The Pentecostal Testimony* (November 1972): 14.
73. "Wilkerson Blasts Established Churches," *The Pentecostal Testimony* (July 1972): 24.
74. "C.P.C. President Assesses Year," *The Pentecostal Testimony* (September 1971): 11.
75. Douville, "The Uncomfortable Pew," 486. In my own conversation with Personal conversation with Albert Vaters, Cobourg, Ontario, August 8, 2014.
76. Watsons, discussion, August 23, 2012.
77. Albert Vaters, discussion with the author, Cobourg, ON, August 8, 2014.
78. Douville, "The Uncomfortable Pew," 488.
79. Harpur, "Fervent teenagers."
80. Ibid.
81. Ibid.
82. Douville, "The Uncomfortable Pew," 479.
83. Watsons, discussion, August 23, 2012.
84. Ibid.
85. Preston Shires, *Hippies of the Religious Right* (Waco, TX: Baylor University Press, 2007): 68.
86. Ibid., 64.
87. Ibid., 65.
88. Ibid., 198.
89. Douville, "The Uncomfortable Pew," 491.
90. Ibid.

91. Sture, discussion, June 2, 2014.
92. Ibid.
93. James Craig, telephone discussion, August 20, 2014.
94. Douville, "The Uncomfortable Pew," 499.
95. Shires, *Hippies of the Religious Right,* 38ff.
96. Douville, "The Uncomfortable Pew," 501.
97. Ibid.
98. Ibid., 501-502. *Toronto Star* religion editor, Tom Harper highlighted this phenomenon in Canada in his article "Jesus People blend into the 'straight' churches," May 11, 1974.
99. Robert Skinner, discussion with author, Cobourg, ON, September 8, 2014. Skinner, a cousin to Jim McAlister noted that McAlister's father, Hugh, was also believed to have been attracted to Beall's teachings.
100. Archibald Thackery, "The Latter Rain Movement of '48'" http://lrm1948.blogspot.ca/2013/05/mom-beall-and-bethesda.html (accessed September 8, 2014). See also http://lrm1948.blogspot.ca/2014/01/the-chronology-of-latter-rain-revival.html (accessed September 8, 2014).
101. Watsons, discussion, August 23, 2012.
102. Douville, "The Uncomfortable Pew," 504-505.
103. Watsons, discussion, August 23, 2012.
104. Promotion brochure for Shekinah's summer 1974 concert tour of England.
105. Ibid.
106. "Singers, dancers, musicians…Together they praise and worship God," *Markham Economist and Sun* (Wednesday, July 25, 1973): 7.
107. Ibid.
108. Ibid.
109. Ibid.
110. Ibid.
111. Ibid.
112. Watsons, discussion, August 23, 2012.
113. Tom Harpur, "Church puts Metro 'sect' on the street," *The Toronto Star* (Saturday, January 26, 1980): 1,12.
114. Ibid.,12.
115. Jim McAlister, *The Shepherd-Pastor* (1978) in Harpur, "Church puts Metro 'sect' on the street," 12.
116. S. David Moore, *The Shepherding Movement: Controversy and Charismatic Ecclesiology* Journal of Pentecostal Theology Supplement Series 27, eds. John Christopher Thomas, Rickie D. Moore, & Steven J. Land (New York, London: Continuum, 2003): 182-183
117. Ibid., 182.
118. McAlister, *The Shepherd-Pastor* in Harpur, "Church puts Metro 'sect' on the street," 12.
119. Harpur, "Church puts Metro 'sect' on the street."

120. Douville, "The Uncomfortable Pew," 506.
121. Ibid., 507.
122. James Craig, discussion, August 19, 2014.
123. Harpur, "Church puts Metro 'sect.'"
124. Douville, "The Uncomfortable Pew," 509.
125. Ibid.
126. Douville,"The Uncomfortable Pew," 498.
127. C. H. Stiller, "Pentecostal Chaplain Appointed at University" (*The Pentecostal Testimony*, January, 1964): 10.
128. Watsons, discussion, August 23, 2012.
129. Bernice Gerard, "Charismatic Renewal in Vancouver," *The Pentecostal Testimony* (April 1968): 8.
130. Ibid.
131. Ibid.
132. Ibid.
133. Ibid.
134. Ibid.
135. Bernice Gerard, " Pentecostal Evangelism on Campus," *World Pentecost*, issue 2 (1973): 22.
136. Ibid.
137. Ibid., 23.
138. Kevin Flatt, "The Loyal Opposition: A Brief History of the Renewal Movement in the United Church of Canada, 1966–2010," *Church and Faith Trends, A Publication of the Centre for Research on Canadian Evangelicalism: The Evangelical Fellowship of Canada* 3, issue 3 (December 2010): 3.
139. Bernice Gerard, "Pentecostal Evangelism on Campus," 23. In this respect, she points to the research of Luther Gerlach and Virginia Hines' in their landmark work, *People, Power, Change: Movements of Social Transformation* (Bobbs-Merrill Co., 1970). They articulate five factors crucial to the growth and spread of a movement like Pentecostalism, one of which is a commitment act or experience. See also Quebedeaux, *The New Charismatics*, 174.
140. Bernice Gerard, paper given at a Campus Evangelism Seminar, c1973.
141. Bernice Gerard, "Towards Maturity in the Ministry of the Gifts," *World Pentecost,* issue 4 (1974): 13-14.
142. Ibid., 14.
143. "People and Places," *The Pentecostal Testimony* (April, 1973): 13.
144. Ibid.
145. Ibid.
146. Ibid.
147. Correspondence between Derek Prince and the PAOC International Missions Department, PAOC Archives.
148. "People and Places," *The Pentecostal Testimony* (April, 1973): 13.
149. Geoffrey Shaw, "Charisma'73" *Good Tidings*, vol. 24, no. 2 (March-April, 1973): 29.

150. "Prayer Proclamation," *The Pentecostal Testimony* (January 1970): 31.
151. Mainse, discussion, August 8, 2012.
152. PAOC Statistics, 1919-1999, gathered by the PAOC Archives. (reviewed July 1, 2014).
153. Douville, "The Uncomfortable Pew," 489.
154. Ibid., 490.
155. Ibid., 491.

7

Shift in Theological Loci

Disappearance of Doctrinal Emphasis

The second half of the twentieth century saw growing tension within some classical Pentecostal groups between the foundational doctrines upon which they were built and the Charismatic and neo-Charismatic influences that were not historically rooted within those positions. Nevertheless, the various theological tenets that occupied center stage in the life and worship of Pentecostals have generally faded into the background over the past three or four decades. Within the PAOC, they continue to be articulated within the Statement of Fundamental and Essential Truths and to a degree in its other official publications, but they are barely distinguishable in worship, faith-based relationships, or sometimes even in preaching and teaching. As much as those doctrines were held and used to ardently defend against what was perceived as error or threat, they have largely failed to hold up within either ministerial training or church ministry. The result is that the older Pentecostal ethos has been somewhat re-defined so that PAOC churches, despite their early sectarian tendency, have taken on a combination of evangelical and Charismatic traits while ironically, some evangelical churches have begun to appear more "Pentecostal."

The loss of interest in doctrinal focus cannot be attributed only to the religious culture created by subsequent renewal movements. Other factors have surely been at play, not the least of which is the dizzying pace of technology that has helped to totally transform church worship as well as the increased attention and resources given to youth ministry where there is less resistance to, or even awareness of, change and abandonment of the old. In addition, popular culture continues to change with or without those movements. The postmodern view of life as intensely relational tends to dictate the structure of ministry. It might therefore be partially explainable that all of the traditional doctrinal positions have appeared to lose their relevance because of their individual orientations rather than their relationship implications.

In any case, the earlier approach within the denomination to being Pentecostal with a five-fold emphasis on personal salvation, sanctification, baptism in the

Holy Spirit with the initial evidence of speaking with other tongues, divine healing, and the expectation of the imminent return of Christ has declined noticeably from both teaching and practice. Evidence shows that the shift has been significant, at least as indicated by the frequency and characteristics of writings on these subjects in the denomination's official publication, *The Pentecostal Testimony* (now *Testimony*) beginning with the early 1960s. What is not clear is how closely later writings published in the magazine represented the views of leadership on the one hand and constituents on the other. Still, it appears from other evidence such as the structure of Bible college curriculums, where focus has been changed to appear to be more heavily weighted on the side of practical training, that local PAOC churches have been heading in the same direction.

The first edition of *The Pentecostal Testimony* in December 1920 was published by R.E. McAlister who heard about the Azusa Street revival and traveled to Los Angeles to investigate the happenings there.[1] Having experienced the Spirit while returning from Los Angeles to Ontario, he began preaching and pastoring churches. As the official organ of the denomination and despite many changes since its inception, the assumption is that it still would be a fair indicator of the theological direction of the PAOC. What is not always clear is whether the leadership has been pushing against doctrinal trends or simply reflecting reality at any given time. There have been occasions in recent years when one of those five doctrinal positions has suddenly shown up in an issue dedicated to that particular position as its theme. One might reasonably ask whether this represents an attempt to restore or at least to bring readers to an awareness that some recovery of emphasis needs to be made. At any rate, there has been a noticeable loss of the prominence of those five themes, particularly from the 1960s onward. They have continued to be written about, but in a more sporadic way over the succeeding decades.

None of this is to imply that what has transpired is inherently either positive or negative, only that a new reality has emerged. The implications for those who look back to the days when doctrinal substance and clarity were considered paramount are obvious from interviews with retired leaders, pastors, and laypeople. Doctrinal preaching and teaching especially on Spirit baptism and expectation of the return of the Christ appears to have become more incidental to the overall life of the church than deliberately foundational. In its place has arisen the embracing of voluminous teaching and writing on practical Christian living, leadership and mentorship issues. What this shift may mean for the future is a matter of conjecture but there likely is an emerging homogenization of classical Pentecostal, Charismatic, neo-Charismatic, and broader evangelical trajectories.

Five Classical Pentecostal Doctrines and the Charismatic Movement

The five main doctrinal positions held by the PAOC are those common to most other earlier Pentecostal groups. In regard to sanctification, early pioneers of the

PAOC such as A. H. Argue, A. G. Ward, and R. E. McAlister adopted the stance of W.H. Durham in Chicago, namely that no period of preparation was necessary after salvation to become sufficiently sanctified to receive the baptism of the Holy Spirit. Sanctification was seen as a logical consequence of salvation but not as a necessary intermediary step between salvation and Spirit baptism.[2] Furthermore, and similar to the development of Pentecostalism in the United States and elsewhere, it is clear that the early growth of Pentecostalism in this country also arose out of a vibrant proclamation of the gospel driven by the experience of Spirit baptism with speaking in tongues as initial evidence and as an enduement of power for evangelizing the world in anticipation of the soon return of Christ. Canadian PAOC historian, Gordon F. Atter, argued this point firmly:

> [It] has its roots deep in the GREAT COMMISSION... Its very nature is MISSIONARY... The baptism of the Holy Ghost is given primarily as an enduement of power for service in the worldwide propagation of the gospel...It has ever been so, and it most certainly is the case in the PENTECOSTAL REVIVAL OF THIS CENTURY.[3]

Likewise, its inheritance of divine healing as a doctrinal tenet reaches back into its Holiness origins with all their intertwining complexity. Kimberly Ervin Alexander argues that the healing movement is anchored firmly in the Wesleyan tradition but was informed by other streams of thought and experience such as Phoebe Palmer's 'shorter way" and the perfectionistic revivalism of Charles Finney.[4] Finally, the PAOC adopted from the outset a more pessimistic view of the world and its involvement in it, borrowing a premillennial dispensationalist approach to eschatology, though the term 'dispensational' rarely appears. In sum, it inherited from its Holiness-Pentecostal roots all five foci that came together at the Azusa revival. A.W. Orwig, who attended some of the meetings and later became an Assemblies of God minister, recalled the themes of Pentecostal preaching at the revival: "[There was] the teaching that the baptism in the Spirit was upon the sanctified, evidenced by speaking in tongues... as on the day of Pentecost.... The subject or doctrine of divine healing received much attention.... Likewise was the doctrine of the pre-millennial coming of Christ ardently promulgated."[5] It was these fundamental theological viewpoints that slowly began to disappear from view even though attempts were made to defend them from time to time.

Although the PAOC does not hold a monopoly on Pentecostalism in Canada, it is by far the largest classical Pentecostal denomination, originating along with a few other Pentecostal organizations in the early twentieth century revivals.[6] The Azusa Street events and the Toronto Hebden Mission are the two main reference points for PAOC history and the gates to the trail reaching back to the holiness impulse of the nineteenth century. The Methodist-Wesleyan tradition provided its transformational and experiential focus, but its theology was shaped by the modernist tendency to organize and rationalize its beliefs into a tidy system.

Nevertheless, defending long-held doctrinal positions has not proven easy against the emergence of a postmodern climate and the rise of later renewal movements such as The New Order of the Latter Rain, the Charismatic Movement, and neo-Charismatic phenomena where there were obvious differences in perspective. In particular, the stress on miracles, signs and wonders became an attraction for many PAOC people who sensed that they were not seeing enough of such phenomena, a reality that tended to put leadership on the defensive in an effort to avoid extremism. In the case of the later two renewals, a more flexible view of Spirit baptism and the far-reaching impact of innovative music and worship helped to create more generic renewal churches than identifiably classical Pentecostal ones. While little conscious attempt appears to have been made to borrow motifs and ambiance from the Charismatic Movement, in most cases, it seemed best to do so rather than cling to the old.

Traditional evangelistic invitations for conversion still continue in many PAOC churches but seemingly with diminished emphasis on earlier soteriological themes such as atonement and the need for repentance. Spirit baptism with stress on tongues as initial evidence has been largely abandoned especially in more urban churches while remaining surprisingly more common at camps and youth conventions. Attention given to divine healing continues to be substantial though writing and teaching on the subject seems to be minimal. Focus on the premillennial rapture doctrine is arguably less than on any of the other positions considered essential. Sanctification defined in progressive terms has long ago been transformed from concerns for standards of outward holiness to inner holiness and more recently, it seems, toward social holiness understood as engaging with society in addressing justice and poverty issues.

Salvation Through Christ's Atonement

It is not uncommon to hear the sentiment expressed that there is little emphasis anymore on the atoning work of Christ, including the soteriological language of the "cross" and the "blood." What this appears to suggest is that soteriological themes are no longer heard in preaching and teaching; furthermore, it seems that contemporary worship does not replace those themes that were present in traditional hymnody. Former PAON General Superintendent (1980-1996), Roy D. King notes that such focus is sparse at best. Preaching has been condensed so that biblical exposition of repentance and salvation has been omitted in favor of "how to" sermons calling for commitment rather than conversion. Worship (in that context usually defined as singing) has little doctrinal content and has been reduced to "singing to a God who is generalized."[7] He laments the minimal emphasis on Christology as well and argues that early Pentecostals lived with the Bible in one hand and a hymnal in the other indicating that their theology was both spoken and sung.[8] Likewise, Robert Taitinger, a former general superintendent of the PAOC, sees a dramatic decline in doctrinal preaching as it relates to the identification of one's faith position. He continues in his description of this decline: "[There are] more relational type messages...more 'teaching style' preaching and less evangelistic-salvation thrust messages geared to freedom from guilt—remorse or conviction of sin and shortcomings [with] little need for self-examination or repentance."[9]

Interestingly, one lay person observes that the "central theme of the early church's teaching was repentance" which he argues has almost completely disappeared in favor of the creation of a positive atmosphere of faith, thus downplaying the importance of a changed lifestyle.[10] While few if any former leaders would charge the arrival of the Charismatic Movement as being the root cause of such change, they almost invariably conclude that it did not help their evangelistic cause based on the call for repentance and radical life change. In truth, it was the general lack of emphasis on this theme that bewildered many PAOC adherents when they heard about individuals in other denominations speaking in tongues without any apparent evidence of 'getting saved.'

In the early 1960s, *The Pentecostal Testimony* was carrying articles that explicitly affirmed the connection of the cross of Christ with its effect upon humanity. E. A. Francis, PAOC Bible College teacher and missionary, wrote: "There is no obtaining of peace with God, no coming into His holy presence, no knowledge of sins forgiven, save by the way of the Cross, the place of Jesus' vicarious sacrifice.... The Cross of Christ, the greatest victory ever wrought, where Jesus wrung the victory of the grave from Satan's hand and set free all who will believe!"[11]

This trend continued throughout the decade with writings that elevated the cross as the pivotal tenet of the Christian faith. It is noteworthy that such a focus was occurring throughout the year and not just for the issue published for Passion Week. This crucicentric consciousness is evident even in the kinds of books reviewed for the publication.[12]

Addresses given at Bible College graduations at that time were theologically focused rather than practically relevant to pastoral and leadership concerns. One such address in July 1962 talked about salvation as deliverance from sin's power and stated that "Jesus transferred the burden of guilt from men to Himself and bore the whole penalty for that guilt" and that in the act of crucifixion, the blood that was shed was "for the remission of sin. This was death in our place. This was substitution."[13] In 1963, at another graduation, the speaker referred explicitly to the cross again as "the symbol of our purification, our sanctification, and our righteousness, for the blood of Christ spilt there secured our pardon."[14] The same motif making the christological connection between Christ as the God-man and the soteriological significance of the shedding of His blood through death on the cross generally continued throughout the decade.

There appears to have been a need during those years to demonstrate the roots within and continuing relationship with the soteriology heritage of the Reformation. Several issues of the publication either examined and reaffirmed the theology of the Reformers or directly reprinted their writings. The April 1964 issue reprinted John Calvin's "Divine Absolution for All Sins" in which Calvin states, "Let us understand the necessity of the redeemer, and that by the price of his blood we are reconciled to God the Father and have free access to Him by prayer."[15] The monthly magazine also commemorated Reformation Sunday, October 25, 1964 by printing an article on the life and contribution of Erasmus, a year later on John Hus, and still the next year on John Knox.[16] However, as the decade of the 1970s approached, there was a decline in focus on Christ's atonement. From February 1964 to November 1970, only one article on the cross and the atonement appeared in the magazine. This was a personal testimony acclaiming Christ as the author's substitute for his sin.

A shift took place toward the meaning, simplicity, certainty and urgency of salvation that continued well into the 1980s. Language changed to that of definitions and scriptural evidences for the new birth: "The new birth is not by reforming yourself... It is on the inside... The new birth is a mystery...by which a hell-deserving sinner receives Jesus Christ, becomes a child of God and begins a new life."[17] The substance of these articles was reflective of the rapidly growing "born again" movement at the time. Wayne Dawes, a former PAOC pastor and academic, spoke of "born again" becoming such a popular term as to have begun to lose its meaning. He questioned, "With all of this interest in this popular religious experience, one wonders why there has not been an appreciable influence on morals and ethics."[18] This focus continued into the mid-1980s when an article appeared decrying the loose usage of the term, arguing "fuzzy thinking has come to characterize the term 'born again,'"[19] after which new birth terminology disappeared completely as a subject of reflection in *The Pentecostal Testimony*.

From the mid-1980s to mid-1990s, there appears nevertheless to have been a new attempt to recover soteriological language as a pillar of PAOC faith. As part of a series of articles focusing on the Statement of Fundamental and Essential Truths, Miller referred to justification by faith, defining it as "a judicial act of God on the believer's behalf solely on the merits of Christ" and rooting it not only in the biblical text but also in the Reformation and the history of Pentecostalism. Miller argued that because the movement has its roots in the Holiness and Wesleyan traditions, the doctrine became one of its cardinal tenets from the very beginning.[20] He further proposes that as early as 1906 when Seymour first published his periodical magazine on the new movement, he included a statement of faith that defined justification by faith in orthodox Protestant terms: "Justification is the act of God's free grace by which we receive remission of sins." (Acts 10.42-43; Romans 3.25).[21]

Other articles with an intentionally apologetic tone appeared in the denomination's publication such as "The Stripes of Jesus" referring to Calvary as "our base of operation against every ill which beleaguers mankind,"[22] and "Is the Blood of Christ an Offense?"[23] Further reflections came in quick succession such as "The Long Arm of God" in which "Christ's death on the cross, with the shedding of His blood" is seen as making it "possible for man to reach up in faith, taking hold of God's long arm of grace."[24] Other articles continued the theme: "The Meaning and Importance of the Blood of Jesus"[25] and "The Cleansing of the Conscience through the Blood of Jesus."[26] From 1994 to 2001, there is no further evidence of attention given to the substitutionary work of Christ on the cross and its implications for salvation. Former General Superintendent William D. Morrow, wrote a short editorial item in November 2001 in which he reflected on the grace of God, referring to the believer's justification "by his grace through the redemption that is in Christ Jesus."²⁷ Following this, the thrust shifts largely toward missions, church planting, and other practical concerns.

Caution needs to be exercised in any attempt to draw firm lines between this change and any emphases or influences of the Charismatic Movement that supposedly caused it. Notwithstanding, the Charismatic Movement clearly appears to have prompted the PAOC to a re-articulation of its core doctrines, an attempt that in the end, does not seem to have been altogether successful. While not often explicitly stated, it was a period when there was obvious concern that the core positions of the denomination were slowly slipping into the background. Perceived deficiencies and aberrations in a new renewal movement tended to provoke efforts to make up for them through meetings, conferences and publications. Just as PAOC constituents were convinced of the necessity of individual conversion, so they were also persuaded of the need for personal holiness.

Sanctification

The perceived lack of preaching on the cross, salvation, and repentance has led to the making of an immediate connection with a lack of concern about living out what is believed in a life of purity of heart and action. It is observed that the shift is toward letting God meet personal needs and, further, that the common allegation of legalism within the earlier years of the PAOC has seen a pendulum swing toward a total embracing of popular culture.²⁸ Emphasis is no longer seen to be on conversion and repentance, but rather on commitment and decisions about life and God that one makes for oneself, thus resulting in a substantial decline in the stress on holiness. King observes that the next generation of Pentecostals looks back on what was preached as holiness and calls it legalism and, as a result, this generation has lost sensitivity to God and to a personal relationship with God. The earlier approach stressed the believer keeping his/her conscience sensitive to the Spirit.²⁹ George Power, a retired PAOC pastor and church pioneer, laments the lack of preaching against sin and recalls that during the 1960s, he believes that he was called to do that very thing, not just to preach the love of God in an attempt to please everyone. He insists that ethical issues such as co-habitation and abortion have now been ignored.³⁰ Likewise, Taitinger notes that there is "not a lot of strong preaching on holiness of lifestyle. Much preaching stresses God's love, forgiveness, grace, mercy" and lacks the elements of "sin-consciousness and eventual judgment day reality."³¹ He believes that a balance is necessary between the fear of God and the love of God as it relates to the outworking of an individual's faith.³²

Reflections on holiness continued throughout the years under consideration but drastically changed their shape over time. A July 1965 article in *The Pentecostal Testimony* asked the question as to what holiness is and proceeded to itemize specifics such as "the 'beat' of the *modern music* (so-called)" being of "satanic origin," alcohol, narcotics, and nicotine being harmful to the human body and "filthy literature...flooding our news stands across the land."[33] Another article in the same issue asked, "What's wrong with a good movie? Where do we draw the line?"[34] Believing that there was such a serious drift away from biblical morality in the mid-1960s, the PAOC prepared an official statement publishing it in the magazine in May 1966. The statement opened with the following resolution:

> Whereas there is every evidence of a serious and continued drift from the basic standards of righteousness as taught in the Bible, and whereas the trend is most clearly evident in the moral breakdown within our present society, and whereas this attitude has clearly affected the thinking of some Christians, therefore we, the Pentecostal Assemblies of Canada, go on record as publicly reaffirming our faith in the teaching of the Bible on these matters. [35]

The position taken at that point stressed the teaching of the Bible in matters of sex, marriage and morals, particularly in view of the "New Morality" which the PAOC saw as encouraging "uninhibited sexual expression." This statement continued, "We cannot accept the modern view of society that divorce should be granted for such reasons as cruelty, incompatibility, non-support, and drunkenness."[36] The fear of growing secularism was precipitating responses that essentially communicated the message that adopting such a view of divorce, for example, would be capitulating to the moral decline of the culture.

The same sentiments continued to be expressed into the 1970s with arguments made that "society is reaping today the harvest of permissiveness, compromise and apathy. So far as morals are concerned there are many who no longer believe that there is any absolute right or wrong."[37] Views were expressed regarding responsible choices and the profiling of celebrities who were seen as turning the Gospel into entertainment. As a result, a resolution was adopted by the PAOC in March 1971: "RESOLVED that we reaffirm our stand against theatre attendance by Pentecostal Christians, especially in view of the attempts being made to entice Christians to attend the movie version of 'the Cross and the Switchblade' which is being released in theatres only, and other movies advertised as 'good' and 'responsible' entertainment."[38] One exception was a lone article by Atter in which he called for a return to true biblical holiness: "I do not mean to return to old-fashioned dress, conversation and deed, but rather to maintain godliness in thought, word, and deed."[39] However, the trend generally continued late into the decade when attention turned toward a more comprehensive view of personal holiness. In the October 1977 issue, one writer pointed out that "the real truth about holiness has nothing to do with the proverbial list of do's and don'ts.... When we seek to legalize personal conduct with rules and regulations, there is a danger of catastrophic failure and discouragement and eventually 'giving up trying to be a Christian.'"[40] A noticeable change of direction was taking place that tended to prefer abandoning focus on traditional taboos in order not to appear as not being too conservative on many social issues, especially within the PAOC's official publication with its wide national audience.

In a 1987 study of the denomination's pastors, Carl F. Verge, a former Bible college president, educator, and missionary, found that there were noticeable trends developing among more highly educated pastors: "They are not as dogmatically opposed to social drinking, smoking, movie attendance, or the fact that Sunday should be strictly observed. They are more active than other clergy in attending movies and drinking alcoholic beverages."[41] Verge concluded that the PAOC had a dilemma, namely, that "if it accommodates a liberal shift in values, members will separate from it and form groups to bring it back on track. On the other hand, if it does not allow change, other members will separate to find the freedom to express these changes."[42] Although no formalized studies have been made to this point to measure the projections of this study, there has been considerable shifting of classical Pentecostal people to and from less organized Charismatic-type groups and other evangelical churches with a Charismatic flavor.

Holiness soon begins to be interpreted in terms of Christlikeness as an ongoing process.[43] As part of a series on the Statement of Fundamental and Essential Truths, Roy Upton, PAOC missionary in Kenya at the time, referred to real holiness as being of the heart: "True holiness can only be achieved when Christ flows through the inner life by the power of the Holy Spirit. There can be no sanctification without *The Sanctifier*."[44] Although, as far as writers for *The Pentecostal Testimony* were concerned, holiness was still viewed as a Pentecostal distinctive, there developed a propensity to dwell on the larger principles of holiness while stressing that sin was still sin.[45] The attempt to take the more moderate approach to holiness is evident in an essay by Richard L. Dresselhaus, an Assemblies of God pastor, reprinted in *The Pentecostal Testimony*, July 1989 where he called for balance between the extremes of legalism and antinomianism.[46]

Throughout the 1990s, the threat of New Age philosophies and the decline in sexual morality within the larger society elicited writings with such titles as "Living Clean in an Unclean World" and "No, No! Don't Go to the Show," the latter in particular encouraging the reader not to compromise convictions despite the increasing prominence of sexual content in the media.[47] Ronald Kydd argued that although Pentecostals had enriched the Church by bringing back the idea that people could experience God, he believed that "we have defined spirituality in terms of experiences, and it has hurt us" and called for a *"spirituality of lifestyle, not of crisis"* (his emphasis).[48] Kydd seems to have come closest to linking a loss of holiness focus within PAOC life to an overemphasis on a Charismatic experience. The tenor of the time was one of recovering a greater experience of the Spirit, a message that the Charismatic Movement was projecting as being the primary concern, and thus explains Kydd's call for a spirituality of personal lifestyle.

The focus on holiness continued at least until the end of the century with the pervading question being that since the old legalism had disappeared, had Pentecostals gone too far the other way? Homer Cantelon, former district superintendent, captured the developing angst over what constituted holiness, arguing:

> ...we have...criticized the outward trappings of holiness adhered to by more legalistic groups. Sombre dress, outdated hairstyles and other "touch not, handle not" rules of this circumscribed life style, scorned by us, has freed us to adorn ourselves

pretty much as we choose. This freedom is carried into practically all aspects of our life. Aware of the restrictions which hold others so securely, and being inwardly grateful for our detachment from this concept of Christian living, what standards, scripturally based, are we to follow?[49]

The question increasingly seemed to become not so much whether holiness should be stressed, but what it meant. By 1995, Rick Hiebert, the editor was arguing that because of the PAOC's traditional stance on Hollywood shows, the denomination had no platform from which to speak and so advocated the support of believers involved in the arts[50]—a difference in approach from previous decades that could not be more apparent. There continued to be concern about the reality of sin and the need for holiness to be viewed primarily as a state of the heart.

As late as 2001, an entire issue was devoted to the subject. A couple of articles took a more traditional view but one writer Tom Morrow, pastor of a more contemporary church in Calgary, Alberta, asserted that holiness is a question of perspective on Scripture. He called for the reader to understand that this is the post-modern world and that instead of "making truth hard edged and absolute in nature, we need to be present and confident in the truth of God's Word within us…our first response should be an active demonstration of grace and an understanding of the presuppositional underpinnings."[51] Morris's perspective was a radical departure from previously held understandings of holiness and represented a new generation that tended to think from a postmodern worldview.

Baptism in the Spirit and Initial Evidence

There is an acute sense among some middle-aged to older adults within the PAOC that Spirit baptism with the accompanying initial evidence of speaking in other tongues has all but disappeared from practice. This is attributed to a general lack of certainty among pastoral leadership regarding their own position on this defining Pentecostal distinctive resulting in a lack of clear verbalization of it within preaching and publication. Although there is perceived to be somewhat less decline in the practice of speaking in tongues, its connection with the baptism in the Spirit as initial evidence is now largely avoided. Verge concluded in his study of PAOC pastors, "They are less likely to insist that one is not filled with the Spirit unless one has spoken with tongues."[52] The assertion is also made that there are so few Spirit baptisms simply because it is not preached and taught to the extent that it once was and should continue to be. King adds with concern that the older generation is not disgruntled, just mourning the loss of what they understood to be the substance of being Pentecostal.[53] While it is unclear whether this development is directly attributable to the influence of the Charismatic Movement, the parallel is striking. Over time, there has been an undeniable retreat in arguing for tongues as initial evidence but not so much in the validity of glossolalia itself as a 'prayer language' as well as a charism.

A former professor at Eastern Pentecostal Bible College (now Master's College and Seminary), Scott Bullerwell observes that Spirit-baptism has taken a secondary place in the denomination. He argues that it is now a "hard sell" and believes that the Holy Spirit is viewed as playing a greater role in praise and worship than in the preaching of the Word.[54] Taitinger concurs that there is less emphasis on the baptism of the Holy Spirit with the initial evidence of speaking with tongues but adds that the prayer room, the altar call, and the laying on of hands for the infilling of the Spirit seems to have declined as well. He notes, "This ministry seems to be left more and more to the 'camp meeting' where young people get revived, filled, taught and encouraged in the Pentecostal experience that was once practiced in the local assembly."[55]

Baptism in the Spirit with the initial evidence of tongues occupied the minds of PAOC leadership throughout the 1960s. No less than one hundred articles appeared in *The Pentecostal Testimony* over that period focusing on such topics as celebrating Pentecost, defining Holy Spirit baptism, experiencing the power of Pentecost, and seeking to defend it by attempting to make a direct link with the life of the apostolic church. It attempted to reinforce its position by adding other non-Pentecostal voices. In April 1962, it reprinted an article by Alan Redpath, pastor of Moody Memorial Church titled, "The Dynamics of Apostolic Christianity" in which Redpath highlighted the life-transforming impact of the experience of the Holy Spirit but does not mention Holy Spirit baptism as such nor speaking in tongues. The purpose here seems to have been to try to reinforce the historical connection with apostolic Christianity while leaving arguments for initial evidence to other writers. Most writers simply discussed the importance of receiving the baptism in the Spirit itself and its trans-generational and global implications. Much of the content at the time was borrowed from British Pentecostals, particularly the writings of Donald Gee. Even the magazine's book review section was significantly weighted in the direction of pneumatology.[56]

Following news of the outbreak of neo-Pentecostalism in the traditional churches, the PAOC began to recognize the outpouring of the Spirit among those outside its ranks and generally applauded it. In June 1962, *The Pentecostal Testimony* published an address given at the Pentecostal Fellowship of North America Convention (PFNA), Moody Church, Chicago 1961, relating the story of California Episcopalians receiving the Pentecostal baptism. The following year it ran a two-part series on glossolalia by David du Plessis. In the latter case, though, the second of the two-part series was introduced with a disclaimer stating that the views expressed by the writer did not reflect the official position of the PAOC in every particular.[57] Two years later, it published a full page copy of the *Toronto Daily Star*, March 7, 1964 edition announcing that Rev. Dennis Bennett, an Anglican priest, had "spoken in tongues" sending shock waves through Anglicanism within the United States and Canada.[58] There was an obvious desire for Pentecostals, at least within the PAOC, to see themselves as part of a much bigger work of the Spirit and that any echoes of their own theology in other traditions validated their own. "What the Archbishop said about The Holy Spirit," a sermon preached by F.D. Coggan, Anglican Archbishop of York appeared in the June 1966 issue in which Coggan posed the questions, "Is it possible that Pentecostals have gifts of the Spirit which we have not? Do we need to heed the reminder of Bishop Stephen Neill that 'not infrequently true religious life is to be found in the sects when it has died in the orthodox; the nonconformists have been from time to time the salvation of the church?'"[59] In 1967, *The Pentecostal Testimony* was continuing to reprint news of the spread of the Charismatic Movement within the broader Christian world. In October of that year, it reprinted a news item from the Religion section of TIME describing the move of the Holy Spirit in Brazil. The following year, it published an evaluation of the Pentecostal movement by Kilian McDonnell, an internationally known Roman Catholic Charismatic scholar, where he noted that glossolalia was decreasing as Pentecostalism grew, making the "question of tongues essentially peripheral" while the deep interior work of the Spirit had become central.[60] The intention seemed to be to affirm the global spread of renewal but with a growing tinge of self-protective introspection. As time passed, however, the PAOC began to more overtly defend itself against what it deemed to be aberrant doctrinal positions that had developed within the Charismatic Movement.

Reflections on the heritage of the Pentecostal movement and an on-going re-articulation of what Pentecostals believed about the Holy Spirit had begun to appear in the early 1960s as well.[61] R. J. White, a PAOC credential-holder, presented a paper called "Pentecost Today and Ecumenicity," at a minister's institute in Calgary, Alberta, January 16, 1963, in which he sought to show that Pentecost was not just another religious institution. He argued, "It is not the perpetuation of Pentecost as a denomination that interests us particularly. History has shown us too many denominations that originated in revival fires and became, in a few generations, stereotyped, static, and sterile."[62] The doctrine of the work and ministry of the Spirit was so central in the thinking of the denomination at the time that even a Christmas issue of *The Pentecostal Testimony* would tend to be pneumatologically focused.[63] It tended to view Christology in direct relationship to the work of the Spirit as evidenced by one view in which the suddenness of the first and second advents was compared with the suddenness of the "Holy Ghost advent,"[64] thus apparently attempting to anchor the Spirit's action within a christological center.

In 1969, the PAOC reached its jubilee year and emphasized, throughout the ensuing months, its heritage and the danger of losing the simplicity of its humble beginnings. One intriguing item attempted to articulate the lessons that could be learned from the ancient charismatic phenomenon of Montanism. Unless there was awareness and alertness, it would be natural for "charismatic leadership" to give place to "bureaucratic institutionalism" which Montanism resisted. Furthermore, the article warned of the necessity to transmit the experience of Pentecost rather than merely trying to preserve the continuity of any system. Affirmation of the wider moving of the Spirit was given by arguing that "should He tarry, and Pentecostalism pass into history, we can rest assured that future generations will continue to enjoy the waves of Holy Ghost revival."[65] These kinds of apparent contradictions in sentiments indicate the ambivalence that both PAOC leadership and constituents experienced during that era.

By the time of the denomination's fiftieth anniversary, however, awareness had grown that the landscape had changed significantly from its early beginnings. Whereas being identified as Pentecostal had been a matter of personal conviction, one that often had incurred hostility and misunderstanding from mainline denominations, association had now become more routinized, resulting in passing on to the next generation a sense of duty rather than an internalized individual need to belong. Many young people attending church with their parents had experienced conversion and the Spirit-baptism, while others were merely being compelled by their parents to be a part of church life. At this juncture, there was also a sense that the PAOC had lost its original fervor and that a fresh outpouring was needed.[66] Upon the marking of its eightieth year in 1987, the question was asked, "Have we reached a plateau where we can rest at ease? There are beautiful churches, colleges and benevolent institutions.... The best of facilities and electronic media cannot bring revival apart from God, the Holy Spirit."[67] As much as this was admitted, there was never any indication, explicit or implied, that the Charismatic Movement ought to be embraced in whole or in part. Conversely, it appears that the hope was for a resurgence of the earlier Pentecostal revivals at the beginning of the century.

From the 1970s to the end of the century, the actual coverage given to the doctrine of baptism in the Spirit became half of what it had been in the 1960s. Nevertheless, some of the traditional topics continued to be subjects of reflection such as the question of tongues, the true purpose of Spirit baptism as power for witness, and how to receive the Spirit. Amaro Rodriguez, a former Roman Catholic priest, wrote in August 1970 that the move of the Spirit among Catholics had created an appropriate environment for dialogue but also implied that Pentecostals have the task of "taking the Bread of Life and the real testimony of our lives..." to them rather than waiting for Catholics to join Pentecostals.[68] Thomas F. Zimmerman, then General Superintendent of the Assemblies of God, in a sermon delivered August 24, 1972 and reprinted in *The Pentecostal Testimony*, spoke of the "current outpouring of the Holy Spirit in the historic churches" so making it "possible for most Spirit-filled believers to remain in their own churches."[69] By 1973, it was clear that the influence of renewal among Roman Catholics had expanded remarkably with the movement having spread all over the United States from its beginnings at Duquesne and Notre Dame Universities and even to Europe and Asia.[70]

In the mid to late 1970s, a clearly articulated fear of actually losing the classical Pentecostal identity had begun to set in. There was concern that

> some people lack sound conviction concerning Pentecostal doctrine. Our longstanding position that speaking in tongues is the initial evidence of the incoming and fullness of the Holy Spirit is at least questioned by others if not considered unimportant.... The tendency to generalize and to gravitate to purely an evangelical or a comfortable community-oriented doctrinal position is ultimately to fail in the specific message that God has entrusted to us.... If we do not have identity here, we have little reason to exist within the framework of the Fellowship of the Pentecostal Assemblies of Canada.[71]

In attempting to maintain the doctrine of speaking with tongues as the "initial physical sign" of baptism in the Spirit, the fact that some Pentecostals would seem to "downgrade the value of tongues in the name of a 'baptism of love'" was considered to be an unfortunate development. To compromise the truth including that of tongues as the initial physical evidence of having received the Holy Spirit was seen as serious business.[72] In the final analysis, the PAOC found itself in a battle not so much to defend the theology of Spirit baptism, as much as the initial evidence as its pivotal doctrinal distinctive.

Whereas the PAOC seemed to applaud the new wave of the Spirit among Roman Catholics and Protestant denominations in the 1970s, this response began to change as the difference between the Charismatic view of the work of the Spirit and the classical Pentecostal perspective became clearer. Deliberate efforts continued to be made to defend the distinctive doctrinal position of speaking in tongues as the initial evidence. Keith R. Balkwell, a PAOC pastor and child evangelist, expressed the commonly held concern: "There are a number of well-known evangelists who declare publicly that you don't have to speak in tongues to prove that you have received the baptism.... To heighten this dilemma, many 'charismatics' claim to be filled with the Spirit and openly announce that they have never spoken in tongues."[73] The situation spurred on a new attempt to defend the heritage of the PAOC and its doctrine of Spirit-baptism based on the Acts instances connecting the infilling of the Spirit with glossolalia.[74]

Writing just after the 13th Pentecostal World Conference in Nairobi, Kenya in 1982, R. J. White expressed delight that Baptists, Roman Catholics and others had spoken in tongues and claimed the experience of the baptism in the Holy Spirit. Still he expressed concern that with the growth of the Charismatic Movement in historic churches many people who claimed to have received the Spirit also claimed not to have spoken in tongues. The question, therefore, would be whether the traditional stance of Pentecostals was valid and whether the baptism in the Spirit was a post-conversion experience. White continued, "Pentecostals are right to insist upon the evidence of tongues, even if this insistence results in their separation at this point from the main stream of Evangelicalism."[75] Another contributor, Teresa Ter Hoek wrote, "The fact is that we are beginning to have even more unwholesome elements infiltrating our Pentecostal fellowship. The merchandising of miracles, which is big business today, prophecy performances that are spreading..."[76] Alarm within PAOC circles regarding the new view of Spirit baptism was beginning to manifest itself along with a determination to resist extremism and deviation from the accepted norms regarding the operation of miracles, prophecy, and signs and wonders.

The nervous relationship between the Charismatic Movement and the PAOC was expressed nowhere more succinctly than by PAOC historian Thomas Miller who wrote, "The charismatic movement has been undergoing a process of continual change and development, while the Pentecostal movement has been assessing this process and trying to determine how to react to it."[77] He also highlighted the different terminology used by Charismatics such as "renewal" versus "revival," the claim that any gift of the Spirit can be considered evidence of reception of the Spirit rather than just speaking in tongues, and the continuance of Roman Catholic Charismatics to live in scriptural error.[78] Miller seemed to have been as perplexed as anyone in the PAOC, torn between loyalty to the older Pentecostal way and affirmation of the new work of the Spirit:

> The charismatic movement of the past 20 years has served to strengthen the doctrinal position of the Pentecostals and to create even greater worldwide interest in Pentecostalism. While we rejoice at what God is doing among the charismatics, we must ask ourselves what He will do for us in the future. How can Pentecost be perpetuated without that loss in spiritual vitality and evangelistic fervor which has so often overtaken revival movements in the past. No doubt, the answer lies in our following the same paths that led the Pentecostal pioneers to the experience of Azusa Street.[79]

A decade later when Miller published his history of the PAOC his tone seemed to have become less sympathetic as there were growing concerns over differences between the Charismatic Movement and classical Pentecostals. In comparing the impact of both the Jesus People movement and the Charismatic Movement, he wrote, "Where the former movement generally had a beneficial but limited influence on Pentecostalism, the impact of the latter has been the subject of an ongoing debate." He devoted minimal space to the issues but observed, "Throughout the 70's, the differences between the 'classical' and the new Pentecostals gradually replaced 1960s emphasis on their similarities." This he believed was because "many traditional Pentecostals were puzzled at the reluctance of the charismatics to abandon their 'dead' churches...." The differences were becoming obvious: "the Pentecostals became less enamored with the Charismatic Movement and the charismatics began to distinguish themselves from one another along denominational lines—'Catholic charismatics,' 'Lutheran charismatics' and so on."[80] Nowhere did Miller expound on the notion that the Charismatic Movement had served to strengthen the doctrinal position of the PAOC but he seemed to want to affirm the existence and effectiveness of the new renewal on the one hand while calling classical Pentecostals back to their former days on the other.

Throughout the late 1980s and early 1990s, there was a repeated calling for a return to old-fashioned Pentecostal revival and prayer that God would "do it again." It could be surmised that impulse was in part precipitated, ironically, by a positive reaction to the Charismatic climate that involved a desire to see the work of the Spirit again within more formalized Pentecostalism. Kydd agreed but also believed the prayer might be answered in new and surprising ways. With the strong connection in his thinking between the move of the Spirit and its inevitable impact upon society through the church, he argued that "the Spirit may urge someone to move into a condominium, in the heart of one of our great cities, so that the gospel can be preached to the thousands who live stacked on top of each other."[81] Apart from foreign missions that had always been combined with a humanitarian and educational focus, the relationship between the Spirit's renewal and social engagement had not been at all strong.

On the eve of the 1990s, the PAOC's Decade of Destiny was launched with the intent to make greater progress in nationwide evangelism. The coordinator of this focus, George W. Grosshans, voiced the concern of many of his contemporaries noting that after seventy years of remarkable growth and the move of the Spirit since the signing of the PAOC charter, the most recent statistics revealed a "serious plateauing of our growth and effective outreach."[82] He reported that over the last half of the 1980s, growth had all but leveled out and that any growth was largely "biological or transfer."[83] In clear contrast to the picture of the 1960s and 1970s, he made this alarming claim: "We in the Pentecostal Assemblies of Canada have found ourselves at the watershed of our growth. Pentecost, with its power infillings, signs, wonders, healings and miracles, has become more of a memory than a present experience in a number of our churches. We are dangerously close to becoming a 'has-been' Pentecostal movement."[84]

Such awareness in the early 1990s resulted in a renewed desire for revival and along with writings in *The Pentecostal Testimony* on issues such as subsequence and tongues, an effort was made to address other lingering doctrinal and practical concerns regarding the Charismatic Movement. In early 1991, the magazine published two articles by the General Superintendent of the Assemblies of God (USA) in which he argued that the Pentecostal /Charismatic movement was facing divided interpretations concerning the place of ministry gifts with some wrongly declaring that unless an assembly has a designated prophet, it is not an apostolic church. He saw arbitrary and absolute direction by a prophetic gift as not being in accordance with New Testament teaching.[85] Concern was expressed that in some PAOC circles only a minority of members and adherents had ever experienced Spirit baptism with the initial evidence of speaking in other tongues and knew little about it.[86] By this time, writers were also lamenting more and more the loss of what used to be, as a result of increasing secularization, the perceived need for relevancy and widespread moral compromise.

Divine Healing

Some Pentecostals have become disheartened over time with the seeming lack of healings taking place or at least reported, expressing the concern that genuine miracles used to accompany the preaching of the gospel in the their early days. They perceive healings as having made the Pentecostal message of supernatural power legitimate. Presently, divine healing continues to be viewed as being a formally held historic position and assumed to be part of practice, but perceived as unfortunately not expounded, taught or experienced often enough. A retired pastor, George Power views the doctrine as having all but disappeared due to a lack of dependence on God and too much on self, noting that in the PAOC's beginnings, the number of people healed became a "faith builder," which encouraged others to believe for personal healing. He recalls incidents within his own ministry and especially his own healing from tuberculosis in 1955 to the astonishment of his doctors.[87] For older Pentecostals, in speaking of divine healing, 'genuine' was often the operative description as miracles of healing tended to be viewed as exceptional, powerful, and readily verifiable. There was a sense among some Pentecostals, on the contrary, that Charismatic-type 'healings' were inclined to be overplayed and open to suspicion of manipulation. Gordon R. Upton, a national PAOC executive member prepared a document for the biennial leadership council at Winnipeg, Manitoba in which he wrote:

> 1. Records and personal accounts indicate that healings and the working of miracles were common in the early days of the movement.
> 2. There did not seem to be an attempt to "specialize" in these areas, but these acts were spontaneous and accompanied the preaching of the gospel.
> 3. These acts still occur on the widespread scale among us but we now tend to "specialize" these ministries.[88]

Upton was representing a wider held sentiment that the Charismatics were compartmentalizing the Pentecostal message and practice, giving greater profile to some giftings over others.

On the other hand, Ted Yuke, pastor emeritus and co-founder of the Rock Church, Halifax Nova Scotia, with deep family roots in the PAOC, is representative of a pastor who early became attracted to the Charismatic Movement through visiting Pittsburg's Duquesne University, and became captivated with its environment of healing and deliverance. He remembers, "People would come to the altar with such simple faith. There were healings and restorations and deliverance. I have been religious my whole life but it changed. It was almost unexplainable what was happening."[89] As a result Yuke began to invite Charismatic speakers to his church, which soon became a Charismatic congregation, eventually leaving the PAOC. He laments the loss of what he remembers from his earlier days with his parents as PAOC pastors, which in some ways he saw the Charismatic movement as restoring.

As with other classical Pentecostal movements, the doctrine of divine healing has remained an official part of the theology and practice of the PAOC. *The Pentecostal Testimony,* especially in the 1960s and 1970s, frequently published testimonies of healing, but in comparison with the other foundational doctrines, few writers over the past decades have engaged in serious reflection on divine healing as a theological position and coverage in the magazine dedicated to both declined after the 1960s. This trend may at least be partially due to the fact that within many evangelical groups and even mainstream denominations, physical, emotional, and mental healing is considered possible, even if not explicitly taught. Hence, the need to defend it was not nearly as urgent. Many have been cessationists on the doctrine of Spirit-baptism with initial evidence of tongues but not so much on divine healing. There has not seemed to be an overwhelming need to defend this doctrine against possible detractors. C. M. Ward, speaker of the Assemblies of God's international radio broadcast, *Revivaltime,* quoted statements on healing from Martin Luther, George Fox, and Andrew Murray, as well as John

Wesley, which was perhaps an indication of classical Pentecostals' propensity towards rooting this distinctive much deeper than just in its Methodist-Holiness beginnings.[90] Nevertheless, it is interesting to note that the traditional tendency to clearly link healing to Christ's atonement has diminished.

Divine healing as bound up with atonement theology rather than with supernatural power encounters as was more characteristic of the Charismatic Movement was discussed in the early 1960s, but the subject has not been given significant attention since that time.[91] Furthermore, only one writer drew any relationship between the work of the Spirit and divine healing. George C. Smith, an Edmonton, Alberta pastor wrote: "The Holy Spirit's ministry is not limited to the conviction of sin…[he] is involved in the total life of the believer, and one of His ministries is divine healing…. The church was vibrant with the presence of the Holy Spirit. It was in that atmosphere that the healing ministry became a daily occurrence."[92]

Most authors simply affirmed God's will to heal based on the ministry of Jesus, the practice of the early church, and the earliest beginnings of the PAOC itself. Randall Holm, a PAOC minister and educator, argued that Pentecostalism, taking its cue from the Holiness Movement, has "boldly marshaled the message that God desires to heal all manner of sickness, not unlike that evidenced in the early church."[93] At any rate, there were continued efforts in *The Pentecostal Testimony* to remind readers that healing is still possible and available while also attempting to grapple with such questions as "Is it God's will to heal everybody now?"

In 1981, concern began to be expressed over "Faith Preaching" and "positive confession." The phenomenon was considered to be extreme and ought to be rejected as unbiblical. Such preachers were accused of coming to the conclusion that "Paul's and Peter's teaching on suffering was a mistake."[94] By the late 1990s, the PAOC, though holding still to biblical and historical precedent for divine healing, seems to have begun to recognize that God's sovereignty is always involved and that theological issues exist that "deal with God's ability and willingness to supernaturally intervene and do a miracle of healing."[95] Another confessed that although in some cases, people have witnessed divine healing, in others, "if there is no healing apparent, we keep looking to the Lord for further revelation."[96] The expectation of divine healing has softened and moved toward greater focus on divine sovereignty when no answer has been forthcoming.

Expectation of Christ's Second Coming

From its inception, the PAOC has held to a pre-tribulation rapture position. In contrast to an earlier era when the expectation of Christ's return was always in front, presently it seems, as evidenced through the infrequency of preaching and writings in *The Pentecostal Testimony* on the subject, that many no longer think in terms of a pre-tribulation rapture. The perception expressed is that the change is obvious not so much by what is contained in preaching and teaching, but by what is not.[97] The loss of this expectation is believed as well to be evident in the "daily deportment" of Pentecostals who convey the impression that they believe it will happen some day but not today whereas early Pentecostals lived each day as if it might be the day of Jesus' return.[98] The underlying thought appears to be that since it is rarely talked about publicly, one might infer that it is not likely any longer a seriously held belief:

> The return of Christ—the doctrine of the Second Coming—seems notably lacking as the theme of a given sermon. As opposed to the early days when we are told that nearly every sermon, or message preached, made some reference to the baptism of the Holy Spirit or the second coming... It could be that the lack of reminding the church of this cardinal truth might account for, what seems to be a lessening of commitment to a separated lifestyle. The affluence of the 20th and 21st century—our comfortable lifestyle—Hollywood's unquestionable influence on western culture—idolizing the world and the pleasure it offers perhaps in part accounts for change over the last four decades.[99]

The view that people no longer seem to expect the imminent return of Christ is widespread and is theorized to be the result of living in close attachment to the present age. As a result, even local church leadership appears to prefer to steer the theological ship in other directions.

Yet, it is intriguing that for the most part, PAOC leadership through *The Pentecostal Testimony* has over the past decades continued to carry writings on the second coming of Christ, though in an uneven manner. Clearly, they have been aware of the need to reiterate the doctrine and so have attempted to keep it central in the life of the denomination. A significant amount of material on the subject appeared in the 1960s as well as in the 1980s and 1990s. It was quite popular in the 1960s to talk about the coming world church and the rise of the European Common Market headed by a great gentile ruler "satanically inspired."[100] Books promoted tended to be about biblical prophecy and other teachings regarding the second coming and its relationship to events in the Middle East. By late 1967, connections were being made between Bible prophecy and the Arab-Israeli conflict.[101]

At the time, there was a preoccupation with the urgency of being ready and with the signs that were pointing to Christ's imminent return.[102] While The Catacombs frequently referred to the imminent return of Christ and its prophetic connection with Israel, a focus spurred on in part by the apocalyptic impulse of much of the Jesus Movement, most early Charismatic groups did not seem to emphasize it much. PAOC writers expressed in positive terms the hope of the second coming whereby the believer would "see Jesus face to face...behold His wounds, but ... also hear His welcome. Then too, we shall behold the whole Christian Church adorned as a bride to meet the bridegroom."[103] Everything about the second coming was clearly within the context of a pre-millennial rapture.[104]

Writings on the subject tapered off significantly in the 1970s with just a total of nine articles appearing in the denomination's publication for the entire decade, but they increased by five-fold (a total of forty-seven items) during the 1980s. It likely suggests a new awareness of the rapidly approaching close of the twentieth century with the thought that it might signal the end of the age, in addition to the concern that the Charismatic Movement was not holding strongly to this doctrine. There was articulation of the pre-tribulation rapture position with its two phases of Christ's return [105] and perceived signposts to the imminent return of Christ and the revelation of the Antichrist.[106]

This trend continued throughout the decade with various topics relating to the end of time which clearly seems to be, at least in part, also a response to the popular 'Kingdom Now" theology,[107] that became intertwined with the Charismatic Movement. Yuke was influenced by this theology: "We were teaching a lot about the kingdom. That became a major issue. But what we were teaching about the kingdom was no different than what the word of God talked about."[108] General Superintendent, James McKnight, responded directly to the 'Kingdom Now' theology by expounding on the "Statement of Faith" in the May 1985 edition of *The Pentecostal Testimony*, an effort to affirm it and stand against what he saw as error: "There are a number of things that contribute to the cohesiveness of 1000 churches working together as a cooperative fellowship. I am persuaded, however, that '...those things which are most surely believed among us...' (Luke 1:1)... is basic to our existence as a fellowship...." He argued:

> We strongly contend and plead for revival and encourage spontaneous worship in our lives individually and corporately in our churches. In our longing for revival and a great move of God, however, it is possible to be caught up in emotionalism, misplaced zeal which leads to pride and vindictiveness, where an objective understanding of Scripture is waived in lieu of this perceived new revelation. All that has been tried and proven in God's Word suddenly becomes rather outdated and ineffective. The claim is made that God is doing a new thing in a new way in His church.
> They suggest this last-day outpouring is sent by God to equip the Church to convert the world and bring in the kingdom of God on this earth. They arrive at this error by faulty interpretation in the use of allegorical imagery rather than the correct use of hermeneutics.[109]

McKnight then proceeded to outline five areas relating to the *Statement of Fundamental and Essential Truths* where he saw "Kingdom Teaching" as being contrary to a proper biblical interpretation and therefore unacceptable to the PAOC—the church, worship, truth, the sovereignty of God, and Christ's imminent return. In regard to worship he continued:

> We must avoid dividing congregations by demanding of God's people an outward conformity to a certain type of praise in order to identify with and receive approval of the Restoration Movement. We must avoid an emphasis that members of a certain select minority, elitist class—godly remnant—are the real children of God. We must not be deceived into basing unity on experience rather than truth and developing a critical attitude which breeds disunity, the very opposite of the restoration of the unity the restoration movement avows. Let us "...contend for the faith which was once delivered unto the saints" (Jude 3).[110]

MacKnight's commentary followed a letter that he had sent to all PAOC ministers in February 1985. An unnamed district dealing with the teaching that had surfaced in some of its churches had appealed to the national executive for direction. MacKnight had accompanied his official response to the constituency with a document opposing "Kingdom Now" teaching about which he had stated at the time, "It is presented without bias, with the prayer that it will be helpful to you" and concluded by stating, "This is not a time to get sidelined on a tangent. There is too much to do and so little time in which to do it."[111]

At the beginning of the 1990s, the impending prospect of the transition into a new millennium began to emerge[112] although the amount of writing on the end times dropped to half of what it had been in the 1980s. Miller observed, "Now as the twentieth century draws to a close, there has arisen a new interest in the subject of prophecy, Last Things and the Second Coming of Jesus Christ."[113] Larry Willard, PAOC member and Vice President of Tyndale College and Seminary, Toronto, even used the title "Is Disaster Imminent?" in warning of the Y2K bug that supposedly threatened to cripple computers worldwide.[114] Connections with the year 2000, Israel and the Middle East continued to be made until the close of the decade.

However the lines are drawn between the changes in doctrinal focus and the Charismatic Movement or any other influences, it is clear that there was at least a significant shift in emphasis that can in part be attributed to a new spiritual climate. Perhaps, it may also be the product of a secular cultural outlook that was no longer as sympathetic toward institutions and firm non-negotiable guiding statements.

Notes

1. Douglas Rudd, "How Pentecost Came to Ontario," *The Pentecostal Testimony* (September 1978): 32.

2. Thomas Miller, " Five Pillars of Pentecostalism," *The Pentecostal Testimony* (October 1992): 8.

3. Gordon F. Atter, *The Third Force*, (Peterborough, Ontario: The College Press, 1962): 247.

4. Kimberly Ervin Alexander, *Pentecostal Healing: Models in Theology and Practice*, Journal of Pentecostal Theology Supplement Series (Deo Publishing, 2006): 10-13.

5. A. W. Orwig, *The Weekly Evangel* (March 18, 1986): 4 in *NIDPCM*, s.v. "Dispensationalism," (by French L. Arrington).

6. http://www.thecanadianencyclopedia.ca/en/article/pentecostal-movement/ (accessed September 28, 2014).

7. Roy D. King, discussion with author, Dartmouth, NS, February 2008.

8. Ibid.

9. Written comments by Robert Taitinger, former general superintendent of the PAOC, February 2008.

10. Howard Winsor, discussion with the author, Dartmouth, NS, January 2008. Winsor is a layperson and former PAOC church deacon.

11. E. A. Francis. "The Cross of Christ," *The Pentecostal Testimony* (November 1961): 6.

12. The March 1964 issue highly recommended a book of sixteen sermons on the cross titled "The Cross Still Stands" by Alfred Doerffler, a Luthuran pastor in St. Louis, MO.

13. Don Schellenberg, "Transcendent Grace," *The Pentecostal Testimony* (July, 1962): 11.

14. Emma Giesbrecht Butcher, *The Pentecostal Testimony* (April 1963): 11.

15. John Calvin, "Divine Absolution for All Sins." *The Pentecostal Testimony* (February 1964): 3.

16. James E. Adams. "The Gentle Erasmus." *The Pentecostal Testimony* (October 1964): 6; S.H.Thompson, "The Heritage of John Hus." *The Pentecostal Testimony* (October 1965): 7 and F.W. Boreham, "John Knox's Text." *The Pentecostal Testimony* (October 1966): 3.

17. Henry Gagne, "The New Birth." *The Pentecostal Testimony* (February 1973): 7.

18. Wayne Dawes, "When the Term 'Born Again' Becomes a Syndrome," *The Pentecostal Testimony* (August 1979): 28.

19. Thomas Miller, "Born Again or Saved?" *The Pentecostal Testimony* (September 1985): 38.

20. Thomas Miller, "Jesus Our Justification," *The Pentecostal Testimony* (March, 1985): 10.

21. William J. Seymour, *The Apostolic Faith*, Vol.1 No. 1 (September 1906): 2.

22. Al Werbiski, "The Stripes of Jesus," *The Pentecostal Testimony* (April 1987): 4.

23. Terry Damm, "Is the Blood of Christ an Offense?" *The Pentecostal Testimony* (April 1988): 16.

24. Clinton L. Ward, "The Long Arm of God," *The Pentecostal Testimony* (May 1990): 33.

25. J. Giraldo Prieto, "The Meaning and Importance of the Blood of Jesus," *The Pentecostal Testimony* (March 1991): 8.

26. Edwin Martin, "The Cleansing of the Conscience Through the Blood of Jesus," *The Pentecostal Testimony* (October 1993): 16.

27. William D. Morrow, "Marvelous, Infinite, Matchless Grace," *The Pentecostal Testimony* (November 2001): 30.

28. Winsor, discussion, January 2008.

29. King, discussion, February 2008.

30. George Power, telephone discussion with author, February 2008.

31. Taitinger, written comments, February 2008.

32. Ibid.

33. Hope Smith, "Holiness: What is it?" *The Pentecostal Testimony* (July 1965): 29.

34. Rev. J. Montgomery, "Worldliness," *The Pentecostal Testimony* (July 1965): 28.

35. Official statement by the Youth and Family Commission of the PAOC and approved by the General Executive, "The Biblical Standards of Morality," *The Pentecostal Testimony* (May 1966): 7.

36. Official statement, *The Pentecostal Testimony* (May 1966): 7.

37. Paul C. Sorenson, "Spiritual Drift and Drive," *The Pentecostal Testimony* (March 1971): 6.

38. *The Pentecostal Testimony* (June 1971): 9.

39. Gordon F. Atter, "Is Biblical Holiness Obsolete?" *The Pentecostal Testimony* (February 1974): 6. He states,

40. Ron Reid, "Chosen to be Holy," *The Pentecostal Testimony* (October 1977): 30.

41. Carl F. Verge, "A Comparison of the Beliefs and Practices of Two Groups to Pentecostal Assemblies of Canada Ministers: Those with a Masters Degree and the Those with Only Three Years of Bible College Training," Unpublished dissertation, New York University, 1987: 192.

42. Ibid., 197.

43. Articles appeared such as "In His Likeness" by Samuel M. Buick (August 1982) and "Aim at Perfection" by Clinton L. Ward (February 1983).

44. Roy E. Upton, "We Believe in Holy Living." *The Pentecostal Testimony* (February 1985): 18, (his italics).

45. Michael P. Horban, "Principles of Holiness for Today," *The Pentecostal Testimony* (March, 1985): 18 and "We Live in an Unholy World and the Church is Worldly," *The Pentecostal Testimony* (April 1985): 46.

46. Richard L. Dresselhaus, "Pentecostal Balance: Four critical balance points in Pentecostal theology and practice," *The Pentecostal Testimony* (July 1989): 7.

47. Roy E. Upton, "Living Clean in an Unclean World," *The Pentecostal Testimony,* (August, 1990):22 and Doreen Halliwell, "No, No! Don't Go to the Show," *The Pentecostal Testimony* (September 1991): 9.

48. Ronald Kydd, "Walking Straight in a Crooked World," *The Pentecostal Testimony* (August 1990): 18-19.

49. Homer Cantelon, "HOLINESS: Without Which No Man Shall See the Lord", *The Pentecostal Testimony* (October 1993): 33.

50. Rick Hiebert, "Living Between Two Worlds," *The Pentecostal Testimony* (July 1995): 4.

51. Tom Morris, "Holiness: It's in the View" *Testimony* (May 2001): 14.

52. Verge, "Comparison of the Beliefs and Practices,"184.

53. King, discussion, February 2008.

54. Scott Bullerwell, telephone discussion with author, February 2008.

55. Taitinger, discussion, February 2008.

56. The January 1962, March 1963, and August 1965 issues carried reviews of *The Holy Spirit—His Gifts and Power* by John Owen, *The Third Force* by Gordon F. Atter and *Spiritual Gifts in the Work of the Ministry Today* by Donald Gee respectively.

57. Jean Stone, "More Than 1300 California Episcopalians Receive Pentecostal Baptism" *The Pentecostal Testimony* (June 1962): 8 and David J. du Plessis, "Glossolalia" *The Pentecostal Testimony* (February 1963): 4 and (March 1963): 7.

58. "Priest 'speaks in tongues' now everyone's doing it" *Toronto Daily Star* (March 7, 1964) in *The Pentecostal Testimony* (June 1964): 7.

59. "What the Archbishop said About the Holy Spirit" *The Pentecostal Testimony* (June, 1966): 8. This was a reprint of a sermon preached by Archbishop Coggin at St. Paul's Cathedral, October 24, 1964.

60. Kilian McDonnell, "The Ecumenical Significance of the Pentecostal Movement," *The Pentecostal Testimony* (June 1968): 8.

61. Ray Austin, "Our Pentecostal Heritage," Stuart Mulligan and David Crabtree, "What We are and Who We Are", and G.P.Tunks, "I Believe in the Holy Ghost" all appeared in the June 1963 issue of *The Pentecostal Testimony.*

62. R. J. White, "Pentecost Today and Ecumenicity" *The Pentecostal Testimony* (March 1964): 8.

63. Philip Duncan, "The Two Advents of the Ministry of the Holy Spirit." *The Pentecostal Testimony* (December 1963): 6.

64. F.G. Fleming, "The Advent of Christ and of the Holy Ghost," *The Pentecostal Testimony* (December, 1968): 6. Also, W. H. Moody, "The Holy Spirit and Christmas," *The Pentecostal Testimony* (December 1975): 10.

65. H. P. B. Benney, "The Lessons of Montanism," *The Pentecostal Testimony* (June 1969): 6.

66. George R. Upton, "Jubilee—retrospect and prospect," *The Pentecostal Testimony* (November 1969): 6.

67. Douglas Rudd, "After Eighty Years, What?" *The Pentecostal Testimony* (January 1987): 39.

68. Amaro Rodriguez, "The Spirit of God is Moving," *The Pentecostal Testimony* (August 1970): 9.

69. Thomas F. Zimmerman, "The Wind Bloweth Where it Listeth," *The Pentecostal Testimony* (September 1972): 4.

70. Peter Prosser, "Roman Catholic Charismatic Impact Increases," *The Pentecostal Testimony* (September 1973): 5.

71. R.W. Taitinger, General Superintendent, "Priorities," *The Pentecostal Testimony* (June 1976): 8.

72. Howard D. Honsinger, "Single-Tongued Pentecostalism," *The Pentecostal Testimony* (January 1979): 7.

73. Keith R. Balkwell, "Distinctive," *The Pentecostal Testimony* (May 1980): 26.

74. Burton K. Janes exemplified this idea in his writing, "Acts Reviewed for an Experience Today," *The Pentecostal Testimony* (November 1981): 20.

75. R. J. White, "What Makes A Person Pentecostal?" *The Pentecostal Testimony* (November 1982): 11.

76. Teresa Ter Hoek, "Stranger Fire," *The Pentecostal Testimony* (May 1987): 16.

77. Thomas Miller, "Pentecostals and Charismatics," *The Pentecostal Testimony* (November 1983): 14.

78. Ibid.

79. Ibid.

80. Thomas A. Miller, *Canadian Pentecostals*, 298, 300-301.

81. Ron Kydd, "Do it Again! Do it Again!" *The Pentecostal Testimony* (May 1989): 19. In July 1991, Robert Skinner wrote an editorial by the same title.

82. George W. Grosshans, "Why a Decade of Destiny?" *The Pentecostal Testimony* (September 1989): 24.

83. Ibid.

84. Ibid.

85. G. Raymond Carlson, "The Role of the Prophet Today," *The Pentecostal Testimony* (January 1991:22-24); "Christ's Gifts to His Church," (March 1991:28-30).

86. William A. Griffin, "Real Pentecostals, Please Stand," *The Pentecostal Testimony* (June 1998): 19.

87. George Power, discussion with author, Dartmouth, Nova Scotia, February 2008.

88. Gordon R. Upton, "Pentecostal Distinctives and Charismatic Focus," (Paper prepared for the Biennial Leadership Council at Winnipeg, Manitoba November 15-17, 1977), PAOC Archives

89. Ted Yuke, discussion with the author, The Rock Church, Halifax, Nova Scotia, February 25, 2014.

90. C. M. Ward, "Do You Need Healing?" *The Pentecostal Testimony*, (August 1965): 5 & 26.

91. There were only a minimal number of writings on the subject in *The Pentecostal Testimony* during that period. These included "Is Healing in the Atonement?" by W. Cornish Jones (September 1961): 6, "Healing by the Power of the Resurrection" by Lilian B. Yeomans (April 1962): 8 and "Why I Believe in Divine Healing" by Victor G. Brown (November 1967): 7.

92. George C. Smith, "The Quickening Spirit in Healing," *The Pentecostal Testimony* (May 1977): 22.

93. Randall Holm, "Developing an Understanding of Divine healing," *The Pentecostal Testimony* (October 1992): 18.

94. Kenneth B. Birch, "Faith or Presumption," *The Pentecostal Testimony* (February 1981): 3.

95. William A. Griffin, "When Healing Doesn't Come," *The Pentecostal Testimony* (July 1999): 20.

96. Garth Leno, "Healing and the Prayer of Faith," *Testimony* (June 2001): 14.

97. Winsor, discussion, January 2008.

98. King, discussion, February 2008.

99. Taitinger, discussion, February 2008.

100. F. H. Parlee, "Europe—The Rising Deterrent," *The Pentecostal*

Testimony (July 1962): 4.

101. Wilbur M. Smith, "The Middle East Crisis in the Light of the Bible," *The Pentecostal Testimony* (November 1967): 3.

102. Titles such as "As it was in the Days of Noah", "As ye see the Day Approaching", and "And the Door was Shut" were common themes.

103. Alexander Tee, "Looking for that Blessed Hope," *The Pentecostal Testimony* (August 1967): 5.

104. Alfred F. Missen, writing about the resurrection of believers in March 1970 explicitly stated that "it will be a pre-millennial resurrection," *The Pentecostal Testimony* (March 1970): 7.

105. Thomas Holdcroft, "The Two Phases of Christ's Second Coming," *The Pentecostal Testimony* (November 1983): 16-17, "Evidence for a Pre-Tribulation Rapture," *The Pentecostal Testimony* (December 1986): 26, and "God's Purposes in the Tribulation," *The Pentecostal Testimony* (February 1984): 24.

106. Examples include Abraham Kudra, "Five Signs that Point to Christ's Imminent Return," *The Pentecostal Testimony* (November 1983): 8 and Mervin Thomas, "For Minutes Before Midnight," *The Pentecostal Testimony* (November 1983): 4. Charles G. Enerson in "Christ is Coming Soon" notes "fifteen signs that the return of Christ is near." (January 1988): 4-7.

107. Paul Lowenburg, "Message Under Siege—The Pre-millennial Return of Christ," *The Pentecostal Testimony* (January 1988): 24-26. Lowenburg wrote that for Pentecostals, "the glorious hope of the rapture is being challenged by 'Kingdom Now' proponents."

108. Yuke, discussion, February 25, 2014.

109. James M. MacKnight, "Statement of Faith," *The Pentecostal Testimony* (May 1985): 14.

110. Ibid., 16.

111. James M. MacKnight, correspondence to PAOC ministers, February 1985, PAOC Archives.

112. Bernice M. Gerard, "The Terrors of the Year 2000," *The Pentecostal Testimony* (January 2000): 34.

113. Thomas W. Miller, "Canada and the Coming 'New World Order,'" *The Pentecostal Testimony* (June 1993): 8.

114. Larry Willard, "Is Disaster Imminent," *The Pentecostal Testimony* (December 1998): 8.

8

Facing the Dilemma

Douville is quite accurate in his assertion that PAOC people were not unanimous in their views of the Charismatic Movement. More specifically, differences in acceptance, however, lay at least somewhat horizontally along urban-rural lines and vertically from adherents to top PAOC leadership. Urban congregations would have generally been more accepting and open to new expressions of worship than more rural churches where traditional Pentecostal worship style had deep roots and would be maintained for many years to come. Lay people seemed to have been embracing what appeared to them to be an old-fashioned Pentecostal revival breaking out in the other churches. At the same time their pastors, especially district and national leadership, were attempting to navigate their way through uncharted territory and to determine a response, sensing the need to guard the PAOC *Statement of Fundamental and Essential Truths*. The ways in which a religious organization grapples with its challenges are often best reflected in the structures of its official publications and boardroom decisions.

Vacillating Perspectives

With the intermingling of counter-cultural influence represented by the Jesus People with interdenominational openness to the Spirit in the Charismatic Movement, many PAOC laity, clergy and leadership imagined an absence of parameters around the Charismatic Movement and were therefore exceedingly uneasy and sometimes critical, if not cynical. There was fear that with no apparent accountability structures there would be theological excess and extremism, not to mention a lack of direction in channeling new experiences of the Spirit and adjustments in lifestyle. Added to this was concern over a Charismatic push toward some kind of 'ecumenical' union–an extremely negative word within much of sectarian Pentecostalism. The PAOC stood in alignment with the Assemblies of God (USA) in this regard, reporting on the release of its "Charismatic Study Report." The AG statement opposed "organic ecumenism" but declared, "We do believe in the institution of the Church. We trust the Holy Spirit to bring the members of the Body of Christ into a true unity of the Spirit . . . which transcends but does not destroy existing organizational bounds."[1] The conviction was clearly articulated at the time by C.H. Bronston, president of one of the largest PAOC training institutions, Eastern Pentecostal Bible College, Peterborough, Ontario. He argued the urgent need for a solid, classical Pentecostal biblical education:

> In an age of evangelism and church growth, of charismatic renewal and revival, there exists a great need for those who are sound in basic Christian doctrine. Someone must train Holy Spirit filled young people for leadership and guidance in this great move of God's Holy Spirit. For this reason there must be a Pentecostal Bible college, a college that is concerned about charismatic ministries and a continued outpouring of the Holy Spirit in the Church of Jesus Christ.
> Not only must they be knowledgeable in this area of doctrine, but they must be knowledgeable in all areas of doctrine, in order for our Pentecostal Assemblies of Canada churches to remain theologically sound.[2]

Whereas the Charismatic Movement appeared to be unconcerned about theological differences, at least along lines of pneumatology, the PAOC saw as more imperative than ever its mandate to guard its theological distinctives.

Ironically, few Pentecostals seemed to realize that, while they were trying to protect themselves against the fluidity and perceived excesses in doctrine and practice of the Charismatic Movement, Charismatics were rejecting the cultural baggage of classical Pentecostalism. Quebedeaux observes: "Renewal is particularly attractive to the middle class because of its legitimate, rational, educated clergy and lay leadership, and because of its well-conceived, well-ordered evangelism without the revivalistic extremes of classical Pentecostalism."[3] While The Catacombs was perhaps the most visible example of Charismatic expression, it was not the only one as older and newer forms of Pentecostalism in some instances had deep misunderstanding and suspicion of each other.[4]

Yet, the mixture of response to the Charismatic Movement is reflected in the lack of a uniform stand on the phenomenon even in *The Pentecostal Testimony* itself. The publication reported numerous Charismatic happenings in Canada, some of them having taken place in cooperation with local PAOC churches, as well as Charismatic events around the world. It reported on the "Catholic Pentecostal Movement" in Canada that had spilled over from the United States and was resulting weekly in "over 5,000 Roman Catholics... meeting from coast to coast in more than 100 *Pentecostal* prayer groups" (emphasis added).[5] Well before the new renewal was considered a challenge this report was anchoring the Movement to a prayer meeting held at Combermere, Ontario in August 1968. It highlighted the fact that Canada's most populated province was the "most fertile ground for the growth of the movement" and that other groups were spreading throughout other provinces, so much so that *Renewal* magazine, the official journal of the Catholic charismatic movement in the United States referred to it as having "hardly begun."[6] At the top of its international news section in August 1973, it included a report on the seventh annual international conference of the Catholic Charismatic Renewal at the University of Notre Dame where 22,000 attended, twice as many as the previous year.[7]

Although it was not altogether common, there were a few Charismatic events in various Canadian cities in which local PAOC pastors participated and at times even initiated. Area churches in Prince George, British Columbia in 1973 planned what they labeled 'Key 73,' a festival held at Prince George Pentecostal Tabernacle with emphasis on "evangelism plus ecumenicity plus the charismatic."[8] Spirit filled Roman Catholic priests, Salvation Army officers and leaders of other groups were represented in an event that was reported to have had "remarkable harmony."[9] This kind of cooperation in the midst of a Charismatic climate seems to have been particularly true in Quebec (see Chapter Four).

Another event illustrative of the blending of the Jesus People atmosphere, the Charismatic Movement, and the PAOC was reported by the *Catholic Register* and re-printed in *The Pentecostal Testimony*. In the summer of 1972, hundreds of French and English youth from many denominations and nationalities joined in a large parade of Jesus People beginning at the PAOC Evangel Pentecostal Church in downtown Montreal and marched to the Lafontaine Park in the city's east section singing, "We are one in the Spirit, we are one in the Lord."[10] The march had been organized by Evangel Church along with André Gagnon, a PAOC pastor from Quebec City who spoke to the crowd in French and Robert Johnson, PAOC pastor of Trinity Pentecostal Church in La Salle, a suburb of Montreal, who addressed the audience in English.[11] A report of this type indicates a level of acceptance of the Charismatic Movement, especially if the PAOC was directly involved.

Not all PAOC adherents, however, were as quick to embrace the new wave of renewal that was making itself felt in mainline churches and on some college campuses. Some contributing writers to *The Pentecostal Testimony* were not as positive in their assessment. By the time the Charismatic Movement was at its height in Canada about 1973, the PAOC felt it necessary to address a phenomenon that seemed to be pulling the denomination in different directions, demonstrating the challenge of maintaining unity in a geographically expansive country with so much regional diversity, even in ecclesiastical matters. The cover of the September 1973 issue boldly asked, "Is the Catholic Charismatic Renewal Real?" and an additional question was then posed by PAOC pastor, Jack Ozard, as to whether the work of the Spirit in the Reformation was being undone, or even if indeed the Reformation was a mistake. In response, he clearly expressed his personal consternation over evangelism efforts between Charismatic Catholics and Pentecostals: "In a full gospel youth crusade in a U.S. city recently, a priest sat among the sponsoring pastors, many of whom were Pentecostal. When the priest was introduced amidst cheers, he promised to pray for the success of the crusade in a special mass. That lost me! Conscious involvement and enjoyment in the rest of the service was difficult."[12] He continued, "I am frankly worried about getting under 'an umbrella raised high enough so that under it we can all gather without sacrificing our particular heritage,'" deferring to biblical precedent regarding the futility of believers attempting to work in harmony with unbelievers (2 Cor. 6:14).[13] One wonders how widespread this perspective may have been.

Classical Pentecostals have usually been concerned over any emphasis on the

Spirit or its operation that does not have the biblical text as its reference point, arguing that the Spirit and the written Word work in tandem. Ozard reflected:

> From my understanding of any wind of the Spirit blowing in past history, and of the Word of God, the Holy Spirit always blows us on course. It is His purpose always to bring us back to the Scriptures from which it seems so easy to wander. Though we may be thrilled with every new report of God's blessing, we need to be careful lest the devil lead us down the garden path of compromise to liberalism, formalism or some other position contrary to Holy Scriptures.[14]

Ironically, while the PAOC is rooted in the Methodist and Holiness revivals of the nineteenth century, if *The Pentecostal Testimony* is any indication, some of its constituents have found comfort in times of theological uncertainty in its Reformation heritage.[15] This tendency will be discussed later in this chapter. Ozard exhorts, "Let's not forget that we are Christians, yes, but also Pentecostal, evangelical and Protestant! We have a time to *protest,* and keep the Word of God open before us."[16] Ozard was one of several writers for the publication who alluded to or reiterated the centrality of the Reformation for Pentecostal thinking.

Amaro Rodriguez, a former Roman Catholic priest who experienced a conversion in 1961 and became director of a Bible school in the Argentinian Assemblies of God, wrote twice for *The Pentecostal Testimony* in 1970 when the Charismatic Movement was gaining momentum. He too affirmed the legacy of the Reformation in giving "the Bible the value and importance that it deserved as the only infallible rule of faith and fountain of revelation"[17] and for making it accessible to the people. Ironically, however, Rodriguez was advocating that Pentecostals should also seize the opportunity to participate in the growing spirit of ecumenism. He conceded that although "the situation in the Roman Catholic Church has never been so complicated and critical," he saw positive changes beginning to take place and articulated what seems to have been an astonishing perspective to appear in the PAOC's official magazine in 1970:

> The spirit of ecumenism and efforts toward unity of all Christians are every day more notable and growing.... Since the historic embrace of Pope Paul VI and Athenagoras, orthodox patriarch of Constantinople, it would seem that the barriers of separation, which for centuries differentiated the groups of nominal Christendom, are falling to the ground. We do not ask for the formation of a super-church or a religious superstructure which would absorb small groups and bring out the realization of ecumenical hope.... But true Christians must take advantage of the favourable atmosphere, where there is a mutual coming together of various groups, to reach those who are seeking the truth.[18]

Rodriguez had left the Catholic Church and though he was sympathetic to the need to influence from within, he demonstrated his belief that inevitably Catholic Charismatics would have to leave the mother church.

Meanwhile, Ozard was unflinching in his opposition to Pentecostals risking any compromise with Catholics. He argued, "We may thank God for the Roman Catholic friend who professes an experience with the Holy Ghost. But let us remember that the Roman Catholic church hasn't changed its position on many matters of eternal importance!"[19] He categorized the areas of concern and those that needed to be cherished in two extensive lists of "we protest" and "we still believe. " It is not entirely clear how widely his fear was shared in his attempt to entrench the denomination in its traditional stand, but was probably representative of a significant segment of its constituents.

Differences between Rodriguez and Ozard's perspectives represent ambivalence in the PAOC toward developments in the Charismatic world. Uncertainty and fear of doctrinal compromise were prevalent but in varying degrees as indicated by such points of view and other references to the Charismatic Movement in *The Pentecostal Testimony*, not to mention individuals who unofficially, perhaps even secretly, attended Charismatic events such as The Catacombs. For example, Rodriguez's more moderate position stands in stark contrast to Ozard's unyielding classical Pentecostal apologetic. While Rodriguez admits that "in the majority of cases," those who experience the Holy Spirit would need to "go out of the church of Rome," he celebrated what he saw happening in the Catholic Church as evidence of divine work. He wrote:

> Another of the evidences of a loving providence in the actual religious process is, without doubt, the notable fact of the outpouring of the Holy Spirit on monks, nuns and priests and the Roman Catholic laity of our day.... In a Roman Catholic magazine Esquiu, a Jesuit writes of priests "speaking in new tongues." A letter from a North American friend tells of being in a meeting where Roman Catholics and evangelicals participated and all worshipped and praised God in other tongues.[20]

Yet, Rodriguez reveals some vacillation on another level. PAOC leaders and adherents were unsure of how to respond to the new wave of renewal, whether to ignore or celebrate it, or to defend their own ground. Even where they saw engagement with Charismatics as having some merit, there was still a clear tendency to assume that Charismatic Catholics especially would want to, and ought to embrace what Pentecostals had to offer them, even to the extent of leaving the mother church and joining the PAOC. Lines of communication needed to be developed as far as Rodriguez was concerned, but he seemed to be contradictory in arguing for "open dialogue" while also expecting Catholics to receive the Word as Pentecostals presented it to them: "Also today, this hour of open dialogue, of mutual coming together, and of sincere conversation without prejudices, puts on us the task of taking the initiative to take the Bread of Life and the real testimony of our lives to help hungry and thirsty Roman Catholics."[21] Although Rodriguez was not a member the PAOC, he clearly represented the reticence of the denomination toward the Charismatic Movement during this period.

A similar but more sympathetic view was expressed by Peter Prosser whose thought demonstrated a firm grasp of the significance of the ecumenical work done by du Plessis and the importance of the work of Vatican II in the birth of Catholic renewal. Nevertheless, he did not assume or expect that Catholics having experienced the Spirit would leave their church, arguing, "However, I do not think most of us had thought that the Catholics could receive the Spirit without 'coming out.' Yet here is a movement which for the most part is based on biblical doctrine."[22] In an effort perhaps to help ease any suspicion or fear on the part of his PAOC readers, he defended the Charismatic Movement as being more evangelical than what most thought it to be. Having already attended many Catholic Charismatic retreats, prayer meetings and other events, he reported: "The movement has a healthy evangelistic emphasis, calls people to repent, turn from sin to Jesus Christ and ask Christ to become their Saviour. They perform exorcisms, pray for the sick, and are excited about the return of the Lord.... Strong emphasis is placed on the power of Christ to deliver, fill with the Holy Spirit and develop gifts and graces in the whole man."[23]

Prosser was calling for patience and a wait-and-see attitude for Pentecostals as they tried to determine their place in the new movement that he seemed to have prematurely overstated as being evangelical. Pentecostals, he was requesting, should reach out to Charismatics wherever possible:

> As I have become involved more and more in the Charismatic movement I have come to realize that there is a wide open door for Pentecostals to minister and teach in this renewal and to share our doctrine in the light of the Bible. There is much that we do not understand but the worst we can do is to ignore it or stand on the outside and criticize... In the Roman Catholic church this evangelical wing has developed and is steadily growing... As Pentecostals let us give them a helping hand and show them our Christian love.[24]

The sentiment was clear: Pentecostals ought to do everything they could to facilitate the new wave of renewal.

Ozard, on the other hand, left no room for cooperation or dialogue with Charismatic Catholics and warned against any form of cooperative evangelism in the interest of fidelity to biblical truth:

> Our word of warning today is to hold fast to the Word of God and to the faith "once delivered unto the saints" (Jude 3). We cannot in the name of cooperative evangelism or charismatic revival or anything else, depart from those foundational truths "delivered to the saints." Any evangelism that breaks away from its evangelical moorings is set adrift upon a sea where the winds are contrary and the ships are broken up by the raging seas. We must insist upon the purity of the gospel.[25]

Although it was not likely a majority opinion, Ozard took liberty to raise the possibility that such aberrations that were characteristic of the Charismatic Movement might be the work of Satan: "Not all who change their names or their terminology have experienced a changed heart. Old Bible words are being vested with new meaning by wolves in sheep's clothing. So subtle is the working of Satan that he comes dressed up as an angel of light and sometimes even talking in tongues."[26]

Yet, Ozard's observations appeared astonishingly contradictory in his assertion, "Without letting prejudice, preconceived ideas or our dignity stand in the way, we must be prepared to move with God."[27] Such was the typical wavering in response to the emerging movement that ranged from acceptance in some quarters to hesitation and even refutation in others. Those who tended to oppose the new wave of renewal defaulted to a fundamentalist-evangelical position on the place of the written Word, seeing it as the ultimate source for the validation of its own distinctives and therefore leaving no space for negotiation nor a new in-breaking of the Spirit. Ozard's dual concern for uncompromising loyalty to the Bible and caution in all interdenominational evangelism efforts was driven home in his final statement—a stand that would have resonated with many readers at this early stage in the Charismatic Movement:

> But let us remember God never works apart from His Word.... How important it is in seasons of refreshing to keep the Book open so that we are led by the Spirit and the Word. Let us be careful that the new and exciting acceptance of our Pentecostal position and our love for evangelism doesn't lure us into a compromising position, which could be the beginning of the end for this revival we have enjoyed.[28]

In retrospect, it appears that misunderstanding and fear had led to the notion that the Charismatic Movement might indeed prove to be an eventual threat to the classical Pentecostal revival.

Protestant renewal did not appear to have given PAOC leadership and adherents cause for the same level of consternation, as did news of the Catholic Charismatic Renewal. One leader, Howard D. Honsinger, Superintendent of the Western Ontario District, in the early 1970s expressed in an opinion column for *The Pentecostal Testimony* that while Catholics and Pentecostals had discovered a common denominator in the experience of baptism in the Spirit and consequently with speaking in tongues becoming widely acceptable, he was nonetheless dismayed and described the changes with some cynicism: "In fact the general attitude has so altered that this phenomenon has become in some instances the criteria whereby it is established that the contemporary churchman has 'arrived.'"[29] Honsinger's viewpoint was a follow-up to the annual Charismatic conference held at Notre Dame University in 1973 at which among the thousands in attendance there were eight bishops and archbishops, one cardinal, and six hundred priests.[30]

Leaders of Honsinger's generation understandably found it difficult, if not impossible, to refrain from applauding and encouraging others to find joy when people of any Christian tradition experienced the Spirit. Yet, the perceived distance between the realities of the Catholic tradition and the Pentecostal movement was too wide for them to ignore without raising alarm. Honsinger was referring to what he believed to be the troubling news report contained in the August 1973 edition of the magazine on the conference at Notre Dame, specifically the closing "mass" at which Cardinal Leo-Joseph Suenens addressed the crowd and where "during the mass, worshippers repeatedly broke into the language of tongues in which they praised God in unintelligible voices."[31] Honsinger then expresses the common concern for most Pentecostals:

> Tongue speaking at a mass? I suppose that we should all rejoice? Or should we? Or is there a possibility that the uneasiness in my heart over reports like this is shared by others? How can this be reconciled with the teaching of Scripture? These

are serious questions. Should they be suppressed? Or do they deserve an answer? I think they should be answered, especially when they are considered in the light of the statements made by Kevin and Dorothy Ranaghan in the book Catholic Pentecostals. This book should be more properly titled Roman Catholic Pentecostals because it deals with the experience of Roman Catholics exclusively and describes the attitude of Roman Catholic Pentecostals toward the baptism with the Holy Spirit in particular. [32]

He then proceeded to draw attention to what he considered to be unacceptable sections of the Ranaghans' book, that Catholic renewal "began not through any Protestant Pentecostal proselytization but because some renewal-minded Catholics prayed to the Holy Spirit that they might become better Catholics "[33] and their claim that precise language about the Spirit would be talk not of "receiving the baptism in the Spirit but of renewing the baptism in the Spirit."[34] Honsinger was further alarmed by their statement that "the phrase 'baptism in the Spirit' has been borrowed from fundamentalist Pentecostals who don't have the sacramental theology needed to relate it to the whole context of water baptism."[35] He appeared to have had no reference point from which to judge these assertions in a reasoned manner and so surrendered to the temptation to dismiss and oppose them. His point was clear: the Catholic mass and Pentecostal baptism are entirely incompatible. His analysis conveyed a distinct air of closure:

> These statements trouble me. Inherent in them is a subtle reference to the primacy of the Roman church and the right to spiritual privileges through baptism by water into it. Shrouded discreetly in the cloak of dualism which has always been characteristic of Rome is the subtle emphasis that its membership can be loyal to the sacramental system of Rome and enjoy more fully the experience which has been that of fundamentalist Pentecostals. Why entertain a second rate experience outside the church when a first rate experience can be enjoyed within? [36]

It seems this was as close as any PAOC writer at the time came to asserting that Spirit baptism was the exclusive domain of classical Pentecostals.

Honsinger then came to the conclusion to which many of his contemporaries arrived, namely, that proof of the authenticity of Spirit baptism for a Catholic would necessitate an exit from the Catholic Church and the mass:

> Here is the heart of the dilemma. It is not difficult to understand how a Roman Catholic may continue for a time, because of ignorance of the Scriptures, in the pursuit of sacramental error. But as new light reaches his heart surely it will be impossible for him to pursue that which purports to be the actual repetition of the sacrifice of Calvary for the living and the dead every time it is celebrated by the priest. I do not hesitate to take this position because this practice constitutes a forthright denial of the finished work of Calvary and the "once for all" sacrifice which Christ made of Himself.[37]

Deeply embedded in PAOC history have been christological and soteriological motifs to which the work of the Spirit has been seen as integrally related. Honsinger remained true to this as he repeated the common line that the Holy Spirit would point to and glorify Christ and his salvific activity. For him, the Spirit would draw people away from the mass, not towards it. So, he claimed:

> I do not believe that the mass will become more beautiful and meaningful to the one who receives a genuine baptism with the Holy Spirit.... The Holy Spirit does not come to make better Catholics, or for that matter better Pentecostals. He comes to glorify Christ in the all-sufficiency of His finished work, and by a baptism of power to make better Christians. To me, there is something more important than an experience of speaking in tongues particularly if that experience ignores the principles of biblical Christianity and provides the means whereby baptized believers are incorporated into the church of Rome.[38]

Finally, Honsinger echoed the same uncertainty as some others regarding the entire validity of such an argument by admitting the freedom of the Spirit to work as he wills but only in accordance with the written Word. Like Ozard, he seemed to want to affirm both openness and closure simultaneously and argued thus:

> We should be ready to acknowledge the sovereignty of the Holy Spirit. He may bless whom He will. But, at the same time, we must never allow the true Pentecostal baptism with the Holy Spirit to become the guinea pig of a sort of ecclesiastical ecumenism whose existence depends upon the vagaries of shifting experience apart from obedience to the written Word of God. Religious experience is one thing. Obedience to the Word is something else.[39]

The overriding impression these documents convey is that there was immense ambivalence and ambiguity regarding the Charismatic Movement with a wide range of views and little clear sense of what the impact might be. Other considered and more official responses came through conferences, resolutions and correspondence from the national PAOC leadership.

Official Responses

The global spread of renewal in the latter half of the twentieth century, particularly as it emerged within the broader Christian and evangelical world of the West, had a far-reaching impact on the PAOC, as a classical Pentecostal movement. The environment necessitated a rethinking of its praxis and how its foundational doctrines with their traditional terminology might fit with the new reality. Kydd used Bruce Reed's interpretive model of human behavior as oscillating between independence and dependence allowing him to argue that the PAOC, previous to the emergence of the Charismatic Movement had become "intra-dependent," that is to say, it had come to consider itself as having a healthy confidence with its future firmly in its own hands.[40] The Charismatic Movement, nonetheless, changed all of that with its bold new trans-denominational approach to the Spirit life, the timing of which corresponded roughly to the beginning of a decline in doctrinal emphasis that was taking place within the PAOC. Kydd further observed, "The Pentecostals tended to assume that they would be able to provide teaching for the Charismatics, but the Charismatics, unfortunately in a number of cases, were not asking questions or showing any inclination to be taught."[41] As noted previously,

Pentecostals initially were applauding the move of the Spirit outside their own ranks as if what God was doing simply validated what he had done among them at the beginning of the century and for which they had endured much misunderstanding. Kydd portrayed the scene: "Pentecostals... saw what they perceived as their youth being replayed in Charismatic spontaneity.... There was a sense of novelty among the Pentecostals in seeing 'mainline' Christians doing the things for which they had previously been called 'holy rollers,' and there was a sense of being justified."[42]

The threat to its intra-dependency compelled the PAOC to look backward and attempt to regain and rearticulate what had been part of its own experience. The initial celebration of the outbreak of Pentecostalism elsewhere turned to an accent being placed on the differences, as Miller stated, "Canadian Pentecostals moved from enthusiastic approval of the new Charismatic Movement in the 1960s to a more wary assessment of it by the end of the '70s."[43] In essence, as interaction with the Charismatic Movement increased, it provoked a re-examination and re-affirmation of the fundamental doctrines of the PAOC.

However, few leaders seemed to realize that their own early history was not one of defending doctrinal distinctives as a priority. With the formation of the denomination in 1919, every effort was made to prevent anything from hampering the move of the Spirit, particularly ecclesiastical organizations. Robert Higgs, a PAOC graduate student, observes correctly, "What resulted from this reluctance to organize was the refusal to solidify a common stance."[44] Suspicion of ecclesiastical and doctrinal organization was reflected in a resolution in a statement published in 1926 just seven years following its formation as a fellowship of Canadian Pentecostal churches: "...We disapprove of making a doctrinal statement a basis of fellowship and co-operation but that we accept the Word of God in its entirety, conducting ourselves in harmony with its defined principles and Apostolic example endeavoring to keep the unity of the Spirit in the bond of peace until 'we all come in the unity of faith.'"[45] During its infancy, the PAOC's self-understanding was that it was part of a loose fellowship of Pentecostal groups.

As the period of the Charismatic Movement reached its apex, several official responses were forthcoming. In the 1977 National Leadership Council in Winnipeg, Manitoba the leadership openly discussed its concerns with the ongoing influence of a renewal phenomenon that it believed was already affecting its churches. Gordon R. Upton, the Eastern Ontario District Superintendent stated:

> It would be superfluous for us to indicate our great rejoicing in the light of the current widespread outpouring of the Holy Spirit among people of every denomination and which has given rise to the so-called "Charismatic Movement." The positive aspects need not be outlined here. There are several areas of concern which come into focus as we view this interdenominational and parachurch movement.[46]

Upton saw two of the PAOC distinctive positions as being more at risk than the others, namely divine healing and the expectation of Christ's imminent return. In addition to a shift in physical healings understood as being more spontaneous events to a focus on those who "specialize" in healing, he expressed great concern for the lack of attention given to the imminence of Christ's return and therefore an alleged failure on the part of Charismatics to be aggressive in missionary outreach. He addressed other relevant matters:

> The Charismatic Movement appears not to hold our distinctive position regarding the initial evidence or sign.... There is not an aggressive attempt to establish new churches.... There does not appear to be an emphasis upon holiness or separated living... Of greater concern, however, is the matter of Bible doctrine. This is particularly of concern in the Roman Catholic Charismatic Renewal. Does it really matter what people believe? Is experience sufficient to counteract doctrinal error? Should we be concerned about unsound doctrine in the light of the multitudes who are enjoying an unusual experience?[47]

Indicative again of the reticence of PAOC leadership regarding the new renewal, Upton admitted: "However, perhaps the plan of God is for recipients of the Pentecostal experience to remain within their churches."[48]

Examination of Catholic Charismatic Renewal documents that indicated devotion to the Eucharist as traditionally understood, the rosary, and especially a view of Spirit baptism as a part of conversion-initiation was confirmation enough for PAOC leadership that extreme vigilance must be exercised. Upton concluded: "The question that remains is related to how far we can go in our patronage without compromising our part. How closely can we become associated if we do not have opportunity to assist with Bible teaching? Already there is evidence among some of our people that experience covers any lack in doctrinal soundness? This could lead to the writing of our epitaph."[49]

It appeared that the PAOC was substantially less comfortable with the Charismatic Movement than was the Assemblies of God (USA). Knowing and following these developments, the question was asked at the PAOC Winnipeg meeting, "Does the attitude of some in the Assemblies of God lead to an accommodation of too many viewpoints? Do we give sanction to error in our patronage of the Charismatics?"[50]

Accommodation seems to have been more easily made by AG leadership than that north of the border. During the mid-1970s the General Council had passed a resolution appointing a commission "to explore areas of cooperation and avenues of communication in the various charismatic communities" and to report back to the executive presbytery. At least as far as the resolution was concerned, the AG was expressing complete openness to dialogue with what was amended to read "various charismatic movements" (not an insignificant change) rather than focusing on doctrinal differences. It affirmed the manifestation of the Spirit's gifts by members of the historic churches where such members had been tolerated and encouraged to practice their beliefs within their respective denominations. The resolution was driven partially by the growing interest shown by some charismatic groups already in fellowship and dialogue with the AG and by the belief that "The Assemblies of God has been raised up to witness to the power of the Holy Spirit in the twentieth century and is in position to provide sound biblical teaching to the numerous converts in the current revival wherever possible." It resolved to do three important things: first, to appoint an executive officer of the General Council to serve as liaison with charismatic groups to report quarterly on problems and opportunities; second, that the Assemblies of God accept invitations to participate in various inter-denominational charismatic conferences, and third, that a conference on the Holy Spirit be convened by 1978 or as soon as possible inviting leaders of the various charismatic movements to participate and be available to answer questions, to conduct workshops on problems and opportunities.[51]

The assessment report from the 1977 Winnipeg meeting revealed perhaps more than anywhere else the apprehension that the PAOC was experiencing over the growing Charismatic influence.[52] It noted that the denomination's early history showed that it came from a non-doctrinal emphasis to a very definitely stated position, a notion that presumably legitimized its stand that all renewal movements should do likewise. It asserted that doctrine was not established by trends but "anchored in the word of God." First, the Leadership Council affirmed that the word "regularly" in its constitution item called "Baptism of the Holy Ghost" meant "normally"—an attempt to firm up its position on initial evidence. Second, it resorted to a christological rather than pneumatological argument for its position by pointing out, "…our fellowship with believers is in Christ and not in experimental phenomena." It also noted a quite common sentiment at the time: "It is an amazing fact that we accept doctrinal error because some speak with tongues." Third, it questioned whether, since the Holy Spirit was given to 'speak of Christ' and 'lead into all truth,' Catholic Charismatic leaders were trying to tie Charismatics most closely to the Catholic Church. Fourth, it expressed dismay over the failure to see lifestyle changes in those who had professed to speak in tongues. A specific example was offered of an individual who came into a PAOC church from a Charismatic group but who allegedly "gave no evidence of any separated life," had "a wrong influence upon others," and openly criticized the church, saying that it was "not emotional enough" and had "not enough evidence of the gifts of the Spirit in action." Fifth, it observed that Charismatics tended to be often divisive and dependent on "inspired utterances," with led to confusion in determining doctrines and attitudes.[53]

Yet the leaders at that time affirmed the openness of worship and the enthusiasm of the Charismatic Movement; while holding firmly to the denomination's doctrinal heritage, they called for "a real climate of love." In the end, there were several practical challenges with which the leaders saw themselves having to grapple. Bible college presidents attending the Winnipeg event raised concerns relative to their students over challenges in the uncertainty about initial evidence and the loss of holiness as exhibited in character and lifestyle, further defined as dress, appearance, and activities such as theatre attendance and the use of alcoholic beverages. Furthermore, from the leaders' perspective, guidance needed to be given in approaching the plethora of Charismatic literature, suggesting that more carefully crafted writing from a classical Pentecostal perspective was essential. A final emerging challenge needing to be confronted was that all applicants for credentials be compelled to affirm the PAOC doctrinal position as well as an annual reaffirmation be required by current credential holders. The concluding sentiment provided a definitive summary: "It was agreed that we need to be aggressive in our position, positive in our actions, and selective in our speakers."[54]

Nevertheless, in 1978, General Conference members received a report from the leadership with a surprisingly more positive tone as "an expression of our attitude towards those who call themselves 'charismatic' people or groups in Canada today."[55] Although the document nowhere indicated, it was a verbatim appropriation of the earlier Charismatic Study Report adopted by the 35th General Council of the Assemblies of God in August 1973. In any case, the report interestingly was a warm embrace of what the PAOC saw as happening across Canada as well:

> There is thrilling evidence that God is moving mightily by his Spirit throughout all the earth. The winds of the Spirit are blowing freely outside the normally recognized Pentecostal body...Thousands of people have prayed for years that this would come to pass. The Pentecostal Assemblies of Canada wishes to identify with what God is doing in the world today.... [It] does not place approval on that which is manifestly not scriptural in doctrine or conduct. But neither do we categorically condemn everything that does not totally or immediately conform to our standards. No genuine spiritual movement in church history has been completely free of problems or above criticism. The Pentecostal movement of the century has experienced its problems relating both to doctrine and conduct.... We place our trust in God to bring his plan about as He pleases in his sovereign will. It is important that we find our way in a sound scriptural path, avoiding the extremes of an ecumenism that compromises scriptural principles and exclusivism that excludes true Christians.[56]

From the picture emerging, this apparently warm embrace did not seem to last.

Uncertainty and inconsistency in response to the Charismatic Movement continued into 1980 as the denomination at its General Conference revised its position on tongues as initial evidence by changing the wording in its *Statement of Fundamental and Essential Truths*. This change was from tongues as "the initial *physical* sign" of the baptism in the Holy Spirit to simply "initial evidence" of the baptism in the Holy Spirit,[57] an attempt possibly related to growing pressure from some areas of the constituency to soften the expectation of immediacy in speaking in tongues as evidence.

In the context of increased interest in demonology, the PAOC also introduced a statement articulating the denominational stand that although demons were real and attempted to oppose God's purpose, they could not possess believers.[58] The official position of the AG on the question, "Can Born-Again Believers Be Demon Possessed?" had already been adopted in 1975. In its publication the PAOC was clearly identified the source of this stance, "This statement reprinted from the Pentecostal Evangel represents the official position of the Assemblies of God USA.... As a sister organization, the Pentecostal Assemblies of Canada has adopted the statement as its position also."[59]

Before 1980, "demon" does not appear anywhere in *The Statement of Fundamental and Essential Truths,* only reference to the "devil and his angels."[60] That year, a new section called "Angels" was introduced under which was added the item "The Believer and Demons."[61] It stated, "Demons attempt to thwart God's purpose. However in Christ, the believer may have complete liberty from the influence of demons. He cannot be possessed by them because his body is the temple of the Holy Spirit in which Christ is Lord."[62] While the belief that 'demons,' traditionally referred to as 'fallen angels,' sought to possess humans for evil purposes was not generally controversial for most PAOC people, it was the extent of the demonic influence that was the point of contention. Most likely, this was the result of the influence of certain segments of the Charismatic Movement, more specifically, that a Christian could be possessed by one or more demons.[63] The PAOC articulated its firmly held belief that this was an impossibility.

Furthermore, the PAOC recognized a need to clarify and perhaps re-affirm the purpose of spiritual gifts in the face of what it deemed to be their excessive and unwise use in some circles. This may not have been traceable to any specific Charismatic occurrence but they were aware that the gate had probably been opened wide to a variety of approaches to the use of the *charismata*. Thus, they seemed to sense a need to try to close the gate or certainly to guard it. The PAOC having historically defended Spirit baptism against its detractors who criticized glossolalia as fake or those who practiced it as being demonically influenced, now had to contend with a new view on Spirit baptism.[64] In response to Charismatic pneumatological thought that a sign of having received the Holy Spirit was not limited to tongues but could involve any gift of the Spirit, the PAOC clarified its position by stating, "The gifts of the Spirit are supernatural abilities given by God through the exercising of which believers are enabled to minister effectively and directly in particular situations."[65] Classical Pentecostals were charging Charismatics with confusion or misrepresentation of tongues as one of the ministry gifts as opposed to tongues as evidence of having received Spirit baptism. It can be concluded with a reasonable degree of certainty that this was an effort at an apologetic not only for the Pentecostal distinctive of Spirit baptism with tongues, but a clarification regarding the purpose of the other spiritual gifts, none of which were to be viewed as initial evidence of thaving received the Spirit.

The impulse to protect its own reached a height for the PAOC in the early 1980s. At the beginning of the decade, the General Conference also requested that the name "Pentecostal" be displayed clearly on all local churches. This was in direct response to the growing nonsectarian trend inherent in the Charismatic climate. The resolution in part stated:

> WHEREAS we believe that in the light of the current Pentecostal and charismatic emphasis in the world today, it is of great importance to identify our assemblies as being "Pentecostal," and WHEREAS in view of the growing favour with which we are regarded, ...BE IT RESOLVED that we encourage that the name "Pentecostal" be displayed prominently, either in the specific name of the assembly or use of the phrase "affiliated with the Pentecostal Assemblies of Canada" (not abbreviated) in connection with the actual name...[66]

The PAOC had come full circle from its original resistance to institutionalization and identification as one of the major features of the Canadian ecclesiastical landscape.

Finally, the most definitive expression of difficulty with the direction of the Charismatic Movement, in particular as it related to renewal within the Catholic Church, came from the PAOC General Conference in 1982. A resolution had been presented to the Resolutions Committee August 18, 1982:

> WHEREAS, There is a degree of fraternization between some PAOC credential holders and some leaders of the Roman Catholic Church which results;
> (a) a clouding of the differences in doctrine and practice
> (b) confusion among Protestants, and
> (c) deep concern on the part of ex-Roman Catholics; and
> WHEREAS, The Bible states, "That if it were possible the elect will be deceived" in the last days; and
> WHEREAS, There was a Protestant Reformation; therefore be it
> RESOLVED, That we:
> (a) reaffirm our belief in the Statement of a Fundamental and Essential Truths of the PAOC will see and especially in the doctrines of:
> (1) justification by faith alone
> (2) the finished work of Christ; one sacrifice, once and for all
> (3) one mediator between God and man—Jesus Christ
> (4) the Word of God as our final of Authority in faith and practice
> (5) the priesthood of the believer.[67]

The resolution then listed twelve doctrines of the Catholic Church to which the PAOC did not adhere such as the infallibility of the pope and the veneration of Mary, and then continued, "and be it RESOLVED FURTHER that we remind our constituency that the charismatic renewal has not changed the above basic doctrines and dogmas of the Roman Catholic Church."[68]

While the form of the resolution that was eventually presented to the membership had by then some modifications, thus making the document's language admittedly less stark, the intent had not changed and was adopted by the Conference. There was little official activity in response to the Charismatic Movement subsequent to that action.

Impact of Changes

Defending theological constructs in response to renewal movements did not tend to meet with significant and measureable success. One thing is certain, however: the ethos of the Charismatic Movement was not friendly toward any impetus to protect theological systems at the risk of stifling spiritual renewal. Endeavors to reinforce the five doctrinal points proved to be an extraordinarily formidable task in an age when social thought patterns were shifting toward less systematization rather than more. In that regard, the extent to which the deepening post-modern era has impacted the PAOC is also difficult to measure. However, the loss of emphasis on objective truth expressed in propositional doctrinal statements certainly correlates with the post-modern worldview where truth and meaning tend to be subjective with no obvious overarching meta-narrative. Although such speculation may be reasonable, it is current PAOC culture and practice that provides the clue to the impact of subsequent renewal movements.

There is no aspect of PAOC climate where the transformation is more evident than in the worship patterns borrowed from Charismatic, as well as neo-Charismatic influences, both of which blended together to produce a very different PAOC than that to which its older generation was accustomed. Traditional hymnody with its theoretical and rhythmical style, chordal progressions, and themes that reflected and promoted the doctrinal basis of the Pentecostal movement were evident in the early days of the PAOC. Kydd argues that Pentecostals have now become concerned with what they get out of worship as opposed to what God receives, a trend that developed in the late 1960s and 1970s as the Pentecostal church adopted musical styles from society that reflected popular culture with its "individualistic, narcissistic self-gratification."[69] Essentially, if PAOC churches have turned to society to find what Kydd refers to as a "musical idiom in which to worship,"[70] it has likewise resulted in the charge that there has been a loss of the singing of doctrine that, from the perspective of some older Pentecostals, has replaced gospel proclamation that once took place through singing as well as preaching. Furthermore, if singing songs and hymns with theological substance is believed to have played such a major role in the culture and heritage of the PAOC but has now been lost, it is plausible that some may similarly conclude that such a shift toward the embracing of popular culture has also affected preaching and teaching, as demonstrated through the self-help, user-friendly, and human-centered emphases as opposed to theological and doctrinal reflection. As in other contexts, some PAOC ministers have also begun to see and refer to themselves as "emergent" though no one has attempted to determine how the term fits into a classical Pentecostal model.

With the decline in doctrinal certainty and emphasis at all levels of its life, the PAOC in the second decade of the millennium now finds itself struggling with its identity. The movement has long ago left its isolation and been compelled to abandon any so-called 'intra-dependent' position. It has moved toward the middle of the evangelical stream while having selected from both the substance and style of the Charismatic and later neo-Charismatic movements. The original doctrines are on the books, taught in Bible colleges, and assumed to be adhered to for ministerial leadership but are largely out of view within the PAOC grassroots environment. Ian Rennie, a non-Pentecostal evangelical, observes that for Pentecostals emerging from relative isolation, "it can be a shock to find gifted and dedicated Christians in other communions, even in those most obviously in need of renewal, and can result in a sense of deprivation and inferiority."[71] The answer may be found somewhere in pointing the next PAOC generation toward neither isolationism nor the abandonment of its roots but rather toward the meaningful contribution it can make to the broader evangelical and Christian world with its heritage of emphasis on the work of the Holy Spirit as God in action in the world, though now in a post-modern one.

Notes

1. News item, *The Pentecostal Testimony* (November 1972): 12.
2. C. H. Bronsdon, "Why a Pentecostal Bible College?" *The Pentecostal Testimony* (January 1973): 11.
3. Quebedeaux, *The New Charismatics*, 183.
4. While a university student in the early 1970s, the author experienced this scenario when renewal broke out in segments of the UCC. It took several years for suspicion as to its authenticity to dissipate. The Pentecostal Assemblies of Newfoundland slowly began to more readily accept the renewal especially as some of the participants ended up in PAON churches. For several decades following the beginnings of UCC renewal, the group would make use of the PAON provincial camp and convention facilities for its annual renewal retreat.
5. "Catholic Pentecostal Movement in Canada," *The Pentecostal Testimony* (May 1973): 17-18.
6. Ibid.
7. "Catholic Pentecostals' Largest Meeting," *The Pentecostal Testimony* (August 1973): 10.
8. "Challenging Campaigns," *The Pentecostal Testimony* (June 1973): 14.
9. Ibid.
10. This was a frequent theme song of the Charismatic Movement written by Peter Scholte in 1966.
11. "Youth Parade in Montreal," *The Pentecostal Testimony* (October 1972): 12-13.
12. Jack Ozard, "Let's Stay on Course," *The Pentecostal Testimony* (September 1973): 4.
13. Ibid.
14. Ibid.
15. The November 1982 edition of *The Pentecostal Testimony* included a feature article by a well-respected PAOC pastor, Michael Horban entitled "Our Pentecostal Heritage." On the title passage was included Resolution 15 passed at the PAOC General Conference that year:

> WHEREAS, There is an awareness among us that God is working in our unusual manner among members of many denominations today; and
>
> WHEREAS, *The charismatic renewal has not changed their basic doctrines and dogmas;* therefore be it
>
> RESOLVED, That we reaffirm our belief in the Statement of Fundamental and Essential Truths of the PAOC and especially in the doctrines of:
>
>   (a) justification by faith alone
>   (b) the finished work of Jesus Christ; one sacrifice, once and for all
>   (c) one mediator between God and man—Jesus Christ
>   (d) the Word of God as our final authority in faith and practice

    (e) the priesthood of the believer. (my italics)
 16. Ozard, "Let's Stay on Course," 4.
 17. Amaro Rodrigues, "The Spirit of God is Moving," *The Pentecostal Testimony* (August 1970): 8.
 18. Ibid., 8-9.
 19. Ozard, "Let's Stay on Course," 4.
 20. Rodriguez, "The Spirit of God is Moving," 9.
 21. Ibid.
 22. Peter Prosser, "Roman Catholic Charismatic Impact Increases," *The Pentecostal Testimony* (September 1973): 5.
 23. Ibid.
 24. Ibid., 26.
 25. Ozard, "Let's Stay on Course," 4.
 26. Ibid.
 27. Ibid., 4, 26.
 28. Ibid., 26.
 29. Howard D. Honsinger, "The Ecumenical Guinea Pig," *The Pentecostal Testimony* (November 1973): 26.
 30. Prosser, "Roman Catholic Charismatic Impact Increases," 5.
 31. "Catholic Pentecostal Largest Meeting," *The Pentecostal Testimony* (August 1973): 10.
 32. Honsinger, "The Ecumenical Guinea Pig," 26.
 33. Kevin & Dorothy Ranaghan, *Catholic Pentecostals* (Paramus, NJ, New York, NY & Toronto, ON: Paulist Press Deus Books, 1969): 153.
 34. Ibid., 151.
 35. Ibid., 142.
 36. Honsinger, "The Ecumenical Guinea Pig," 26.
 37. Ibid.
 38. Ibid.
 39. Ibid.
 40. Kydd, "The Impact of the Charismatic Renewal on Classical Pentecostalism," 59.
 41. Ibid., 63.
 42. Ibid.
 43. Thomas Miller, *Canadian Pentecostals*, 301.
 44. Robert Higgs, "Pentecostal History—1980 Statement of Fundamental and Essential Truths." (unpublished paper): 2.
 45. "Minutes of the Pentecostal Assemblies of Canada," *The Pentecostal Testimony* (February 1926).
 46. Upton, "Pentecostal Distinctives," PAOC Archives.
 47. Ibid.
 48. Ibid.
 49. Ibid.
 50. Assessment Committee Report, Leadership Council, November 15-17,

1977, Winnipeg, Manitoba. PAOC Archives.

51. A/G Resolution 7, Charismatic Movement, 1977. PAOC Archives.

52. Assessment Committee Report, Leadership Council, November 15-17, 1977, Winnipeg, Manitoba. PAOC Archives.

53. Ibid.

54. Ibid.

55. "Charismatic Study Report," PAOC General Conference, August 1978. PAOC Archives.

56. Ibid.

57. *Statement of Fundamental & Essential Truths* (Toronto, Ontario, Canada: PAOC, 1980), PAOC Archives. (original italics)

58. Ibid.

59. *The Pentecostal Testimony* (June 1975): 16.

60. James Craig, correspondence with the author, July 1, 2014.

61. Higgs, *Pentecostal History*. Higgs interviewed Charles Yates, General Secretary of the PAOC at the time of the revision who stated that he had no knowledge as to the reasons for the inclusion of this article, 8. Higgs' interview with Charles Yates, April 12, 2006.

62. *Statement of Fundamental & Essential Truths*, (Toronto, Ontario, Canada: PAOC, 1980), PAOC Archives.

63. Higgs, *Pentecostal History,* 9.

64. Ibid., 14.

65. Ibid.

66. Official Minutes of the 32nd Biennial PAOC General Conference, August 1980, PAOC Archives.

67. Official Minutes of the 33rd Biennial PAOC General Conference, August 1982, PAOC Archives.

68. Ibid.

69. Kydd, "The Impact of the Charismatic Renewal on Classical Pentecostalism in Canada": 63.

70. Ibid.

71. Ian Rennie, "Pentecostalism and Christianity," *Testimony* (June 2001): 8.

9

Reflections and Recommendations

It is tempting to speculate whether what has transpired in the PAOC over the decades and likely in other classical Pentecostal groups might be the expected cycle of a renewal movement from a free-flowing spontaneous fellowship of the Spirit to dependence on a series of doctrinal reference points in order to safeguard against the threat of error. Ironically, however, emphasis on a body of teaching now appears to inevitably take second place to worship and relationships. It can obviously be debated whether such change in an era of spiritual renewal conditioned by post-modern thinking is unavoidable and desired, or should be resisted and challenged.

Although in its official publication, *The Pentecostal Testimony*, the PAOC has held to the five essential doctrinal points and at times over the past four decades has seen the need to reaffirm those positions, the coverage devoted to them has dwindled over time. Former leaders, pastors and laypeople also recognize the loss of focus in practice. The attempt to respond to the doctrinal influences of the Charismatic Movement seems to have all but failed to stem the tide of cultural and religious change. A missions spotlight has continued to be in the forefront but writings on the doctrinal tenets of the denomination have dwindled in favor of more on leadership, testimonies, social involvements, and practical living subjects.

Official attempts by PAOC leadership to address the challenges of the Charismatic Movement were ongoing for several years as evidenced by segments of its conferences, executive meetings, and communiqués which betrayed an understandable uncertainty. On the one hand, the PAOC saw the need to hold to the agreed foundations upon which it believed it was built and on the other, it felt the need not to be viewed as rigid and unresponsive to the Spirit's work in the world.

Renewal in Canada began long before the early years of the last century. The First Great Awakening of the mid-eighteenth century that had arisen against the backdrop of political upheaval in America sent ripples into parts of eastern British North America. It signaled the initial stages of a complex process in which renewal impulses would continue to influence Canada from the two other corners of what is frequently known as the North Atlantic Triangle.[1] As for modern Canadian Pentecostalism, the more pronounced influences came from the south with the development of the American Holiness movement and its Pentecostal offshoot.

While some renewal forces had their origin in Britain, the free flow of Methodist, Holiness, Pentecostal, and Charismatic preaching and teaching, publications, and music would continue into the next century and beyond from the south, and to some degree, return in a reciprocal way.

The holiness environment set the stage for the rise of Pentecostalism in Canada as it did south of the border. The PAOC founders had deep holiness roots with at least a couple of them being directly impacted by the events at Azusa Street. As an array of fundamentalist, dispensationalist, and pneumatalogical beliefs coalesced, the PAOC came to see itself as the guardian of Pentecostal orthodoxy. Later renewal phenomena such as the New Order of the Latter Rain, the Charismatic Movement, and the more recent neo-Charismatic renewal were often seen as deviations from accepted classical Pentecostal doctrine and practice, thus putting the PAOC in an overall defensive position while it attempted to navigate through what it could and could not affirm in the new. Leadership believed that they had successfully weathered the Latter Rain storm that had arisen from within, but it was the emergence of the Charismatic Movement from without, with no connection to the older Canadian Pentecostalism, that would confront the PAOC with a wider challenge.

It did not take long for the Charismatic Movement and the events surrounding Dennis Bennett's experience of the Spirit, as well as the later developments at Duquesne and Notre Dame to make their presence felt on the Canadian side, mainly through American Charismatic leaders being invited to share with churches and university audiences in Canada as well as through individuals visiting the original places of the Charismatic phenomenon. In particular, growing secularization in Quebec and rejection of institutional religion in the 1960s, known as the Quiet Revolution appears to have left a spiritual vacuum into which the Charismatic Movement was able to find a place, where at the height of the renewal in 1977, the largest Charismatic conference perhaps ever held in Canada occurred in Montreal drawing 50,000 francophones.[2] The free flow of people and ideas to and from the United States along with the expanding power of television had a transforming impact, chiefly among a younger generation of PAOC churchgoers along with adherents of the traditional churches. Ted Yuke recalled how, having heard about the events at Duquesne University, he travelled there with a group from his congregation. He described the experience that changed the direction of his ministry:

> We went there and God was moving on people, I mean, big time. I sat there and I struggled at first because what I saw, things I had never seen before in my life..... But what I struggled with, I saw God moving on people that I was kinda taught God shouldn't be moving on. Women had make-up, earrings, all the stuff. I grew up without any of that. And I'm watching the mascara all being ripped apart and ladies faces just weeping in the presence of God. I knew God was there. So no matter. I was going through this turmoil. This is the way I was brought up all along. But it started something in our hearts and we came back ...we just opened up and said, "God, there's something more...." Watching people...there was an openness and there was an excitement for God. They didn't care what somebody thought.

They would get out in the aisle and start dancing. It wasn't a show. It wasn't a performance. It was not orchestrated. It was just an exuberance for God. People would come to the altar with such simple faith. There were healings and restorations and deliverance. I have been religious my whole life but it changed. It was almost unexplainable what was happening… I'm standing there as a Pentecostal looking at this, attracted to it because I'm saying at the same time what I grew up in, as good as it was, is not cutting it. We have nice churches but there is no impact. There is no life.... [But] it was just the momentum of the Spirit that was driving [this]. It was not a good idea. It was not a slick preacher. It wasn't charisma. I mean, some of the stuff that was being preached wasn't even what we would call great oratory. God was in the house. There was an expectancy.[3]

Representative of many from his generation, Yuke was not rejecting his Pentecostal heritage, but rather was frustrated over the loss of what he believed Pentecostalism to have originally been. From whence renewal came was of no consequence to many as long as it was genuine and restored what had disappeared over time.

What some PAOC leaders and pastors believed privately regarding the authenticity and positive potential of the Charismatic Movement, once it was clear that most Charismatics would not be looking to the PAOC for direction, is a matter of speculation. District and national leadership was called to respond to a phenomenon that seemed to have no parameters, direction, or accountability; they were often under pressure from local pastors who found themselves obligated to deal with those Charismatics who did frequent their churches, or with some of their own adherents influenced by Charismatic experiences. There was serious uneasiness about where the Charismatic Movement was going and the long-range impact it would have upon the PAOC churches. Fear of losing its own and of aberrations from long established doctrinal positions compelled responses that betrayed misunderstanding and isolationism. There is no evidence that any attempts were initiated to dialogue with mainstream Charismatic groups, leaving the impression with many Charismatics that the PAOC believed it had a monopoly on the Spirit. There was, however, much less apprehension with ministry involvement to Charismatics and cooperation with them as long as one of its own trusted leaders was at the helm. An example of this affirmation took place in late 1973 when William Prankard, a PAOC evangelist opened The Charismatic Centre in Ottawa, Ontario. Several well-known PAOC pastors attended and showed their support. Upton remarked, "…prophecy is being fulfilled as people are being brought together from many backgrounds into the fullness of the Holy Spirit." The stated purpose of The Charismatic Centre was to provide "a place of worship, study and fellowship for people of all denominations who have become interested in a practical supernatural 'charismatic' experience in their lives." [4]

Two Generations Encounter Renewal

The generation born before 1945, commonly known as the 'builder' generation, was characterized by focus on group goals, intense loyalty to institutions, and resistance to change. PAOC people from the builder generation had seen their denomination generally flourish during the years of the Great Depression, World War II and beyond. Like classical Pentecostals elsewhere, they tended to see their version of revival as the final outpouring of the Spirit before Christ's return. Few expected renewal to arise from within mainstream denominations and so the PAOC was caught in a position of not knowing how to respond to such a development. For decades, it had already become an established Canadian denomination with firm and explicitly stated doctrinal distinctives. The impulse of the builder generation was to protect those propositions and, by implication, to preserve the revival that had produced the denomination. To venture into other Christian traditions except for openly evangelistic purposes was tantamount to risking compromise of biblical standards.

Nevertheless, David Mainse as one of the most visible national spokespersons for that generation of PAOC constituents had few misgivings about engaging fully with other denominations, which in turn, perplexed and worried many of his contemporaries. That he was able to speak so openly about the need to engage with other Christian persuasions, was either because of his disarming personality and sincerity, or perhaps because there were many people in PAOC ranks who were responding positively to his approach even though they may not have said so publicly. It is possible that the freedom and spontaneity associated with the spiritual identity of early Pentecostals may have resonated with some PAOC people, awakening a longing for what they felt had been all but lost. It was not altogether difficult for many to appreciate Gordon Williams, the Charismatic UCC minister on Mainse's staff, as being close to their own tradition, representing a revivalist past with which they could identify.

While Mainse was sympathetic to what was happening in the Charismatic Movement, he never did become a Charismatic nor did he actively promote the Movement but remained loyal to the PAOC. His focus instead was on affirming and cultivating everything that he saw in any Christian tradition as the Spirit's work. In that sense, he was more of a 'middle-of-the-road' evangelical who was able to cross all lines and to be accepted in practically every denominational tradition. Any detractors have long been silenced by Mainse's exceptionally respectable record of national ecumenical ministry of over half a century.

Perhaps the only other visible locus of PAOC-Charismatic encounter of that generation was the Full Gospel Businessmen Fellowship (FGBMFI) as previously alluded to in Chapter Four. Originating as it did in the classical Pentecostal tradition, its nondenominational affiliation provided a comfortable environment for those from other denominations who had encountered the Spirit through the Charismatic Movement. It became a place of freedom and understanding where acceptance was largely guaranteed. The context was similar to what social-judgment theorists, Hovland and Sherif (1961) refer to as 'the latitude of acceptance,' defined as "the range of positions on an issue ... an individual considers acceptable to him (including the one 'most acceptable' to him)" and on the opposite end of the continuum 'the latitude of rejection' as "positions he finds objectionable (including the one 'most objectionable' to him»."⁵ The FGBMFI was one of the few environments where for a Charismatic that range was expanded. On the contrary, in a long established revivalist denomination with clearly defined doctrinal distinctives, the range would have been much narrower along the continuum. For some Charismatics who eventually ended up in PAOC churches, the FGBMFI became a stepping-stone or middle ground between the Charismatic Movement and classical Pentecostalism. They were able to mingle with Pentecostals, many who regularly attended FGBMFI events and some who were the leaders and organizers. In this way, they subsequently found in some PAOC churches the kind of environment closest to what they now enjoyed most at the FGBMFI rather than in their traditional churches. The Charismatic Movement in Canada was, in essence, a general environment of spiritual renewal that blended into its own identity influences from both the Jesus Movement and the FGBMFI. It was a phenomenon of national interdenominational activity bringing people from mainline churches into new spiritual experiences, many of whom became part of the PAOC or of independent Charismatic churches.

Those in the PAOC born after 1945 (the 'boomer' generation) were far less concerned about loyalty to leadership structures and institutions in general. Yet, they had a keen spiritual appetite and recognized in their own heritage what they wished to retain and what they believed was transferable to every generation. For some youth in the Toronto area, The Catacombs was exposure to the familiar and the unfamiliar simultaneously, a mix that was attractive as they witnessed a focus on experiencing the Spirit occurring in a radically different context from anything to which they had been accustomed. The excitement of hundreds of youth from the counterculture and from traditional churches worshipping and associating in an environment of love and acceptance was new, but palpable.

For hundreds of other PAOC youth in colleges and universities across Canada, the same enchantment was evident as they heard about experiences of the Spirit occurring in contexts that were totally non-traditional Pentecostal. The fact that the Charismatic Movement, especially the Catholic renewal, emerged among the educated gave it special credence. While some PAOC youth may have already been experiencing some uncertainty about tongues as necessarily initial evidence, they had no similar uncertainty about the reality of the Spirit for their time. Yet, they were faced with the appeal of popular culture with its materialism that, in subsequent years, would threaten their passion for renewal and for some, would transform their renewal experience through the attraction of the success and prosperity gospel.

Two Generations Changed by Renewal

Many of the builder generation are still bewildered by the dramatic changes they have seen within the PAOC during their lifetime, especially in music and worship style, dress, appearance, and the substance of preaching that often omits explicit attention to the basic doctrines of the denomination as stated in its *Statement of Fundamental and Essential Truths* or sometimes even little biblical reference. A worldview that observed biblical truth through a rational, systematic lens met a generation that yearned for freedom from traditional church dogma, structure and authority resulting in the loss of what an older generation believed to be essential as the defining parameters of its denomination. The demise of emphasis on the major doctrinal positions of the PAOC is attributable to the accompanying environment of the Charismatic Movement which seemed to permit a freedom to experience and believe that did not previously exist. In effect, the climate perhaps overpowered and displaced any tendency to hold to non-negotiable theological positions. It is not at all clear, for example, why the PAOC appeared in its official publication to have dispensed with lending much attention to pneumatology, a trend that continues to the present day. It might be conjectured that it was a reaction to the excesses of previous movements and an attraction to a safer evangelical path.

There may also be other ways to view this astonishing development whereby the attempt to protect doctrinal integrity met with apparent failure. Changes were in the making whereby the PAOC would become much less monolithic in style and substance than what it had been in its infancy. In the ensuing years, a variety of trajectories have emerged within the denomination. Especially in some rural areas, an older style Pentecostalism continues to persist with little change over the decades, although this would be a shrinking minority of churches. In other contexts, Pentecostal-Charismatic style churches are popular that mix classical Pentecostal motifs and style with those of both the Charismatic and neo-Charismatic movements. The third trajectory has been the rise within the PAOC of thoroughgoing evangelical congregations based on models of contemporary American evangelicalism and emergent church trends. The latter direction for the PAOC might possibly be a reaction to the perceived primitive nature of classical Pentecostalism, on the one side, and the excesses of later renewal movements on the other. Thus, the denomination perhaps exists as a safe place for the expression of basic Christianity without the need for focus on clear-cut doctrines and provision of charismatic space. Admittedly, there is considerable overlap among them with discernible elements of each in the other, especially of the Charismatic Movement in the older strains of Pentecostalism. The hypothesis must await further research.

Notwithstanding, the PAOC has veered significantly toward the evangelical mainstream and seems to find a significant level of comfort in aligning itself with Canadian evangelicalism and the broader evangelical world.[6] With the PAOC having been instrumental in bringing the Evangelical Fellowship of Canada (EFC) into existence in 1964 and its continued alliance with the evangelical world, the question remains whether it was perhaps more comfortable in becoming more evangelical and less Pentecostal, or at least becoming more generically 'Pentecostal' in its ambiance, rather than promoting and emphasizing its traditional distinctives.

Other forces were converging that ran counter to the early preoccupation with carefully articulated doctrine. As the anti-intellectualism of the past began to decrease and increasing numbers of PAOC minsters and leaders enrolled in higher education, there tended to be a growing discomfort with firm doctrines substantiated by an array of isolated biblical texts. Some of these doctrines lost their impact because of a generational change in which higher education produced thinkers who were not prepared to hold too tightly to definitive theological statements. Bible college training no longer transferred those positions to their students *ex cathedra*. Furthermore, the improvement in the socio-economic status of many Pentecostals made them want to be seen as less sectarian, thus making it difficult to make predetermined doctrines a priority that might make Pentecostals appear more parochial. Growing secularization, the power of the media, and suspicion of institutions all worked together to create an environment within the PAOC that was no longer conducive to doctrinaire ways of doing theology and church life.

In an effort to respond to the need to be contemporary during the era of the 1960s and 1970s, there was an inclination among youth to select from the culture what was palatable, convenient, and what conveyed a sense of freedom and openness. The same perspective on reality appears to have found its parallel in the way PAOC youth saw and responded to the Charismatic Movement. They were comfortable embracing what they saw as being of value while leaving behind its more distasteful aspects. The end result was an environment that overpowered focus on the PAOC's central doctrines and consequently, pulled into its ethos a spontaneity in thought, action, and in overall climate that it had not previously known.

The Road Ahead

An attempt has been made to discern and articulate areas of actual interface between classical Pentecostalism as represented by the PAOC and the Charismatic Movement during the 1960s to 1980s and, in turn, the transformational influence of the latter movement upon the PAOC. The result in practically all of its churches to a lesser or greater degree has been a transformation in its worship and teaching style and in attention given to its traditional doctrinal loci. Uniformity ironically exists only in the varying mixture of diverse elements borrowed from the Charismatic Movement and subsequent renewal movements as well as the evangelical mainstream.

The PAOC found itself in the most difficult dilemma of wanting to affirm the work of the Spirit wherever it was taking place while clinging to its own historical heritage. Astonishing ambivalence is manifested in its publications, its participation in Charismatic events and in its leadership consultations. Because the Charismatic Movement never became a denomination nor did Canadian charismatics flock to PAOC churches, statistics and other data are sparse. Determining where charismatics ended up would be a rewarding area of research. Nevertheless, many did eventually find their way into PAOC churches, established themselves as leaders and loyal supporters, some of whom the author is personally aware.[7] It has been expressed by some in PAOC ranks that the denomination has benefited greatly from the Charismatic Movement more than perhaps is recognized through both the direct and indirect addition of its members to their churches.

It is doubtful that ambiguity in relationship between the two movements would have occurred if the Charismatic Movement had emerged prior to the crystallizing of definite Pentecostal positions in the PAOC's early days when there was internal resistance to organizing a revival movement into a denomination. One is left only to imagine the landscape had there been openness to the later renewal regardless of where it originated. Gradual departure from emphasis on some of its distinctive positions despite occasional attempts to sustain them took place in the context of an era when there was a return to the center of what birthed classical Pentecostalism in the first place, the experience of the Spirit.

Reformulating its theological distinctives to accommodate current trends may not be the way forward for the PAOC, but neither is retreating behind a wall of doctrinal protection. New approaches that aim at better understanding of the history and theology behind those positions, consideration of reasonable latitude in some areas, and communication of the same that cause those distinctives to be lived out within the post-modern context need to be considered. Although seemingly a contradiction from the perspective of its history, the PAOC will need to see itself within the broader context of what God is doing globally and contribute willingly from its own theology and experience to the wider church.

If it is to continue as a robust revival movement, the PAOC must not cease to network closely with global Pentecostalism. There are some encouraging signs such as its active participation in *Empowered21*, a consortium of Pentecostal-Charismatic groups aiming to promote global renewal. The denomination must see itself as part of the ecumenical global activity of the Spirit notwithstanding its position on such issues as initial evidence and eschatology, none of which must be allowed to ultimately define its existence. Attempts can be made to prevent fragmentation by rediscovering the dynamic of the energizing Spirit that created the PAOC. There is the ever-present tendency within classical Pentecostalism to become locked inside a theological construct that misses the larger global Pentecostal phenomenon. Established Pentecostal denominations and subsequently renewalists would do well to remember that the Spirit cannot be confined and encapsulated in theological or ecclesiastical structures: "The wind blows where it chooses"(John 3:8 NRSV).

Notes

1. The North Atlantic Triangle is a term often used in Canada to refer to the importance of the United States-United Kingdom-Canada relationship.

2. Catholic Register Staff, "Charismatics Gifted by the Holy Spirit for 40 Years," *The Catholic Register* (October 5, 2007), http://www.catholicregister.org/item/8376-charismatics-gifted-by-the-holy-spirit-for-40-years (accessed

September 20, 2014).

3. Interview with Ted Yuke, pastor emeritus of The Rock Church, Halifax Nova Scotia, February 25, 2014.

4. *The Pentecostal Testimony* (January 1974): 9.

5. Carl I. Hovland and Muzafer Sherif, *Social Judgment: Assimilation and Contrast Effects in Communication and Attitude Change,* reprint from 1961 edition (Westport, Connecticut: Greenwood Press, 1980): 129.

6. It was a PAOC pastor in Toronto who initiated the Evangelical Fellowship of Canada (EFC) in 1964. Harry Faught noticed his colleagues tended to stay within their own denominations: "There were so many good men, but it seemed to me they weren't having anything to do with each other.... They all worked independently of each other." http://www.evangelicalfellowship.ca/page.aspx?pid=286 (accessed September 21, 2014). Today the EFC has become the national evangelical voice in Canada with most evangelical denominations, including the PAOC as members. Furthermore, many PAOC ministers and leaders have been trained at the graduate and post-graduate levels at evangelical educational institutions including Wycliffe College (University of Toronto); Tyndale University College, Toronto; and McMaster Divinity School, Hamilton, Ontario.

7. Marilyn Stroude, former head archivist at the PAOC Archives experienced baptism in the Spirit through a United Church of Canada Renewal prayer group and later became an active member of the Catacombs. Until her death in 2013 she had been a longtime member of Portico, a PAOC church in Mississauga, Ontario. The author is also acquainted with other Charismatics who came to the PAOC via the FGBMFI.

Bibliography

Primary Sources

Adams, James E. "The Gentle Erasmus." *The Pentecostal Testimony*, October 1964, 6,33.

Argue, A. H. "After Twenty-Five Years." *The Pentecostal Testimony*, June 1932, 13.

_____. "Azusa Street Revival Reaches Winnipeg." *The Pentecostal Testimony*, May 1956, 9.

Argue, Robert M. "HOME MISSIONS from Report to General Conference." *The Pentecostal Testimony*, October 1972, 10.

_____. "A Bomb Bursts in Quebec." *The Pentecostal Testimony*, December 1972, 10-11.

_____. "General Conference Reports, Executive Director of Home Missions, Bible Colleges and Men's Fellowship Departments." *The Pentecostal Testimony*, October 1982, 21.

_____. "The Answer—French Scholarships." *The Pentecostal Testimony*, February 1970, 10.

Asbury, Francis. The Journal and Letters of Francis Asbury 2, ch. 12 , Sept. 1, 1811. The Wesley Center Online. http,//wesley.nnu.edu/other-theologians/francis-asbury/the-journal-and-letters-of-francis-asbury-volume-ii/francis-asbury-theletters-vol-2-chapter-12/ (accessed May 8, 2013)

Atter, Gordon. "Is Biblical Holiness Obsolete?" *The Pentecostal Testimony*, February, 1974, 6.

Austin, Ray. "Our Pentecostal Heritage." *The Pentecostal Testimony*, June 1963, 5.

Balkwell, Keith R. "Distinctive." *The Pentecostal Testimony*, May 1980, 26.

Bartleman, Frank. *Azusa Street, the Roots of Modern-day Pentecost*. Plainfield, NJ, Logos International, 1980.

Benney, H. P. B. "The Lessons of Montanism." *The Pentecostal Testimony*, June 1969, 6.

Birch, Kenneth. "Can We Learn From The Jesus People?" *The Pentecostal Testimony*, December 1971, 24-25.

———. "Faith or Presumption." *The Pentecostal Testimony*, February 1981, 3, 30.

———. "From Lennoxville to Drummondville." *The Pentecostal Testimony*, March 1972, 10.

Boehm, Henry. Reminiscences, Historical And Biographical of Sixty-Four Years in the Ministry. Edited by Joseph B. Wakeley. New York, Carlton & Porter, 1865 and Nelson & Phillips Cincinnati, Hitchcock & Walden, 1875. http,//books.google.ca/books/about/Reminiscences_historical_and_biographica.html?id=QR0RAAAAIAAJ&redir_esc=y (accessed May 4, 2013).

Boreham, F. W. "John Knox's Text." *The Pentecostal Testimony*, October 1966, 3, 33.

Bowen, Allan D. "Quebec City at the Crossroads." *The Pentecostal Testimony*, July 1972, 9.

Boyd, David P. "Quebec, Canada's Samaria." *The Pentecostal Testimony*, September 1984, 24-25.

Bronsdon, C. H. "Why a Pentecostal Bible College?" *The Pentecostal Testimony*, January 1973, 11.

Brown, Victor G. "Why I Believe in Divine Healing." *The Pentecostal Testimony*, November, 1967, 7, 35

Buick, Samuel M. "Challenge of Quebec." *The Pentecostal Testimony*, July 1967, 11, 31.

———. "In His Likeness." *The Pentecostal Testimony*, August 1982, 8-9, 26.

Burns, Nelson. *Divine Guidance, or the Holy Guest*. Brantford, ON, The Book and Bible House, 1889.

Burns, Terry. "Emerging Confusion?" *enrich* 6, no.1, 21.

Butcher, Emma Giesbrecht. "Christ Crucifies." *The Pentecostal Testimony*, April 1963, 11.

Calvin, John. "Divine Absolution for All Sins." *The Pentecostal Testimony*, February 1964, 3, 32.

Cantalon, Homer. "HOLINESS, Without Which No Man Shall the Lord." *The Pentecostal Testimony*, October 1993, 33.

Carlson, Raymond G. "The Role of the Prophet Today." *The Pentecostal Testimony*, January 1991, 22-24.

———. "Christ's Gifts to His Church." *The Pentecostal Testimony*, March 1991, 28-30.

Clarke, Marguerite. "Revival in French Canada." *The Pentecostal Testimony*, June 1983, 23, 30.

Coggin, Donald. "What the Archbishop said About the Holy Spirit." *The Pentecostal Testimony*, June 1966, 8, 33. Sermon Reprint.

Cressman, Salome. "A Half Century of Pentecost in Quebec." *The Pentecostal Testimony*, September 1964, 4-7, 33.

Crossley, Hugh T. *Practical Talks on Important Themes*. Toronto, Wm. Briggs, 1895.

Damm, Terry. "Is the Blood of Christ an Offense?" *The Pentecostal Testimony*, April 1988, 16-17.

Dawes, Wayne. "When the Term 'Born Again' Becomes a Syndrome." *The Pentecostal Testimony*, August 1979, 28-29.

Dresselhaus, Richard L. "Pentecostal Balance, Four critical balance points in Pentecostal theology and practice." *The Pentecostal Testimony*, July 1989, 7-8.

Duncan, Philip. "The Two Advents of the Ministry of the Holy Spirit." *The Pentecostal Testimony*, December 1963, 6-7.

du Plessis, David. "Glossolalia." *The Pentecostal Testimony*, February 1963, 7, 9, 34 and, March 1963, 4-5, 34.

_____. *The Spirit Bade Me Go*. Plainfield, NJ; Logos International, 1970.

Enerson, Charles G. "Christ is Coming Soon." *The Pentecostal Testimony*, January 1988, 4-7.

Fleming, F. G. "The Advent of Christ and of the Holy Ghost." *The Pentecostal Testimony*, December 1968, 6-7.

Francis, E. A. "The Cross of Christ." *The Pentecostal Testimony*, November 1961, 6.

Gagne, Henry. "The New Birth." *The Pentecostal Testimony*, February 1973, 7.

Gagnon, Mlle. Marie-Paule. "Tenth Anniversary for French Telecast." *The Pentecostal Testimony*, February 1971, 10.

Gee, Donald. *Trophimus I Left Sick: Our Problems of Divine Healing*. London, Elim Publishers Co. and Springfield, MO, Gospel Publishing House, 1952. http,//www.sermonindex.net/modules/articles/index.php?view=article&aid=1367 (accessed May 24, 2014).

Gerard, Bernice. "The Terrors of the Year 2000." *The Pentecostal Testimony*, January 2000, 34.

_____. "Charismatic Renewal in Vancouver." *The Pentecostal Testimony*, April 1968, 8.

_____. Paper given at a Campus Evangelism Seminar, c1973.

_____. "Pentecostal Evangelism on Campus." *World Pentecost* 2 (1973): 22.

_____. "Towards Maturity in the Ministry of the Gifts." *World Pentecost* 4 (1974): 13-14.

Griffin, William A. "Real Pentecostals, Please Stand." *The Pentecostal Testimony*, June 1998, 19.

_____. "When Healing Doesn't Come." *The Pentecostal Testimony*, July 1999, 20.

Grosshans, George W. "Why a Decade of Destiny?" *The Pentecostal Testimony*, September 1989, 24-25.

Halliwell, Doreen. "No, No! Don't Go to the Show." *The Pentecostal Testimony*, September 1991, 9.

Harpur, Tom. "Church puts Metro 'sect' on the street." *The Toronto Star*, Saturday, January 26, 1980, 1,12.

──────────. "Fervent teenagers, Isn't Jesus wonderful?" *The Toronto Star*, February 19, 1972, *The Toronto Star*, Saturday, February 19, 1972, 84-85.

──────────. "Priest 'speaks in tongues' now everyone's doing it." *Toronto Daily Star*, March 7, 1964. *The Pentecostal Testimony*, June 1964, 7.

Hiebert, Rick. "Living Between Two Worlds." *The Pentecostal Testimony*, July 1995, 4.

Hill, Donald G. "Christian Healing in the Present Age." *The Pentecostal Testimony*, September 1976, 7.

Holdcroft, L. Thomas. "Evidence for a Pre-Tribulation Rapture." *The Pentecostal Testimony*, December 1986, 26.

──────────. "God's Purposes in the Tribulation." *The Pentecostal Testimony*, February 1984, 24-25.

──────────. "The Two Phases of Christ's Second Coming." *The Pentecostal Testimony*, November 1983, 16-17.

Holm, Randall. "Developing an Understanding of Divine Healing." *The Pentecostal Testimony*, October 1992, 18-19.

Honsinger, Howard D. "Single-Tongued Pentecostalism." *The Pentecostal Testimony*, January 1979, 6-7.

──────────. "The Ecumenical Guinea Pig." *The Pentecostal Testimony*, November 1973, 26.

Horban, Michael P. "Our Pentecostal Heritage." *The Pentecostal Testimony*, November 1982, 24-26.

──────────. "Principles of Holiness for Today." *The Pentecostal Testimony*, March 1985, 18-19.

──────────. "We Live in an Unholy World and the Church is Worldly." *The Pentecostal Testimony*, April 1985, 46-47.

Hornby, E. A. "The Word of God is Relevant." *The Pentecostal Testimony*, December 1970, 8.

Horner, Ralph C. *Evangelist*. Brockville, Ontario, 1926.

──────────. *Pentecost*. Toronto: William Briggs, 1891.

──────────. *Reminiscences From His Own Pen*. Brockville, Ontario, n.d.

Hoskins, John. "An Account of Mr. John Hoskins, in a Letter to the Rev. John Wesley." *Arminian Magazine* 8, 1785, 24-27, 85-88, 143-44, 194-96. http,//www.mun.ca/rels/meth/texts/hoskins/hoskins2.html (accessed April 4, 2013)

Hunter, Stewart. "QUEBEC—Canada's Sleeping Giant Awakens." *The Pentecostal Testimony*, November 1987, 6-7.

Janes, Burton K. "Acts Reviewed for an Experience Today." *The Pentecostal Testimony*, November 1981, 20-21.

Jones, W. Cornish. "Is Healing in the Atonement?" *The Pentecostal Testimony*, September 1961, 6, 8.

Kudra, Abraham. "Five Signs that Point to Christ's Imminent Return." *The Pentecostal Testimony*, November 1983, 8-9.

Kulbeck, Earl N. O. "Canada's National Birthday." *The Pentecostal Testimony*, July 1963, 2.
———. "What God Hath Wrought in Quebec." *The Pentecostal Testimony*, September 1964, 2, 32.
Kydd, Ronald. "Do it Again! Do it Again!" *The Pentecostal Testimony*, May 1989, 18-19.
———. "Walking Straight in a Crooked World." *The Pentecostal Testimony*, August 1990, 18-19.
Lane, Grace. "Catholic Charismatic Movement Flourishes in Western Canada." *The Christian Century*, May 24, 1972, 618.
Leno, Garth. "Healing and the Prayer of Faith." *Testimony*, June 2001, 14.
Lowenburg, Paul. "Message Under Siege—The Pre-millennial Return of Christ." *The Pentecostal Testimony*, January 1988, 24-26.
MacGowan, W. H. Ken. "Quebec's Greatest Need." *The Pentecostal Testimony*, April 1976, 18-19.
Mainse, David. *100*. Burlington, Ontario: Crossroads Christian Communications, 1999.
Mainse, Roy Lake. *A Happy Heart, One Man's Inspiring Story of God's Fulfillment in His Life.* Burlington, Ontario: Crossroads Christian Communications, 1988, 29-58.
Martin, Donald R. "Aboard!...Calling for Quebec Flite." *The Pentecostal Testimony*, May 1975, 16-17.
———. "FLITE Celebrates Anniversary." *Pentecostal Testimony*, June 1980, 24.
———. "Formation Timothée." *The Pentecostal Testimony*, August 1980, 10-12.
Martin, Edwin. "The Cleansing of the Conscience Through the Blood of Jesus." *The Pentecostal Testimony*, October 1993, 16.
McAlister, R. E. "Have Ye Received the Holy Ghost Since Ye Believed." *The Good Report*, no.1 (May 2011): 2.
McDonnell, Killian. "The Ecumenical Significance of the Pentecostal Movement." *The Pentecostal Testimony*, June 1968, 8.
Miller, Thomas. "Born Again or Saved?" *The Pentecostal Testimony*, September 1985, 38.
———. "Canada and the Coming 'New World Order.'" *The Pentecostal Testimony*, June 1993, 8.
———. "Five Pillars of Pentecostalism." *The Pentecostal Testimony*, October 1992, 8-9.
———. "Jesus, Our Justification." *The Pentecostal Testimony*, March 1985, 10-11.
———. "Pentecostals and Charismatics." *The Pentecostal Testimony*, November 1983, 13-14.
Missen, Alfred F. *The Pentecostal Testimony*, March 1970, 6-7.
Montgomery, J. "Worldliness." *The Pentecostal Testimony*, July 1965, 28.

Moody, W. H. "The Holy Spirit and Christmas." *The Pentecostal Testimony*, December 1975, 10.

Morris, Tom. "Holiness, It's in the View." *Testimony*, May 2001, 14.

Mulligan, Stuart and Crabtree, David. "What We Are and Who We Are." *The Pentecostal Testimony*, June 1963, 5.

O'Connor, Edward. "The Canadian Renewal." *New Covenant*, 1, no.7 (January 1973): 11-13.

Ozard, Jack. "Let's Stay on Course." *The Pentecostal Testimony*, September 1973, 4, 26.

Parlee, F. H. "Europe—The Rising Deterrent." *The Pentecostal Testimony*, July 1962, 4, 31.

Prieto, Giraldo J. "The Meaning and Importance of the Blood of Jesus." *The Pentecostal Testimony*, March 1991, 8.

Prosser, Peter. "Roman Catholic Charismatic Impact Increases." *The Pentecostal Testimony*, September 1973, 5, 26.

Randall, Herbert E. "The Comforter Has Come to Herbert E. Randall." *The Promise*, no.2 (June 1907): 1-2.

Redpath, Alan. "The Dynamics of Apostolic Christianity." *The Pentecostal Testimony*, April 1962, 6-7, 32-33.

Reid, Ron. "Chosen to be Holy." *The Pentecostal Testimony*, October 1977, 30-31.

Reimers, Al. *God's Country, Charismatic Renewal*. Toronto. G.R. Welch, 1979.

Rennie, Ian. "Pentecostalism and Christianity." *Testimony*, June 2001, 7-8.

Rodriguez, Amaro. "The Spirit of God is Moving." *The Pentecostal Testimony*, August 1970, 8-9.

_____. "What is Happening in the Roman Catholic Church." *The Pentecostal Testimony*, April 1970, 6-7.

Rudd, Douglas. "After Eighty Years, What?" *The Pentecostal Testimony*, January 1987, 39.

_____. "How Pentecost Came to Ontario." *The Pentecostal Testimony*, September 1978, 32.

Schellenberg, Don. "Transcendent Grace." *The Pentecostal Testimony*, July 1962, 11.

Seymour, William J. "Justification is the act of God's free grace by which we receive remission of sins." *The Apostolic Faith* 1, no 1 (September 1906): 2.

Shaw, Geoffrey. "Charisma '73" *Good Tidings* 24, no. 2 (March-April 1973): 29.

Smith, George C. "The Quickening Spirit in Healing." *The Pentecostal Testimony*, May 1977, 22.

Smith, Mrs. Hope. "Worldliness, What is it?" *The Pentecostal Testimony*, July 1965, 28-29.

Smith, Wilbur M. "The Middle East Crisis in the Light of the Bible." *The Pentecostal Testimony*, November 1967, 3, 31.

Solmes, Reg and Doris. "Gaspé Calls." *The Pentecostal Testimony*, March 1962, 10.

Sorenson, Paul C. "Spiritual Drift and Drive." *The Pentecostal Testimony*, March 1971, 6-7.

Stiller, C. H. "Pentecostal Chaplain Appointed at University." *The Pentecostal Testimony*, January 1964, 10.

Stone, Jean. "More Than 1300 California Episcopalians Receive Pentecostal Baptism." *The Pentecostal Testimony*, June 1962, 8.

Taitinger, R. W. "Priorities." *The Pentecostal Testimony*, June 1976, 8.

Tee, Alexander. "Looking for that Blessed Hope." *The Pentecostal Testimony*, August 1967, 5, 22.

Ter Hoek, Teresa. "Stranger Fire." *The Pentecostal Testimony*, May 1987, 15-17.

The Promise, no. 12 (February 1909): 3.

Thomas, Mervin. "For Minutes Before Midnight." *The Pentecostal Testimony*, November 1983, 4-5.

Thompson, S.H. "The Heritage of John Hus." *The Pentecostal Testimony*, October 1965, 7, 37.

Truax, Albert, ed. *Autobiography of the Late Nelson Burns*. Toronto, The Christian Association, n.d.

Tunks, G. P. "I Believe in the Holy Ghost." *The Pentecostal Testimony*, June 1963, 8, 34.

Upton, George R. "A Race Against Time." *The Pentecostal Testimony*, January 1983, 10, 21-22.

_____. "Jubilee—retrospect and prospect." *The Pentecostal Testimony*, November 1969, 6-7, 28.

_____. "Mission Canada." *The Pentecostal Testimony*, April 1984, 17, 35.

Upton, Roy E. "Living Clean in an Unclean World." *The Pentecostal Testimony*, August 1990, 22-24.

_____. "We Believe in Holy Living." *The Pentecostal Testimony*, February 1985, 18-19.

Verhulst, Rev. and Mrs. Carl. "Quebec's Hour." *The Pentecostal Testimony*, June 1965, 10.

Ward, A. G. "A New Year." *The Pentecostal Testimony* 27, no.1 (January 1, 1946): 2.

Ward, C.M. "Do You Need Healing?" *The Pentecostal Testimony*, August 1965, 5, 26.

Ward, Clinton L. "Aim at Perfection." *The Pentecostal Testimony*, February 1983, 6, 15.

_____. "The Long Arm of God." *The Pentecostal Testimony*, May 1990, 33.

Werbiski, Al. "The Stripes of Jesus." *The Pentecostal Testimony*, April 1987, 4-6.

Wesley, John. "The Signs of the Times." *The Sermons of John Wesley*, Sermon 66, August 25, 1787. Wesley Center Online. http,//wesley.nnu.edu/ johnwesley/thesermons-of-john-wesley-1872-edition/sermon-66-the-signs-of-the-times/ (accessed December 22, 2013).

Wheatley, Richard. *The Life and Letters of Mrs. Phoebe Palmer*. New York, W.C. Palmer Publisher, 1881.
White, R. J. "Pentecost Today and Ecumenicity." *The Pentecostal Testimony*, March 1964, 8, 33.
White, R. J. "What Makes A Person Pentecostal?" *The Pentecostal Testimony*, November 1982, 11-13.
Willard, Larry. "Is Disaster Imminent?" *The Pentecostal Testimony*, December 1998, 8.
Wilson, Ruth E. "Are You With Us?" *The Pentecostal Testimony*, July 1969, 11.
Yeomans, Lilian B. "Healing by the Power of the Resurrection." *The Pentecostal Testimony*, April 1962, 8, 34.
Zimmerman, Thomas F. "The Wind Bloweth Where it Listeth." *The Pentecostal Testimony*, September 1972, 4-5.

News Items with No Author Listed

"Dateline, World of Religion." *The Pentecostal Testimony* 54, no. 9 (September 1973): 11.
"Dateline, World of Religion." *The Pentecostal Testimony*, November 1973, 18.
"Catholic Pentecostal Movement in Canada." *The Pentecostal Testimony*, May 1973, 17-18.
"Catholic Pentecostals' Largest Meeting." *The Pentecostal Testimony*, August 1973, 10.
"Challenging Campaigns." *The Pentecostal Testimony*, June 1973, 14.
"Charismatic Centre Opened." *The Pentecostal Testimony*, January 1974, 9.
"Charismatic Study Report." *The Pentecostal Testimony*, November 1972, 12.
"Church Growth, Bilingual Style." *The Pentecostal Testimony*, June 1980, 13.
"C.P.C. President Assesses Year." *The Pentecostal Testimony*, September 1971, 11.
"Jesus People at the Olympics." *The Pentecostal Testimony*, November 1972, 14.
NEWSLINES, "100 Huntley Street-French." *The Pentecostal Testimony*, September 1984, 26.
"Olympic Outreach." *The Pentecostal Testimony*, October 1976, 16-19.
"Pentecostal Pioneer." *The Pentecostal Testimony* 42, no. 4 (April 1961): 9.
"People and Places." *The Pentecostal Testimony*, April 1973, 13.
"Prayer Proclamation." *The Pentecostal Testimony*, January 1970, 31.
"The Holy Spirit Falls on Yale Students." *The Pentecostal Testimony*, June 1963, 6.
"The Time for Prayer, The Third Great Awakening." *Christian History*, Summer 1989, 32-33.
"What the Archbishop said About the Holy Spirit." *The Pentecostal Testimony*, June 1966, 8.
"Wilkerson Blasts Established Churches." *The Pentecostal Testimony*, July 1972, 24.
"Youth Parade in Montreal." *The Pentecostal Testimony*, October 1972, 12-13.

Official Documents

Canadian Bishops Statement on the Catholic Charismatic Renewal, "The Charismatic Renewal in Canada 2003." *Catholic Charismatic Renewal Services of Canada,* Pentecost 2003, 1-20. http,//www.catholiccharismatic.ca/index_files/BishopsofCanadaStatementBooklet.pdf (accessed June 10, 2014).

Fourth Census of Canada 1901, vol 1, *Population*. Prepared by S. E. Dawson. Printer to the King's Most Excellent Majesty, 1902. http,//archive.org/stream/fourthcensusofca01canauoft#page/144/mode/2up (accessed September 4, 2013).

"Minutes of the 101st General Assembly of the Presbyterian Church of Canada," 1976, 375-393. Presbyterian Church, Canada, 1976. "The Work of the Spirit." Reprinted in *Presence, Power, Praise, Vol.II*. Continental, National, Regional Documents. Edited by Kilian McDonnell. Collegeville, MN, The Liturgical Press, 1980, 221-255.

Minutes of the 26th General Conference of the Pentecostal Assemblies of Canada. Windsor, Ontario, August 22-26, 1968. PAOC Archives.

Minutes of Joint Meeting of the PAOC and the Crossroads Christian Communications Incorporated Board of Directors. PAOC National Office, September 16, 1979. PAOC Archives.

Minutes of the Joint Meeting of the Pentecostal Assemblies of Canada General Superintendent and National Officers with Crossroads Christian Communications Incorporated Board of Directors. 100 Huntley Street, Toronto, Ontario, April 6, 1979. PAOC Archives.

"Minutes of the Pentecostal Assemblies of Canada." *The Pentecostal Testimony*, February 1926.

Official correspondence from General Superintendent James M. MacKnight to PAOC ministers, February 1985.

Official correspondence from the PAOC General Secretary, Charles Yates, to the General Executive, June 1, 1977. PAOC Archives.

Official Minutes of 32nd Biennial the PAOC General Conference, August 1980. PAOC Archives.

Official Record of the Anglican Church of Canada. General Synod, May 1973, Act 42/43.

Official Record, "House of Bishops." February 1984. Resolution 15-2-84.

Official statement by the Youth and Family Commission of the PAOC and approved by the General Executive, "The Biblical Standards of Morality." *The Pentecostal Testimony*, May 1966, 7, 31.

Presbyterian Church, Canada, 1976. "The Work of the Spirit." Cited in *Presence, Power, Praise Vol II*. Continental, National, Regional Documents. Edited by Kilian McDonnell. Collegeville, MN: The Liturgical Press, 1980, 221-255.

Roman Catholic Church, Canada 1975. "Charismatic Renewal, Message of the

Canadian Bishops Addressed to all Canadian Catholics." *Presence, Power, Praise. Vol.II.* Continental, National, Regional Documents. Edited by Kilian McDonnell. Collegeville, MN: The Liturgical Press, 1980, 84-98.

Statement of Fundamental & Essential Truths (Toronto, Ontario, Canada: PAOC, 1980). PAOC Archives.

Text of resolutions taken from "ACC-5: Anglican Consultative Council: Report of Fifth Meeting. Newcastle upon Tyne, England 8-18 September, 1981." London. Published by the Anglican Consultative Council, c1981.

Upton, Gordon R. "Pentecostal Distinctives and Charismatic Focus." Paper prepared for the biennial leadership council at Winnipeg, Manitoba November 15-17, 1977. PAOC Archives.

Secondary Literature

Monographs

Aikens, Adlen. "Christian perfection in central Canadian Methodism, 1828-1884." PhD dissertation. McGill University, 1987.

Airhart, Phyllis D. *Serving The Present Age, Revivalism: Progressivism, and the Methodist Tradition in Canada.* Montreal: McGill-Queen's University Press, 1992.

Alexander, Kimberly Ervin. *Pentecostal Healing: Models in Theology and Practice.* Journal of Pentecostal Theology Supplement Series. Deo Publishing, 2006.

Atter, Gordon F. *The Third Force.* Peterborough, Ontario: The College Press, 1962.

Blumhofer, Edith L. *The Assemblies of God: A Chapter in the Story of American Pentecostalism.* 2 vols. Springfield, MO: Gospel Publishing House, 1989.

Butchart, Reuben. *The Disciples of Christ in Canada Since 1830.* Churches of Christ, 1949.

Cerillo, Augustus Jr. and Wacker, Grant. "Bibliography and Historiography of Pentecostalism in the United States." *New International Dictionary of Pentecostal and Charismatic Movements.* Edited by Stanley M. Burgess and Eduard M.Van Der Maas. Revised edition. Grand Rapids, MI: Zondervan, 2003, 397-405.

Chagnon, Robert. *Les charismatiques au Quebec.* Montreal, Quebec/Amerique, 1979.

Cox, Harvey. *Fire From Heaven: The Rise Of Pentecostal Spirituality And The Reshaping Of Religion In The 21st Century.* De Capo Press, 2001.

Csordas, Thomas J. *Language, Charisma, and Creativity: The Ritual Life of a Religious Movement.* Berkeley, Los Angeles, Oxford: University of California Press, 1997.

Dayton, Donald. *Theological Roots of Pentecostalism.* Peabody, Massachusetts: Hendrickson Publishers, 2007.

Di Giacomo, Michael. "Les Pentecôtistes Québécois, 1966-1995: Historie d'un Réveil." PhD dissertation. Université Laval, October, 1999.

di Sabatino, David. *The Jesus People Movement: An Annotated Bibliography and General Resource.* 2nd Edition. Jester Media, 2003.

Dieter, Melvin Easterday. *The Holiness Revival of the Nineteenth Century.* 2nd Edition. Metuchen, N.J.& London: The Scarecrow Press, 1996.

Douville, Bruce. "The Uncomfortable Pew, Christianity, the New Left, and the Hip Counterculture in Toronto, 1965-1975." PhD dissertation. York University, August 2011.

Fairweather, Eugene R. "Canadian Catholics Offer Milestone Conference on Renewal." *The Christian Century.* October 4,1967, 1261-1265.

Faupel, D. William. *The American Pentecostal Movement: A Bibliographical Essay.* Vol. 2. Asbury Theological Seminary, May 2012.

_____. The Everlasting Gospel: The Significance of Eschatology in the Development of Pentecostal Thought. *Journal of Pentecostal Theology.* Supplement Series 10. Sheffield, England: Academic Press, 1996.

Fortune, Clifford Roy. "Ralph Cecil Horner: Product of the Ottawa Valley." Unpublished master's thesis. Carleton University, 1999.

Foster, Douglas A., Dunnavant, Anthony L., Blowers, Paul M., and Newell, Williams, D., eds. *The Encyclopedia of the Stone-Campbell Movement.* Wm. B. Eerdmans, Publishing Co., 2004.

Fuller, Clare. "The Effect of the Pentecostal Movement on Canadian Methodist and Holiness Churches, 1906-1930." Unpublished paper. Ontario Theological Seminary, May 1986.

Garrett, Leroy. *The Stone-Campbell Movement: The Story of the American Restorationist Movement.* Joplin, MO: College Press Publishing Company, 1981.

Gerlach, Luther and Hines, Virginia. *People, Power, Change: Movements of Social Transformation.* Bobbs-Merrill Co., 1970.

Grant, John Webster. *The Church in the Canadian Era.* Vancouver: Regent College Publishing, 1988.

Harrell, David Edwin Jr. *All Things Are Possible: The Healing and Charismatic Revivals in Modern America.* Indiana University Press, 1979.

Hollenweger, Walter J. *The Pentecostals.* Peabody, MA: Hendrikson Publishers, 1988.

Hovland, Carl I. and Sherif, Muzafer. *Social Judgment: Assimilation and Contrast Effects in Communication and Attitude Change.* Reprint from 1961 Edition. Westport, Connecticut: Yale University Press, 1980.

Janes, Burton K. *History of the Pentecostal Assemblies of Newfoundland.* St. John's NL: Good Tidings Press, 1996.

Jones, Charles Edwin. *Perfectionist Persuasion: The Holiness Movement and American Methodism, 1867-1936.* Metuchen, 1974.

Kee, Kevin B. "The Heavenly Railroad, Ernest Crossley, John Hunter and Canadian Methodist Revivalism, 1884-1910." Master's thesis. Kingston:

Queen's University, 1994.

Kulbeck, Gloria Grace. *What God Hath Wrought.* Edited by Walter E. McAlister and George R. Upton. Toronto: The Pentecostal Assemblies of Canada, 1958.

Linteau, Paul-Andre Robert, Jean-Claude, Durocher, Rene & Ricard, Francois. *Quebec Since 1930.* Les Editions du Boreal Express. 1986. Translated by Robert Chodos & Ellen Garmaise. Toronto, James Lorimer & Company Publishers, 1991.

Lockwood, Glenn. *Smiths Falls: A Social History of the Men and Women in a Rideau Canal Community, 1794-1994.* Corporation of the Town of Smith's Falls, 1994.

McAllister, L.G. and Tucker, W.E. *Journey in Faith: A History of the Christian Church.* Disciples of Christ, 1975.

McLeister, Clara. *Men and Women of Deep Piety.* Edited by E.E. Shelhamer. Syracuse, NY: Wesleyan Methodist Publishing Association, 1920.

Miedema, Gary. "For Canada's Sake, the Re-visioning of Canada and the Restructuring of Public Religion in the 1960's." PhD dissertation. Queen's University, 2000.

Miller, Thomas William. *Canadian Pentecostals: A History of the Pentecostal Assemblies of Canada.* Edited by William A. Griffin. Mississauga, ON, Full Gospel Publishing House, 1994.

Moore, S. David. *The Shepherding Movement, Controversy and Charismatic Ecclesiology.* Journal of Pentecostal Theology. Supplement Series 27. Edited by John Christopher Thomas, Ricker D. Moore, and Steven J. Land. London & New York: T&T Clark International, 2003.

Noll, Mark A. *A History of Christianity in the United States and Canada.* Grand Rapids, MI: Eerdman's, 1992.

Orr, Edwin J. *The Event of the Century: The 1857-1858 Awakening.* Pennsylvania State University: International Awakening Press, 1989.

Playter, George F. *The History of Methodism in Canada: With an Account of the Rise and Progress of the Work of God Among the Canadian Indian Tribes.* Toronto: The Wesleyan Printing Establishment, 1862.

Poewe, Karla. *Charismatic Christianity as a Global Culture: Studies in Comparative Religion.* University of South Carolina Press, 1994.

Poloma, Margaret, M. *Charismatic Movement: Is There a New Pentecost? Social Movements Past and Present.* Twayne Publishers, 1982.

Prosser, Peter. "An Historical and Theological Evaluation of the Charismatic Renewal." Unpublished Master's thesis. University of Montréal, 1978.

Quebedeaux, Richard. *The New Charismatics: The Origins, Development, and Significance of Neo-Pentecostalism.* New York: Doubleday and Company, 1976.

Ranaghan, Kevin and Dorothy. *Catholic Pentecostals.* Paramus, NJ, New York, NY & Toronto, Ontario: Paulist Press Deus Books, 1969.

Rawlyk, George A., ed. *Aspects of the Canadian Evangelical Experience.*

McGill-Queen's University Press, 1997.

———. *Ravished by the Spirit: Religious Revivals, Baptists, and Henry Alline*. Kingston & Montreal: McGill-Queen's University Press, 1985.

———. *The Canadian Protestant Experience 1760-1990*. McGill-Queen's University, 1990.

Reed, Bruce. *Dynamics of Religion: Process and Movement in Christian Churches*. London: Darton, Longman and Todd, 1978.

Riss, Richard M. *The Latter Rain Movement*. Honeycomb Visual Productions, 1987.

Rudd, Douglas. *When the Spirit Came Upon Them: Highlights from the Early Years of the Pentecostal Movement in Canada*. Edited by William A. Griffin. Mississauga, ON: The Pentecostal Assemblies of Canada, 2002.

Semple, Neil. *The Lord's Dominion: A History of Canadian Methodism*. McGill-Queen's University Press, 1996.

Shires, Preston. *Hippies of the Religious Right*. Waco, TX: Baylor University Press, 2007.

Stevens, Abel. *History of the Methodist Episcopal Church in the United States of America*. 4 vols. New York: Carlton & Porter, 1866-1868.

Stewart, Adam ed. *Handbook of Pentecostal Christianity*. DeKalb, Illinois: Northern Illinois University Press, 2012.

Synan, Vinson, ed. *Aspects of Pentecostal-Charismatic Origins*. Plainfield, NJ: Logos International, 1975.

———. *The Holiness-Pentecostal Tradition: Charismatic Movements in the Twentieth Century*. Grand Rapids, MI: Eerdmans's, 1971,1997.

Tentler, Leslie Woodcock. "Les pentecôtistes québécois, 1966-1995, histoire d'un réveil." PhD dissertation. Université Laval,1999.

———. ed. *The Church Confronts Modernity: Catholicism Since 1950 in the United States, Ireland, and Quebec*. Washington, D.C.: The Catholic University of America Press, 2007.

Trouillot, Michel-Rolph Trouillot. *Silencing the Past: Power and the Production of History*. Boston, MA: Beacon Press, 1995.

Weber, Max. *The Theory of Social and Economic Organization*. New York, NY: The Free Press. 1947.

Whitaker, Colin. *Great Revivals*. Revised edition. London: Marshall Pickering, 1990.

Wigger, John. *American Saint: Francis Asbury & the Methodists*. Oxford University Press, 2009.

Wilkinson, Michael, and Althouse, Peter, eds. *Winds From the North: Canadian Contributions to the Pentecostal Movement*. Brill, 2010.

Wood, Laurence W. *The Meaning of Pentecost in Early Methodism: Rediscovering John Fletcher as John Wesley's Vindicator and Designated Successor*. Lanham, MD: Scarecrow Press, 2002.

Verge, Carl F. "A Comparison of the Beliefs and Practices of Two Groups to Pentecostal Assemblies of Canada Ministers: Those with a Masters

Degree and the Those with Only Three Years of Bible College Training." Unpublished PhD dissertation. New York University, 1987.

Journals, Periodicals, and Unpublished Papers

Atanasoff, Don. "Singers, dancers, musicians…Together they praise and worship God." *Markham Economist and Sun*, Wednesday, July 25, 1973, 7.

Bebbington, David W. "The Holiness Movements in British and Canadian Methodism in the late Nineteenth Century." *Proceedings of the Wesley Historical Society,* 50. Edited by E. Alan Rose. October 1996, 203-228.

Catholic Register Staff. "Charismatics Gifted by the Holy Spirit for 40 Years." *The Catholic Register,* October 5, 2007. http,//www.catholicregister.org/item/8376-charismatics-gifted-by-the-holy-spirit-for-40-years (accessed September 20, 2014).

Dayton, Donald. "The Doctrine of the Baptism of the Holy Spirit, It's Emergence and Significance." http://www.freerevivalcd.com/cdlive/2/holyspirit.htm (accessed September 27, 2014).

Di Giacomo, Michael. "FLITE, Religious Entrepreneurship in Quebec in the 1970's and 1980's." *Journal of the Canadian Church Historical Society* 46, no.1 (Spring 2004): 49-88.

_____. "La Vieille Capitale, son importance pour le pentecôtisme au Canada français dans les années 1970." SCHEC. *Études Histoire Religieuse* 70 (2004): 81-96. https://www.researchgate.net/publication/216168969_La_vieille_capitale_son_importance_pour_la_croissance_du_pentectisme_canadien-franais?ev=prf_pub (accessed June 24, 2014).

_____. "Pentecostalism, Nationalism, and Quebec Culture." *PNEUMA* 28, no.1 (Spring 2006): 33-58.

Di Giacomo, Michael and Rust, Ronald. "Quebec, Mission not Impossible." http://dqpaoc.org/?s=QUEBEC%2C+MISSION+IS+NOT+IMPOSSIBLE (accessed June 25, 2014).

Doucet, Daina. "The Day When Hamilton Changed the World." http://www.christianity.ca/page.aspx?pid=11878 (accessed August 21, 2013).

Fairweather, Eugene R. "Canadian Catholics Offer Milestone Conference on Renewal." *The Christian Century,* October 4, 1967, 1261-1265.

Ferrrante, Angela. "The New Believers." *Macleans*, January 1, 1979, 26.

Fieguth, Debra. "A Church You Should Know: Eglise Nouvelle Vie, Longueuil, Quebec." *Faith Today*, Nov-Dec. 2006. http://www.evangelicalfellowship.ca/NetCommunity/Page.aspx?pid=761&srcid=384 (accessed June 25, 2014).

_____. "Fire and Ice." *Christianity Today*, October 23, 2000, 20.

Flatt, Kevin. "The Loyal Opposition: A Brief History of the Renewal Movement in the United Church of Canada, 1966–2010." *Church and Faith Trends: A*

Publication of the Centre for Research on Canadian Evangelicalism, *The Evangelical Fellowship of Canada* 3, no. 3 (December 2010): 1-18.

Fontalvo, Luis C. "Hispanic Pentecostals in a Canadian Anglo-Franco Environment." *PNEUMA* 13, no. 2 (Fall 1991): 73-81.

Giguère, Hermann. "Notes Historiques sur les Debuts du Renouveau Charismatique." *Selon sa Parole* 25, no. 6 (June-July 1999). http://selonsaparole.tripod.com/gig996.htm (accessed June 17, 2014).

Hanrahan, James. "The Nature and History of the Catholic Charismatic Renewal in Canada." *CCHA Study Sessions* 50 (1983): 307-324.

Higgs, Rob. "Pentecostal History—Statement of Fundamental and Essential Truths." Unpublished paper.

Holdcroft, L. Thomas. "Strange Fire: The New Order of the Latter Rain." http,//www.spiritwatch.org/firelatter2.htm (accessed May 24, 2014).

———. "The New Order of the Latter Rain." *PNEUMA* 2, no. 2 (Fall 1980): 46-60.

Kydd, Ronald A. "Pentecostals, Charismatics, and Canadian Denominations." *Eglise et Theologie* 13, no. 2 (May 1982): 211-231.

———. "The Impact of the Charismatic Movement upon Classical Pentecostalism in Canada." *PNEUMA* 18, no.1 (Spring 1996): 55-67.

Lane, Grace. "Catholic Charismatic Movement Flourishes in Western Canada." *The Christian Century,* May 24, 1972, 617-618.

Mainse, David. Unpublished paper given at the Congress on Pentecostal Leadership (*COPL*). Toronto, Ontario. Fall 1987.

Menzies, William W. "Reflections of a Pentecostal at the End of the Millennium: An Editorial Essay." http://www.apts.edu/aeimages/file/ajps_pdf/98-1-menziesw.pd (accessed April 20, 2015).

Mussio, Louise A. "The Origins and Nature of the Holiness Movement Church, A Study in Religious Populism." *Journal of the Canadian Historical Association/Revue de la Societe historique du Canada* 7, no.1 (1996): 81-104.

O'Leary, Denyse. "A Velvet Oppression." *Christianity Today*, April 2, 2001. http,//www.ctlibrary.com/ct/2001/april2/7.75.html (accessed July 16, 2014).

Reed, David. "From Movement to Institution: A Case Study of Charismatic Renewal in the Anglican Church of Canada." *American Theological Library Association Summary of Proceedings* 45 (1991): 173-194.

Ross, Brian. "Ralph Cecil Horner: A Methodist Sectarian Deposed 1187-1895." *Journal of the Canadian Church Historical Society* 19, no. 2 (1977): 94-103.

Sawatsky, Ron. "'Unholy Contentions about Holiness: The Canada Holiness Association and the Methodist Church." *Canadian Society of Church History Papers,* 1982.

Smith, Peter T. "Major Signs of Religious Revival Seen in France and Quebec." May 26, 2006. https://www.lifesitenews.com/news/major-signs-of-religious-revival-seen-in-france-and-quebec (accessed April 20, 2015).

Stiller, Karen. "The Man Next Door: Billy Graham's Impact on Canada." *Faith*

Today, July-August 2009, 20.

Thackery, Archibald. "The Latter Rain Movement of '48.'" http://lrm1948.blogspot.ca/2013/05/mom-beall-and-bethesda.html http,//lrm1948.blogspot.ca/2014/01/the-chronology-of-latter-rain-revival.html (accessed September 8, 2014).

"25 years ago, December 1974." *The Anglican Journal*, December 1999. http,//www.anglicanjournal.com/articles/100-years-ago-december-1899-377 (accessed June 11, 2014).

Audio/ Visual

Context with Lorna Dueck. http,//www.contextwithlornadueck.com/episodes/davidmainse-crossroads-cts-tv (accessed August 12, 2014).

Orr, Edwin J. "The Awakening of 1858 in America. Audio lecture. http,//archive.org/details/TheAwakeningOf1858InAmerica-ByJEdwinOrrBroughtByPeterjohn_658 (accessed August 16, 2013).

Watson, Merv and Merla. *Toronto Catacombs: St. Paul's Cathedral, Toronto, 1974, Maranatha & Sunday Morning Communion*. Abbotsford, B.C.: Catacombs Productions Ltd., 1998. Compact disc.

Other Websites Consulted

Anglican Renewal Ministries of Canada. "History of Anglican Renewal Ministries." http,//armcanada.org/history.htm (accessed June 9, 2014).

Bethany Charismatic Catholic Church. http,//bethanyccc.org/CCCChistory.htm (accessed April 20, 2015).

Catholic Charismatic Renewal Council. http,//www.ccrctor.com/ (accessed September 24, 2014).

Dictionary of Canadian Biography Online. http,//www.biographi.ca/en/index.php (accessed May 14, 2013).

"French-Speaking Cursillo Movement of Canada." http,//www.cursillos.ca/en/cursillo.htm (accessed June 11, 2014).

Gordon Williams Evangelistic Association. http,//gordwilliams.com/revgordonwilliamsc242.php (accessed July 16, 2014).

History of Anglican Renewal Ministries. http,//www.cyberus.ca/~arm/history.htm (June 9, 2014).

Lausanne Occasional Papers. http,//www.lausanne.org/en/documents/lops/73-lop-2.html (accessed July 21, 2014).

Merv and Merla Watson. http,//www.mervandmerla.com/home.cfm (accessed July 1, 2014).

Madonna House. www.madonnahouse.org (June 16, 2014).

"Sentiers de la spiritualité chrétienne." http,//www.michel-lafontaine.com/sentiersspirituels_christ_jeanpaulregimbal.html (accessed June 17, 2014).

Street Level Consulting: The Jesus Movement. http,//streetlevelconsulting. ca/www.streetlevelconsulting.ca/newsArticlesStats/Jesus_Movement.htm (accessed August 14, 2014).
The Canadian Encyclopedia. http,//www.thecanadianencyclopedia.com/en/ (accessed August 28, 2013).
The Evangelical Fellowship of Canada. http,//www.evangelicalfellowship.ca/page.aspx?pid=286 (accessed September 21, 2014).
The Hollywood Free Paper. http,//www.hollywoodfreepaper.org/portal.php?id=2 (accessed August 19, 2014).
The New York Times, March 20, 1858. http,//query.nytimes.com/mem/archive-free/pdf?res=F40B1FFF3E581B7493C2AB1788D85F4C8584F9 (accessed August 22, 2013).
The Winnipeg Free Press. http,//passages.winnipegfreepress.com/passage-details/id-91315/name-Robert_Macdougall/ (accessed July 15, 2014).

www.ingramcontent.com/pod-product-compliance
Lightning Source LLC
Chambersburg PA
CBHW061937220426
43662CB00012B/1941